College Typewriting: A Mastery Approach

Comprehensive

William M. Mitchell
James E. LaBarre
University of Wisconsin—Eau Claire
K. A. Mach
Saddleback Community College

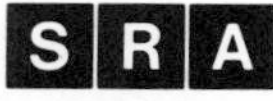

SCIENCE RESEARCH ASSOCIATES, INC.
Chicago, Palo Alto, Toronto
Henley-on-Thames, Sydney
A Subsidiary of IBM

Acquisition Editor	Susan L. Fisher
Project Editor	James C. Budd
Compositor	House of Graphics
Designer	Alex Teshin
Cover Designer	Don Fujimoto
Mechanical Art	House of Graphics

Library of Congress Cataloging in Publication Data

Mitchell, William Martin, 1932-
College typewriting, a mastery approach: comprehensive.
Includes index.
1. Typewriting. I. LaBarre, James E. II. Mach, K. A.
(Kaye A.) III. Title.
Z49.M68 1982 652.3 81-23248
ISBN 0-574-20650-7 AACR2

Printed in the United States of America.

10 9 8 7 6 5 4 3 2 1

Contents

Learning to Type

You are ready to begin learning a skill that will benefit you in many ways. Your goal in learning to type may be for personal reasons—typing your class notes, a term paper, report, letters, and so on—or you may wish to continue building your skills and eventually obtain an office position in which you can use them. In adddition, the growth of electronic keyboards in a wide range of automated office equipment and personal computers has made keyboarding mastery desirable for a much broader segment of our population. Regardless of your individual goal, learning to type will provide you with a valuable skill.

Thousands of people have learned to type. You will have little difficulty in learning to type if you always try to maintain a positive attitude. Never say, "I can't." The "I can't" attitude is exactly what has happened to those individuals who have failed to become good typists. So always try to keep a positive attitude. (You may find, however, that you do have some days when you are not able to type as well as you would like. Don't despair—every typist, even an expert one, has "bad" days, so don't let it bother you.)

Read the following introductory pages very carefully. Make a mental note of what is included, since later on in the book you will need to refer to these pages for some of the information.

Ready? There is no better time than right now for you to begin to learn how to type.

Getting Ready to Type

Some of the popular brands and models of typewriters are illustrated. Find the illustration of your machine and place a paper clip on the edge of the page so that you may refer to it easily whenever necessary.

If you are unable to find the illustration of your machine: (1) check with your instructor for the manual that accompanies your particular machine; or (2) find the illustration that most closely resembles your machine.

IBM CORRECTING "SELECTRIC" (NON-CARRIAGE MACHINE)*

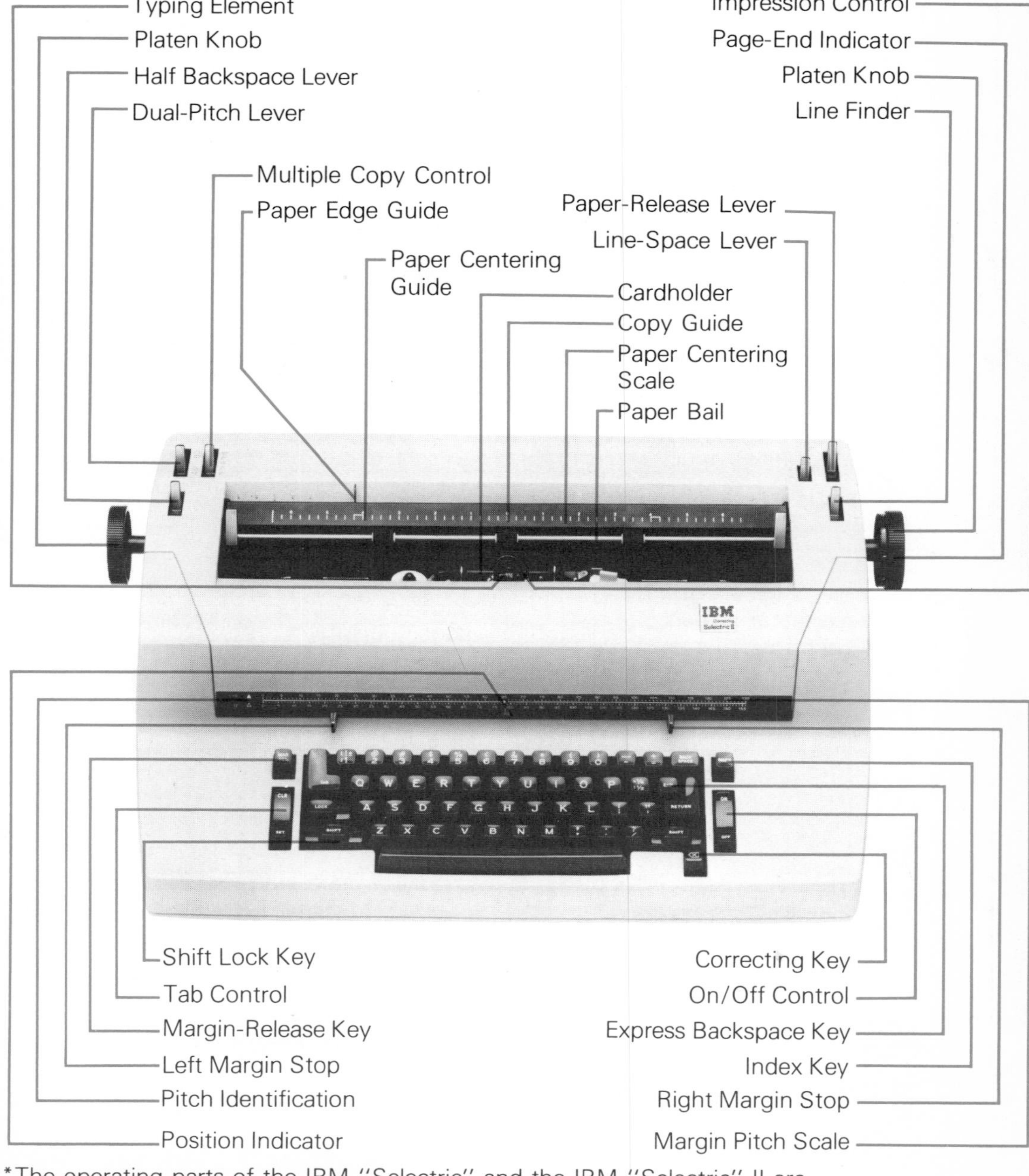

*The operating parts of the IBM "Selectric" and the IBM "Selectric" II are quite similar.

Courtesy of IBM

ROYAL ELECTRIC (SE 5000 CD)

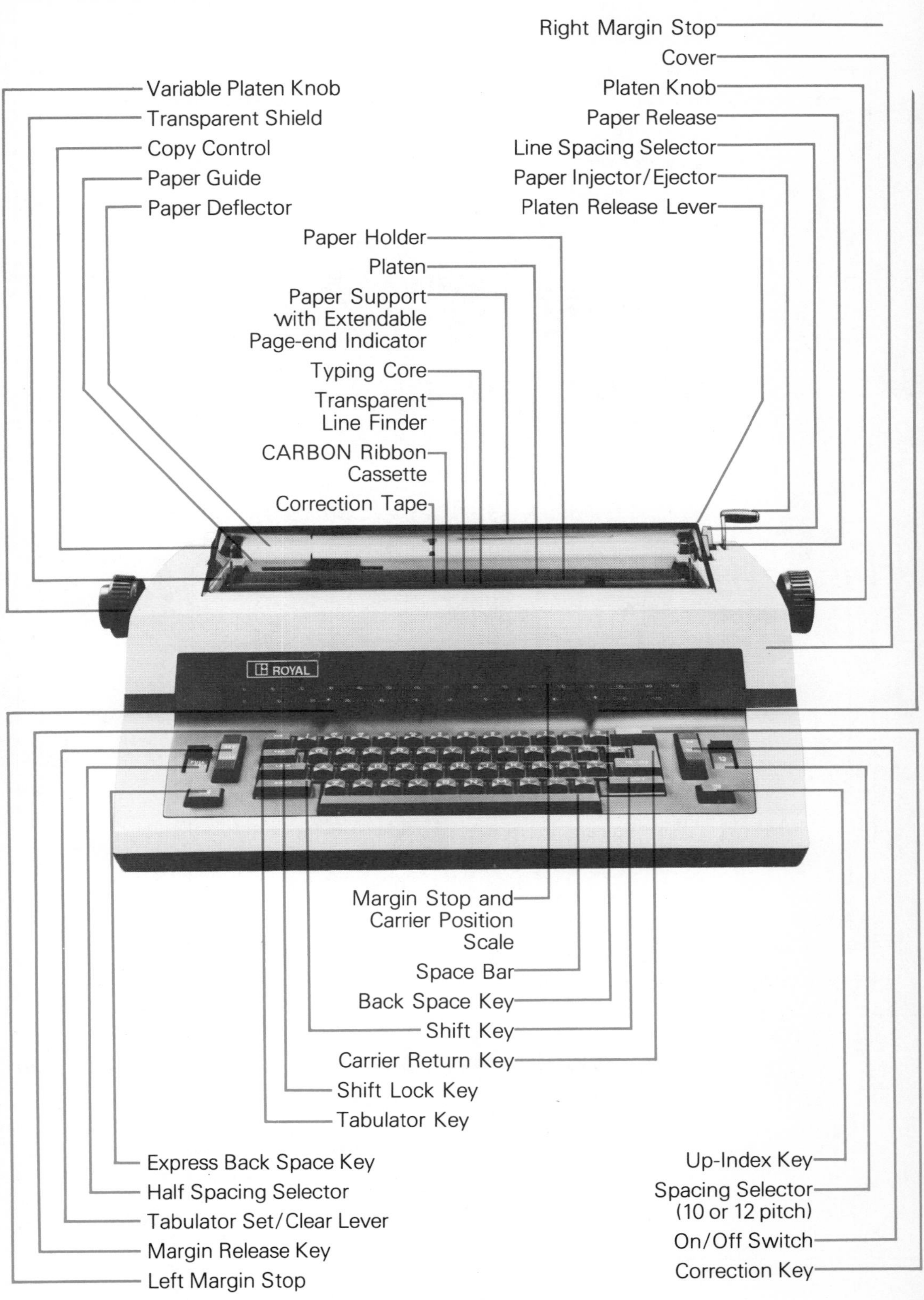
Right Margin Stop
Cover
Variable Platen Knob
Platen Knob
Transparent Shield
Paper Release
Copy Control
Line Spacing Selector
Paper Guide
Paper Injector/Ejector
Paper Deflector
Platen Release Lever
Paper Holder
Platen
Paper Support with Extendable Page-end Indicator
Typing Core
Transparent Line Finder
CARBON Ribbon Cassette
Correction Tape
ROYAL
Margin Stop and Carrier Position Scale
Space Bar
Back Space Key
Shift Key
Carrier Return Key
Shift Lock Key
Tabulator Key
Express Back Space Key
Up-Index Key
Half Spacing Selector
Spacing Selector (10 or 12 pitch)
Tabulator Set/Clear Lever
On/Off Switch
Margin Release Key
Correction Key
Left Margin Stop

Courtesy of Royal Business Machines, Inc.

ELECTRONIC KEYBOARD OF THE IBM PERSONAL COMPUTER

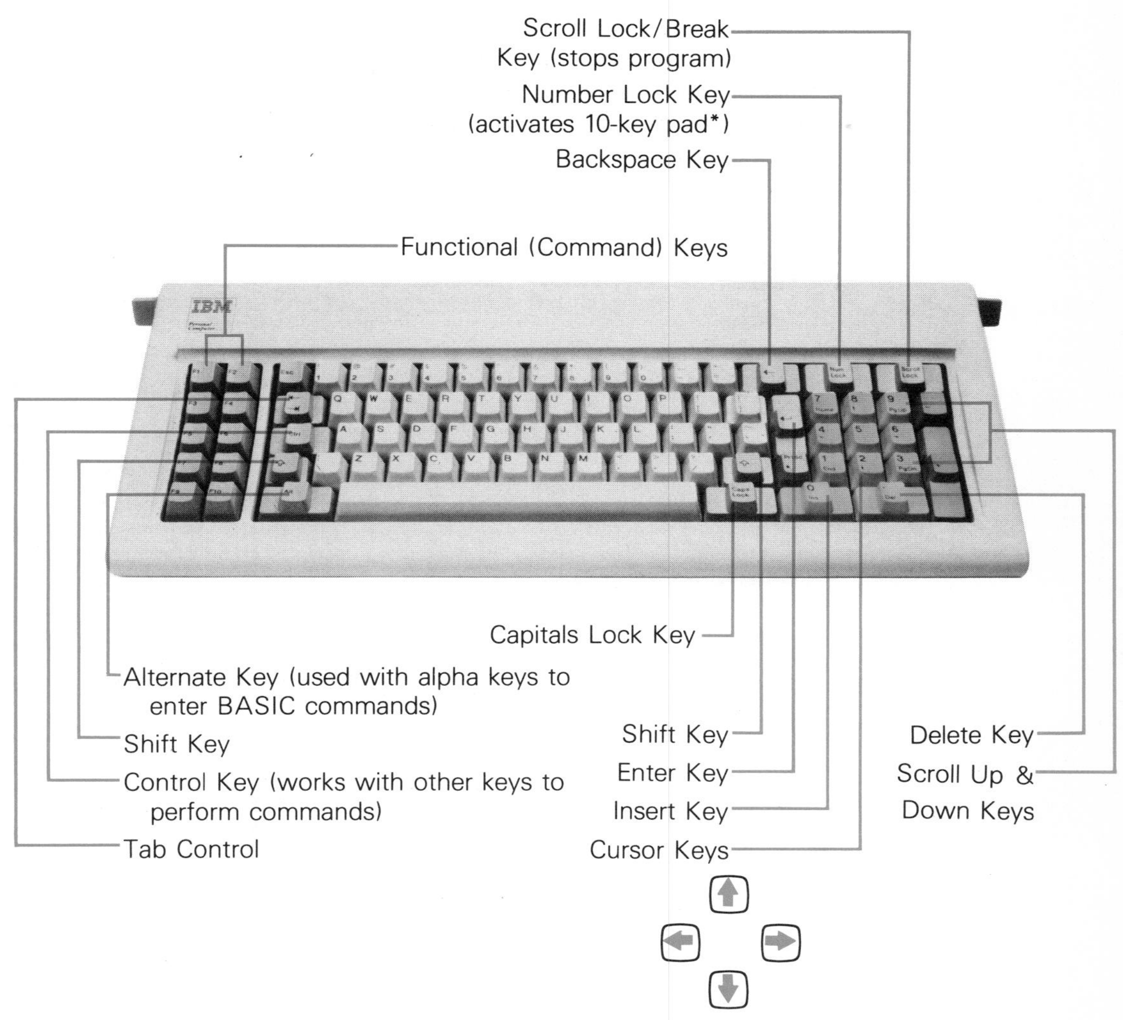

*10-Key Pad is shaded; it operates when Number Lock Key is depressed; when Number Lock Key is released, the editing keys are operative.

Courtesy of IBM

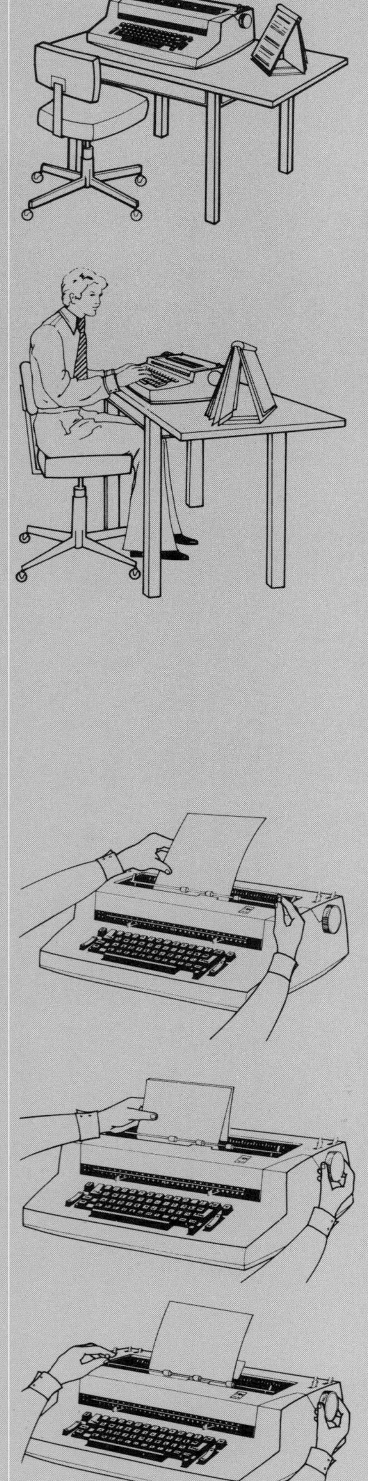

Your Working Area. Remove all items from your desk except the book support, which should be placed on the right side of your machine. Place your book on the support in a position so that you can clearly see the printed material.

Position at the Machine. Before beginning to type, check your position in front of the machine. Your body should be a little to the right of the center of the keyboard and back from the machine far enough so that your elbows are in a comfortable position at your sides.

Your feet should be flat on the floor, and you may find it more comfortable to place one foot slightly ahead of the other.

Paper Insertion and Removal. Look back at the illustration of your typewriter and locate the following parts:

1. Paper table
2. Cylinder (platen)
3. Paper bail
4. Paper guide
5. Right cylinder knob
6. Paper-release lever
7. Line scale

To insert paper into your machine:

1. Pick up the paper with your left hand.
2. Pull paper bail toward you with your right hand.
3. Place paper between cylinder and paper table. Line left edge of paper against paper guide—be sure that the paper guide is positioned so that the left edge of the paper will be on zero on the line scale.
4. Turn the paper in with the right cylinder knob — be sure the paper has advanced enough to be covered by the paper bail after completion of the next step.
5. Push paper bail forward toward the paper with left hand.

6. If your paper is crooked, pull the paper release toward you, straighten the paper, and return the release to the position away from you.

To remove the paper from your machine:

1. Pull paper bail toward you with left hand.
2. Pull paper release toward you with right hand.

3. Remove paper with left hand.

4. Push paper release forward with right hand.
5. Push paper bail forward with right hand.

Insert and remove a sheet of paper several times, until you can do both operations very smoothly and quickly.

Line-Space Regulator. Using the illustration of your machine, locate the ***line-space regulator.*** Most machines can be set on single (type on every line), double (type on every other line), or triple (type on every third line) spacing. You can see the difference in spacing in the examples below:

Single Spacing	*Double Spacing*	*Triple Spacing**
XXXXXXXXX	XXXXXXXXX	XXXXXXXXX
XXXXXXXXX		
XXXXXXXXX	XXXXXXXXX	
XXXXXXXXX		XXXXXXXXX

Margins. To set the margins on your machine to the correct line length, it is necessary that you know which type (Pica or Elite) your machine has. Each time you use a different machine, be sure that you check to determine which type the machine has. Pica letters take up more space on the sheet of paper than Elite letters. There are 10 letters to 1 inch with Pica type and 12 letters to 1 inch with Elite type.

aaaaaaaaaaaa Elite

aaaaaaaaaa Pica

1″

*Some machines are equipped so that you can single and double space automatically only. If your machine is set for single spacing, return the carriage three times; if set for double spacing, return it once and turn the cylinder knob away from you once.

A standard sheet of typing paper is 8½" wide and 11" long. There are 85 Pica spaces (8½" x 10 spaces = 85) and 102 Elite spaces (8½" x 12 spaces = 102) across a sheet of paper. Before setting your margins, you must know where the center of the paper is:

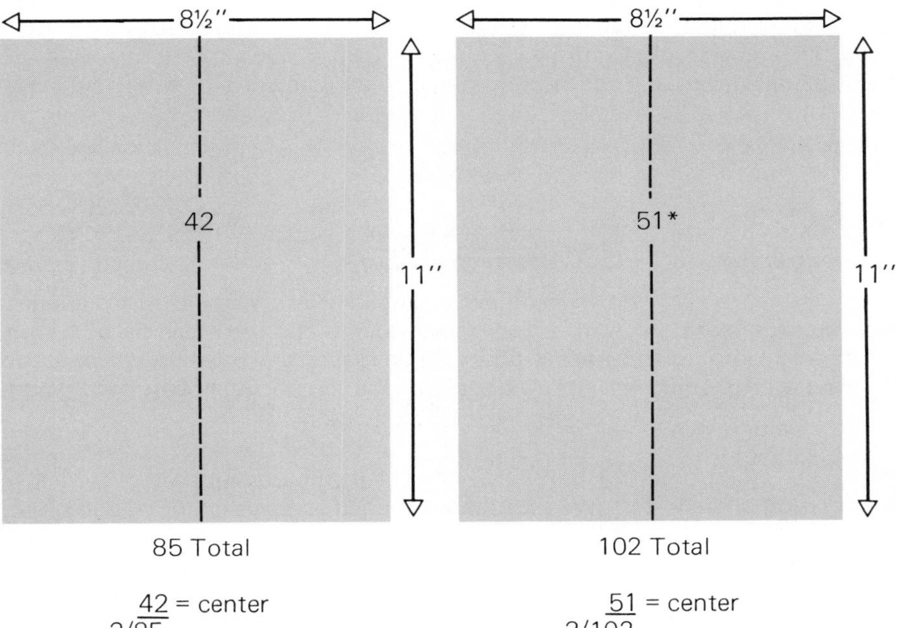

When setting the margins, you want to set them so that the left and right margins are approximately even. To do this, ***subtract*** one-half of the desired line length from the center point to set the left margin. ***Add*** one-half of the desired line length to the center point to determine the right margin. The following examples show the margins for various space lines:

	Pica		Elite[†]	
	Left	Right	Left	Right
40-space line	22	62	30	70
50-space line	17	67	25	75
60-space line	12	72	20	80
70-space line	7	77	15	85

Practice setting the margins for your machine for each of the example line lengths given above. Refer to the illustration of your machine and locate the margin-setting mechanism.

---

*You may find that using space 50 is more convenient.

[†]Using space 50 as center.

Hands. Place your fingers on the home row of the keyboard as shown here:

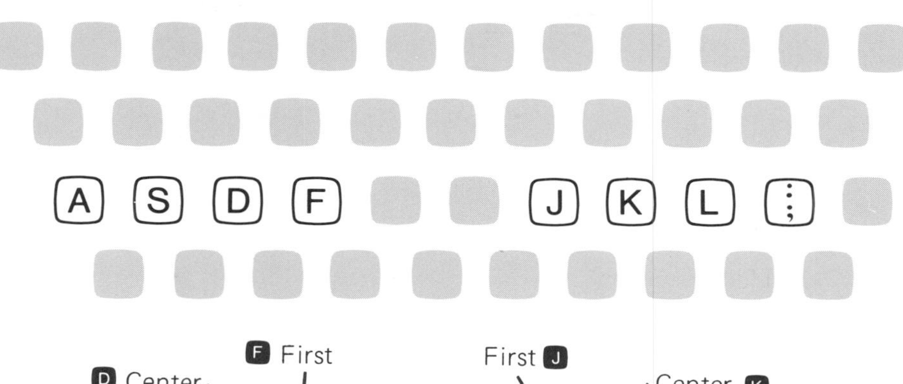

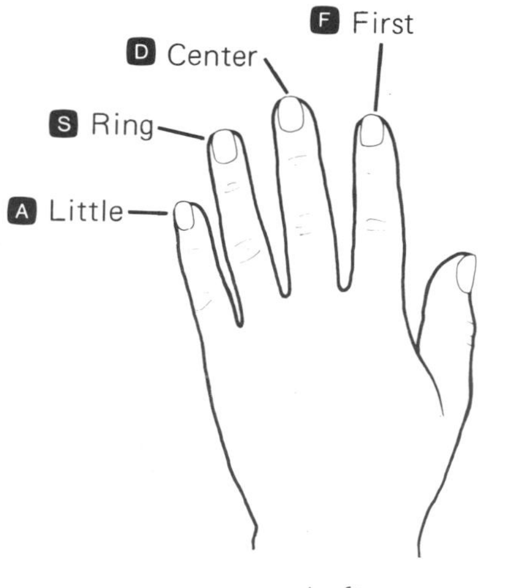

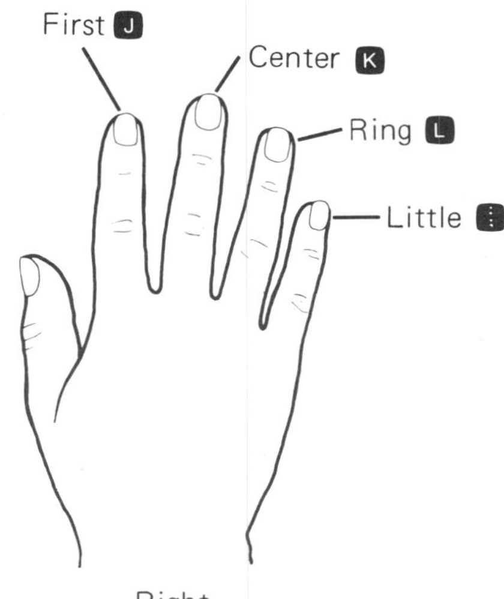

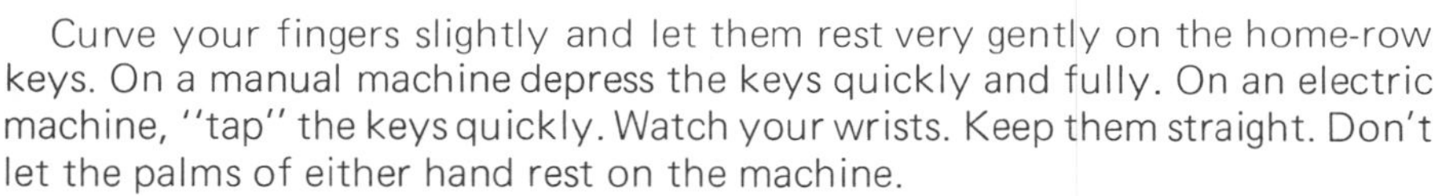

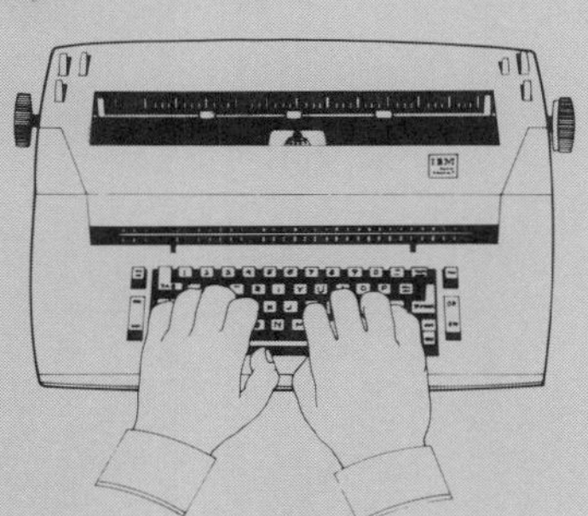

Curve your fingers slightly and let them rest very gently on the home-row keys. On a manual machine depress the keys quickly and fully. On an electric machine, "tap" the keys quickly. Watch your wrists. Keep them straight. Don't let the palms of either hand rest on the machine.

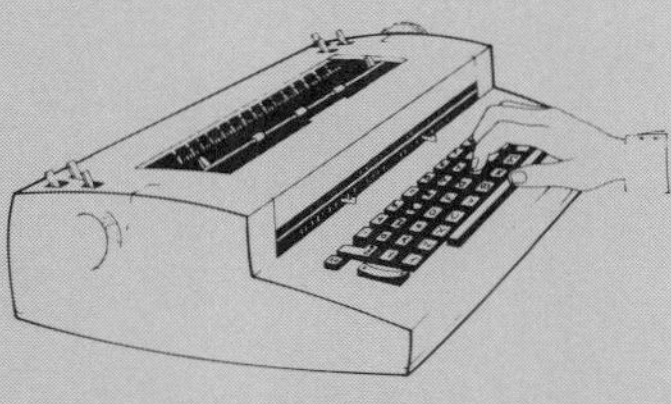

The space bar is struck with either your right or left thumb. If you are right-handed, you will probably find it is more natural to use your right thumb. If you are left-handed, you will probably want to use your left thumb. Keep the thumb you are not using to strike the space bar close to your first finger of that hand. Tap the space bar quickly.

Carriage Return. On a manual machine:

1. Move left hand from home row.
2. Place side of first finger against lever and move carriage quickly and smoothly to the right.
3. Return hand to home-row position.

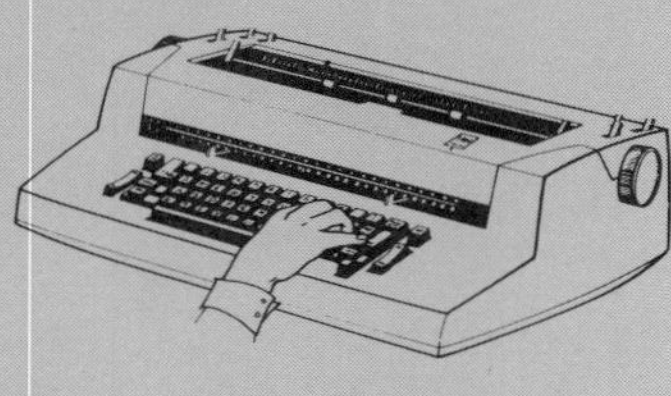

On an electric machine:

1. Move right little finger to "return" key and "flick" gently.
2. Return finger to home-row position.

On an electronic machine:

1. Electronic keyboards have a feature called ***word wraparound.*** Once the right margin has been set, the system returns to the next line automatically.
2. For a short line, it is necessary to "flick" the key for return to the next line.

Practice returning the carriage until you can do it quickly and smoothly.

Touch Typing. You are now ready to begin the process of learning to become a touch typist. Touch typing means that you will be able to read the copy and type it without having to look at the keyboard or your hands. At the time a new letter is introduced, however, it is a good procedure for you to look at your hands as you practice the new reach. As soon as you are confident that you know the reach, return to the habit of keeping your eyes on the copy and not on the keyboard or your hands.

A Final Word. This text has been designed so that you may begin learning the alphabetic or the numeric keys first. Your instructor will tell you which method will be used in your class. If you will be learning the alphabetic keys first, turn to page 1 and proceed. If you will be learning the numeric keys first, turn to page 51 and proceed.

The Keyboard

Alphabetic Keys

The Home Row

Remember—your left hand covers the ***a s d f***. Your right hand covers the ***j k l ;*** . Curve your fingers slightly, as shown in the illustration below.

Margins
Elite: 30 and 70
Pica: 22 and 62

Strike each key with a firm, quick motion. Practice striking each home-row key several times. When completed, continue on to the drill material below. Follow the instructions shown in the left-hand portion of the page.

Lines 1-3 once
Lines 1-3 again

```
1   a s d f j k l ; aa ss dd ff jj kk ll ;;
2   aa ss dd ff jj kk ll ;; asdf jkl; af j;
3   aaa sss ddd fff jjj kkk lll ;;; sd kl ;
```

Lines 4-7 once
Lines 4-7 again

```
4   a ad a ad add add adds adds a ad add ad
5   a as as a ask ask asks asks a all all a
6   a all all a alas alas a as ad add ask a
7   ad add as ask all alas adds asks all ad
```

Lines 8-12 once
Lines 8-12 again

```
8   d dad d dad dads dads s sad sad f fad f
9   fads fads fall fall falls falls fad fad
10  flak flak flask flask lad lad lads lads
11  lass lass lad lad lads dad dads ask ask
12  falls flask alas fads dads asks all sad
```

Situation

When you arrive at the office at 8:45 a.m., Tuesday, May 4, there is a note on your desk from Kathy stating that she will be at a meeting with Ms. Barron and a client. Kathy and Ms. Barron can be reached at 784-9618. They expect to be back in the office by 1:30 p.m.

In addition to your regular typing activities, Kathy left you several items that she would ordinarily handle. Proceed as follows:

1. ***Remove from your working papers those sheets identified for the in-basket.***
2. Carefully read each item.
3. Divide the work into three groups:

   Priority 1: Rush; urgent; must be done immediately; must be done before Kathy and Ms. Barron return.

   Priority 2: Important, but can be done ***after*** you have completed Priority 1 items.

   Priority 3: Routine; can be done ***after*** you have completed Priority 1 and 2 items.
4. After completing each item, turn your paper over and write in the upper left-hand corner the number indicating the order in which the item was completed.

Names and titles of selected Modern Office Systems personnel and a calendar for the month of May follow:

Judy Barron	Partner
Charles Bradshaw	Partner
Kevin Heyden	Office Layout Specialist
Betty Kronenberg	Supervisor of Duplication Services
Pam Rineck	Office Systems Project Coordinator
Frank Tuttle	Accountant
Kathy Watts	Administrative Secretary
You	Corresponding Secretary

MAY

S	M	T	W	T	F	S
						1
2	3	4	5	6	7	8
9	10	11	12	13	14	15
16	17	18	19	20	21	22
23	24	25	26	27	28	29
30	31					

Lines 1-4 once. At end of each line return carriage quickly and immediately begin typing on next line. Then do again.

DRILL

```
1   all all
2   sad sad dad dad
3   fad fad alas alas
4   fall fall lad lad add add
```

Lines 1 and 2 once
Lines 1 and 2 again

REVIEW

```
1   a s d f j k l ; aa ss dd ff jj kk ll ;;
2   aa ss dd ff jj kk ll ;; a s d f j k l ;
```

The Shift Keys Make Capital Letters

Depress right shift key *firmly* with right little finger. Type capital letter with correct finger of left hand. *Release* shift key and return quickly to home-row position.

Lines 1 and 2 once
Lines 1 and 2 again

RIGHT SHIFT KEY

```
1   aA sS dD fF Aa Ss Dd Ff AsDf aA fF sS D
2   Add Sad Dad Fad Ask Salad Dads Flak All
```

Introduction to H

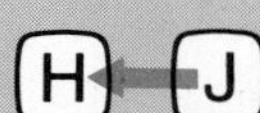

Home-row *j* finger moves left to the letter *h*. Place both hands on the home row and practice the move from *j* to *h*. Look at your hands and watch your finger make the motion. Do this several times; then look away and try the same motion.

activities. For instance, keyboarding words and data, such as a name and address, on a word processing terminal when that information is already in the computer or standing in line at a copier instead of directing the copier via a word processing terminal to reproduce that document are examples of how equipment is not used efficiently. It was not interfaced. The glue that provides the vehicle for office equipment to interact is ***telecommunications.*** Telecommunications media include telephone lines, cable, satellites, and microwave transmission.

Background

Assume you are employed by Modern Office Systems Associates, Incorporated, a consulting firm that designs office systems for reducing paperwork costs. The address and telephone number of the firm are:

12 Appletree Court
St. Paul, MN 55420
(612) 853-2398

You report to Ms. Judy Barron, one of the owners of Modern Office Systems. In addition to her responsibilities as a partner and consultant, she is an author and lecturer in the area of office systems and word processing.

Ms. Barron has designed the word-processing system used by Modern Office Systems. In your office area, Ms. Barron has set up an administrative support team, consisting of yourself as corresponding secretary and Ms. Kathy Watts as the administrative secretary.

Your basic responsibility is the keyboarding function, while Kathy Watts is responsible for all other support functions. Your work stations are located side by side, close to the entrance to Ms. Barron's work area. Ms. Barron has designed the system so that you and Kathy know both jobs and can cover for each other at any time.

H

Line 1 twice

Lines 2-3 once
Lines 2-3 again

```
1  jj hh jh jh hj hj jj hh jh jh j h jh jh
2  jh has has has had had had h has had jh
3  jh hall hall hall sash sash has sash jh
```

Lines 4-7 once
Lines 4-7 again

```
4  ash ash ash ha ha ha jhjh ash ha ash ha
5  half half half lash lash lash half lash
6  dash dash dash hash hash hash dash hash
7  shall shall shall flash flash flash has
```

The Shift Keys Make Capital Letters

Depress left shift key ***firmly*** with left little finger. Type capital letter with correct finger of right hand. ***Release*** shift key and return quickly to home-row position. The shift of the ***semi*** key will produce a ***colon.***

LEFT SHIFT KEY

Lines 1 and 2 once
Lines 1 and 2 again

```
1  jJ kK lL ;: Jj Kk Ll ;: JkL; jK lL :;:;
2  jJ hH jH aA sS dD fF jJ kK lL ;: jJ hH:
```

After typing the colon, tap the space bar twice.

DRILL

Line 1 twice

```
1  Lass Lad Lads Flask:  All:  Sad:  Lads
```

DRILL

Lines 1-3 once. At end of each line return carriage quickly and immediately begin typing on next line. Then do again.

```
1  half:  half:
2  flash:  flash:  shall:  shall:
3  fall:  hall:  alas:  dash:  half:
```

Remember: Tap space bar TWICE after a colon.

DRILL

Lines 1 and 2 once
Lines 1 and 2 again

```
1  dads:  lads:  hall:  dash:  half:  all:
2  Lads fall:  a lass adds:  ask a Lad:  :
```

Components of a Word Processing System

The components of a word processing system include people, procedures, and equipment. A discussion of these three follows:

PEOPLE

In a word processing system, personnel can be divided into three functions or roles—origination, nonkeyboarding activities, and keyboarding. The first function relates to the creation of the communication —whether oral or written. The terms used to describe the individual creating business communications include ***author, user, principal,*** or ***originator.***

The second function or role of people in a word processing system involves the nonkeyboarding support functions. These include such activities as storing and retrieving information, screening callers and visitors, recordkeeping, coordinating and administering schedules, copying and duplicating, and a variety of research-related activities. In a word processing system in which the nonkeyboard management-support function has been identified as a separate position, titles include ***administrative secretary, administrative specialist,*** or ***administrative assistant.***

The third function, or role, or people in a word processing system centers on keyboarding. In addition to keyboarding itself, proofreading, editing, and revision are included in this function. In organizations where the keyboarding function is designated as a separate position, an individual's job title might be: ***word processor, correspondence secretary,*** or ***word processing specialist.***

In a word processing system where an individual is responsible for keyboarding as well as nonkeyboarding functions, job titles include ***stenographer, secretary,*** or ***executive secretary.***

PROCEDURES

The second major component of a word processing system represents the procedures involved in creating and processing business communications. This component includes face-to-face communication, communication by voice (telephone/recording), and written documents. The need for the communication, the steps involved in the origination process, the time and methods involved in processing the information, the flow of work, and the storage and/or eventual destruction of the information all fall within the realm of procedures. Activities to improve the procedures related to a word processing system include:

1. Analyzing oral and written communication to identify activities and documents that need not be created or perhaps reduced
2. Utilizing more effective methods of origination, such as machine dictation
3. Developing charts to trace the flow of work to identify alternative sequences in processing that would be more effective
4. Storing and disposing of documents: method of storage, form of retention (paper, microfilm, magnetic media), process for retrieving and revising, and whether or not the document should be destroyed—if so, the method of destruction

EQUIPMENT

The third and final component of a WP system is the equipment used. With the exception of the telephone, most of the equipment used in an office is in the hands of the management-support staff. In addition, much of the equipment being used serves as a one-function device. For example, in organizations it is not uncommon to find that functions related to computer equipment, electronic word processing equipment, dictation equipment, and copying and duplicating equipment are independent functions.

In many word processing systems, it is desirable to ***interface*** (connect) office equipment to eliminate wasted originating, keyboarding, and nonkeyboarding

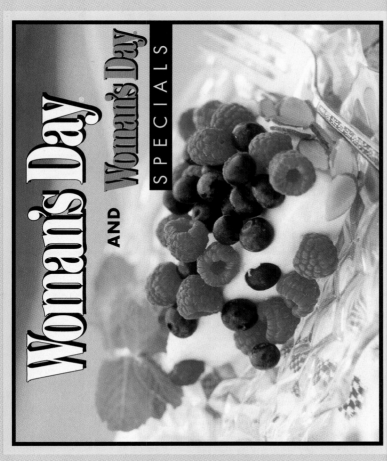

Introduction to the Period

Home-row *l* finger moves down and to the right to the *period* key. Place both hands on the home row and practice the move from *l* to *period*. Look at your hands and watch your finger make the motion. Do this several times; then look away and try the same motion.

Important: Tap space bar TWICE after period at end of sentence. (Note: if you are at the end of your line, return carriage—there is no need to tap the space bar.)

Line 1 twice
Lines 2 and 3 once
Lines 2 and 3 again

```
1   l. l. l.l l.l ll .. ll l. l. .. l. l. .
2   All lads shall dash.  A lad shall fall.
3   Ask a lass.  Ask a lad.  Dad asks lads.
```

Introduction to T

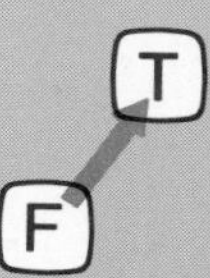

Home-row *f* finger moves up and to the right to the *t* key. Place both hands on the home row and practice the move from *f* to *t*. Look at your hands and watch your finger make the motion. Do this several times; then look away and try the same motion.

Line 1 twice

Lines 2 and 3 once
Lines 2 and 3 again

```
1   ff tt ft ft tf tf ff tt ft ft f t ft ft
2   ft at at hat hat hat hat sat sat sat ft
3   ft fat fat fat aft aft aft t fat aft ft
```

Overview of Word Processing

Word Processing Defined

Word processing is a program designed to improve the efficiency and effectiveness of business communications by the integration of people, procedures, and equipment into an organized and managed system.

The Development of Word Processing

The modern-day concept of word processing originated in Germany in the middle 1960s. The introduction of the IBM Magnetic Tape Selectric Typewriter (MTST) in 1964 provided the impetus for word processing there and quickly spread to other countries. The MTST was equipped with magnetic tape for recording and correcting typographical errors, making revisions, and printing automatically, at a speed of 150 words a minute.

The introduction of the MTST no doubt rekindled the idea that there are alternative methods to support management in an office environment. In the 1960s the most common methods of supporting management included the assignment of one secretary to one or more executives and the "stenopool" method, where management shared the secretarial services provided by the support staff. As word processing has grown, other alternatives for supporting management have evolved. Before identifying the alternatives, however, it is important to recognize the objectives of word processing.

Objectives of Word Processing

1. Increase the productivity of executives, supervisors, and professionals (e.g., attorneys, educators, accountants, doctors, nurses, engineers, architects, etc.).
2. Provide more responsive management support at all levels.
3. Upgrade the quality and quantity of document/message output.
4. Increase the speed of communicating information between sender and receiver(s).
5. Reduce costs of office operations.
6. Improve internal and external oral and written communications.
7. Include the capability to integrate all information processes—word, data, image and voice—so that a single piece of equipment can be used for a variety of tasks.

To apply the objectives of word processing in most organizational settings requires adjustments at all levels in the duties, responsibilities, procedures, and equipment utilized by office personnel. The implementation of a word processing system often involves changes to include support staff location and configuration, job activities, organizational reporting structure, and working relationships.

In most word processing systems, the management-support personnel have an opportunity to become specialists, to become more involved as members of the management team, and to make more meaningful contributions to business—while achieving greater job satisfaction. Through the implementation of a more effective word processing system, management is provided with reduced operating costs, increased office productivity, a higher level of efficiency, and professional management support.

New

ULTRA

Palmolive®

Antibacterial

Ultra Palmolive®
Dishwashing
Liquid
& Antibacterial
Hand Soap

CONCENTRATED
USE 1/3 LESS

The Anti-Germ Palmolive®

© Colgate-Palmolive 1996

MANUFACTURER'S COUPON | EXPIRES 9/30/96

Save 40¢

On any Palmolive® Dishwashing Liquid

Ultra Palmolive® Dishwashing Liquid & Antibacterial Hand Soap

CONSUMER: Do not send this coupon to Colgate-Palmolive. Limit one coupon per purchase of product indicated. You must pay any sales tax.
RETAILER: Colgate-Palmolive will reimburse the face value plus 8¢ handling if submitted in accordance with our Redemption Policy. For policy and/or coupon redemption, send to Colgate-Palmolive, c/o Acu-Trac Services, Inc., P.O. Box 870031, Dept. 35000, Tecate, CA 91987-0031.Cash Value 1/100¢. Void where prohibited.
Redeemable at Food, Drug, Discount and Other Stores accepting coupons.

60666

5 35000 35040 9 (8100)0 60666

Lines 4-7 once
Lines 4-7 again

4 fast fast fast halt halt halt last last

5 lath lath lath salt salt salt flat flat

6 talk talk talk that that that task task

7 slat slat slat data data data tall tall

DRILL

Lines 1-3 once. At end of each line return carriage quickly and immediately begin typing on next line. Then do again.

1 staff staff

2 shaft shaft stalk stalk

3 stash stash atlas atlas fatal fatal

Building speed and accuracy: Try to concentrate for speed or accuracy. Your mind controls your fingers. When the instructions indicate ***speed***, try to think ***speed***. When the instructions indicate accuracy, think ***accuracy***. After you practice setting your "mind" goal several times, you should find that your mind will eventually control your fingers automatically. So try to think ***speed*** or ***accuracy***.

SENTENCES

Lines 1-3 once—speed
Lines 1-3 again—speed

1 A flat flask; a flat hat; a flat atlas.

2 Half a lath; half a slat; half a flask.

3 Dad halts a tall lad; a tall lad halts.

Lines 4-6 once—speed
Lines 4-6 again—speed

4 Stalk a fast lad; a sad lad has a fall.

5 Half a lath; half a slat; half a flask.

6 Dad halts a tall lad; a tall lad halts.

Lines 7-9 once—accuracy
Lines 7-9 again—accuracy

7 Stalk a fast lad; a sad lad has a fall.

8 A lad talks; a lass talks; a dad talks.

9 A dad shall talk; a fat lad shall talk.

Introduction to the Comma

Home-row *k* finger moves down and to the right to the *comma* key. Place both hands on the home row and practice the move from *k* to *,*. Look at your hands and watch your finger make the motion. Do this several times; then look away and try the same motion.

The Word-Processing In-Basket Module

As a further refinement of your secretarial typewriting skills, you are now ready to complete an in-basket. The in-basket is different from the integrated projects you have already completed, in that you must determine the ***order*** in which items are to be prepared.

When you begin working in an office, one of the more difficult things you must adjust to is being able to decide what items must be prepared in what order—in other words, being able to set priorities. Learn to use your common sense when determining the particular order in which you will type the tasks.

When assigned a long project such as an in-basket, you should keep the following items in mind:

1. Understand the purpose of the project.
2. Know the exact due dates.
3. Understand exactly what needs to be done.
4. Be aware of any special requirements.
5. Plan and organize your time to complete the project on time.
6. After the project is completed, check to see that your work is satisfactory.

75-Pc. Bulb Starter Garden

You won't find a better garden value anywhere! This 75-piece bulb garden will come to life every spring all by itself–and for years to come, all without lifting or replanting. Our experts have selected 10 outstanding varieties, including Crocus, Tulips, Daffodils and more! A super value!

FREE Planting Diagram included with this 75-pc. Bulb Garden.

Hydrangea Collection ONLY $9.97

Beautiful...and hardy!

One of the most popular ornamental shrubs in America! Hydrangeas boast big, bold flowers and make excellent borders. Hydrangeas are hardy, so you can plant them and just get out of the way. Nature will do the rest! You get a complete color-balanced collection featuring one plant each of blue, pink and red Hydrangeas. Plant them in a sunny or partly shady location and well-drained acidic soil. You'll enjoy a spectacular color show every May for years to come! 2 1/4" pot.

CAREFREE COLOR FOR YOUR YARD!

◀Creeping Phlox

12 FOR ONLY $4.99

Say goodbye to all those hard-to-mow areas of your yard! This low-growing mat of tufted green spreads vigorously to cover even the most troublesome areas of your yard. In late spring, the foliage gives way to a thick blanket of ankle-high flowers in rose-purple, vivid blue and snowy white. 12 plants cover 20 square feet. Order yours today! 1-year-old plants.

Orange ▶ Candleflower

3 FOR $5.99

The Orange Candleflower just might be the world's perfect flower. It's great for naturalizing, it multiplies every year, it's long-lasting and it makes beautiful cut-flower bouquets. Best of all, it's relatively carefree. Just plant it in the fall and let this candle light up your yard with brilliant color! 10-12cm

The Best Guarantee In the Business!

LIFETIME GUARANTEE

If you're not happy with any item you order from us, simply return it within 15 days for a full refund or replacement, whichever you prefer. What's more, any items that do not grow and flourish to your complete satisfaction will be replaced FREE – with no time limit – for as long as you garden.

FREE Planting Guide Included with Every Order.

MICHIGAN BULB COMPANY F96
1950 WALDORF, N.W., GRAND RAPIDS, MI 49550

YES! Please send my order as indicated for fall delivery. Include all FREE bonus items to which I am entitled. All items are covered by your no-risk LIFETIME GUARANTEE.

MISS / MS. / MR. / MRS. ______ *Please Print* TQ 4055 B 2

ADDRESS ______

CITY ______ STATE ______ ZIP ______

HOW MANY	ITEM #	ITEM	COST
	10637	Mixed Tulips (50/$2.99, 100/$5.88, 200/$11.48)	
	02170	Perennial Starter Garden ($9.99 ea., 2/$18.98)	
	13698	Rainbow Iris (10/$9.99, 20/$18.98)	
	03095	Naturalizing Lilies (10/$7.99, 20/$13.98)	
	11577	Tickled Pink Daffodils (6/$4.99, 12/$7.98, 24/$14.96)	
	08425	75-Pc. Bulb Starter Garden ($9.99 ea., 2/$16.98)	
	09100	Hydrangea Collection. One each of Red, Blue and Pink Hydrangeas - 3 plants in all! ($9.97)	
	02717	Creeping Phlox (12/$4.99, 24/$8.98, 48/$16.96)	
	10405	Orange Candleflower (3/$5.99, 6/$9.98)	
6	FREE	Grape Hyacinths with any order.	0.00
12	FREE	Alpine Rosy Bells if your order totals $10.00.	0.00
12	FREE	Sunny Twinkles (plus 12 Alpine Rosy Bells) if your order totals $20.00.	0.00
1	FREE	Surprise FREE Gift - A $5.00 Value (plus 12 Sunny Twinkles and 12 Alpine Rosy Bells) if order totals $30.00.	0.00

☐ Payment enclosed. ☐ Bill on my credit card below. ☐ MasterCard ☐ American Express ☐ VISA ☐ Discover/NOVUS

Exp. Date ☐☐-☐☐

Credit Card # ☐☐☐☐-☐☐☐☐-☐☐☐☐-☐☐☐☐

Subtotal	$
Postage & handling	4.95
SALES TAX: MI add 6% TN add 8.25% MO add 5.725%	
Grand Total	$

MAIL THIS MONEY-SAVING COUPON TODAY!

M

BIG! SAVINGS

FALL GARDEN SPECTACULAR!

Our Most Popular Plants At Low, Low Prices!

30 FREE BONUS BULBS!

AND A SURPRISE FREE GIFT!

Mixed Tulips

50 FOR ONLY $2.99

Tulips dazzle you with brilliant color every spring but they must be planted in the fall. This incredible offer features our best Flaming Mix assortment of hardy, blooming-size bulbs – for less than 6¢ each! You get glistening whites, fiery reds, bright yellows, pastel pinks, deep purples, gorgeous bi-colors and more. Order 50 Tulips for only $2.99, or 100 for $5.88, or 200 for $11.48. 7-8cm bulbs.

Naturalizing Lilies

10 for $7.99

Transform a forgotten area of your yard into a mass of carefree color that returns year after year – *without lifting or replanting*. Naturalizing lilies produce bigger clumps and more flowers every year. Great for indoor bouquets, too! You get 10-12cm size bulbs that thrive in well-drained soil and sun or partial shade.

A. Creeping Phlox (12 plants)
B. Sweet William (5 plants)
C. Hibiscus, Mixed (3 plants)
D. Mixed Carnations (5 plants)
E. Shasta Daisy (5 plants)
Total number of plants: 30
Approximate planting time: 1 hour
9'
6'
SPECIAL BUY!

Perennial Starter Garden

30 Hardy Perennials $9.99

A fail-proof perennial garden for only $9.99! Perfect for beginners!

If you've admired other people's perennial gardens, yet thought it might be complicated or expensive to put together such a garden of your own, here's great news. This big 9' x 6' **perennial starter garden** will get you off to a sure-fire start! Our professional designers created this delightful bed using 30 of the easiest-to-grow perennial plants — for guaranteed success in your yard. Plant in full sun. You'll have glorious blooms every year for decades to come. 1-year-old plants.

FREE Planting Diagram Included with Perennial Starter Garden.

ADD A SPLASH OF COLOR TO YOUR YARD!

◀Rainbow Iris

10 for Only $9.99

Bearded Iris are tall and stately, versatile, carefree and beautiful beyond compare. Now, you can enjoy them in a rainbow of mixed colors for less than a dollar per plant! Best of all, Bearded Irises multiply, so every year you'll be treated to more lovely blooms!

Tickled Pink ▶ Daffodils

6 for Only $4.99

If you love the beauty and carefree nature of Daffodils, here's a new variety that'll leave you "Tickled Pink!" Tickled Pink is a very special Daffodil. Its soft, pastel pink cups are surrounded by creamy white petals. And it boasts a fresh fragrance that most Daffodils can't match. Order 6, 12 or 24. The more you buy, the more you save! 12-14cm bulbs.

Lines 1-3 once—speed
Lines 1-3 again—accuracy

1 That tall, fat, fast lad shall ask dad.
2 A flat, half lath falls; all lads halt.
3 A flat, fat, sad hall shaft shall fall.

Think—and Type

One of the most important typewriting skills that you will want to develop is that of thinking at the typewriter. After you master the ability to "think" as you type, you will be able to save valuable time by composing directly at the typewriter rather than having to write your thoughts in longhand and then type from your handwritten notes.

You will be given numerous opportunities to develop compositional skills while you are learning the remainder of the letter keys. IMPORTANT: The goal of composing at the typewriter is to get your thoughts on paper quickly. Don't hesitate—begin to type at once as your thoughts begin. Don't worry about errors; you are composing only in rough-draft form. Later you can concentrate on typing a good final copy.

Thinking Drill

LOOK

Look at these five words:

flask *lass* *Dad* *sad* *lad*

SELECT

Now—select the word that best answers each of the following statements. Read each statement, look at the words, and quickly type your selection.

TYPE

1. Opposite of *happy*
2. Another word for your father
3. Another word that describes a girl
4. Another word that describes a boy
5. The name of a container that holds liquids

LOOK
SELECT

How did you do? Remember—type the appropriate response as quickly as you can. Try these:

dash *fat* *hat* *salt* *tall*

TYPE

6. An object that is worn on your head
7. To move quickly
8. Opposite of *short*
9. Flavors food
10. Opposite of *skinny*

REVIEW

Line 1 twice—speed

Lines 2 and 3 once—speed
Lines 2 and 3 again—speed

1 a s d f j k l ; jh jh ;: ;: ft ft jh jh
2 all sad ask fall lad lass dad ha at ash
3 add that has that shall dash last stall

Chicago Athletic Club

Initiation:	$2,250 ($1,000 at initiation and $250 per year for 5 years)
Per Month:	$ 56
Waiting period:	6-12 months

Arbor Forrest Country Club

Initiation:	$5,000 ($1,800 stock plus $3,200 transfer fee)
Per month:	$ 90
Waiting period:	6-12 months

Type in attractive format

¶ In my judgment, Mike should join the Chicago Athletic Club and I should join the Arbor Forrest Country Club in order to effectively develop the Global City Bank presence in Chicago.
c. Mike Fitzsimmons

Item 12

Working Papers, pp. 321-22

TO: J. P. Hopkins, Regional Manager. FROM: Lee Iverson, VP & Gen. Manager. *(spell out)* SUBJECT: Chicago GCB Office Expence Allocation. Following our conversation during your last visit to Chicago, I ~~worked out the following numbers regarding the expense allocation of certain items~~ *analyzed last year's expenses* paid for ~~presently~~ by GCB*, & formulated the following budget for this year:*

Expense Category		Category Detail	Estimated Expense - 19--
Postage	$ 135	meter rental	$2,035
	1,900	postage	
Telephone	$ 850	WATS monthly	12,960
	230	monthly service	
	1,080	x 12 months	
Office Supplies	$ 50	x 12 months	600
Copier	$ .04	x 1,500	600
Depreciation	$6,250	leashold improvements	8,560
	2,310	furniture	
Secretary	$9,300	salary	11,900
	2,600	fringes	
			$35,655

NOTE: Be sure to check multiplication + final total

I checked with ~~Michael~~ *Mike* Fitzsimmons to see what his actual expenses have been in several of the key areas over the past 6 to 12 months and discussed a proper expense allocation with both Mike and Donald Birk. We concluded that the most reasonable approach would be an allocation of 50 percent of the total above expenses, or $17,832. ¶ I feel that actual expenses will be higher than $17,832 this year. However, I think the best we can do at present is to take the estimated fixed allocation approach to assure that our respective Monthly Progress Reports reflect the true expense picture of our businesses. When budget time rolls around in late summer, we can probably refine the allocation process based on a few months *of* experience. ¶ ~~Accounting wise,~~ I propose that the Commercial Banking Department in New York make a monthly charge to the expense code(s) ~~you indicate~~ for one-sixth of the total amount starting July 1, 19__. ¶ Please indicate your agreement with the charges and I will set up the accounting procedures in New York. c: Donald Birk, District Manager, GBCI, Michael Fitzsimmons, Leasing Officer, Jean McDowell, Assistant Vice President

Item 13

Working Papers, pp. 323-24

Reminder -- Send a typewritten memo to Lee Iverson to include: (1) Executive staff meeting, 3:15 p.m., Wed., June 1. (2) Reservations for 5 at Rosewood Inn. (3) Reservations are in your name -- not Iverson's. (4) Meet in rooms 1404 + 1405. (5) dinner at 6:30 p.m. in 1408 + 1409.

Introduction to N

Home-row *j* finger moves down and to the left to the *n* key. Place both hands on the home row and practice the move from *j* to *n*. Look at your hands and watch your finger make the motion. Do this several times; then look away and try the same motion.

N

Line 1 twice—speed
Lines 2 and 3 once—speed
Lines 2 and 3 again—speed

```
1  jj nn jn jn nj nj jj nn jn jn j n jn jn
2  jn an an an and and and an and an an jn
3  jn ant ant ant fan fan fan hand hand jn
```

Lines 4-7 once—speed
Lines 4-7 again—accuracy

```
4  land land land sand sand sand tank tank
5  than than than flank flank flank an tan
6  slant slant slant thank thank thank and
7  nasal nasal nasal stand stand stand fan
```

DRILL

Lines 1-3 once. At end of each line return carriage quickly and immediately begin typing on next line. Then do again.

```
1  sand sand
2  sandal sandal shank shank
3  thank thank annal annal hands hands
```

DETERMINE YOUR SPEED RATE

A "word" in typewriting consists of five letters, digits, symbols, and/or spaces. For example, the words ***I see*** would be counted as one word, not two.

To determine your speed rate, you must use both the ***cumulative*** word count (located at the right of the material) and the ***partial-line*** word count (located across the bottom of the material). Assume you took a one-minute timing on lines 1-4 below. You typed lines 1 and 2 and just typed the word ***sat*** in line 3 when the minute was up. Using the cumulative word count, you find that the last ***completed*** line you typed (line 2) shows a word count of 16. Then, looking at the partial-line count, you find that the word ***sat*** shows that the partial-line count is 3. Adding the two (16 plus 3) gives you a total speed rate of 19 words a minute.

Some timings will be less than one minute. You should always convert these timing rates into your word-a-minute (wam) rate. Use the following table to determine your wam rate when typing for less than one minute.

If You Typed for	Multiply	by			
5 seconds	number words	x	12	=	minute stroking rate
10 seconds	number words	x	6	=	minute stroking rate

3. Opportunity for full-time participation in the 8-day training program (80 percent attendance is a minimum requirement).

4. Participatns should have reached a point in family and career obligations which will allow them to assume expanded community responsibilities. Selection will also be designed, as closely as practicable, to result in a group which includes all fa-ets of the community: emn and women representative of the diverse racial, ethnic, and institutional groups which make up the greater Chicago area. We hope that you will nominate at least one candidate who, in your judgemnt, meets the above criteria. It will be helpful if you would clear your nominations with the persons involved to determine their interest and probably degree of commitment. Remember, your sponsored candidate does not have to be a member of your organization. Thank you for your support. Sincerely. Lee Iverson, Chairman. Civic Awareness Committee. Enclosure.

Item 11

Working Papers, pp. 319-20

TO: John M. Nelson, Vice President. FROM: Lee Iverson, VP & Gen. Manager. SUBJECT: Clubs. Following our discussion regarding clubs during your visit on April 21, I thought a written strategy and recommendation would be appropriate. The Chicago business community is a tight-knit group of executives who eat, live, and socialize in a few exclusive spots in the area:

-- Lunch/Dinner happens at the Chicago Athletic Club and the Executive Club Lounge. The Chicago Athletic Club is by far the better luncheon club. The quality of its food, membership, and facilities are excellent. The Executive Club Lounge has only acceptable food.

-- Socializing is done at private homes and, in large part, at country clubs. Clubs are heavily used for golf, tennis, and evening entertainment. There are three top-rated country clubs: Oak Ridge, Osceola, and Arbor Forrest. Oak Ridge and Osceola Country Clubs are good; the majority of the membership is over 50 years of age, and social activity is limited. Arbor Forrest blends accessibility (a 20-minute drive from downtown), a good mix of members of all ages, and a good middle-market executive and director membership. The GCB-Chicago top priority objective is booking loans. The key strategies are: (1) direct calling on target market prospects, (2) developing referral business, (3) developing a market presence--i.e., developing an awareness that Global City Bank is in the market-place ready and able to fill financial and financially related needs. The first and second strategies are being carried out via direct call and referral programs. It seems to me that the third strategy, market presence, can be rapidly and effectively developed through club membership in a luncheon club and a country club. We could eat and socialize with the middle-market business executives or directors at the clubs they frequent. Michael Fritzsimmons is very effective at developing business through the luncheon/dinner club. He was a member of the New York City Club while in New York. I effectively used the country club as a business development tool during my years in Mexico. Prices here in Chicago are reasonable in comparison to other clube around the United States. For example, it would cost us the following:

(cont'd. on next page)

15 seconds	number words	x	4	=	minute stroking rate
30 seconds	number words	x	2	=	minute stroking rate

Important: Whenever you repeat a timing on the same material, always attempt to:

1. Type more words on the second attempt than you did on the first,

or

2. Have fewer errors on the second attempt than you did on the first.

SENTENCES

Lines 1-8 once—speed

Take:
- Two 15-sec. timings—Line 1
- Two 15-sec. timings—Line 2
- Two 15-sec. timings—Line 3
- Two 15-sec. timings—Line 4
- Two 30-sec. timings—Lines 1-4

Take:
- Two 15-sec. timings—Line 5
- Two 15-sec. timings—Line 6
- Two 15-sec. timings—Line 7
- Two 15-sec. timings—Line 8
- Two 30-sec. timings—Lines 5-8

```
1   Jan shall hand a sad lad an atlas fast.     8
2   Slant that fat lath and add tall slats.    16
3   That tall lad sat and had a fast salad.    24
4   Lana and Sal shall stand and talk last.    32

5   Sad dad had a flat hat that falls fast.     8
6   Hal shall thank that tall and lank lad.    16
7   A tall shaft falls and halts that task.    24
8   Hats and sandals shall stand, as a fad.    32
    ----1----2----3----4----5----6----7----8
```

Thinking Drill

LOOK

Look at these words:

tan hand ant sand thank

SELECT

Now—select the word that best answers each of the following statements. Read each statement, look at the words, and quickly type your selection.

TYPE

1. A small insect
2. During the summer, the hot sun may give you a good______.
3. When you meet someone you may shake his______.
4. What you lie on when you are at the beach
5. It is always good to say_____ you to a person who has done something nice for you.

REVIEW

Margins:
- Elite: 25 and 75
- Pica: 17 and 67

Line 1 once—speed

Lines 2 and 3—speed

Lines 2 and 3 again—speed

```
1   jj nn jn jn askf jkl; jh jh ft ft l.l jj nn jn jn
2   an and ant fan tan sat fat add aft all ask sad at
3   tank land sand than hall tall slat salt lank talk
```

Item 8

Working Papers, pp. 313-14

Mr. David Browne, 813 North 59th Avenue West, Chicago IL 60612. Dear Dave: I would like to take this opportunity to extend to you my congratulations for a truly outstanding term as Illinois State Youth Councelor of Midwest Community Enterprises. Your strong leadership and dedication produced a year of one successful event after another and provided strong momentum for the future. Your future success, Dave, seems assured; I hope that you can from time to time continue to contribute to MCE in some way. Sincerely, Lee Iverson, Chairman, Civic Awareness Committee

Item 9

Working Papers, pp. 315-16

Mr. Bill Godfrey, Jr. Midwest Community Enterprises. 1539 Court House. Chicago, IL 60601 Dear Bill: In response to your request, I am most pleased to communicate with you quarterly with a summary of financial trends and developments for Midwest Community Enterprises. With reference to the financial statements for the six-month period ended March 31 which are enclosed, I would like to draw your attention to the following key points.

1. In 1970, Midwest Community Enterprises realized $24,705 from the sale of land bequested by Ray McAllister. Since 1970, disbursements have exceeded receipts by $10,025, dropping the foundation's net worth to $14,725.

2. In the first six months last year MCE had receipts of $13,400 and disbursements of $17,715, resulting in deficit spending of $4,275.

3. Most of the funds go toward the support of a MCE office, field director, part-time secretary, travel, supplies, etc. None of the funds are going to the club officers or individual chapters.

In January of this year, Midwest Community Enterprises achieved tax-exempt status which is imperative in attracting gifts of quantity and size. The club is now in the prcess of developing programs to encourage individual contributions that are necessary to achieve a balanced budget and to provide momentum for our program of stronger field support, more chapters, and a more widespread public relations program. Sincerely, Lee Iverson, Chairman, Civic Awareness Committee. Enclosures.

Item 10

Working Papers, p. 317

Dear Business Leader: Where will we get our future community leaders in Chicago? Future Focus, sponsored by Midwest Community Enterprises, is an exciting new program of public service leadership training designed to help answer this question. The enclosed brochure describes the basic objectives and outlines the general program, shedule, and fees. We need your help to assure the success of this important undertaking to develop future community leaders. Its long-range success depends on the quality of applicants from whom the final 30 participants will be selected. We ask you to help us by sponsoring a candidate or candidates--young men and women from your organization or some other deserving person from the community. Participants will be selected according to several criteria:

1. Demonstrated ability for leadership as shown by past personal accomplishments in work, community, or education-related activities.
2. Strong interest in community affairs.

(cont'd. on next page)

Introduction to E

Home-row *d* finger moves up and to the left to the ***e*** key. Place both hands on the home row and practice the move from ***d*** to ***e***. Look at your hand and watch your finger make the motion. Do this several times; then look away and try the same motion.

E

Line 1 once

1 d dd de de de dd ed ed de ded ded dd ee de dedede

Lines 2 and 3 once—speed
Lines 2 and 3 again—speed

2 de den den eat eat eel eel ate ate ale ale elf de
3 de let let she she see see the the fee fee elk de

Lines 4-7 once—speed
Lines 4-7 again—accuracy

4 dead dead date date east east else else deaf deaf
5 deal deal ease ease else else desk desk fell fell
6 fade fade feel feel hate hate head head heal heal
7 false false knead knead jeans jeans end end flake

DRILL

Lines 1-14 once. At end of each line return carriage quickly and immediately begin typing on next line. Then do again.

1 He
2 He ate
3 He ate salt.
4 She
5 She has
6 She has land
7 He
8 He tested
9 He tested the
10 He tested the saddle.
11 Send
12 Send a
13 Send a false
14 Send a false flake.

Item 5

Working Papers, pp. 307-8

Ms. Nancy Crosby, CPS / 716 Upton Avenue, Aprartment #203 / Auburn Park, IL 60620

Dear Nancy: welcome to the Global City Bank team in Chicago! I may be prejudiced because of my ten years of experience, but I feel you are about to join the best bank in the world. I wanted to confirm in writing your salary of $445 per month and mention that your position opening date looks firm for June 5. I understand you will be giving a two-week notice to your present employer the week of May 15 and then will be taking a week's vacation. Please fill out the enclosed employment forms and return them to me in a week or so. Also, please mail a copy of your birth certificate. If you can use your imagination in getting the fingerprint card completed, that would be great (The bank will pay for any related expenses). I'm also enclosing copies of two manuals that will help you understand the personnel policies and benefits of Global City Bank a little better. I will give you personal manuals (hopefully newly-revised versions) when you begin work. If you have any questions, don't hesitate to call. Have a pleasant vacation, and we will be in touch soon. Sindreely, Lee Iverson, VP & Gen. Mgr. Enclosures.

Item 6

Working Papers, pp. 309-10

Mr. Nathan Shaw, President / NBS Systems, INc. / 7302 Oakland Ave./ Chicago, IL 60623

Dear Nathan: After giving some thought to your banking problems, we feel more confident than ever that our capabilities and banking systems abroad will be extremely beneficial to your coprorate goals. There are two aspects of our international services which we need to articluate further:

1. The in-country capabilities that we bring to your traveling representative or manufacturing facilities (e.g., structuring deals, competitive pricing, and local modus operandi for contract bidding).
2. The world-wide communication system outlet available to you in Chicago.

To further communicate our banking capabilities, Lee and I would like the opportunity to sit down with you and specifically set up a program for your marketing agents traveling abroad to visit and interface with our overseas network. These arrangments, of course, would be made at your convenience. Enclosed is further economic information pertaining to domestic and foreign monetary policies, money supplies, and foreign currency evaluations. If you would like to receive any of these on a regular basis, please let me know. Sincerely, Jean McDowell, Asst. VP. Enclosures. c: Lee Iverson

Item 7

Working Papers, pp. 311-12

Mr. Ralph J. Benson, President Benson Appliance Center / 444 Main Street / Chicago, IL 60603

Dear Mr. Benson: Global Business Credit recognizes you as one of the Midwest's leading wholesalers. As such, you are probably confronted with the types of dday-to-day needs that we understand: 1. Additional external funding sources 2. Improvement of accounts receivable turnover. 3. A reliable source of funding to keep trade current. 4. Seasonal inventory financing. As an affiliate of New York's Global City Bank, and through our new regional office in Chicago, Global Business Credit is now better able to service the continuing needs of your company. Please call me on my personal line, 662-2101. Sincerely, Donald Birk, District Manager

 Questions? Call **CUSTOMER SERVICE: (402) 474-2161**

THE GREATEST BAG FOR THE GREATEST DRIVERS!

OFFICIAL NASCAR DUFFEL BAG is the gear of champions!

Supercharged rugged 'n colorful nylon duffel features official team colors and number of your favorite NASCAR driver. Jumbo compartment holds all your big stuff while 2 side zip pockets are great for the little things. Adjustable shoulder strap plus carrying handle. 18"L x 10"W x 9"H. Imported. Order #664.

ONLY $19.95

Choose from: **Bill Elliott** **Mark Martin** **Dale Earnhardt** **Jeff Gordon** **Terry Labonte**

FOR FASTER SERVICE ORDER BY PHONE!
(402) 474-0847
Mon-Fri 7AM-12AM
Sat 7AM-4PM CST

Cut Here

CAROL WRIGHT® GIFTS Dept. **F762**
340 Applecreek Road, P.O. Box 8504, Lincoln, NE 68544-8504

Please send me the NASCAR DUFFEL BAGS indicated at right:
☐ Only $19.95 plus $5.95 shipping, handling and safe delivery for one (total $25.90).
☐ **SAVE!** Each additional NASCAR BAG just $18.95 plus $5.95 shipping, handling and safe delivery (total $24.90).

Qty.	Order #	Driver's Name
	664	
	664	
	664	

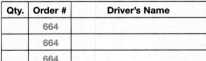

Enclosed is $ ___________. Please make check or money order payable to CAROL WRIGHT GIFTS. Thank you.

Please charge my: ☐ VISA ☐ MasterCard ☐ Discover

Acct. # ________________ Exp. Date Mo. __ / Yr. __

☐ Mr. ☐ Mrs. ☐ Miss ☐ Ms.

NAME (please print)

ADDRESS/Apt. #

CITY/STATE/ZIP

MasterCard
VISA
DISCOVER NOVUS
Carol Wright's
UNCONDITIONAL GUARANTEE
Whenever you buy anything from us, you must be satisfied! Or return your purchase any time for a full refund.

CT and NE residents please add sales tax.
Please allow 4 to 6 weeks for shipment.

SEE OTHER SIDE FOR MORE DETAILS!

THE GREATEST BAG FOR THE GREATEST DRIVERS!

DUFFEL BAG

is the gear of champions!

Supercharged rugged 'n colorful nylon duffel features official team colors and number of your favorite NASCAR driver. Jumbo compartment holds all your big stuff while 2 side zip pockets are great for the little things. Adjustable shoulder strap plus carrying handle. 18"L x 10"W x 9"H. Imported.

Only 19^{95}

Official colors and signature!

Choose from:
Bill Elliott
Mark Martin
Dale Earnhardt
Jeff Gordon
Terry Labonte

Order on other side.

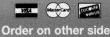

SENTENCES

Lines 1-8 once—speed

Take:
Two 15-sec. timings on Lines 1, 2, 3, and 4. Then take two 30-sec. timings.

1 Jean shall sell the seashells, saddle, and jeans. 10
2 Taste the lean tea; handle the kettle that leaks. 20
3 The athlete tensed a knee as she dashed and fell. 30
4 The eldest, steadfast attendant halted the theft. 40

----1----2----3----4----5----6----7----8----9---10

Take:
Two 15-sec. timings on Lines 5, 6, 7, and 8. Then take two 30-sec. timings.

5 Send the dated lease and halt the endless hassle. 10
6 A talented athlete eats steak and salad at least. 20
7 A flannel hat fell as Allen defended a keen lead. 30
8 The lean hen left the lake and settled at a nest. 40

----1----2----3----4----5----6----7----8----9---10

TAKE A ONE-MINUTE TIMING

Check your stroking rate on the paragraph below. First—type the entire paragraph at a "controlled" rate. A controlled rate is one in which you are typing at a comfortable speed, not concentrating on either speed or accuracy. Second—take a one-minute timing. Determine your word-a-minute (wam) rate. Third, take another one-minute timing. Attempt to get further in the copy (type more words) than you did on your first attempt. REMEMBER—if you get one more letter typed the second time, you are typing faster!

TIMING

Type once at controlled rate.
Take one 1-min. timing.
Take another 1-min. timing.

Ann and Sal attended a feast at the lake estates. 10
The steaks needed salt and the stale salad tasted 20
flat. Ann left a sandal and a hat at the tent. 30

----1----2----3----4----5----6----7----8----9---10

Thinking Drill

LOOK

Look at these words:

heat handle eat fall lake

SELECT

Now—select the word that best answers each of the following statements. Read each statement, look at the words, and quickly type your selection.

TYPE

1. You usually ____ meals each day.
2. The part of a container you grab when you pick it up.
3. The ____ from the stove cooks the meat.
4. It may contain fish.
5. Be careful, he may ____ down.

REVIEW

Line 1 once—speed

Lines 2 and 3 once—speed
Lines 2 and 3 again—speed

1 dd ee de de asdf jkl; jh ft l.l k, et dd ee de de
2 an let see the ale ask and fee fat sad lad all at
3 fell east dates feel desk else deaf eel fade lank

Item 3

Working Papers, pp. 295-96

Send to: John M. Nelson, VP
From: Lee Iverson, VP + Gen. Manager
Subject: New Acct. Manager Position

In the ~~2Q~~ ABQ Position Report, I outlined the rational(e) behind the request for an additional account manager by September or October. The purpose of this memo is to provide more details regarding that request.

Title~~e~~ Experience Level

While a banker from this area with four to five years of lending experience would be preferable, neither my interviewing nor that of Berkeley Associates has turned up a suitable candidate from this area. We will continue to keep our eyes open for a good prospect ~~local man, however~~.

Function

The primary function of the additional account manager would be to develop incremental loan business by calling on assigned prospects and referral sources. We need a confident, outgoing person who is flexible yet persistent enough to learn how to do business in the Upper Midwest.

When the new person develops a potential loan transaction piece of business, he or she can work closely with both Jean and myself in putting the transaction together, getting it approved, and following up. An emphasis on training and production would exist during the first 12 to 18 months here.

If any further details are needed, please let me know.

Item 4

Working Papers, pp. 297-305

TO: ~~Distribution~~

FROM: Lee Iverson, VP & Gen. Manager

SUB. Employment of Ms. Nancy Crosby

I am pleased to announce the expansion of our office staff with the addition of Ms. Nancy Crosby, CPS, who will join us on June 5. ~~within the next few weeks.~~ J. McDowell will be her immediate supervisor.

Nancy comes to us with an associate degree in secretarial science and two years of executive secretarial experience. In addition, she has attained her Certified Professional Secretary rating. More detailed credentials are attached. We are indeed fortunate to obtain someone with her qualifications.

As you know, this position has opened up because of the considerable increase in the volume of work in our office and also in anticipation of the employment of another account manager. I'm sure ~~that~~ each of you will extend a warm welcome to Nancy. Attachments.

~~Distribution:~~ Donald Birk
Michael Fitzsimmons
J. P. Hopkins
Jean McDowell

c. Nancy Crosby

Be sure to make copies for all concerned. Original goes to Jean M. Use internal mail envelopes.

Introduction to I

Home-row *k* finger moves up and to the left to the *i* key. Place both hands on the home row and practice the move from *k* to *i*. Look at your hand and watch your finger make the motion. Do this several times; then look away and try the same motion.

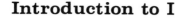

Line 1 once—speed

Lines 2 and 3—speed
Lines 2 and 3 again—speed

1 k kk ki ki ki kk ik ik ki kik kik kk ii ki kikiki
2 ki if if in in it it hi hi kid kid his his ale ki
3 ki sit sit ski ski hit lid lid lie lie ill ill ki

Lines 4-7 once—speed
Lines 4-7 again—accuracy

4 fail fail file file fill fill find find fine fine
5 hill hill tail tail life life said said idea idea
6 this this like like kind kind lift lift dish dish
7 knife knife still still think think kit kit thief

DRILL

Lines 1-14 once. At end of each line return carriage quickly and immediately begin typing on next line. Then do again.

1 aid
2 aid kid
3 aid kid kin
4 aid kid kin tie
5 aid kid kin tie tin
6 diet
7 diet dine
8 diet dine dish
9 diet dine dish lien
10 diet dine dish lien link
11 diet dine dish lien link sail
12 diet dine dish lien link sail skit
13 diet dine dish lien link sail skit thin
14 diet dine dish lien link sail skit thin tile

Item 1

Working Papers, pp. 293-94

TO: Lee Iverson/ Vice President & General Manager. FROM: J. M. McDowell, Assistant Vice President. SUBJECT: Northern Chemical Supply corporation. Lee, attached is a D & B report giving some brief information on Northern Chemical Supply Corporation as of March 18, 19__, ~~with additional financial informationas of December, 19__?~~ An updated report will be available ~~sometime during the month of~~ July 15 Rush!

I will ~~am attempting to~~ obtain additional background information on this company to determine whether our services fit their financing needs. Attachment

---

Item 2

Plain paper

D & B REPORT on NORTHERN CHEMICAL SUPPLY CORPORATION (telephoned ~~in~~ on May 8, 19--)

1. ~~This~~ The report is dated March 18, 19__.
2. They have a rating of 1A2.
3. Corporation is an established business.
4. Principals experienced. Principals' records clear.
5. They have made five (5) payments as of ~~dated~~ January, 19__.
   a. High credit - $18,000
   b. All five payments were prompt.
6. Their financial statement~~s~~ dated ~~December 1, 19???~~ March 1, 19--
   a. Current Assets - $909,470
   B. Current Liabilities - $531,190
   c. Net Worth - $491,190
   d. Sales are $2.5 million
   e. Bank balances - medium six ~~6~~ figures
   f. Loans secured and guaranteed to low six ~~6~~ figures~~.~~
   g. At present, not owing
7. They are a manufacturer and distributor of industrial finishes, plastic coatings, adhesives, and dispersions.
8. Chartered in Illinois - November 9, 1954.
9. Their president is Victor C. Cole.
10. They are now under investigation and will be completing their investigation about ~~the 10th of June.~~ June 10, 19--

Rush! Number + letter these items as indicated.

SENTENCES

Lines 1-8 once—speed

Take:
Two 15-sec. timings on Lines 1-4.
Then take two 30-sec. timings.

1 See, he is ill; his skin is thin; he feels faint. 10
2 The hit thief listened and slid his knife inside. 20
3 Enlist that inside aid that he shall indeed need. 30
4 I dislike that snide kid; he thinks it is a skit. 40
----1----2----3----4----5----6----7----8----9---10

Take:
Two 15-sec. timings on Lines 5-8.
Then take two 30-sec. timings.

5 She is a skilled athlete and likes little detail. 10
6 The kitten is an infant and is a little lifeless. 20
7 The kid thinks I had the idea that he did finish. 30
8 He did ski that hill; that is indeed a fine test. 40
----1----2----3----4----5----6----7----8----9---10

TIMINGS

Type once at controlled rate.
Take one 1-min. timing.
Take another 1-min. timing.

The athlete shall indeed finish last if he falls. 10
His knees and ankles fail at the final line. The 20
defeat is, indeed, a test. 25
----1----2----3----4----5----6----7----8----9---10

Type once at controlled rate.
Take one 1-min. timing.
Take another 1-min. timing.

Jan sat in the shade and listened. As she dined, 10
the island fleas hid in the sand. Allan finished 20
the feast at last and sat as the stillness faded. 30
----1----2----3----4----5----6----7----8----9---10

Thinking Drill

LOOK

Look at these words:

inhale *thief* *island* *kitten* *nail* *diet*

SELECT

Now—select the word that best answers each of the following statements. Read each statement, look at the words, and quickly type your selection.

TYPE

1. **Land surrounded by water**
2. **What you should do if you are too fat**
3. **Opposite of *exhale***
4. **A small cat**
5. **The name of someone who steals**
6. **What you drive into wood with a hammer**

REVIEW

Line 1 once—speed

Lines 2 and 3 once—speed
Lines 2 and 3 again—speed

1 asdf jkl; de ft ki jn k, l. ;: Al Sal Dan Ted Ken
2 the the and and if if it it in in has has had had
3 I see the idle kid, Al, fell at the island slide.

Bank

TYPE OF COMPANY: Commercial Bank

DATE: May 8, 19--

COMPANY NAME/ADDRESS: Global City Bank
480 N. LaSalle Street
Chicago, IL 60606

COMPANY TEL. NO.: 312/662-2100

SITUATION: You are a secretary in the Chicago regional office of Global City Bank, which deals primarily in large commercial loans. You have been employed with the Bank since it opened its Chicago branch nine months ago.

There are four bankers working out of this office for whom you handle office duties:

1. Lee Iverson
   Vice President and General Manager
2. Jean M. McDowell
   Assistant Vice President
3. Mike Fitzsimmons
   Leasing Officer
4. Donald Birk
   District Manager
   Global Business Credit, Inc.
   (a subsidiary of Global City Bank)

Much of the correspondence is sent to individuals at the GCB Headquarters in New York City.

SPECIAL INSTRUCTIONS/EXPLANATIONS:

For this project, assume you called one of the temporary office service agencies, and Mike Niverson was sent to assist you. Assume that you were meeting all morning with the four bankers you work with. Mr. Niverson completed a variety of items, including the preparation of several letters, memorandums, and reports. These items were given for review to the individuals, who dictated them prior to the lunch hour. When you return to your desk after lunch, you find the following items in your In-Basket. These items are to be retyped in the order in which you find them. Be sure to use your initials on each item as the typist.

Items 1 and 2. Jean McDowell has a rush order on a Dunn and Bradstreet report for Northern Chemical Supply Corporation. The information on the report was telephoned in today. Type this information on a separate sheet and attach it to the cover memo from Mr. McDowell.

Items 8, 9, 10. Lee Iverson also holds the position of chairman of the Civic Awareness Committee of Midwest Community Enterprises. This Chicago-based organization is devoted to developing future business and community leaders. Items 8, 9, and 10 deal with correspondence relating to Midwest Community Enterprises; use Midwest Community Enterprise letterhead.

Again, be on the lookout for any and all uncorrected errors.

Introduction to the Question Mark

Home-row ; finger moves down and to the right to the ? key. Since the question mark is located at the top of the key, you must depress LEFT SHIFT before striking the ?. Place both hands on the home row and practice the move from ; to the question mark. Look at your hands and watch your finger make the motion. Do this several times; then look away and try the same motion.

Important: Tap space bar TWICE after question mark at end of sentence.

Line 1 once

Lines 2 and 3 once—speed
Lines 2 and 3 again—speed

1 asdf jkl; ;? ;? ;? ;;; ;? ;? ;?; ?; ?; ;? ;? ;?;?

2 Is Jennie ahead? Is Dennis safe? Is Allen late?

3 Did Jake fall? Did Leslie fail? Did Jan tattle?

DRILL

Lines 1, 2, 3, and 4 once—speed
Lines 1, 2, 3, and 4 again—control

Take two 30-sec. timings.

1 Is Ken late? Is Dale fit? Is Neil in his teens? 10

2 Did she dine? Did the leaf fall? Did Jane flee? 20

3 Has he landed? Has the thief left? Has she hit? 30

4 If Al faints, shall I still slide in the infield? 40

----1----2----3----4----5----6----7----8----9---10

REVIEW

Line 1 once

Lines 2 and 3 once—speed
Lines 2 and 3 again—speed

1 asdf jkl; de ft jn ki l. ;? k, Did I see it skid?

2 the the that that then then than than thank thank

3 a a an an and and ant ant an an ant ant hand hand

Item 13
Plain paper

CLAIM NO. POLICY NO. DATE INCURRED INVOLVING

Use of this form permits us to give your loss prompt attention. We have checked the information needed or action that you should take so that we can satisfactorily service your claim.

__________1. Complete enclosed form and return in the envelope provided.

__________2. "Authorization to Release Information" or "Medical Information Authority" should be signed by the patient, or parent if the patient is a minor, and returned in the envelope provided.

__________3. The "Physician of Supplier Information" section should be completed by the attending physician. Also acceptable is any standard form which agent, doctor, or hospital furnishes.

__________4. Forward the itemized hospital bill.

__________5. Forward the itemized doctor bills.

__________REMARKS: ______________________________

Leave 2 blank lines for remarks

Prompt return of this form together with requested items or information will hasten disposition of this claim. Thank you for your attention.

Mark Evans
Underwriting Supervisor

OMO-314(d)

Here is the info needed for our new form #OMO-314(d) for health claims—(should help to expedite claims) Would you type this form + arrange on a full sheet of paper? Rearrange four items at top so there will be enough room for "fill-in." Leave more room between last line + my name (for signature). P.S. remember -- will need enough line space with heading "INVOLVING" to include name + full address. Make 2 copies. When finished, fill in original as follows

Ⓐ Ms. Shirley A. Novak
23 Circle West
Cincinnati, OH 45211

Ⓑ Claim #K0548E 20884

Ⓒ Policy #B64-10089

Ⓓ Date incurred: Sept. 2

Ⓔ Check items 2, 3, + 5

Ⓕ Remarks: We have not received the radiology bill.

Introduction to G

Home-row *f* finger moves to the right to the *g* key. Place both hands on the home row and practice the move from *f* to *g*. Look at your hands and watch your finger make the motion. Do this several times; then look away and try the same motion.

G

Line 1 once—speed

Lines 2-5 once—speed
Lines 2-5 again—accuracy

1 f ff fg fg ff gf gf fg fgf fgf ff gg fg fg fgfgfg

2 fg gal gal gas gas get get sag sag egg egg gal fg

3 fg keg keg leg leg nag nag jig jig tag tag keg fg

4 fg gang gang gain gain Gale Gale gift gift gag fg

5 fg glad glad gate gate Gene Gene high high gas fg

Lines 6-10 once—speed
Lines 6-10 again—accuracy

6 sign sign sing sing sang sang shag shag hang hang

7 fight fight eight eight light light tag tag night

8 again again sting sting hinge hinge egg egg glass

9 angle angle fling fling ledge ledge get get tight

10 ing seeing taking dealing finding landing talking

DRILL

Type each line once. At end of each line return carriage quickly and immediately begin typing on next line. Then do again.

sag sag
high high
giant giant
taking taking
against against
delegate delegate
delighted delighted
flashlight flashlight
sightseeing sightseeing

the insured and explain the coverage provided. If your state has no-fault insurance coverage, supplemental coverages, or a similar statute, please be sure to explain its options to ~~the insured~~ Mr. Carlson. ¶ The enclosures replace the insured's previous insurance at his former address. Please note the accompanying changes and/or credits and make premium adjustments if necessary. ¶ Since underwriting responsibility for this risk is now yours, be sure to satisfy yourself that the ~~risk~~ client qualifies for continued protection through your agency. If the enclosures inaccurately describe the property which is to be covered, if you decide that the risk does not meet our underwriting requ~~ri~~irements, if the address~~s~~ is incorrect or temporary, or if a change of any kind should be made—please let our office know immediately. ME-US. Enclosures.

Item 12

Working Papers, pp. 291-92

Mr. James P. Cody. 5050 Jersey Ave. West. Ann Arbor, MI 48106 Dear Mr. C. / In your letter of Sept. 16, you asked whether your policy, # 48BD-40517-B, had been canceled + if any refund had been allowed. In checking our records, I find that the policy was canceled effective Aug. 1, as you requested. A refund of $67.30 (check #13467) was issued to you at that time.

In the event you have not received the check +/or notification of cancellation, please contact me; I will make sure the matter is speedily resolved. Sincerely ME US

SENTENCES

Lines 1-10 once—speed

Take:
Two 15-sec. timings on Lines 1 through 5.
Then take two 30-sec. timings.

1 Dennis and Gene nailed a lath in the fallen gate. 10
2 The infant giggles in delight as the sled glides. 20
3 Helen had seen the elegant sign shining at night. 30
4 The endless agenda had eight legal details added. 40
5 A kitten had tangled the thin tinsel in the hall. 50

----1----2----3----4----5----6----7----8----9---10

Take:
Two 15-sec. timings on Lines 6 through 10.
Then take two 30-sec. timings.

6 Kale and Allan ate a salad and a fig and a steak. 10
7 Gina, the gentle giant, giggled at Tina, the elf. 20
8 Dad needs a light flashlight if he skis at night. 30
9 Leslie sang a jingle as she dashed ahead in glee. 40
10 Dan tested his stiff ankle and gnashed his teeth. 50

----1----2----3----4----5----6----7----8----9---10

TIMINGS

Type once at controlled rate.
Take one 1-min. timing.
Take another 1-min. timing.

An idle lad finishes last. He is shiftless as he 10
sits and tells his tales. He needs an insight in 20
the elegant things in life. 25

----1----2----3----4----5----6----7----8----9---10

Type once at controlled rate.
Take one 1-min. timing.
Take another 1-min. timing.

Allan is attaining a skill in legal defense. The 10
giant task is thankless. He insists that all the 20
details heighten his thinking. 26

----1----2----3----4----5----6----7----8----9---10

Push for SPEED. Drive for ACCURACY

The material on the next page has been word counted for 20-, 15-, or 10-second drills (look at the right of the lines): After determining which length timing you will be taking, go to that identified column and go down the row of figures to the one which you think you can "average" a minute. Then type the line to the left of that figure. If you complete the line before time is up, it means that you averaged ***at least*** that many words a minute. Then go to the next line—which is longer—and attempt to complete it before time is called. Repeat the procedure until it is impossible for you to complete the line before time is called.

Remember—Be sure that you are looking at the right time column.

FOLLOW THIS PROCEDURE—For SPEED, let your fingers fly and concentrate on speed; really "push" to finish the line before time is called. Don't worry about errors. For ACCURACY, concentrate on accuracy; attempt to finish the line and have no more than one error before proceeding to the next longer line.

Item 9

Working Papers, pp. 285-86

Mr. Scott Pedderson, 7330 York Avenue, Youngstown, OH 44509. RE. Plicy No. 1616 802 Dear Mr. P: Your agent has advised us that you would like information on the present cash surrender value and loan value of your policy, number 1616 802. ¶ As of September 15, 19__, your policy has a guaranteed cash value of $10,370 ~~which is the cash surrender value at this time.~~ If the September 15 annual premium of $2,998.20 has been paid and the policy is surrendered prior to October 15, the premium will be refunded. ¶ At the present time, your policy has a maximum loan value of $15,340. This amount assumes that the September 15 annual premium has been paid. If this premium has not been paid, it would be deducted from the maximum loan available. ¶ ~~I trust you will find the above information satisfactory. However,~~ if you have any questions, please ~~feel free to~~ contact me. Sincerely, Mark E., Underwriting Supervisor. c. Phil Blooston.

Item 10

Working Papers, pp. 287-88

Mr. Simon F. Gray, Route 3, Box 299, Maple Valley, MN 44320. Dear Mr. Gray: Ohio Mutual has the most competitive program for your automobile coverage. Your present coverage for the two cars would cost $489 annually. ~~The 1977 Elite's~~ insurance on your 1977 Elite would cost as follows:

Liability	-	$ 85
No Fault	-	15
Comprehensive	-	49
$100 Deductible Collision		79
Uninsured Motorist		12
TOTAL		$240

leave more space between the two columns

The total for the three cars is $729 annually. I suggest we submit an application as soon as possible in order to have the policy issued ~~well~~ before October. ¶ I would like to make one observation regarding the coverage you now carry. At present you carry $100 deductible collision. A $250 deductible collision on all three cars would save you $170 annually in premiums. The additional $150 deductible, in effect, would still put you dollars ahead if you had one accident per year. I recommend this change in coverage ~~no matter whom you insure with.~~ ¶ I will await your response and/or questions, Mr. Gray. Sincerely, ME, UN.SUP.

NOTE: the last sentence seems awkward--rewrite, please.

Item 11

Working Papers, pp. 289-90

DATE: Today's. SUBJECT: Dennis Carlson, Jr. POLICY ~~REF.~~ NO.: 12 038156 01 12. TO: Mr. Darrell Egan, 441 South Locust, Newport, KY 41072. To provide service for the above-named insured who formerly lived in another state, we have assigned this client ~~business~~ to your agency. The insured is expecting ~~will welcome~~ your visit; please call as soon as possible and extend assurances that you are now the agent of record and that you can take care of his everyday insurance needs. ¶ We have rewritten the automobile coverage to match, as closely as possible, the policy the insured previously carried. Because of possible statutory coverage differences between states, it is important that you discuss the new policy with

(cont'd. on next page)

SPEED PUSH

	20	15	10
A lank ant ate.	9	12	18
The sail is stained.	12	16	24
Dale ate that stale fish.	15	20	30
Dan and Jane hid in that shed.	18	24	36
That Ted is a tease and a sad fake.	21	28	42
Ski the hills and skate at the fine lake.	24	32	48
The sleet sent Jane and Sean in the tall tent.	27	36	54
That tank seat fit as if it had a snag in the side.	30	40	60

ACCURACY DRIVE

	20	15	10
Design the jig.	9	12	18
A dentist hesitated.	12	16	24
The gaslight is settling.	15	20	30
Essential thinking is gallant.	18	24	36
The legal delegate shall legislate.	21	28	42
The shifting seedling shed is settling.	24	32	48
His flashlight is hanging in the jet infield.	27	36	54
That dashing defendant enlisted in the nineteenth.	30	40	60

Reinforcement Drill Material

CHECK TIMING

Type once at controlled rate.
Take one 1-min. timing.
Take another 1-min. timing.

That gallant knight led the detail. A tall, thin 10
lad assisted at the flank. The knight failed the 20
task and feels the defeat. A sadness sifts in as 30
his shield falls. 33

----1----2----3----4----5----6----7----8----9---10

MORE PRACTICE

Determine the number of words and number of errors for each timing taken on the paragraph above. The material provided on the following three pages is to be used for additional practice on the keys you have learned. There are no instructions on the left side of the page. Use the drills as follows:

1. If you have mastered the keys and do not hesitate when typing any letter, and did not have an excessive amount of errors (your instructor will tell you the maximum number of errors you may have for an acceptable timing), omit this section and proceed to page 18.

HESITATE?

2. If you have not mastered (hesitate before striking the key) the reach to a key(s), type the lines identified as:
   a. balanced-hand words
   b. letter combinations

TOO MANY ERRORS?

3. If you make an excessive amount of errors, type the lines identified as:
   a. double-letter words
   b. longer words

weeks ahead, during that all-important period between graduation from a driver education course and attainment of full driver status, you as a parent can reinforce driving habits. Your beginner will need hours of supervised practice--not only before facing driver license examinations, but also afterward. This practice should include exposure to high-risk situations: after-dark driving, rush-hour traffice, inclement weather, slippery roadways, gravel roads, etc. Depriving a youth of this indispensable type of supervised practice could be a fatal mistake. In view of the critical traffic safety problems facing us, we at Ohio Mutual urge you to make the very most of this opportunity to give your teenager what could turn out to be a priceless advantage in life. Incidentally, if in the process you should pick up some good driving tips from your newly educated young driver, you wouldn' be the first! Good luck, and thank you for your contribution to highway safety in Ohio. sincerely, M.E., Underwriter Supervisor

---

Item 7

Working Papers, pp. 281-82

Mr. Greg Johnson, Alexander Agency, 3004 Madison Avenue, S.E. Cleveland, Oh 44102 RE: Security Protection Devices in the Home of Joseph Newburg. Located at 3441 West 26 Street, Brook Park, Ohio 44142. Dear Mr. Johnson: Mr. Joseph Newburg's home burglar alarm system consists of contacts and window foil on every exterior door and window. Inside protection "traps" are also incorporated into the system. If a break-in should occur, three outside tamper-proof bells will sound and one inside bell. Simultaneously, the signal is transmitted via leased telephone line directly to the Brook Park Police Department's monitoring. In the event the leased telephone line is cut or any other type of violation occurs to the system, an immediate signal will be received by the Police Department. The alarm system also has several stationary silent-signal hold-up buttons permanently mounted in the house, and four portable hold-up buttons. These buttons will transmit an alarm signal to the police from an approximate distance of 300 feet from the house. The stationary buttons also send an instantaneous silent signal to the police. The fire alarm system consists of smoke detectors and heat thermostats mounted throughout the house. There are connected directly to the Police Department by a second leased telephone line. Mr. Newburg has a separate alarm system for his garage area. This equipment consists of electronic photo beams protecting the overhead garage doors, and alarm foil protecting the windows. The garage system is completely independent of the home alarm systems. All alarm equipment is U.L. approved for quality. Sincerely, ME, Underwriting supervisor.

Item 8

Working Papers, pp. 283-84

Mrs. Sheryl Marx, 552 Roosevelt, Cuyahoga Falls, OH 44223. Dear Mrs. M. Enclosed are copies of our checks that have been issued in payment of claims submitted under your insureds' policies with this company. These copies of our checks are being forwarded to you for completion of your records as part of the continuing service provided by Ohio Mutual Insurance Group Sincerely, ME, US. Enclosures

NOT FAST ENOUGH?

4. If you are not able to type as rapidly as you would like, type the lines identified as balanced-hand words.

After determining what you feel you should do, consult with your instructor for permission to proceed.

HELPS BUILD YOUR SPEED

BALANCED-HAND WORDS

1 and the ant tan ale elf end hen she end sigh sign
2 aid fit sit did tie die dig fig and the hang this
3 halt this hand lens lake lane then than ante fish
4 idle file dine hail this dish disk this file lake
5 shake snake title aisle angle fight handle island
6 angle sight digit gland eight slant height sleigh
7 signal giant tight an he if it and elf the and he

HELPS ELIMINATE ERRORS

DOUBLE-LETTER WORDS

1 see glee needs indeed feeling needless teens seed
2 egg sell sniff haggle falling eggshell stall eggs
3 eel keen sheen needle fiddles seedling sleek deed
4 add kiss stiff assist endless lifeless still hill

5 fee need sheet seeing dissent likeness steed heel
6 add fell skill allied skilled settling shell tell
7 see feel teeth indeed gallant sledding sleet knee
8 all hall shall little install knitting stall tall

9 Sadness is a feeling I assess as an alleged need.
10 Assist the skiing attendant and lessen all falls.
11 Did the sleek kitten flee the illegal attendants?
12 Haggling is a senseless dissent that is needless.
13 Flatten the stiff fiddle and install the tassels.

HELPS ELIMINATE ERRORS TOO!

LONGER WORDS

1 endless athlete flatten inflate install dislike
2 lenient distant delight heading inkling digital
3 A lenient athlete has inflated the flattened keg.

4 hesitate likeness definite alkaline initiate
5 heighten stealing gaslight lengthen delegate
6 The hesitating delegate is stealing the gaslight.

7 landslide skinflint stateside essential legislate
8 negligent lightness sightless delighted attendant
9 tasteless steadfast defendant thankless seashells
10 Seashells in the landslide delighted a skinflint.

Item 3

Working Papers, pp. 273-74

Mr. Steven Kuehn, 583 Birch Road, New Rockford, OH 58356. RE: Policy A98-143822

Dear Mr. Kuehn: Like all insurance companies, we have standards which help us determine whether we can provide insurance in individual cases. To our regret, we have concluded that we must ask you to secure insurance coverage through some other source. Coverage under the policy identified above will continue until 12:01 a.m. Eastern Time on November 28, 19__, at which time all coverage will cease. We feel you are entitled to know the reason for our decision. It is due to the combined claims experience in the last year. Claims occurred on April 4, May 17, May 28, and August 23. This action does not imply that you are uninsurable, nor does it prevent you from obtaining other insurance. If your agent has not already done so, he may be able to arrange for continuation of coverage for you through your state's automobile insurance plan. He will be glad to help you in this respect. Since this termination occurs at the end of the policy period, there is no refund due. Sincerely, M.E., Underwriting Supervisor.

Item 4

Working Papers, pp. 275-76

Send the same letter to Mrs. Linda Kuehn as sent to her husband, Steve. Use her policy #, violation dates, expiration date (obtain from info. included in memo to Thayer)

Item 5

Working Papers, p. 277

Dear Customer: We are pleased you have given us the opportunity to serve you. In reviewing your file, recently, we noticed that we are currently handling only a portion of your personal insurance. We feel it is our duty to point out that our agency can serve you best only when all your insurance needs are handled by the same people. Only by looking at your insurance needs as a whole, can your agency be sure that you have the right kinds of insurance protection, in the right amounts, with no duplications or gaps in coverage. Yes, it makes sense to have one agency provide you with total insurance protection. Then you know you are being looked after by insurance professionals who are familiar with you and all your specific requirements. So think about the benefits of total insurance protection. We've outlined many of these benefits in the enclosed brochure, and we've attached a postage-paid reply card for your convenience. Fill it out there is no obligation. But there is a good chance we can show you how to get more for your insurance dollar. Sincerely. Mark Evans, Underwriting Supervisor, Representing Ohio Mutual Insurance Group. Enclosures

NOTE -- This will be a form letter sent to selected customers. Type a final copy (1) Date the letter one week from tomorrow. (2) Leave blank lines so inside address can be typed in (longest inside address will be 4 lines)

Item 6

Working Papers, p. 279

Dear Parent: Knowing that your teenager has successfully completed a driver education course must be a source of satisfaction to you. Yet you may also have mixed feelings, since you know only too well that many critical lessons remain to be learned. In the

(cont'd. on next page)

High Noon™ Western Shirts

BLACK

Special Introductory Price!

Only 14^{95} each

7 DAY FREE WEAR-TEST

High Noon™ Western Shirts

Special Introductory Price!

Only $14.95 each

Trail blazin' good looks are yours — in a High Noon Western Shirt from BLAIR!

Authentic western details include pearlized snaps down the front and on the cuffs and flapped chest pockets, tailored collar with permanent stays, front and back yokes outlined with contrast piping, and long stay-tucked tails.

In rugged woven polyester/cotton, this machine washable Western Shirt will be your reliable pardner for years.

Order yours today for a **Week's Free Wear-Test.** No obligation to keep it if it doesn't meet your expectations.

SATISFACTION GUARANTEED. ABSOLUTELY! If your Western Shirt ever fails to perform to your satisfaction, return it for a full refund or replacement.

WWESTF6 A
BLAIR, WARREN, PA 16366

Detach here and mail today!

YES! Please rush my Western Shirt from BLAIR for a week's FREE WEAR-TEST. Then I'll send just $14.95 plus handling and shipping — or return the Shirt at my expense and owe nothing.

TO SAVE EVEN MORE, I've enclosed my payment now so BLAIR pays ALL handling and shipping costs. All my money will be instantly refunded if I'm not pleased.

DGD-M

☐Miss
☐Mrs.
☐Mr. ____________________

(Please print clearly)

Address ____________________ Apt.# ________

City ____________________

State ____________________ Zip ____________

Home Phone No. (______) ____________________

Credit orders subject to approval WWESTF6 A

TO ORDER: 1. Circle your size.

SMALL (14-14½) MEDIUM (15-15½) LARGE (16-16½)

X LARGE (17-17½) 2X LARGE (18-18½) 3X LARGE (19-19½)

2. Check (✓) color wanted.

BLACK	WHITE	BURGUNDY	ROYAL
02	03	07	09
7938	**ONE WESTERN SHIRT**		**TOTAL $14.95**

18483-CWA

Made in USA Offer good only in USA

Mail today to: **BLAIR®, WARREN, PA 16366**
QUALITY & VALUE SINCE 1910

LETTER COMBINATIONS

HELPS BUILD SPEED

1 de den dead deal desk denial dense deft dental de
2 di dig dish dial digest dislike dine dike disk di
3 I dislike the heat dial that fits the dental fan.

4 fi fish final fine finish fight find fig field fi
5 ga gal gas gag gale gait gallant gasket gadget ga
6 Gal, finish the gasket that the gas gadget needs.

7 ha hate hassle halt hall half hash hang handle ha
8 ki kite kiss kindle kilt kiln king kink kitten ki
9 That hanging kite tail hassels the halted kitten.

10 le lest left lead lend ledge least leaf lessen le
11 li lid lie lied lien link linking linkage like li
12 At least link the left lid and lessen the length.

13 sa sad sat safe sake sale said sang Sal saline sa
14 si sit site sitting signal sighted sill silken si
15 Sad Sal sang a signal as she sighted a safe site.

16 st stead still steal steadiness stateside stag st
17 ta tag talk take tall tale taste task tan tall ta
18 Steadfast Stell still talks and tells tall tales.

19 te tea test tenth tell tend teen tennis tenant te
20 th then that than thing this theft thin thesis th
21 Then that teen tenant, Ted, did a tenth tea test.

Introduction to P

Home-row *;* finger moves up and to the left to the *p* key. Place both hands on the home row and practice the move from *;* to *p*. Look at your hands and watch your finger make the motion. Do this several times; then look away and try the same motion.

Item 1

Working Papers, pp. 269-70

Mr. Thomas Charbonneau, 766 Shorewood Drive, Sayler Park, OH 45233. Dear Mr. Charbonneau: I appologize for the lateness in informing you of the recent rate increase in your homeowners insurance. We just received this notice in the last week. I am enclosing alternate proposals for your consideration. Because of the large rate increases that have occurred in the homeowners insurance market, I am including a proposal for a Form 3 as well as your cuAent coverage, which is a Form 4, so you may compare the prices. There are very important differences in these contracts. Your current coverage is All Risk on the dwelling and the unscheduled personal prAperty. Simply stated, this means that if the cause of the loss is not specifically excluded, it is covered. The Form 3 is identical on the dwelling coverage, but quite different on the unscheduled personal property. There are 18 covered perils listed on the policy form. In order for a loss to be covered, it must fit a covered peril. You will recall that you decided on the Form 4 because of the added coverage you would obtain for unscheduled personal property. I am not now trying to unsell the Form 4 but because of the increased costs, I felt obliged to quote both contract forms. If you have any questions, please call. I would also be happy to stop in and go over this in person if you wish. Sincerely. Mark Evans, Underwriting Supervisor, Enclosures.

Item 2

Working Papers, pp. 271-72

DATE: Today's. SUBJECT: Steven M. & Linda K. Kuehn. Ref. No.: A98-143822 and A98-190071. TO: Mr. Clifford W. Thayer, 424 Madison Street, New Rockford, OH 58356 Cliff, in June I wrote to you regarding the above insured's accident and violation frequency. We now have completed a motor vehicle survey and find that Mr. Kuehn has had even more violations that indicated before. He received a ticket for failure to yeild the right of way with the May 17, 19__, loss. To date, he and his wife have accumulated a total of 36 demerit points. We will be unable to continue both policies and will proceed with expiration on their respective renewal dates. For your infomration, the total record indicates the following:

Date	Violation	Demerits
Linda:		
May 4, 19__	Operating without a license	2
July 18, 19__	Operating while under influence	9
June 30, 19__	Accident	4
July 27, 19__	Driving on wrong side of highway	4
Steven:		
May 17, 19__	Accident	9
April 4, 19__	Failure to yield right-of-way	4
May 28, 19__ and august 23, 19__	Two accidents combined as one	4
	TOTAL	36

Place in chronological order for each individual.

I am sure you can see our concern in the total record of both drivers. Policy A98-143822 will expire November 28, 19__. Policy A98-190071 will expire October 26, 19__. Mark Evans, Underwriting Supervisor.

P

Line 1 once—speed

1 ; ;; ;p ;p ;p ;; p; p; p; ;p; ;p; ;; pp ;p ;P;P;P

Lines 2-5 once—speed
Lines 2-5 again—speed

2 ;p pan pat pea peg pen pep pet pie pig pin pit ;p
3 ;p ape apt dip gap hip lap nap pad sap tap tip ;p
4 ;p deep flap gape help jeep keep leap page lip ;p
5 ;p ship tape pink skip slap taps gads pest sap ;p

Lines 6-10 once—speed
Lines 6-10 again—speed

6 pail pill pain pine pale pest past page plan pile
7 plight paddle peddle pellet planet pet pie peddle
8 depend splash splint elapse happen pen nip staple
9 napkin pledge appeal please dispel peg nap plight
10 peasant pennant pitfall patient pheasant pleasant

DRILL

Type each line once. At end of each line return carriage quickly and immediately begin typing on next line. Then do again.

gasp gasp
leap leap peak peak
snap snap tape tape pile pile
spank spank spike spike aspen aspen
depend depend splint splint dispel dispel
splash splash happen happen sapling sapling

SENTENCES

Lines 1-10 once—speed

Take:
Two 15-sec. timings on Lines 1 through 5.
Then take two 30-sec. timings.

1 Is that dashing pink paint in the shapeless pail? 10
2 Please appease that helpless, pleading plaintiff. 20
3 A sheep passed the pines and plants in the sleet. 30
4 A tall, split, peeling aspen sapling is diseased. 40
5 His pastel napkin keeps dipping in his apple pie. 50

----1----2----3----4----5----6----7----8----9---10

Take:
Two 15-sec. timings on Lines 6 through 10.
Then take two 30-sec. timings.

6 Did Jake pass that fast jeep in his sedate sedan? 10
7 Pat speaks and pleads and defends the plaintiffs. 20
8 The patient is in pain; his left thigh is gashed. 30
9 Did Jane tape that splint and dispense the pills? 40
10 The spaniel has fleas and needs his skilled help. 50

----1----2----3----4----5----6----7----8----9---10

Learn How to Indent Paragraphs

To move the carriage or element to a particular space automatically, locate on your machine:

1. The tab bar or key
2. The tab clear and set keys

If you cannot find them, turn to the front of your book and look at the illustration of your machine.

CLEAR EXISTING TAB STOPS.

1. Return carriage or element to the left margin.

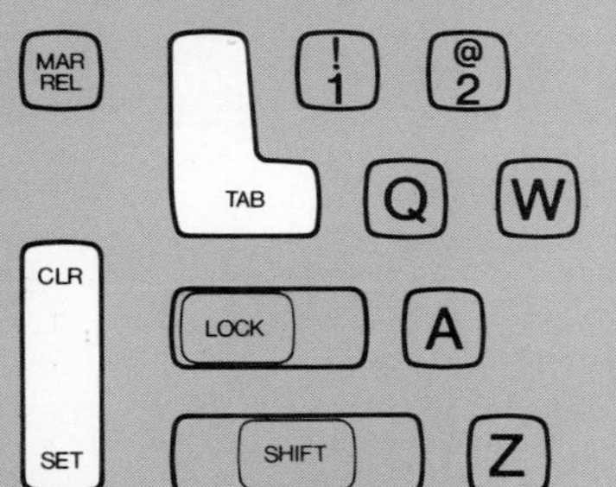

Insurance Agency

TYPE OF COMPANY: Insurance Agency

DATE: September 20, 19 - -

COMPANY NAME/ADDRESS: Ohio Mutual Insurance Group
4058 Elmwood Square
Cincinnati, OH 45219

COMPANY TEL. NO.: 513/488-1303

SITUATION: You are the secretary to Mr. Mark Evans, Underwriting Supervisor, in the home office of Ohio Mutual Insurance Group.

Ohio Mutual has offices located in all major cities in Ohio and five surrounding states. It also employs hundreds of agents in the smaller communities.

SPECIAL INSTRUCTIONS/EXPLANATIONS:

Assume that you have just returned from lunch and that Mr. Evans has given you the following items to be typed in final form. Mr. Evans will be out of the office all afternoon, so you will be on your own. He wants the items completed in the order that he has given them to you. For the letters and items that are complete with enclosures, just sign Mr. Evans' name and place your initials under the signature to show that you were the person who signed the letter. If there is any letter that requires an enclosure which you cannot supply, you will have to hold the completed item until Mr. Evans returns tomorrow morning to obtain the necessary forms or enclosures. Be sure to look for and correct any errors.

2. Depress tab bar or key.
3. If carriage or element stops before reaching the end of the line scale, there is a tab stop already set in the machine. To remove, push tab clear key. Continue this procedure until you have removed all existing stops.

SET TAB STOPS.

1. Return carriage or element to the left margin.
2. Move carriage or element to desired point on line scale.
3. Push tab set key. Continue this procedure until you have put all required tab stops across your sheet of paper.
4. Return the carriage or element to left margin; depress tab bar or key. Carriage or element should move to desired stopping point.

Indent the first line of paragraphs five (5) spaces unless instructed differently.

TIMINGS

Type once at controlled rate.
Take one 1-min. timing.
Take another 1-min. timing.

```
     Taking a jet flight is pleasant.  Despite an      10
initial tense feeling, the steadfast engines sail      20
past the land.  The gentle landing is a delight.       30
----1----2----3----4----5----6----7----8----9---10
```

Type once at controlled rate.
Take one 1-min. timing.
Take another 1-min. timing.

```
     The pitfall in sailing is snapping the final      10
paddles.  The helpless ship spins at a speed that      20
defies the senses and tenses the flesh.                28
----1----2----3----4----5----6----7----8----9---10
```

General Guidelines

ADDING AN *ed* OR *ing* ENDING

There are exceptions to every general guideline. If you are in doubt, consult a good dictionary.

Remember—the vowels are *A*, *E*, *I*, *O*, *U* (and sometimes *Y*). All other letters are consonants.

1. Words ending in a silent ***e***: drop the ***e*** and add the ending. (Example: tape—taping, taped)
2. Words ending in a consonant with ***one*** vowel before the final consonant: double the final consonant and add the ending. (Example: tap—tapped, tapping).
3. Words ending in a consonant with ***two*** vowels before the final consonant: simply add the ending. (Example: dream—dreamed, dreaming).

Type each word and add an *ed* and an *ing* to it.

lean	**fake**
pet	**clean**
dip	**fade**
date	**hate**

REVIEW

Line 1 once—speed
Lines 2 and 3 once—speed
Line 3 again—speed

```
1   asdf jkl; ;p ;p pan pale plea pen ;p ;p asdf jkl;
2   Please pass the pins, tape, paint, snaps and pan.
3   Jane and Allen stapled all the splendid paneling.
```

DEPOSIT: A deposit of $100.00 per person is required to secure reservations on the tour. Balance is due six (6) weeks prior to departure.

FINAL PAYMENT: Due Crossroads Travel Service six (6) weeks prior to departure.

XXBAGGAGE: Limited to 44 lbs. per person in tourist class.

NOTE: Gibson Tours reserves the right to adjust or alter any travel program when necessary or desireable for the protection, safety, or improvement of said travel program or when local conditions do not permit operation of the program as published.

RESPONSIBILITY: CrossXXXXroads Travel Service of St. Louis and Gibson Tours, Inc., Chicago, Ill., the operators of the tour, and/or the suppliers of services act only as agents for the passenger in regards to travel, whether by railroad, motorcar, ship, or plane, and assume no liability for injury, damage, loss, accident, or delay which may be occasioned either by reason of defect in any vehicle or for any reason whatsoever, or through the acts or default of any company or persons engaged in conveying the passenger or in carrying out arrangements of the tour.

Prices are based on tariff in effect January 1, 19__, and are subject to adjustment in the event of any change.

Introduction to R

Home-row *f* finger moves up and to the left to the *r* key. Place both hands on the home row and practice the move from *f* to *r*. Look at your hands and watch your finger make the motion. Do this several times; then look away and try the same motion.

R

Line 1 once—speed
Lines 2-5 once—speed
Lines 2-5 again—speed

1 f ff fr fr fr ff rf rf fr frf frf ff rr fr fr frf
2 fr red rag rid ran rig rip are ear rat sir her fr
3 fr air per era ire jar far par ark fir tar rap fr
4 fr rain rare real rink rake rage rear ripe rip fr
5 fr trap prep near girl pair dare rate rail sir fr

Lines 6-10 once—speed
Lines 6-10 again—speed

6 trip rest tree ring hire fire hard earn dirt fair
7 reign range raise ridge rinse risks art jar right
8 stare there their after pride tired far her press
9 green greed dress large heart after ran fir eager
10 refrain repress release retreat resident register

DRILL

Lines 1-3 once—speed
Line 3 again—speed

1 er era erase per deer tier sneer after farther er
2 re red regal ire hire fire stare spire preside re
3 pert prep steer fresh alert reign eastern printer

Lines 4-6 once—speed
Line 6 again—speed

4 ri rid ridge rip ring rink right rinse printer ri
5 ir ire eerie air fire hair skirt first giraffe ir
6 pair girl arise their trial third aspirin hairpin

SENTENCES

Lines 1-10 once—speed

Take:
Two 15-sec. timings on Lines 1 through 5.
Then take one 30-sec. timing.

1 Rip, the ranger, fell and sprained his left knee. 10
2 An irate diner startled the frightened girl here. 20
3 Dirk did the drill first and drank the tea later. 30
4 Fresh, green grapes are great as a dessert treat. 40
5 Al related the entire tale in the strange letter. 50

----1----2----3----4----5----6----7----8----9---10

MEALS: Will include the modified American Plan of breakfast plus table d'hote dinner (fixed menu meals) on land portion. Full meal service is provided on the cruise.

TRANSFERS: All transfers between airports, rail stations, and a hotels will be provided with two pieces of luggage per person.

SIGHTSEEING: Provided as indicated in each program using late model cars or busses with English-speaking guides. All entrance fees to tour places visited are also included.

BAGGAGE TIPS: Are included at airports, piers, and rail stations for all tour programs. Hotel baggage tips are included.

SERVICE CHARGES AND TAXES: On accommodations and meals that are part of the tour program are included.

REFUNDS: Will not be made for less than 3 days of missed arrangements of a tour and are limited to the net amounts of accommodations, services, and meals. Refunds for occasional missed sightseeing tours or meals are not granted.

CANCELLATIONS: Cancellations may be made at anytime prior to departure. Full reimbursement of the deposit will be made until six (6) weeks before departure. After that time the deposit will be reimbursed less any non-refundable expenses. ON the passenger air fare, 25% is non-refundable if cancellation is received within fifteen (15) days prior to departure.

(cont'd. on next page)

Take:
Two 15-sec. timings on Lines 6 through 10.
Then take one 30-sec. timing.

6 Spread the lard in the skillet and grill a treat. 10
7 He risks great danger if he departs after dinner. 20
8 The eastern ship at sea held pearls and trinkets. 30
9 The sad intern lingered in the garden and rested. 40
10 The raging giraffe splintered that ringside seat. 50
----1----2----3----4----5----6----7----8----9---10

TIMINGS

Type once at controlled rate.
Take one 1-min. timing.
Take another 1-min. timing.

Jane prepares legal papers and letters. She 10
prefers reading ledgers and graphs. It is tiring 20
and drains her. 23
----1----2----3----4----5----6----7----8----9---10

Type once at controlled rate.
Take one 1-min. timing.
Take another 1-min. timing.

If Dan falters at the start, he is risking a 10
defeat. The stern referee sees the sprinters and 20
stresses fairness and praises spirit. 27
----1----2----3----4----5----6----7----8----9---10

Type once at controlled rate.
Take one 1-min. timing.
Take another 1-min. timing.

Print the paragraph in large letters. Raise 10
the title and delete the diagraphs. Insert three 20
fresh phrases at the end. 25
----1----2----3----4----5----6----7----8----9---10

Type once at controlled rate.
Take one 1-min. timing.
Take another 1-min. timing.

It is all right if Dane repairs that rattle. 10
It is a danger and a threat. Perhaps the gear is 20
sheared. He repairs tenders and engines. 28
----1----2----3----4----5----6----7----8----9---10

Thinking Drill

ADDING AN *ed* OR *ing* ENDING

Remember the guidelines. If you have forgotten them, refer to page 20 or consult a dictionary if in doubt.

Remember—the vowels are *A*, *E*, *I*, *O*, *U* (and sometimes *Y*). All other letters are consonants.

Words ending in two or more consonants: simply add the ending. (Example: rest—rested, resting).

Type each word and add an *ed* and an *ing* to it.

sail	sip	relate
nap	seat	arrest
line	pin	resign
nip	dash	retire
peel	sprint	parade

Item 10

Plain paper

(Tour Director's Introduction:)

In the brevity of this brochure, it is impossible to elaborate on the excitement and adventure awaiting you when you visit Europe and the Mediterranean in XXXXXXXX Springtime. Even if you have visited some of the Old World Capitals previously, like an old friend, they always welcome you back. Cruising the Greek Islands is a never-to-be-forgotten experience that returns you through a tunnel of time to the world's cradle of culture. Now read the brochure, let it whet your travel appetite, then make your early reservation.

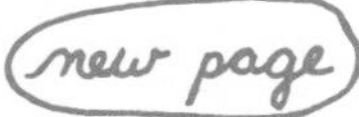

(Conditions and General Information:)

TRAVEL DOCUMENTS: A U.S. citizen must be in possession of a valid passport. No visas are required. Vaccination certificate for smallpox is recommended, but not required.

XXXXXXXX WHAT THE TOUR PRICE INCLUDES:

AIR TRANSPORTATION: Tour price includes round trip economy class jet air fare in accordance with the XX itinerary.

HOTELS: Accommodations will be provided in twin-bedded rooms with bath or shower at the hotels specified in each program listed in this brochure. Category is first class. The right is reserved to substitute hotels specified for others with similar or superior category.

(cont'd. on next page)

REVIEW

Line 1 once—speed

Lines 2 and 3 once—speed
Line 3 again—speed

1 asdf jkl; de fr ft fg jn jh ki k, l. ;p ;: ;? A J

2 and the and the and then and that and then and s;

3 I ran fast; I ran the sideline; he ran past fast;

Introduction to M

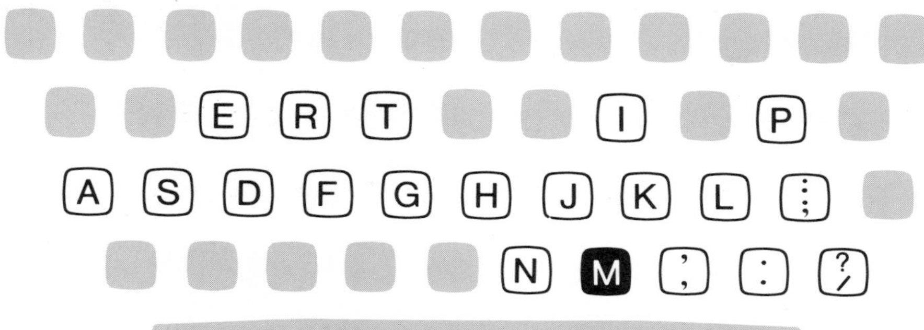

Home-row *j* finger moves down and to the right to the *m* key. Place both hands on the home row and practice the move from *j* to *m*. Look at your hands and watch your finger make the motion. Do this several times; then look away and try the same motion.

M

Line 1 once—speed

Lines 2-5 once—speed
Lines 2-5 again—speed

1 j j jm jm jmj jmj jm mj jm mj jj mm jm mm jm jmjm

2 jm me me dim dim elm elm aim aim arm arm am am jm

3 jm am am him him man man mad mad jam jam me me jm

4 jm farm farm time time mean mean mail mail him jm

5 jm make make same same them them meet meet dim jm

Lines 6-10 once—speed
Lines 6-10 again—speed

6 seem seem miss miss made made game game mate mate

7 might might metal metal dream dream ram ram small

8 admit admit smile smile limit limit mad mad smash

9 theme theme remit remit stamp stamp gem gem ample

10 ed mashed limped harmed minted melted timed named

DRILL

Type each sentence once. At end of each line, return carriage quickly and immediately begin typing on next line. Then do again.

I see him.

He made me miss.

His name is Mr. Marris.

That farmer is smart this time.

She might feel this is a familiar item.

Item 8

Plain paper

List in order indicated

Do not include Numbers!

TRAVEL AGENT'S FACT SHEET

1. Program:	London plus Europe, PanAm (Rex) Holiday 320.
2. Destinations:	London with or without theater, pubs, bus tours, and car; London, Amsterdam, Paris, Copenhagen, and Rome in various one-, two-, and three-week combinations.
3. General Description of Packages:	All essential ingredients: transfers, hotel, sightseeing plus countdown card, and two-for-one dining. Special car and hotel program.
4. Special Value:	All programs include round-trip transfers in all cities. Some competing and higher priced programs do not.
5. More Special Value:	All programs include Travel Assurance Protection.
8. Commission;	Land packages commissionable at 15% from the first booking.
6. Gateway Cities:	All PanAm (Rex) gateways shown in air fare box: New York, Atlanta, Boston, Detroit, Washington. (Some routings on return are via New York and domestic connection.)
9. Reservations:	Call CTS at (816) 263-9901. Spell out – Crossroads Travel Service
7. Group Rates:	Special rates available for groups of 20 or more on most programs.

NOTE: This is more info. for another pamphlet. Set up like you did other one -- only use full sheet of paper.

Item 9

Working Papers, pp. 267-68

Mr. Lee Rubenstein, 812 Wintergreen Terrace, Creve Coeur, MO 63131. Dear Mr. Rubenstein: Thank you for your interest in our vacation package, "In Grand Style." The brochure you requested has not arrived from the printers; we will send you a copy when we receive it. The brochure will tell you something of the elegance and class this program is all about. It is a one-source guide to some of the most luxurious vacations available. The Grand Style program was created for the growing number of discerning people who seek high style vacations. You will find the Grand Style program offers eight exclusive resorts in the Eastern United States with four days and three nights, packages ranging from $192 to $384 per couple, all inclusive. Each resort package includes superb accommodations, gourmet meals, and unlimited sports activities such as tennis or golf. We invite you to spend your next vacation in Grand Style. Call us at 263-9901, and our reservation staff will handle the rest. Sincerely, MP, TM

packages for

SENTENCES

Lines 1-10 once—speed

Take:
Two 15-sec. timings on Lines 1 through 5.
Then take two 30-sec. timings.

1 Mike is making a frame; he needs ample sandpaper.
2 The meat manager made a simple remark and smiled.
3 Did Mamie transmit the message after amending it?
4 Sandman, the fine farm animal, had a marked limp.
5 Pam had made a malt that had milk and mint in it.
----1----2----3----4----5----6----7----8----9---10

Take:
Two 15-sec. timings on Lines 6 through 10.
Then take two 30-sec. timings.

6 Add ample stamps and mail the letter at midnight.
7 The fireman attempted an immense task and missed.
8 Did Sammie eliminate all mistakes in the message?
9 Jim, is that smashed metal mass a damaged helmet?
10 Minne missed the main message as her mind dimmed.
----1----2----3----4----5----6----7----8----9---10

TIMINGS

Type once at controlled rate.
Take one 1-min. timing.
Take another 1-min. timing.

The minimal marks alarmed Mae. She had made 10
three simple, mental mistakes in the math test; a 20
small, grim smile masked the dismal mental image. 30
She had failed the semester. 36
----1----2----3----4----5----6----7----8----9---10

Type once at controlled rate.
Take one 1-min. timing.
Take another 1-min. timing.

Marna smelled the simmering meat. The steam 10
permeated the air. She managed a small taste and 20
smiled. The meat and milk might help that little 30
girl and ease her pain. 35
----1----2----3----4----5----6----7----8----9---10

Type once at controlled rate.
Take one 1-min. timing.
Take another 1-min. timing.

As he firmed the damp earth at the tree, the 10
miser imagined he heard a small sigh. Mirages in 20
the misted marsh alarmed him. Grim fears emerged 30
as his mindless tramping faltered. 37
----1----2----3----4----5----6----7----8----9---10

Type once at controlled rate.
Take one 1-min. timing.
Take another 1-min. timing.

Make that simple diagram first. Then send a 10
message in the mail. Tell that salesman that his 20
latest remarks made the manager mad. The meeting 30
impaired the imminent merger. 36
----1----2----3----4----5----6----7----8----9---10

Item 6

Working Papers, p. 263

Dear Scuba Diver.. Becuase of your past interest in scuba diving, we felt you might be interested in traveling to the Caribbean for a week and enjoy some terrific diving. Many of the resorts are, or course, familiar destinations to divers: Roatan, Cozumel, Grand Cayman, Eleuthera, and an old favorite, Stella Maris. We also feel that Akumalo, located on the Mexican peninsula, will prove to be a popular resort in years to come. You have probably heard that there is some great diving in the Dominican Republic. Well, the Punta Cana Club, located far away from Santa Domingo, has offered us some good rates; we would like to pass these special rates on to you. Because many of you have families, we felt that they, too, had to be taken into consideration, so we have also included destinations that feature great diving, but also provide other activities such as tennis, shopping, sightseeing, and an exciting nightlife. All in all, we feel that we offer something of interest to everyone--both diver and non-diver alike. Should you have any questions regarding the resorts, please feel free to give us a call or drop into our office.

Sincerely, MP, Travel Mgr.

NOTE: prepare for duplication. Leave 6 or 7 blank lines between date and greeting.

Item 7

Working Papers, p. 265

TO: All Employees FROM: Maria Perez, Travel Manager SUBJECT: CAB rulings for OTC/TGC Charters. On all OTC and TGC charters, be sure and remind your clinents to take along numbered identification as well as proof of citizenship. Identification must match exactly with the name on the manifest. In the case of newlyweds, it is necessary for them to have their marriage certificate with them. If a passenger does not have proper identification the airlines are compelled by the Civil Aeronautics Board regulation to deny boarding without liability to the airlines or tour operator. Also, please do not forget to have your clients complete and sign a Participant's Contract (reservation form) and return it to our office with their initial deposit. The completed and signed contract is a requirement of the CAB, and, therefore, must be received by Crossroads Travel Service before your client is manifested.

(i.e., passport, driver's license, or Social Security Card)

Thinking Drill

DOUBLE LETTERS

Each of the following words is spelled incorrectly. Each should have a double letter. Type each word, inserting the needed letter.

mispeled	stemed
matress	metle
maner	meting
imense	midle
hamer	dimer

REVIEW

Line 1 once—speed

Lines 2 and 3 once—speed
Line 3 again—speed

```
1   asdfghjkl; de fr ft jn jm ki k, l. ;p ;: ;? jm jm
2   me dim elm aim arm jam mad man him am time farms;
3   It seems that I missed the game; it makes me mad.
```

Introduction to V

Home-row *f* finger moves down and to the right to the *v* key. Place both hands on the home row and practice the move from *f* to *v*. Look at your hands and watch your finger make the motion. Do this several times; then look away and try the same motion.

V

Line 1 once—speed

Lines 2-5 once—speed
Lines 2-5 again—speed

Lines 6-10 once—speed
Lines 6-10 again—speed

```
1   f f fv fv fvf fvf fv vf fv vf ff vv fv ff fv fvfv
2   fv van van vat vat vie vie via via vim vim van fv
3   fv dive dive five five give give grieve grieve fv
4   fv even even gave gave have have travel travel fv
5   fv leave leave seven seven alive alive seventh fv

6   saving saving eleven eleven selves selves divided
7   shelve shelve invite invite savage savage adverse
8   private private deliver deliver veteran even even
9   prevail prevail seventh seventh arrival vane vane
10  negative negative seventeen seventeen advertising
```

Item 3

Working Papers, p. 259

changed my mind – rather than a memo format prepare as a promotional release. Title in all caps, centered. Doublespace. Get all on one page!! M.P.

TO: Our Missouri Travelers. FROM: Maria Perez, Travel Manager, Crossroads Travel Service, Inc. SUBJECT: "The American Encounter" This year marks the perfect time to re-discover America. What better way to celebrate our historic beginnings than with a "suit yourself" vacation in the cities, towns, and rural communities of the East where the events leading up to our nation's founding all began. ¶ The "American Encounter" is a total vacation package, providing you with all the features you need to plan your own personal holiday. You decide where you want to go, what you want to do, and how long you want to be away. That's the wonderful freedom-of-choice you have with the "American Encounter." You'll find it simple, economical, and highly flexible. ¶ There is also a wide choice of areas to fly to. You can pick and choose just the sort of holiday that suits you best--a fly/drive arrangement with hotels and your own rental car, prearranged sightseeing tours, a dining plan instead of a car, or any combination of these. The choice is up to you.

Item 4

Working Papers, pp. 261-62

Ms. Darlene Ritche, 8 South Center Street, Benton Park, MO 63104. Dear Ms. Ritchie: Our latest tour brochure, the "Golden Prize Tour", is now ready for you to pick up. Prices have been ~~updated~~ revised to reflect the recent increase in air fares. ¶ Our mailings to date have met with great success, and we are receiving many inquiries and bookings for this tour. ¶ We are also pleased to announce a new program arranged in cooperation with Air France and L'Express Cruises. It features a 17-day air/sea itinerary including a delightful cruise from Venice on the S.S. Victoria. We expect to have the brochure available very soon, so please let us know if you would like a copy. ¶ Finally, do not forget us for your special group needs. We can easily handle complex itineraries to any part of the world, with short notice, and at competitive prices. ¶ Your support and loyalty are always appreciated. Sincerely, Maria Perez, Travel Manager

---

Item 5

Plain paper

NOTE: This info will be printed in a pamphlet being prepared by our printer. Type on 1/2 sheet plain paper, single spaced with triple space between paragraphs -- leave room at top so printer can insert title in bold-face type. Use 3/4" side margin.

Pleasure Breaks are operated by Crossroads Travel Service, Inc., who for more than 50 years has been a leader in the group travel field. ¶ Crossroads Travel Service is part of a corporate group with combined resources of over $20 billion. We have financial stability and the ability to package quality travel programs at economy prices. Pleasure Breaks equals quality and economy . . . a sure thing in a successful travel program. Pleasure Breaks OSC's (One-Stop Charters) ~~offered~~ described in this brochure are in response to the many requests received for tours of approximately one week's duration to various European destinations. This is a chance to take advantage of charter savings in air fare and hotels with plenty of free time for individual pursuits at your chosen destination. ¶ Pleasure Breaks group travel services featuring air transportation only are also available with frequent departures on dependable, well-known airlines. Limited space is available. Mail your application today.

DRILL

Type each line once. At end of each line return carriage quickly and immediately begin typing on next line. Then do again.

save saved saving
rave raved raving
serve served serving
shave shaved shaving
vanish vanished vanishing
travel traveled traveling
prevail prevailed prevailing
varnish varnished varnishing
preserve preserved preserving
validate validated validating
ventilate ventilated ventilating
aggravate aggravated aggravating

SENTENCES

Lines 1-10 once—speed

Take:
Two 15-sec. timings on Lines 1 through 5.
Then take two 30-sec. timings.

1 That traveler arrived in a lavish, private plane. 10
2 Seven silver vases vanished at the evening event. 20
3 Did Van ever deliver the varnish and the shelves? 30
4 Vinnie lives in the villa; it has a vast veranda. 40
5 It is evident; the vital lever reverses the vent. 50

Take:
Two 15-sec. timings on Lines 6 through 10.
Then take two 30-sec. timings.

6 The rival divers tried varied dives in the river. 10
7 Val, deliver that vast velvet divan this evening. 20
8 Marvia served vanilla malts at the private event. 30
9 The driver has a grave fever; give him a vitamin. 40
10 The starved vandal evaded five vigilant servants. 50

----1----2----3----4----5----6----7----8----9---10

TIMINGS

Type once at controlled rate.
Take one 1-min. timing.
Take another 1-min. timing.

Traveling in this vast native land is a near 10
marvel. The savage rivers and varied paved miles 20
are impressive. Vivid sights revive the mind and 30
lift spirits. Villages reveal veiled vestiges; a 40
dividend is derived. 44

----1----2----3----4----5----6----7----8----9---10

Type once at controlled rate.
Take one 1-min. timing.
Take another 1-min. timing.

Even if Gavin is vain, she has avid fans and 10
attentive friends. Her singing is sensitive; she 20
reveals her vast talent. She deserves lavish and 30
vivid praise. Her versatile verses are a massive 40
advantage and elevate her fevered fans. 49

----1----2----3----4----5----6----7----8----9---10

Item 1

Working Papers, pp. 255-56

Mr. Earl P. Saunders, President, St. Louis Optimist Club, 3641 Michigan Avenue, St. Louis, MO 63128. Dear Mr. Saunders: I would like to take a few minutes of your time to discuss how we might service your group travel requirements. ¶ The group travel services of our company cover the full range of your group's needs. We can not only handle all basic domestic and international group travel efficiently, but also your special needs, such as travelers cheques and insurance. And, because all these services are essentailly free to your group, we can save you substantial amounts of money compared to the cost of providing these arrangements on your own. ¶ "Insert A below" This year's travel season should be a very exciting experience for the traveling public because of the many new places that are being discovered as destinations. Here are just a few of the offerings: Rio de Janeiro (check sp.), Cancun, Honh Kong, India, East Africa, Leningrad/Moscow, Cartegena, Grand Canary Islands, Freeport, Lima, Europe, Hawaii, Mexico, and more. Or, if you wish, we have the facilities to plan an exclusive tour for your organization. ¶ Join with friends in the travel experience and see the world. If you have any questions regarding group programs, please give me a call. Sincerely, Maria Perez, Travel Manager

Insert "A" ¶ Because of our international scope, Crossroads' services extend in many ways beyond the obvious. Known and respected throughout the world travel community, the Crosoroads name stands behind every airline, cruise, + hotel reservation we make. In addition, our worldwide office structure provides unparalleled service to travelers while enroute.

Item 2

Working Papers, p. 257

Dear Traveler: In this issue of our Newsletter, you will find advance listings of the very best values in tour and cruise offerings for the coming year. ¶ Our judgment, as usual, is based primarily on first-hand information gathered by our staff members who make frequent survey trips to different areas of the world. ~~These~~ Our staff members have personally cruised on many of the ships listed in our cruise section for the purpose of inspecting accommodations and evaluating the ship's cuisine, service, seamanship, and shipboard activities. In addition, before any tour or cruise offering is ~~even~~ considered for listing in our Newsletter, it is carefully researched and compared with similar offerings of other major companies. ¶ Because of the great care taken in making our selections and preparing our recommendations, Crossroads' clients can be certain only those tours and cruises that offer the best itineraries and routings, the best in sightseeing, escorts, hotel accommodations, and other services--in short, the best in value--are featured in our Newsletter. ¶ If you wish to receive ~~a copy~~ information about any of the tours or cruises, please ~~stop in to see us~~ write or call me. Sincerely, Maria Perez, Travel Manager

This will be a dup. form letter - use February 1 date - leave enough line spaces to accommodate a 4-line address (inside)

Type once at controlled rate.
Take one 1-min. timing.
Take another 1-min. timing.

```
     Navigate the even trail in life.  Derive all        10
things that are pleasant and reap the advantages.        20
Preserve the vital past and evade vile evils.  An        30
avid, aggressive striving is needed in all lives.        40
A varied and diverse path prevents grief.                48
----1----2----3----4----5----6----7----8----9---10
```

Type once at controlled rate.
Take one 1-min. timing.
Take another 1-min. timing.

```
     The vessel vanished in the savage river.  An        10
adept diver salvaged several parts.  Seven native        20
men assisted him.  The added strength gave him an        30
advantage.  He saved the silver investment.              39
----1----2----3----4----5----6----7----8----9---10
```

Thinking Drill

LOOK

Look at these words:

shave *village* *liver* *vase* *alive* *evening*

SELECT

Now—select the word that best answers each of the following statements. Read each statement, look at the words, and quickly type your selection.

TYPE

1. What many men do each morning
2. Opposite of *morning*
3. Some people like it with onions!
4. Opposite of *dead*
5. Another name for a small town

REVIEW

Line 1 once—speed

Lines 2 and 3 once—speed
Line 3 again—speed

```
1   asdf jkl; de fr ft fg fv jn jm ki ;p ;? ;; fv fvf
2   eleven even save give travel leave five sensitive
3   The eleven travelers arrived at the lavish haven.
```

Introduction to O

Home-row *l* finger moves up and to the left to the *o* key. Place both hands on the home row and practice the move from *l* to *o*. Look at your hands and watch your finger make the motion. Do this several times; then look away and try the same motion.

Travel Agency

TYPE OF COMPANY: Travel Agency

DATE: January 19, 19 - -

COMPANY NAME/ADDRESS: Crossroads Travel Service, Inc.
400 Metro Drive
St. Louis, MO 63144

COMPANY TEL. NO.: 816/263-9901

SITUATION: You are employed as secretary to Ms. Maria Perez, Travel Manager in the St. Louis office of Crossroads Travel Service, Inc.

Crossroads enjoys a fine reputation in their industry. They are specialists in making the following arrangements for both domestic and international travel:

Cruises/tours/independent itineraries
Airline/steamship reservations
Hotel/resort reservations
Auto rentals
Traveler's checks
Charters

SPECIAL INSTRUCTIONS/EXPLANATIONS:

For this project, assume that Ms. Perez is out of the office on business today and tomorrow. A number of edited materials have been left for you to retype. You have been instructed to sign and mail out the letters to individual customers. Those letters and promotional materials which will be sent out in bulk mailings may be signed with Ms. Perez's signature stamp and sent to the printer.

Item 10: Ms. Perez is working on materials to be included in a tour brochure entitled, "Springtime in Europe and the Mediterranean." The tour, arranged by Crossroads Travel Service in cooperation with Gibson Tours, runs from March 20 to April 8.

Type the Tour Director's Introductory Statement and the "Conditions and General Information" in a rough draft. While she is away, Ms. Perez would like you to go over these materials and make any corrections (spelling, grammar, or communication) that you feel are necessary or would improve the text. Then retype the materials for her final ok.

Ms. Perez is currently writing the itinerary for the brochure. All materials will be sent to the printer at the end of the week. Again, be sure to correct any errors that have been overlooked.

O

Line 1 once—speed

Lines 2-5 once—speed
Lines 2-5 again—speed

1 l l lo lo lol lol lo ol lo lo ll oo lo ll lo lolo
2 lo do for hop log one old not off pot son golf lo
3 lo go too one oil ego odd top sod ton rot horn lo
4 lo no host moan more good roll hope joke floor lo
5 lo of loan knot post love from done vote stood lo

Lines 6-10 once—speed
Lines 6-10 again—speed

6 order prove among noise loose store flavor inform
7 along avoid drove prior other toast option oppose
8 stove movie shove floor front stole region reform
9 polite proper report remove lesson shovel opinion
10 endorse diamond another visitor develop insertion

DRILL

Type each line once. At end of each line return carriage quickly and immediately begin typing on next line. Then do again.

Deliver
Deliver melons
Deliver melons and
Deliver melons and onions
Deliver melons and onions to
Deliver melons and onions to the
Deliver melons and onions to the renovated
Deliver melons and onions to the renovated hotel.

SENTENCES

Lines 1-10 once—speed

Take:
Two 15-sec. timings on Lines 1 through 5.
Then take two 30-sec. timings.

1 He does not fool me; he is not an honest senator. 10
2 Ora ordered the onions and olives from the store. 20
3 That old man stooped among the roses and groaned. 30
4 The golden moon shone on the old prison rooftops. 40
5 The soft fog floated aloft over the lone trooper. 50

----1----2----3----4----5----6----7----8----9---10

Take:
Two 15-sec. timings on Lines 6 through 10.
Then take two 30-sec. timings.

6 Someone noted the stolen passport photos at noon. 10
7 The senior pilot spotted an airport in the gloom. 20
8 Jo dropped the looped rope at the rodeo and lost. 30
9 A violent storm moved along the remote oak grove. 40
10 Did the florist remove the thorns from the roses? 50

----1----2----3----4----5----6----7----8----9---10

INN Staff Members
Page 2
July 30, 19__

Condo Rentors/Owners:
$3/court hour (add'l 1/2 hour same as above)
Outsiders:
$4.50/court hour

HORSEBACK RIDING: $4.00/hour
Free transportation to stables

GAMES: Available at no charge to registered guests. (See Social Director.) Includes: ping pong, checkers, monopoly, ring toss, scrabble, dominos, cards, poker chips, dice, backgammon, chess, fishing poles.

Item 15

Working Papers, pp. 253-54

Mr. Kenneth Jackson, Glendale Chamber of Commerce, 7333 West 42nd Street, Glendale, AZ 85304 Ken, attached is a letter from a training firm that conducted a program at Zurich's Denver Inn, an Atlas Resort proerty. I spoke with Brian at last week's General Managers Meeting, and he felt the program was quite whorthwhile for supervisory levels and up. From our previous discussions of training and motivation, I thought you might want to follow up on this as a chamber-wide program. At Zurich's Denver Inn, they had two groups of 20 each. The cost for that number, I believe, was $100 per person. Tim Aubrecht, GM, Attachment.

TIMINGS

Type once at controlled rate.
Take one 1-min. timing.
Take another 1-min. timing.

It is good to have honest goals. Nothing is 10
gained if one goes forth in pointless roaming. A 20
major effort is needed to prosper. Isolate those 30
foolish errors and avoid them. Hold to a strong, 40
firm hope and move along. 45

----1----2----3----4----5----6----7----8----9---10

Type once at controlled rate.
Take one 1-min. timing.
Take another 1-min. timing.

Floss shook in terror as the tornado stormed 10
along the shore. The radio droned on foretelling 20
doom and gloom. The phone popped in her ear as a 30
torrent of rain fell. Alone in the lone mansion, 40
her fear overtook her for a moment. 47

----1----2----3----4----5----6----7----8----9---10

Type once at controlled rate.
Take one 1-min. timing.
Take another 1-min. timing.

Ron is fond of opera. The golden tones of a 10
violin smooth his tense nerves. Visions arise in 20
his mind as the viola responds to the mood. Soft 30
tones float in the air as the piano renders notes 40
of dimension and diversion. 45

----1----2----3----4----5----6----7----8----9---10

Type once at controlled rate.
Take one 1-min. timing.
Take another 1-min. timing.

Oatmeal is often a good food to eat. Add an 10
orange, hot toast, and milk to a morning meal for 20
digestion. It is important to eat in the morning 30
to avoid tension. Restore vim and vigor at noon; 40
do not overeat. 43

----1----2----3----4----5----6----7----8----9---10

Thinking Drill

LOOK
SELECT
TYPE

Look at these words:

Senator *envelope* *sirloin* *opened* *editor* *airport*

Now—type each sentence below, using one of the words to fill in the blank.

1. The __________ of the paper resigned.
2. __________ James remained in the state to vote.
3. Fold the letter and insert it in the __________.
4. The __________ ramp is not long or large.
5. Lots of people like __________ steak.
6. Rain pelted into the __________ door.

Item 14
Working Papers, p. 251

TO: All INN Staff Members

FROM: Daniel Stearns
Social Director

DATE: July 30, 19__

SUBJECT: Recreational Rates

The following recreational rates are in effect until further notice

GOLF: Palms and Pines Courses

Weekdays:	Greens	$6.00	10.
	Cart	$3.00	5.
	Tax	$ .45	.75
Weekends:	Greens	$7.00	15.
	Cart	$3.00	7.
	Tax	$ .50	1.10

Put a "total" line for each one

Guests of our hotel may charge their green fees and cart by obtaining a validated golf voucher from myself or the front desk before they go over to the Pro Shop. Transportation is provided by INN station wagon or ferryboat.

SAILBOATS: & PADDLEBOATS Available for rent from 9 a.m. to 5 p.m. daily (later hours during summertime).
Rates are ~~valid~~ in effect until January.
Guests at hotel and Tennis & Swim Club members:
$ 8/hour
$15/half day (9 a.m. to 1 p.m. or 1 p.m. to 5 p.m.)
$25/full day (9 a.m. to 5 p.m.)
Outsiders and Ranch Residents:
$10/hour
$20/half day
$30/full day
Employees:
half the price of Outsider/Resident rates.

BICYCLES: Available for rent from 9 a.m. to 5 p.m. daily.
$2.50/hour
$8.00/day

TENNIS: Hotel Guests:
$~~3~~ 8/court hour (additional half hour at no charge at descretion of Pro Shop based on court demand) ← check spelling!
Ranch Residents:
$~~3~~ 8/court hour (add'l 1/2 hour same as above)

Group these 2 plus 1st item on 2nd page into one category

(cont'd. on next page)

Introduction to B

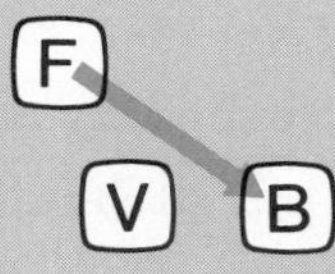

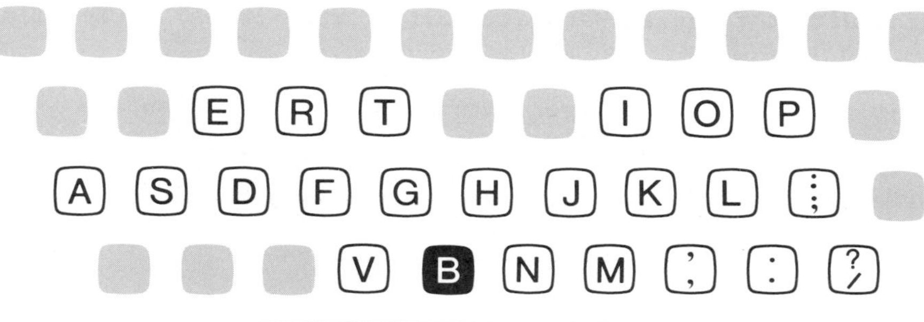

Home-row *f* finger moves down and to the right to the *b* key. Place both hands on the home row and practice the move from *f* to *b*. Look at your hands and watch your finger make the motion. Do this several times; then look away and try the same motion.

B

Line 1 once—speed

Lines 2-5 once—speed
Lines 2-5 again—speed

```
1  f f fb fb fbf fbf fb bf fb fb ff bb fb ff fb fbfb
2  fb bad bag ban bar bat bed bee beg Ben bet bid fb
3  fb be bid big bit Bob bop dab mob lob job limb fb
4  fb bank barb lamb best bake bank bear bite rob fb
5  fb bald best bias herb book bend able brag rib fb
```

Lines 6-10 once—speed
Lines 6-10 again—speed

```
6  libel fiber broil amber begin labor label algebra
7  bread bingo label brave alibi blast debit vibrate
8  barter member harbor banker ballot border benefit
9  verbal emblem better before absorb absent tremble
10 alphabet basement neighbor remember remarkable be
```

DRILL

Type each line once. At end of each line return carriage quickly and immediately begin typing on next line. Then do again.

```
bad bag bat
bail bait bake
badge barge baste
banish banker basket
bandage bailiff barrage
baseball bailment barefoot
```

Type each line once. At end of each line return carriage quickly and immediately begin typing on next line. Then do again.

```
beg bed bet
beat belt beaf
beast berth beard
behalf bedlam behave
believe belated bearing
befriend bearable behavior
```

Item 11

Working Papers, p. 245

TO: Accounting, Dining Room, Front Desk, Lounge, Night Auditor, Reservations, Dan Stearns, Social Director, Susan Marshall, Director of Sales FROM: Tim Aubrecht, General Mgr. SUBJECT: Credit Cards. ~~Please be advised that~~ we now accept Diners Club and Carte Blanche credit cards for any charges within the hotel. These are in addition to American Express, Master Charge, and Bank Americard. ¶ All cashier stations should have the necessary supplies charge vouchers, "bad card" lists, etc. If you do not have these materials, please advise your supervisor immediately. When stamping these cards, please be sure to use the ~~proper~~ ~~corresponding~~ appropriate voucher.

Item 12

Working Papers, pp. 247-48

Mrs. Donna Sylvester, McMurphy Travel Agency, 85 East Main Street, Union City, NY 07087 Mrs. Sylvester, Misses Jane Gallagher and Carrie Hamilton are confirmed at our resort on a Summer Holiday Package booked through your office. Reservations are for August 26 through September 1. ¶ I'm sorry, but we do not offer any packages that include horseback riding ~~as part of the package~~. However, horseback riding is available at $~~4~~ 8 an hour with free transportation to the stables. In addition, breakfast and dinner rides can be arranged at a cost of $~~8~~ 15. This would include the price of the meal. A minimum of six people is necessary, ~~to do this,~~ but we would try to organize the group. ~~collect enough people to make this possible.~~ Timothy Aubrecht, Gen. Mgr.

Item 13

Working Papers, pp. 249-50

Send a copy of the updated application form you revised earlier to: Mr. Dale Pearson
399 Hawthorne Ave
Glendale, CA

Include a cover letter asking him to sign + return the form. Be sure to acknowledge his inquiry, add a few lines about the many advantages of the resort, and stress the need for his signature and return of form asap.

SENTENCES

Lines 1-10 once—speed

Take:
Two 15-sec. timings on Lines 1 through 5.
Then take two 30-sec. timings.

1 Bev gobbled broiled beef, bread, and baked beans. 10
2 A nimble rabbit nibbles bean blossoms and blinks. 20
3 Debbi observed a brash bandit robbing a big bank. 30
4 I grabbed a dab of bread and biked to the harbor. 40
5 The bears bathed beneath the bridge in the brook. 50

----1----2----3----4----5----6----7----8----9---10

Take:
Two 15-sec. timings on Lines 6 through 10.
Then take two 30-sec. timings.

6 Babe is baffled; the beverage bottles are broken. 10
7 The dark banjo is broken; he is bitter and bleak. 20
8 The big battered barrels bent the riverbed barge. 30
9 Barb babbles to her bored brother; she is a snob. 40
10 Barni, the beagle, barks and begs for a big bone. 50

----1----2----3----4----5----6----7----8----9---10

TIMINGS

Type once at controlled rate.
Take one 1-min. timing.
Take another 1-min. timing.

Labor to do a noble job. Bosses like brains 10
and ambition. A blend of both brings a desirable 20
habit that boosts a beginner. A babbling boaster 30
absorbs a bore. The absent laborer blemishes his 40
possible bankroll boost. 45

----1----2----3----4----5----6----7----8----9---10

Type once at controlled rate.
Take one 1-min. timing.
Take another 1-min. timing.

Bif booked a berth on the battered boat. As 10
he bragged to his somber brother, the boom of the 20
harbor bells vibrated. Beneath the boasting, Bif 30
began to babble. A belated bolt of disbelief and 40
brooding stabbed at him. 45

----1----2----3----4----5----6----7----8----9---10

Type once at controlled rate.
Take one 1-min. timing.
Take another 1-min. timing.

Barbi is able to make edible spareribs. She 10
blends the best herbs and parboils the ribs. The 20
ribs are broiled and basted. She adds vegetables 30
and bread to the elaborate meal. The first bites 40
are a believable treat. 45

----1----2----3----4----5----6----7----8----9---10

Type once at controlled rate.
Take one 1-min. timing.
Take another 1-min. timing.

Bo is indebted to Ben, the able banker. The 10
liberal loan is to brighten a drab sailboat. Big 20
debts are a problem to Ben, the banker. Sensible 30
debtors absolve all debts. Bo might have a habit 40
of breaking his verbal bindings. 46

----1----2----3----4----5----6----7----8----9---10

Item 10

Working Papers, p. 243

Make an original and one copy. The copy will be used in Item 13, even though the copy is not on letterhead.

Membership Application Form

THE INN TENNIS & SWIM CLUB
~~1978–79 Season~~
September thorugh April

Omit dates here. At bottom right hand corner of page, type today's dates in figures.

Name____________________ Address____________________

City_______________ State__________ zip ________ Telephone_______________

No. Adults________ No. Children________ Wife's Name_______________

Children's Names: _______________ Age(s)________ Birthdate(s)_______________

_______________ ________ _______________

_______________ ________ _______________

Family Membership . . . . $~~45.00~~ 50. Deposit . . . . . . $~~45.00~~ 50 per month

Single Membership . . . . $~~35.00~~ 40. Deposit . . . . . . $~~35.00~~ 40 per month

Guest Fee . . . . $ ~~1~~ 3.00 per person

#

All memberships must be paid in advance. No refunds will be made. The Club reserves the right to refuse any application for membership or to cancel a membership in case of violation of Club rules.

Because the Tennis Club courts are a hotel facility, it will sometimes be necessary to use the courts for a hotel function or tournament.

Because there is no initiation fee, any overdue bill in excess of 60 days will immediately drop the family or individual from the membership list. The deposit is to be used for the last month of the family's or individual's membership dues. Two weeks' prior notice of cancellation of membership must be given, or the member will be charged for the following month.

_______________ ____________________
Date Applicant's Signature

The above signature indicates that I have read and agree to abide by all the rules and regulations of THE INN Tennis and Swim Club as defined above.

Sold by_______________ Total Amount Paid $__________ Date_______________

Approved by____________________ Membership Expires_______________
Membership Begins_______________
Membership Card# _______________

By_______________ Date_______________

Thinking Drill

LOOK
THINK
TYPE

Type as many words as you can think of that begin with:

bo bl
bi br

REVIEW

Line 1 once—speed

Lines 2 and 3 once—speed
Line 3 again—speed

1 asdf jkl; de fr fv ft fg fb jh jn jm ki lo ;p ;?;
2 be gab drab debit obtain ambition probable broken
3 His ambition enables him to obtain great diamonds.

Introduction to W

Home-row *s* finger moves up and to the left to the *w* key. Place both hands on the home row and practice the move from *s* to *w*. Look at your hands and watch your finger make the motion. Do this several times; then look away and try the same motion.

W

Line 1 once—speed

Lines 2-5 once—speed
Lines 2-5 again—speed

1 s s sw sw sws sws sw ws sw sw ss ww sw ss sw swsw
2 sw jaw wag raw two war wet saw hew how new sew sw
3 sw wig won few awe law wit win now owl wan web sw
4 sw down draw news town walk when twig wish dew sw
5 sw word plow west twin with swim week know now sw

Lines 6-10 once—speed
Lines 6-10 again—speed

6 white grown waist drown waken swamp elbow welfare
7 brown water twine where swell write frown awkward
8 review warmer bowler wiring inward wisdom preview
9 window follow waiver jigsaw within warmth lawless
10 hardware workable followed weakness endowment two

Item 9

Working Papers, p. 241

TO: THE INN Employees

FROM: Tim Aubrecht
General Manager

DATE: July 30, 19__

SUBJECT: Tennis

Spell out "one-half"

1. Effective September 7, guests of THE INN will be charged a tennis court fee of $3 [$8] per court hour. An additional 1/2 hour can be added at no charge at the discretion of the Pro Shop based on court demand. The free 1/2 hour cannot be reserved.

2. The Summer Tennis and Swim Club memberships expire on September 7. As of this date, individuals no longer have use of the pool or health clubs and should be charged the guest rate of $3 [$8] an hour for tennis court use upon presenting their expired Summer Tennis and Swim Club card. The rate will be re-evaluated on December 15.

3. Residents of Sawyer Ranch will be charged the guest rate of $3 [$8] per court hour when playing tennis. The free 1/2 hour is not extended.

4. Annual membership in the Tennis and Swim Club is available at the following rates:

   Family: $50 deposit* $50 each month
   Single: $40 deposit* $40 each month
   *Deposit to be used for last month of membership dues.
   Guest Fee: $1 [3] per person

   Individuals must have a valid membership card with them to enjoy the Club privileges. # Inquiries should be directed to Dan Stearns or Ann Lambert.

5. [Family] Membership in THE INN Racquet Club for Condo owners/renters: [costs $35.] There is no deposit or guest fee.
   ~~Family: $35 No Deposit No Guest Fee~~

6. Employees of THE INN at Sawyer Ranch can play tennis at no charge on a space-available basis. If a court time is reserved, the employee should be prepared to pay the guest rate of $3 per court hour. Employees should also relinquish their court, unless paying, if a guest is waiting for a court. Do you know a better way of stating this?

urs

Review pages 19 and 20 for setting tabs.

Set tabs every 10 spaces. Type once and then do again.

TAB DRILL

I	like	to	feel	good.
When	one	feels	good,	one
will	attempt	to	feel	good
at	all	times.	Shall	we
all	attempt	to	feel	good?

SENTENCES

Lines 1-10 once—speed

Take:
Two 15-sec. timings on Lines 1 through 5.
Then take two 30-sec. timings.

1 Will Marlow wash that wool sweater in warm water? 10
2 Their nephew was a fellow bowler with the winner. 20
3 Wear a warm gown if it snows; the weather is raw. 30
4 The new lawn will grow when watered well at dawn. 40
5 Warren wiped the jeweled bowl with a white towel. 50
----1----2----3----4----5----6----7----8----9---10

Take:
Two 15-sec. timings on Lines 6 through 10.
Then take two 30-sec. timings.

6 Is Win wasting water if he washes the new window? 10
7 It is wise to wire the news to the waiting woman. 20
8 The wealth of the world will not wield wiser men. 30
9 He saw few minnows swimming in the shallow water. 40
10 Widen the wooden window and rewire the two bells. 50
----1----2----3----4----5----6----7----8----9---10

TIMINGS

Type once at controlled rate.
Take one 1-min. timing.
Take another 1-min. timing.

We will await the word of warning in the new 10
tower. The wise stalwart leader wants to preview 20
the writings of men of worth. He frowns on wrong 30
narrow views. We will follow wise wishes and win 40
a wearisome war and bestow a renewed foothold. 49
----1----2----3----4----5----6----7----8----9---10

Type once at controlled rate.
Take one 1-min. timing.
Take another 1-min. timing.

Will reviewed the written words. He did not 10
wish to show that witless newsman how shallow his 20
words were. However, he wanted to warn the world 30
of the wasted wealth in the wages of the man. He 40
showed the network the handwriting on the wall. 49
----1----2----3----4----5----6----7----8----9---10

Type once at controlled rate.
Take one 1-min. timing.
Take another 1-min. timing.

Barlow, a shrewd fellow, winked as he waited 10
in the shadows. A whistle warned him of the slow 20
walk of his fellow worker. As he wallowed in the 30
warmth of that workshop, Will worked in the wild, 40
blowing wind. Barlow was worthless. 45
----1----2----3----4----5----6----7----8----9---10

Item 8

Working Papers, pp. 239-40

Dear Golfing Guests: Thank you for making your reservations here at THE INN at Sawyer Ranch. If you would like a tee time for the day of your arrival or the following day, please fill out and return the ~~enclosed~~ below form so that we can make these arrangements for you in advance. Sawyer Ranch Golf Courses are very busy this time of year; unless we receive this form prior to your arrival, we cannot guarantee your desired starting time. ¶ If you would like a golf schedule set up with confirmed tee times during your visit with us, please see me upon your arrival; I will be most happy to help you. For our guests who would like to charge their green fees and carts to their room bill, stop by our front office or my desk in the lobby and obtain your validated Golf Voucher before going to the Pro Shop to play golf. ¶ I look forward to welcoming you personally to our resort. Sincerely, Daniel Stearns, Social Director, Enclosure.

NOTE: leave enough room at bottom of letter so can type following item. Include a "tear off" line ----------

---

Mail to: Daniel Stearns, Social Director, THE INN at Sawyer Ranch, 7402 Logan Road, Glendale, AZ 85301

Please make a tee time for:

Name ______ Arrival Time ______ Arrival Date ______

Address ______ City ______ State ______ Zip ______

Tee Date (first choice) ______ Tee Time ______ # Players ______

Tee Date (Sec. choice) ______ Tee Time ______ # Players ______

Date ______ Guest Signature ______

Thinking Drill

LOOK

Look at the words listed below. Select a word from each list to make a compound word.

SELECT
TYPE

ward	lash	*Example*
whip	horse	wardrobe
wind	robe	
home	down	
saw	work	
snow	mill	
team	work	
mark	storm	
soft	wear	

Reinforcement Drill Material

CHECK TIMING

Type once at controlled rate.

Take one 1-min. timing.
Take another 1-min. timing.

```
     When the winter snow thaws, warm rain washes      10
the world.  Wild flowers begin to weave in a slow      20
swing with the wind.  Whiffs of a meadow awakened      30
swirl down at the dawn.  The dew is a rainbow and      40
twinkles as a jewel.  Winter has blown onward.         49
----1----2----3----4----5----6----7----8----9---10
```

MORE PRACTICE

Determine the number of words and number of errors for each timing taken on the paragraph above. The material provided on the following three pages is to be used for additional practice on the keys that you have learned. There are no instructions on the left side of the pages. Use the drills as follows:

1. If you have mastered the keys and do not hesitate when typing any letter—and did not have an excessive amount of errors—omit this section and proceed to page 37.

HESITATE?

2. If you have not mastered (hesitate before striking the key) the reach to a key(s), type the lines identified as:
   a. speed push (review)
   b. speed push (balanced-hand words)
   c. speed push

TOO MANY ERRORS?

3. If you made an excessive amount of errors, type the lines identified as:
   a. accuracy drive (double-letter words)
   b. accuracy drive (longer words)

NOT FAST ENOUGH?

4. If you are not able to type as rapidly as you would like, type the lines identified as:
   a. speed push (balanced-hand words)
   b. speed push

After determining what you feel you should do, consult with your instructor for permission to proceed.

Item 6

Working Papers, pp. 235

CERTIFICATE

We are pleased to present to you a complimentary

WEEKEND FOR TWO

at

THE INN

Sawyer Ranch

To be given away Sept. 1 at Casino Night, Arizona State University. ¶ These accommodations are for a two-night/three day stay, + may be used anytime before Dec. 30. ¶ Please present this certificate to our front desk upon your arrival. We suggest that you make reservations in advance to assure availability for the time of your choice. ¶ It will be our pleasure to welcome you to THE INN at Sawyer Ranch.

Timothy Aubrecht
General Manager

NOTE: Use letterhead and type in an attractive format.

Item 7

Working Papers, pp. 237-38

Mr. and Mrs. Paul Broderick, 344 Division Street, Las Vegas, Nevada 89112. Mr. and Mrs. Broderick, we are pleased that you have been able to take advantage of the Atlas Resort Club Programs that have been presented to you in the past. ¶ We are enclosing for your information our summer club program. As indicated in the program bulletin, the special rates ~~to which you are entitled~~ are effective seven days a week at our resort hotels; you may also enjoy these special rates at non-resorts during the weekends. ¶ Check over your Atlas Resort Country Directory which was mailed to you, and call me for your reservations. If you do not have a directory, ~~at this time,~~ please let us know; we would be most happy to ~~forward one to you.~~ send you one. ¶ Once again, we appreciate your membership and ~~believe~~ know you will enjoy taking advantage of these special rates on your vacation and traveling. T.A., Gen. Mgr. Enclosure.

HELPS BUILD YOUR SPEED

SPEED PUSH (REVIEW)

1 asdf jkl; ;p; frf jmj fvf lol fbf sws pr mv db ww
2 p pad pan peg pen pin pit pie plan phase pledge p
3 r rap ran red rip rent rests real repels refers r
4 m ham hem hen him mate mind mesh manage mandate m
5 v vat vim vet vise vent vane vigil valid veneer v
6 o oh or odd old one oaf opens omit ogle oval of o
7 b bah beg bid bop brag blend board brake better b
8 w was wed who win woe were when went where with w
9 Janell Kenneth Morris William Shanon Olan Bronson

STOPS HESITATION

SPEED PUSH (BALANCED-HAND WORDS)

1 lamb blend blank blame amble emblem problem bible
2 lap nap pen paid pane flap span pale spent dispel
3 air par sir risks lair heir pair hair flair widow
4 map maid mane melt sham lame mend firm make flame
5 vie via viva vivid pelvis disown pens laps disown
6 fog sod oak rod foam fork form foam odor soak rod
7 bow wig wow vow down gown wisp with wish when wit
8 Did the lame lambs amble down near the west oaks?
9 The pale widow paid for the vivid gown and a wig.
10 When did Vivian mend the pair of problem emblems?

HELPS ELIMINATE ERRORS

ACCURACY DRIVE (DOUBLE-LETTER WORDS)

1 slipping sipping happen flipping appease shipping
2 terriers irritates terrains follow all narratives
3 dimmer dinners hammering manners immense immerges
4 moon roof pool hood hook loot took mood root door
5 gobble rabble hobble babble pebble nibbles rabbit
6 Janell slipped the irritated terrier in the door.
7 That immense rabbit emerged and nibbled a bottle.
8 She will be shipping the poor winter winner soon.

Item 2

Working Papers, pp. 225-26

Mr. Bradley Dirk, 4560 Jersey Avenue, Phoenix, AZ 85040 Mr. Dirk, ~~just a short note to say~~ "thank you" for allowing us to serve as your hosts this past week. We hope to be able to serve you again in the ~~very near~~ future when you are in need of a hotel or banquet facility. If you are traveling to other areas of Atlas Resort Country, we invite you to ~~use the directory enclosed~~ stay with us and enjoy ~~the~~ our same fine service and hospitality. ¶ With the details of your recent visit still fresh ~~in your~~ mind, would you kindly complete the enclosed questionnaire regarding our services. This questionnaire is ~~perhaps~~ our most important source of corrective information. ¶ Thank you again for your confidence in THE INN at Sawyer Ranch. We look forward to your return and the opportunity of serving you again. ~~in the near future.~~ Timothy Aubrecht, General Manager, Enclosure

Item 3

Working Papers, p. 227

Type following questions on letterhead. Leave enough space for a full-line response. Make 2 originals and 2 copies.

1. Were we properly prepared for you according to your instructions?
2. Was our housekeeping + cleanliness satisfactory?
3. Was the quality of our food to your pleasure?
4. Was all service prompt + courteous?
5. Was there a representative of the management available when needed?
6. What changes do you suggest be made to more expertly meet our guests' comforts + needs?
7. May we serve you again?
8. Please add any other comments/observations that you may have.

Thank you for your time in assisting us.

THE INN at S.R.

Item 4

Working Papers, pp. 231-32

Send same letter as Item 2 to: Ms. Robin McCarthy, 612 Fourth Street, Newport, Beach, CA 92663--be sure to enclose copy of questionnaire.

Item 5

Working Papers, p. 233

Mr. Arthur Lange, Palmer Hall, Arizona State University, P.O. Box 175, Tempe, AZ 85281 Mr. Lange, enclosed is a certificate from THE INN at Sawyer Ranch for a complimentary weekend for two. This certificate will be valid until December 30. The accommodations may be enjoyed anytime during that period, subject to availability. We do suggest that the winner make reservations in advance. ¶ Thank you for asking THE INN to participate. Susan Marshall (Mrs. Director of Sales. Enclosure. c. Tim Aubrecht

CONCENTRATE

ACCURACY DRIVE (LONGER WORDS)

1 elephant dependent safekeeping plaintiff pipeline
2 standard registrar parenthesis telegrams resident
3 That resident registrar sends standard telegrams.

4 familiar eliminate sentimental dependent estimate
5 retrieve primitive advertising privilege negative
6 Eliminate that sentimental, familiar advertising.

7 rational tradition imagination negotiate renovate
8 ambition elaborate observation establish possible
9 stalwart knowledge handwriting wholesale whenever
10 Establish rational imagination whenever possible.

THINK SPEED

SPEED PUSH

1 pe peg pen pest peeps peddles pellet pets peep pe
2 pi pin pie piles pills pitfall pipes pink pine pi
3 That pill peddler peddled piles of pinkish pills.

4 ra ran rap ranks rake rates raised range rapid ra
5 ri rid rip rises ripe right ridges rigid rinse ri
6 Rapid Red ran to the raised ridges on that range.

7 ma man mat math make mail marsh manager margin ma
8 mi mid mild mind mint midst might misting mire mi
9 The manager might mail the mild mints to the man.

10 va van vat vane vases vast valid varied vanish va
11 vi vie vim vise vile vine visits vital vintage vi
12 The vital vintage vases vanished from a vast van.

13 oa oak oats oath oatmeal load toad roast float oa
14 of off offers offends offset offense offensive of
15 Those offensive oats floated off of that oatmeal.

16 ba bad bag bail balk bath badge barks bandages ba
17 bl blade bleak blast blank blight blind blinks bl
18 The babe blinked at a baboon blinded in bandages.

19 wa was war wag wade wait wane wash waste waves wa
20 wi win wit wig wide wipe will wise wield wiper wi
21 Winna washed and wiped her wig; she wasted water.

Item 1

Working Papers, pp. 223-24

Current Date

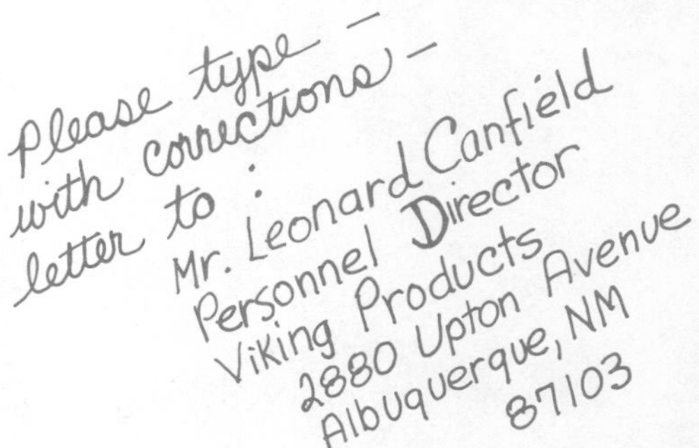

Please type —
with corrections —
letter to :
Mr. Leonard Canfield
Personnel Director
Viking Products
2880 Upton Avenue
Albuquerque, NM
87103

, thank you for your inquiry regarding company rates at THE INN at Sawyer Ranch.

Our criteria for extending company rates to a company are cimple. We require a letter of request typed on your business letterhead in advance of your first visit. The letter should express your company's intent to use the lodging facilities of THE INN at Sawyer Ranch along with an indication as to the approximate frequency of use. A minimum of two visits per month is required from your company. All reservations are made on a guarantee basis; the company will be responsible for paying for any person who does not show, unless cancelled 24 hours in advance of arrival.

All of our commercial rooms overlook beautiful Camelback Mountain. The following rates are extended Sunday through Friday:

Dates	Single	Double
January 15 - April 30	$37.00	$47.00
May 1 - June 4	26.00	36.00
June 5 - September 14	11.00	14.00
September 15 - January 14	26.00	36.00

Upon receipt of your letter, we will place your company's name on file at our front desk. Support and use of the facilities will be reviewed semi-annually for continuing the rate privilege.

Again, thank you for yoru interest. If you would like more information, please feel free to contact me. We look forward to serving you in the future. You may be assured that our staff will do its utmost to make your stay with us enjoyable.

Susan Marshall (Mrs.)
Director of Sales

REVIEW

Line 1 once—speed

Lines 2 and 3 once—speed
Line 3 again—speed

```
asdf jkl; sw de fr ft fg fv fb jh jn jm ki lo ;p;
as ask asked saw seen seem sent dare darn door is
and the when where this there their those gone at
```

Introduction to U

Home-row *j* finger moves up and to the left to the *u* key. Place both hands on the home row and practice the move from *j* to *u*. Look at your hands and watch your finger make the motion. Do this several times; then look away and try the same motion.

U

Line 1 once—speed

Lines 2-5 once—speed
Lines 2-5 again—speed

```
1  j ju ju jj ju uj jj uu juj juj ju ju juj juj juju
2  ju up up us us due due out out use use rub rub ju
3  ju put put sun sun fun fun mud mud gum gum sum ju
4  ju just just jump jump junk junk jug jug judge ju
5  ju rust rust sure sure turn turn pull pull but ju
```

Lines 6-10 once—speed
Lines 6-10 again—speed

```
6  duel shut gulf fund dump bulb hunt must rude true
7  build fault under usual until awful insure budget
8  vault audit rumor truth about nurse sprung refund
9  adjust endure refuge manual fourth versus publish
10 fusion lawful nature urgent plural module suppose
```

DRILL

Type each line once. At end of each line return carriage quickly and immediately begin typing on next line. Then do again.

```
Sue rubbed
Sue rubbed the
Sue rubbed the furred
Sue rubbed the furred pup.
```

Type each line once. At end of each line return carriage quickly and immediately begin typing on next line. Then do again.

```
Bud tugged
Bud tugged and
Bud tugged and lugged
Bud tugged and lugged the
Bud tugged and lugged the rug.
```

Resort

TYPE OF COMPANY: Resort

DATE: July 30, 19 - -

COMPANY NAME/ADDRESS: THE INN at Sawyer Ranch
7402 Logan Road
Glendale, AZ 85301

COMPANY TEL. NO.: 602/972-6060

SITUATION: You are employed as secretary in the Front Office of THE INN at Sawyer Ranch. In this position, your chief supervisor is Mr. Timothy Aubrecht, General Manager. You also assist Mrs. Susan Marshall, Director of Sales, and Mr. Daniel Stearns, Social Director.

THE INN at Sawyer Ranch is a property of Atlas Resorts and offers a variety of lodging, dining, and recreational facilities.

SPECIAL INSTRUCTIONS/EXPLANATIONS:

For this project, assume that on Friday, July 27, you typed up a number of items for your three supervisors and left the materials with them for their review over the weekend. In addition to the correspondence, the materials included updated rates, forms, and policy information. On Monday morning, you come to work and find the following items in your in-basket.

Item 8: In the past, two items were mailed to guests who had indicated an interest in playing golf at the resort—a short informational letter and a separate form. Mr. Stearns believes the two items could easily and conveniently fit on one page.

Item 10: A few changes have been made in last year's Membership Application Form for THE INN Tennis and Swim Club. Retype the form that is to be duplicated in quantity.

Note: Be sure to read each item carefully. Even though an item has been edited, there are some errors that have ***not*** been corrected. Be sure to correct these.

SENTENCES

Lines 1-10 once—speed

Take:
Two 15-sec. timings on Lines 1 through 5.
Then take two 30-sec. timings.

1 The guest menu featured halibut and autumn fruit. 10
2 Louis hunts for sunken ruins and hauls treasures. 20
3 Sue slumps and sulks as she slurps the sour soup. 30
4 Just be sure to return that blouse to the bureau. 40
5 That auto bumper is a hunk of junk; it is ruined. 50

----1----2----3----4----5----6----7----8----9---10

Take:
Two 15-sec. timings on Lines 6 through 10.
Then take two 30-sec. timings.

6 Buff found a huge bug on the shrub in the puddle. 10
7 A stout runner shouted and slumped to the ground. 20
8 The group hummed a rousing tune during the stunt. 30
9 Susan put tuna on a bun and built a super supper. 40
10 The pup dug around in the mud and found a peanut. 50

----1----2----3----4----5----6----7----8----9---10

TIMINGS

Type once at controlled rate.
Take one 1-min. timing.
Take another 1-min. timing.

The blunt auditor suggested to Duke that the 10
business returns were a fraud. The usual routine 20
of minimum turnovers of funds had been sound, but 30
that fortune of thousands paid to a juror had not 40
been inserted in the annual input. Duke presumed 50
he was ruined and flushed with guilt. 57

----1----2----3----4----5----6----7----8----9---10

Type once at controlled rate.
Take one 1-min. timing.
Take another 1-min. timing.

Ruth sulked as her aunt poured a dose of the 10
awful blue fluid. The sour stuff was supposed to 20
be used for fatigue from the flu. She paused for 30
a minute, and gulped it down. Her aunt found two 40
lumps of sugar for a bonus. Sullen disgust would 50
turn into a laugh as a result. 66

----1----2----3----4----5----6----7----8----9---10

Type once at controlled rate.
Take one 1-min. timing.
Take another 1-min. timing.

Muffin is a genuine bulldog. Although he is 10
a plump pup, he bounds about with a flourish. It 20
is fun to see him plunge around, indulging in the 30
pure pleasure of running. He huffs and puffs and 40
slumps to the ground. No doubt, he will jump and 50
lunge again after a pause and find trouble. 59

----1----2----3----4----5----6----7----8----9---10

Jill E. Simmons
Personal Data Sheet
Page 2

Chairman, AV Committee, 1973 Secretarial Seminar; Chairman, Hostess Committee, 1973 Secretarial Seminar.
A Cappella Choir, 1972-76.
Beta Upsilon Sigma, undergraduate business fraternity, 1973-76.
Placed first at Beta Upsilon Sigma State Leadership Conference in Extemporaneous Speaking event, 1976.
Third place, Outstanding School of Business Senior, 1976.
Graduated Summa Cum Luade.

REFERENCES

Dr. Elizabeth Howard, Chairman
Department of Office Administration
McMurray College
Abilene, TX 79605
713/704-3876

Mr. Wilbur C. Beach, Administrator
Houston Lakeside Hospital
80 First Street
Houston, TX 77011
712/924-6011

Dr. Lorraine Brauer, Professor
Department of Office Administration
McMurray College
Abilene, TX 79605
712/704-3891

A complete set of my credentials is available upon request from:
Career Planning & Placement Office
McMurray College
Abilene, TX 79605
713/704-2319

Type once at controlled rate.

Take one 1-min. timing.
Take another 1-min. timing.

```
     Russel bought a used auto from a true fraud.      10
Although the bumper and the trunk were ruined, he      20
assumed that it would run.  If he would flush the      30
rust from the lumbering hulk of junk, he might be      40
able to use it.  His woeful anguish spurred a new      50
thought; perhaps it was useless.                       56
----1----2----3----4----5----6----7----8----9---10
```

Thinking Drill

LOOK
THINK
TYPE

Using each word beginning given below, make up new words. Set tabs 10 spaces apart. Be sure that you have a three-letter word, a four-letter word, and a five or six-letter word for each beginning. See how many you can do in five minutes. Do not use the letters, *q*, *y*, *x*, or *c*.

	3 letters	*4 letters*	*5 or 6 letters*
hu—	hug	hunk	human
bu—			
du—			
gu			
ju			
fu			
us			
pu			
tu			
nu			
ru			

REVIEW

Line 1 once—speed

Lines 2 and 3 once—speed

Line 3 again—speed

```
1  asdf jkl; ju ju juj ju uj su us ug um ud up ul ur
2  us use turn spurt endure routing suspend thousand
3  Endure the thousand, routine, suspended sunrises.
```

Introduction to Z

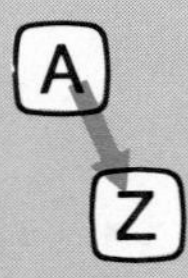

Home-row ***a*** finger moves down and to the right to the ***z*** key. Place both hands on the home row and practice the move from ***a*** to ***z***. Look at your hands and watch your finger make the motion. Do this several times; then look away and try the same motion.

Item 11

Plain paper

PERSONAL-DATA SHEET

Jill E. Simmons
714 Lyndale Avenue, Apt. #204
Houston, TX 77010-1126
Telephone: 713/924-6296

Jill Simmons, an employee candidate, has asked you, as a favor, to retype her data sheet.

PERSONAL DATA

move this section after Activities & Honors

Age: 22
Height: 5 feet 8 inches
Weight: 130 pounds

Marital Status: Single
Health: Excellent
G.P.A.: 3.83

EDUCATION

McMurray College, Abilene, Texas. 79605-1410

August, ~~1972~~ 1978, to May, ~~1976~~ 1982.
Received a Bachelor of Business Administration degree.
Major: Office Administration.
Courses in major included Advanced Typewriting, Advanced Shorthand, Administrative Transcription Techniques, Business Communications, Office Management, Records Management, Word Processing Office Simulation, and Office Systems, Layout, and Design.

East Memorial High School, Houston, Texas.

August, ~~1968~~ 1974, to June, ~~1972~~ 1978.
College-preparatory graduate.

WORK EXPERIENCE

September, ~~1973~~ 1978 - May, ~~1976~~ 1982	Department of Office Administration McMurray College Abilene, TX 79605-1410	Student Secretary
June, ~~1971~~ 1977 - August, 1981	Houston Lakeside Hospital 80 First Street Houston, TX 77011-3306	Office Work

ACTIVITIES AND HONORS

National Honor Society.
Outstanding Senior Secretarial Sequence Student.
Senior Class Treasurer. 1976
Texas State Honor Scholar, ~~1972~~.
Dean's List, ~~1972-75~~ 1978-82
Dormitory Resident Assistant, ~~1973-74~~. 1980-81
Student Advisory Committee, Department of Office Administration, member and secretary, ~~1973-74~~ 1981-82

(cont'd. on next page)

Z

Line 1 once—speed

Lines 2-5 once—speed
Lines 2-5 again—speed

1 a aa az az zz za aza aza az aza az az zz aza azaz
2 az zig zig zip zip zoo zoo buzz buzz daze daze az
3 az fizz fizz fuzz fuzz gaze gaze haze haze zoo az
4 az jazz jazz maze maze doze doze raze raze zip az
5 az size size whiz whiz zeal zeal zest zest zig az

Lines 6-10 once—speed
Lines 6-10 again—speed

6 zing zone zoom zero blaze gauze glaze graze prize
7 seize breeze amaze razor pizza hazel zombi wizard
8 bronze wheeze frozen nozzle zipper fizzle seizing
9 freeze bazaar hazard puzzle zealot zinnia sneezed
10 trapeze zealous pretzel drizzle horizon embezzler

DRILL

Review pages 19 and 20 for setting tabs.

Set tabs every 10 spaces. Type once and then do again. Type each line across the page.

I	ate	a	pizza	with
zest	at	the	zoo.	The
zebra	was	grazing;	the	lizard
was	dozing;	I	zipped	home.

SENTENCES

Lines 1-8 once—speed

Take:
Two 15-sec. timings on Lines 1 through 4.
Then take two 30-sec. timings.

1 Liz seized that sizzling pizza and ate with zeal. 10
2 Hazel embezzled a zillion and has been penalized. 20
3 He authorized Zeb to organize the bronze nozzles. 30
4 The zinnias were glazed in that freezing drizzle. 40
----1----2----3----4----5----6----7----8----9---10

Take:
Two 15-sec. timings on Lines 5 through 8.
Then take two 30-sec. timings.

5 Minimize the hazard and stabilize that bulldozer. 10
6 Dozens of zealous buzzards whizzed over the zone. 20
7 Buzz gazed with amazement as Hazel won the prize. 30
8 Zeb baked a dozen pretzels in the sizzling blaze. 40
----1----2----3----4----5----6----7----8----9---10

TIMINGS

Type once at controlled rate.
Take one 1-min. timing.
Take another 1-min. timing.

Zeb zipped to that zoo with zest and nuzzled 10
the zebras. He sneezed in the breeze and went to 20
see the lizards. He wants to be a zoologist when 30
he gets older. He knows a zillion things and his 40
dazed and puzzled parents are amazed. 47
----1----2----3----4----5----6----7----8----9---10

Item 10

Plain paper

OFFICE PERSONNEL SERVICES FEE SCHEDULE

Office Personnel Services is licensed, bonded, and operates under the laws of the State of Texas and is regulated by the Department of Labor and Industry.

EMPLOYER-PAID FEE SCHEDULE

1. Office Personnel Services (a division of Management Recruiters Corporation) will refund placement fees which have been paid by an employer, should the employee voluntarily leave said employer without just cause (as defined by Texas law) or be discharged for cause within 30 days from the date of starting work, if Office Personnel Services is notified in writing within 5 working days of this employee's separation from the employer.

2. In the event a refund is made, Office Personnel Services may retain 25 percent of the gross earnings of the employee as a temporary placement fee.

3. FEES

   a. For a position paying less than $8,000 per year, 8 percent of the first year's gross earnings

   ~~b. From $5,000 to $5,999 per year, 9 percent of first year's gross earnings~~

   c. From $6,000 to $9,999 per year, 10 percent of first year's gross earnings.

   d. From $10,000 to $12,999 per year, 12 percent of first year's gross earnings

   e. For a position paying over $13,000 per year, 15 percent of first year's gross earnings

   In the event that compensation for the position is based in whole or part on commission or performance bonuses, the above fee schedule shall apply, except that "earnings" shall be construed to mean a reasonable estimate of the compensation for the first year of employment as agreed upon by the employer and Office Personnel Services at the time of acceptance. This estimate is not subject to reduction or increase thereafter.

4. Fees shall be billed when the applicant begins work.

5. Terms: Net 10 days

Type once at controlled rate.

Take one 1-min. timing.
Take another 1-min. timing.

```
     Zelda gazed in amazement as Zip, the wizard,      10
seized a wand.  It was ablaze with a maze of fire      20
and lights.  He did dozens of hazardous feats and      30
puzzled all at the bazaar.  He also was a trapeze      40
whiz and dazzled folks.                                45
----1----2----3----4----5----6----7----8----9---10
```

Thinking Drill

Review general guidelines on pages 20 and 22.

LOOK—THINK—TYPE

Set tabs for 15 spaces. Type the word, tab over, type the word with an *ing* ending; tab again and type the word with an *ed* ending.

doze	seize
graze	amaze
waltz	sneeze
zoom	zigzag

REVIEW

Line 1 once—speed

Lines 2 and 3 once—speed
Line 3 again—speed

```
1    asdf jkl; z w e r t g v b h u n m i o p ; . ? : z
2    zip buzz blaze prize puzzle trapeze minimize zest
3    Hazel, the zealous zebra, won the nuzzling prize.
```

Introduction to C

Home-row *d* finger moves down and to the right to the *c* key. Place both hands on the home row and practice the move from *d* to *c*. Look at your hands and watch your finger make the motion. Do this several times; then look away and try the same motion.

C

Line 1 once—speed

Lines 2-5 once—speed
Lines 2-5 again—speed

```
1    d dd dc dc dc dd cc dcd dcd cd cd dcd dc dc ddccd
2    dc cod cat car cap can cab cut cow cup cop cue dc
3    dc card came care cast calm cask call cash cur dc
4    dc calk cane case calf camp carp cave cede cad dc
5    dc coke cord come coin coil cool corn cook ace dc
```

3. What supervisory or leadership roles have you held?

4. What qualifications do you have that make you feel that you will be successful in your field?

5. How do you spend your free time?

6. What have been your most satisfying and most disappointing school and work experiences?

7. What are your strongest and weakest personal qualities?

8. What were the major duties and responsibilities in your previous jobs?

9. Why do you think you might like to work for our company? What do you know about our company?

10. What courses in school did you like best and least? Why?

11. What did you learn or gain from your part-time and summer-job experiences?

12. What can you do for us? What can I do for you?

13. What are your plans for continued education?

14. Why did you choose your particular field of work?

15. Tell me about your extracurricular activities and interests.

16. Which geographic location do you prefer? Why?

17. Tell me about your home life during the time you were growing up.

18. Do you have any questions?

Group the questions into 6 groups of 3 each.

Single space within groups + double space between them.

If the interview has reinforced your genuine interest in what the organization has to offer, make a statement to that point. Also, as you leave, make sure that you thank the interviewer for his or her time.

Finally, we urge you to report back to us as soon as possible after each interview with your feedback as to how the interview went and your general reactions to the company and the position that is available. We will then contact the organization to discuss their reactions and "match notes."

We wish you the best of luck in your job search and your future career.

Lines 6-10 once—speed
Lines 6-10 again—speed

6 chain notch chute touch cheap since chase ancient
7 career public credit police carpet income decease
8 camera notice commit impact circle decide attract
9 compute deceive collate finance climate placement
10 compare produce consult service council enclosure

DRILL

Type each line once. At end of each line return carriage quickly and immediately begin typing on next line. Then do again.

The
The consulting
The consulting service
The consulting service produced
The consulting service produced income.

Type each line once. At end of each line return carriage quickly and immediately begin typing on next line. Then do again.

Notice
Notice how
Notice how the
Notice how the camera
Notice how the camera attracted
Notice how the camera attracted attention?

SENTENCES

Lines 1-10 once—speed

Take:
Two 15-sec. timings on Lines 1 through 5.
Then take two 30-sec. timings.

1 Carlton, the cat, curled in comfort in the chair. 10
2 Can Carrie cure colds with tonic and citric acid? 20
3 A lack of ethics caused the doctor to face scorn. 30
4 Clarice recalled the basic facts of the accident. 40
5 Chris decided to purchase a record and a picture. 50
----1----2----3----4----5----6----7----8----9---10

Take:
Two 15-sec. timings on Lines 6 through 10.
Then take two 30-sec. timings.

6 Cecelia consumed a rich chocolate ice cream cone. 10
7 The clever client could conceal crucial evidence. 20
8 Carol watched a cautious crow circle the cottage. 30
9 The wicked witch cackles as she concocts recipes. 40
10 Can Cam choose music as a classic school subject? 50
----1----2----3----4----5----6----7----8----9---10

TIMINGS

Type once at controlled rate.
Take one 1-min. timing.
Take another 1-min. timing.

A cookout on the beach could include cheese, 10
carrots, meat sandwiches, and cold juice. If the 20
chill of the ocean is too much, hot chocolate and 30
hot coffee can chase the cold chills. The decent 40
lunch and a chat with chums can enrich affection. 50
----1----2----3----4----5----6----7----8----9---10

Item 9

Plain paper

HOW TO ~~SNOW~~ PREPARE FOR YOUR JOB INTERVIEW

The job interview is the most crucial part of the hiring process. It probably causes the greatest amount of anxiety amongst all job seekers. It is really not much more than a social interchange between people, one looking for a job and the other wanting to hire someone. Interview skills can be learned, but preparation is needed.

Office Personnel Services has provided these interview tips and questions for your consideration in order that you might make the best possible impression on your job interview.

Before you even set out for the interview, we will have given you a thorough overview of the organization--what they do, the services they provide, the products they manufacture, the type of working environment they promote, etc.

You will be expected to have a resume and/or some type of completed biographical application form filled out prior to the interview. If it is an application form, make sure you fill in all relevant information. Be sure it is neat and spelling is correct. Use your resume to aid you in completing the form.

Once in the interview room or office, relax as much as possible. Most of the questions you will be asked during the interview will concern you. These will deal with your background, the reasons why you have done things, what your likes and dislikes are, how you feel about working for that employer, etc.

The following list of frequently asked interview questions has been compiled for your careful review and preparation. The questions have been designed to test your self-confidence, your realistic knowledge of yourself, your ability to communicate, and ~~to determine~~ your overall employment suitability.

1. Tell me about yourself. Expand on your resume.
2. What are your long-term career goals? Where do you want to be in 5 years? 10 years?

Retype this material. Single space with double space between paragraphs. Cut this down to two pages. Type the material "back to back". When finished, the material should be read just as a textbook that is bound at the side. Remember—1 sheet of paper—type on both sides.

(cont'd. on next page)

Type once at controlled rate.
Take one 1-min. timing.
Take another 1-min. timing.

```
     An office clerk who lacks basic ethics could      10
become the subject of scorn. Those who persist in      20
cruel and careless attacks on certain new workers      30
can cause havoc.  It is logical to follow strict,      40
concise rules concerning office tact.  Choose the      50
right track and be sincere.                            55
----1----2----3----4----5----6----7----8----9---10
```

Type once at controlled rate.
Take one 1-min. timing.
Take another 1-min. timing.

```
     A career in science includes certain choices      10
to consider.  One could choose to become a doctor      20
in a clinic or a teacher in a medical school.  An      30
active search of a current college catalog should      40
indicate which courses to select.  Contact campus      50
finance officers to check cost factors.                58
----1----2----3----4----5----6----7----8----9---10
```

Type once at controlled rate.
Take one 1-min. timing.
Take another 1-min. timing.

```
     Mack, a black Scottie, is a champion canine.      10
A constant companion is the chocolate colored cat      20
called Chicco.  Crowds chuckle as Mack and Chicco      30
do their tricks to music.  Mack can count objects      40
and prance on a bench.  Clever Chicco climbs upon      50
Mack and adds a certain clownish touch to the act.     60
----1----2----3----4----5----6----7----8----9---10
```

Thinking Drill

Review general guidelines on pages 20 and 22.

LOOK
THINK
TYPE

Set tabs for 15 spaces. Type the word, tab over, type the word with an *ing* ending; tab again and type the word with an *ed* ending.

cure	pack
curl	face
sack	chop
back	slap
tack	kick

REVIEW

Line 1 once—speed

Lines 2 and 3 once—speed
Line 3 again—speed

```
1  asdf jkl; juj aza dcd a z a j u j d c d dcd cd dc
2  car clip curb bunch curve wreck place crowd scrap
3  The wrecked cars are in the ditch near the curve.
```

me, the realistic first-year earning range for this position is from ~~$5,500~~ $8,000 to $~~7~~9,200. This range of figures includes all compensation--i.e., salary, draw, estimated bonuses, commission, and so on. ¶The service charge which you agree to pay, only in the event you haire a person referred by us in this earning range, shall be from ~~$600~~ $800 to ~~$720.~~ $920 Please note that the attached schedule ~~which includes~~ fees, terms, and guarantees. You will be billed when the applicant begins work, and (stet) the service charge will be due and payable ten days thereafter (stet) ¶This letter is written confirmation of our verbal agreement should you haire a person referred to you by our firm for this position. ~~Therefore,~~ if there is any misunderstanding regarding this aggreement, please ~~noticy~~ notify us immediately in writing. Allan Seymour, Account Executive. Enclosure.

Item 7

Working Papers, pp. 221-22

TO: All Account Executives, Deborah Bergman, Manager Director. INTERVIEWING TIPS. Hardly a day goes by when we aren't asked for suggestions on proper interviewing techniques or questioned ~~regarding~~ about what to expect in an interview. Because of the large demand for this type of information, I have prepared a handout on "How to ~~Snow~~ Prepare for Your Job Interview." This information is attached. ¶~~A large quantity of~~ this handout is being duplicated in large quantities so that you may pass them out to ~~any~~ individuals who would like a copy. ¶I think you will find this ~~tool~~ material to be both a timesaver and an aid to our employee candidates. attachment

---

Item 8

Plain Paper

Please proof and type this info that Shelly King has provided regarding a new listing—double space between headings—single space other info. D.B.

Position: Secretary (to the V.P. of Marketing)

Firm: Neptune Paint Co.
5048 Greenwood Dr.
Fairbanks, Texas 77040

Attention: Herb Thompson

Job Description: typing/shtd, greet clients, plan meetings, travel arrangements, supervise two other secretaries, asst. in market research.

Hrs: 8:30-5 (1 hr. lunch) Start: May 5

- -

Office Information

Job No: 5778
Accepting Counselor: S. King
Fee Status: Fee pd. by employer 10% ($960)

Introduction to Y

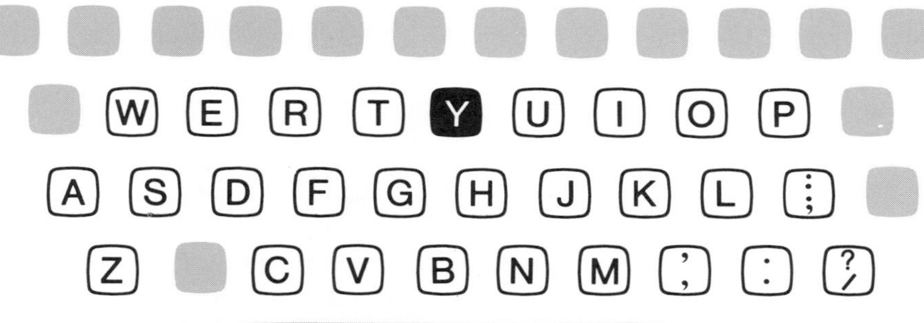

Home-row *j* finger moves up and to the left to the *y* key. Place both hands on the home row and practice the move from *j* to *y*. Look at your hands and watch your finger make the motion. Do this several times; then look away and try the same motion.

Line 1 once—speed

Lines 2-5 once—speed
Lines 2-5 again—speed

1 j jj jy jy jy jj yy jyj jyj yj yj jyj jy jy jj yj
2 jy you yes yet yew yaw yea spy shy sky may key jy
3 jy yarn they yawn gray your type year stay lye jy
4 jy yard play yowl very yolk away yell lazy sly jy
5 jy stay only defy easy rely vary obey hazy pay jy

Lines 6-10 once—speed
Lines 6-10 again—speed

6 angry rhyme daily enjoy fancy happy leaky yowling
7 allay spray dairy entry foggy handy lucky staying
8 alley stray daisy essay fiery heavy loyal yawning
9 assay style dandy every fifty hasty lowly defying
10 alloy yearn decay empty forty hurry lousy playing

DRILL

Type each line once. At end of each line return carriage quickly and immediately begin typing on next line. Then do again.

The
The yowling
The yowling stray
The yowling stray enjoyed
The yowling stray enjoyed the
The yowling stray enjoyed the alley.

Type each line once. At end of each line return carriage quickly and immediately begin typing on next line. Then do again.

Type
Type your
Type your essay
Type your essay every
Type your essay every day.

Item 5

Enclosure 2 for Item 3
Plain paper

(Brochure Ad for Employer Candidates):

Please type - double space (enclosure 2 for creative printing)

WHO WE ARE

Triple space

Office Personnel Services is the largest clerical employment agency service in Texas and one of the most successful in the country. Just four years old, we've enjoyed tremendous growth in the Houston area. In our brief history, we've already gained three national awards: "Manager of the Year" in ~~1974~~ 1980 and ~~1976~~ 1982 and "Office of the Year" in ~~1975.~~ 1981

OUR STAFF > *Triple space before and after.*

Many of our staff counselors 1980 are recognized as among the best in the United States. In ~~1975,~~ 1979 the Texas Employment agencies Association recognized eight of our counselors as among the most outstanding of the member agencies represented (and only 17 such awards were given). Our multiple offices in downtown Houston, Almeda, and Harrisburg (with Southmore soon to follow) aid us in securing the finest talent available, *for our clients.*

A UNIQUE ORGANIZATION > *Triple space before and after.*

What sets us apart? Among other things, we really care--about our applicants and their career objectives, and our clients' exacting employee criteria. We see our selves as members of a profession vital to the local business community. We bring the highest level of integrity to our industry. Our counselors are bright, well-educated, results-oriented individuals. As a member division of one of the world's largest employment placement corporations, we are dedicated to absolute professionalism and incorporate the latest methods of securing and screening candidates for our clients. Our total ~~whole~~ effort is aimed at both attracting and representing the finest possible applicants available in this market.

↓ *Add last paragraph (& phone numbers of all three offices) from Ad for Employee Candidates that you just typed.*

Item 6

Working Papers, p. 219-20

(Address on Index Cards)

Mrs. Pamela Windsor, Office Manager, P & B Fabricating, Inc., 1484 Hamline Avenue, Houston, Texas 77001-6604 Mrs. Windsor, thank you for your cordial reception on the telephone. I look forward to helping you fill your present personnel needs. ¶ In our phone conversation, ~~you will recall that~~ we discussed our office's policy of working on an "employer-paid service charge basis. This allows me to spend my time selecting and presenting to you only the best candidates for your position. I want to reiterate that your agreement to pay this service charge takes effect only in the event we refer a person to you that you in turn hire. ¶ This letter will ~~is to~~ confirm the agreement we made over the telephone regarding the service charge for the position of corresponding secretary. According to the specifications that you gave

(cont'd. on next page)

SENTENCES

Lines 1-10 once—speed

Take:
Two 15-sec. timings on Lines 1 through 5.
Then take two 30-sec. timings.

1 The sassy gray puppy plays daily in a sunny yard. 10
2 Why did that shy boy enjoy the truly scary story? 20
3 A nearby sentry eyed a hungry baby in the subway. 30
4 The hungry boy easily ate one cookie at the curb. 40
5 The kitty and the puppy may not enjoy happy play. 50
----1----2----3----4----5----6----7----8----9---10

Take:
Two 15-sec. timings on Lines 6 through 10.
Then take two 30-sec. timings.

6 It is only your duty to obey every law of safety. 10
7 An early yellow lily may defy a wintry windy day. 20
8 Silly Sally annoys that friendly young boy, Gary. 30
9 Billy is ready to carry the heavy load Wednesday. 40
10 Accuracy at a typewriter keyboard may imply zest. 50
----1----2----3----4----5----6----7----8----9---10

TIMINGS

Type once at controlled rate.
Take one 1-min. timing.
Take another 1-min. timing.

Basically, employers like a loyal secretary. 10
Honesty and courtesy always pay off in any job or 20
duty. Apathy and sloppy typing are always likely 30
to be very costly to a company. Any employee who 40
displayed a steady style will be properly awarded 50
and enjoy a fairly large salary. 56
----1----2----3----4----5----6----7----8----9---10

Type once at controlled rate.
Take one 1-min. timing.
Take another 1-min. timing.

There is simply no key to easy money. A bad 10
agency may say that you are lucky and a legacy of 20
wealthy glory is yours. Yet, if you try fancy or 30
phony schemes, you will be mighty sorry. Steady, 40
weekly saving is the thrifty means to easy money. 50
Lay a penny away a day and be happy. 57
----1----2----3----4----5----6----7----8----9---10

Type once at controlled rate.
Take one 1-min. timing.
Take another 1-min. timing.

A lazy bicycle ride in the country is surely 10
a healthy and worthy activity. A sunny sky and a 20
dry day is surely an omen to any type of cyclist. 30
Be wary of cloudy and windy days. A daily remedy 40
for a healthy and spry body is a ride on a cycle. 50
Energy is enjoyed by young and not so young. 59
----1----2----3----4----5----6----7----8----9---10

Item 3

Working Papers, pp. 217-18

Mr. ~~Wayne Meyers~~ Julian Kycia, Creative Printing Services, Inc., P. O. Box 17064, Houston, TX 77082-3008 Wayne, enclosed are the ~~text materials for the~~ typewritten portions of two advertising brochures which your agency is printing for us. As soon as you have the graphics work completed along the lines of what we discussed last week, please give me a call at 918-4801. At that time I will stop by your office to give the final okay for the materials to be sent to press. ¶ We look forward to having these materials available for public distribution by May ~~10~~ 15. Deborah Bergman, Manager. Enclosures

Item 4

Enclosure for Item 3
Plain paper

(Brochure Ad for Employee Candidates):

Please type—double space, text, triple space before & after headings.

WHO WE ARE

Office Personnel Services is the office and clerical placement arm of Management Recruiters Corporation--a personnel placement network of nearly 200 offices located throughout the United States and Canada.

We believe you *challenging & interesting* should use your talents to ~~do your~~ *in a* job, *suited to you* working with your type of people. We believe ~~in having~~ that ~~new~~ *a* job *should* be ~~an adventure.~~ We also think that finding that "just-right" position should be just as much an adventure as the work itself. That's our job. . . making your job search a pleasant and worthwhile experience leading to a position that's an adventure, not a labor.

HOW OFFICE PERSONNEL SERVICES WORKS FOR YOU

We do more than match your skills with a company's requirements--although that's important, too. We match you with people, your personality with a company's personality, your likes and dislikes with the best possible office environment for you!

First we find out what you want and what's right for you. ~~A~~ *One of our* professional Account Executive*s* asks you questions about the type of work you've done before, what you like in a job, and what you don't like, but knowing you is only half the job. Your Account Executive has also learned the needs of local business and industry, the working environment offered by companies in your area. We get to know the job.

IT HAPPENS!

Office Personnel Services brings you together with the company that best fulfills your goals and objectives. . . ~~with~~ no cold calls on your part, no uncertainty in answering vague classified ads, no wasted interviews.

Sound like what *all* you want, like the opportunity you've been looking for? It happens with Office Personnel Services. Call us today and let it happen for you.

Downtown Houston	713/918-4801
Almeda	713/911-2323
Harrisburg	713/976-4660

Type once at controlled rate.
Take one 1-min. timing.
Take another 1-min. timing.

```
     That overly busy lady is not tidy.  She pays      10
dearly for her folly and hasty ways.  A sloppy or      20
dirty habit will always imply a lazy personality.      30
In theory, a neatly and correctly done job hardly      40
portrays apathy.  The lady is in a hurry and only      50
makes costly errors for her employer.                  57
----1----2----3----4----5----6----7----8----9---10
```

Thinking Drill

LOOK

Look at these words:

jockey *guilty* *yellow* *bicycle* *empty* *birthday*

SELECT
TYPE

Now—type each sentence below, using one of the words to fill in the blank.

1. The pail was full; now it is ______ .
2. ______ is usually not a favorite color.
3. The ______ fell off the horse.
4. Someone stole my ______ .
5. If he is not innocent, he must be ______ .
6. Ted is going to have a ______ party.

REVIEW

Line 1 once—speed

Lines 2 and 3 once—speed
Line 3 again— speed

```
1    asdf jkl; juj aza dcd jyj ju jy jyj jyj jyj jj yyj
2    lazy busy daddy tray yowl rely happy noisy yelling
3    Sally is too busy yelling and yowling to be happy.
```

Introduction to X

Home-row *s* finger moves down and to the right to the *x* key. Place both hands on the home row and practice the move from *s* to *x*. Look at your hands and watch your finger make the motion. Do this several times; then look away and try the same motion.

Neptune Paint Company
5048 Greenwood Drive
Fairbanks, TX 77040-1922 — Herb Thompson
714/654-1692

Pamela Windsor (Mrs.)
P+B Fabricating, Inc.
1484 Hamline Avenue
Houston, TX 77001-6604
713/772-4926

Item 2

Working Papers, pp. 215-16

Please type this letter to Mr. Robert Krause at Fremont Chemicals (address on index cards)

April 30, 19__

Mr. Krause, thanks for talking with me on the phone today. I will send you our new brochures just as soon as they have been returned from the printer.

I would like to re emphasize that we do provide interviewing facilities in each of our branch offices in the event you wish to conduct a confidential interview away from your own offices or just wish to conduct an interview without any interruptions.

Isn't it true that you want the finest possible employee for your recruitment dollars? More than any other, Office Personnel Services will help you achieve that objective.

We welcome the opportunity to prove this claim.

Debarah Bergman
Manager

X

Line 1 once—speed
Lines 2-5 once—speed
Lines 2-5 again—speed

1 s ss sx sx sx ss xx sxs sxs xs xs sxs xs sx ssxxs
2 sx axe box fix fox lax mix six tax wax exhaust sx
3 sx axle next exam flex text hoax apex expedite sx
4 sx affix excel index toxic latex annex sixteen sx
5 sx fixed mixed boxer exist relax exact mixture sx

Lines 6-10 once—speed
Lines 6-10 again—speed

6 sixty extra sixth borax waxen vixen luxury export
7 deluxe excise expand export prefix excite example
8 oxygen reflex exotic expert boxing expire textile
9 explain extinct perplex mixture expense expecting
10 explode exhaust toolbox examine anxiety exporting

DRILL

Set a tab at space 50. Begin the left-hand column words at the left margin—the other column of words at 50. Type each line across the page. Concentrate on smooth motions to tab button or bar and carriage return.

Explore	the
deluxe	duplex
next.	Then
expect	to
relax	and
explore	the
perplexing	and
exciting	exhibits.

SENTENCES

Lines 1-10 once—speed

Take:
Two 15- sec. timings on Lines 1 through 5.
Then take two 30-sec. timings.

1 Maxine was exposed to smallpox; examine her next. 10
2 Six expert boxers were boxing in the extra annex. 20
3 Did excess oxygen explode during that experiment? 30
4 The textbook explained the new relaxing exercise. 40
5 Explain the context and expedite that experiment. 50

----1----2----3----4----5----6----7----8----9---10

Take:
Two 15-sec. timings on Lines 6 through 10.
Then take two 30-sec. timings.

6 Did Baxter excuse the next six tax experts, then? 10
7 Maxim exchanged a box of textiles for a textbook. 20
8 Is the lynx an exotic pet or is it a vexing jinx? 30
9 Fix the exhaust and examine the axle of the taxi. 40
10 Did experts exclude the existence of an appendix? 50

----1----2----3----4----5----6----7----8----9---10

Employment Agency

TYPE OF COMPANY: Employment Agency

DATE: April 30, 19 - -

COMPANY NAME/ADDRESS: Office Personnel Services
310 Marshall Building
1422 France Avenue South
Houston, TX 77001-4320

COMPANY TEL. NO.: 713/918-4801

SITUATION: You are the secretary/receptionist in the downtown Houston office of Office Personnel Services. Your supervisor is the manager, Ms. Deborah Bergman. Ms. Bergman generates the bulk of your workload. However, you also perform secretarial duties as required for a number of Account Executives.

In addition to the downtown office, there are also two other Office Personnel Services offices currently in the Houston area and numerous offices operating throughout the United States and Canada. Office Personnel Services is affiliated with Management Recruiters Corporation.

SPECIAL INSTRUCTIONS/EXPLANATIONS:

While away from your desk for lunch, your in-basket has accumulated the following items. Assume that you have grouped them in the priority that each item should be done and proceed to complete the items.

Do not sign any of the correspondence. This will be done by the individuals identified on each item. Be sure to use your initials in the reference position.

Item 1

½"

Mr. Robert Krause
Fremont Chemicals, Inc.
2180 Third Street/Houston, TX 77020
713/509-8799

½"

Please type this information on index cards—be sure to include firm name, address, phone # + contact person

Mr. Robert Krause/Fremont Chemicals, Inc.
2180 Third Street/Houston, TX 77020-3746
713/509-8799

Mr. Julian Kycia/Creative Printing Services, Inc.
P.O. Box 17064
Houston, TX 77082-3008
713/929-3422

(cont'd. on next page)

TIMINGS

Type once at controlled rate.
Take one 1-min. timing.
Take another 1-min. timing.

Max expects to chop those six boxes with the 10
old ax. This excellent exercise helps flex those 20
lax muscles. He plans to exchange the boards for 30
deluxe mailboxes. His fixed expenses perplex him 40
and influence his expansion. 46

----1----2----3----4----5----6----7----8----9---10

Type once at controlled rate.
Take one 1-min. timing.
Take another 1-min. timing.

An extra exercise to help your mind relax is 10
inhaling and exhaling deeply. It extends all the 20
oxygen capacity before it is expelled. Choose an 30
exact time each day to expedite an extra relaxing 40
exertion. Your anxieties and vexations disappear 50
and you relax. Try this exciting experience. 59

----1----2----3----4----5----6----7----8----9---10

Type once at controlled rate.
Take one 1-min. timing.
Take another 1-min. timing.

Exercise an extreme caution before investing 10
in an old duplex. Have an expert examine all the 20
existing details and explain them to you. It may 30
be easier to buy a luxurious and deluxe apartment 40
house. An experienced land expert knows if it is 50
an expensive venture. 54

----1----2----3----4----5----6----7----8----9---10

Type once at controlled rate.
Take one 1-min. timing.
Take another 1-min. timing.

An excursion into an old cave excites expert 10
explorers. The expedition offers mixed anxieties 20
and an extreme joy. Excavating an old cave takes 30
dexterity and complex reflexes to examine ancient 40
examples of a past existence. Some old caves are 50
a hoax and are a pretext to extract extra cash. 60

----1----2----3----4----5----6----7----8----9---10

Thinking Drill

LOOK
THINK
TYPE

Type each word below, inserting an appropriate letter. Use the letter *a*, *b*, *c*, *e*, *o*, *t*, or *x*.

b_x	rel_x
ax_	six_een
ta_	to_lbox
si_th	text_ook
ex_use	dupl_x

Integrated Projects Module

The integrated projects give you the opportunity to refine the production skills that you have built previously. In addition, you will have the opportnity to refine your proofreading and grammar skills.

Typist Responsibility

Each of the projects in this module represents a different type of business. You will be able to complete some of the tasks following the handwritten instructions shown on each task. On others, it will be necessary to follow the special instructions illustrated on the cover sheet.

Decisions concerning style formats for correspondence, manuscripts/business reports, and tabulation are the responsibility of the typist. Unless directed by your instructor, you should select the styles that facilitate your productivity. Efficient style formats allow you to type more letters and reports in a shorter period of time. Always remember that the style you select must be acceptable to the business or industry in which you are working. When on an actual job, you should consult the office manual or look in files containing previously typed letters to see what is the predominant style used by the office support personnel.

Complete each project as efficiently as possible. Remember that each task you complete must be "mailable." You must proofread carefully so that each completed task is free of typographical errors and has been prepared according to the specific instructions. Important: There are some errors that have *not* been corrected. It is your responsibility to edit all materials.

REVIEW

Line 1 once—speed

Lines 2 and 3 once—speed
Line 3 again—speed

1 asdf jkl; juj aza dcd jyj sxs sx sx sxs sxsx sxsx

2 six boxer reflex complex extra axes next exciting

3 Six complex exercises for sixty boxers are extra.

Introduction to Q

Home-row *a* finger moves up and to the left to the *q* key. Place both hands on the home row and practice the move from *a* to *q*. Look at your hands and watch your finger make the motion. Do this several times; then look away and try the same motion.

Q

Line 1 once—speed

Lines 2-5 once—speed
Lines 2-5 again—speed

1 a aa aq aq aq aa qq aqa aqa qa qa aqa aq aq aaqqa

2 aq quid quip quit quiz quack quail quake quart aq

3 aq queen quell quest quick quill quire require aq

4 aq quote quire squid quiet squaw query qualify aq

5 aq equip equal squat squad queer quilt acquire aq

Lines 6-10 once—speed
Lines 6-10 again—speed

6 quartz acquit squash unique squeezing questioning

7 quench equate squeak equity squelching quarreling

8 squawk liquid squeal queasy inquiring acquainting

9 square opaque squint equate antiquated conquering

10 squire quarry quaver quorum quartering requesting

DRILL

Type each line once. At end of each line, return carriage quickly and immediately begin typing on next line. Then do again.

The guest
The guest acquired
The guest acquired a
The guest acquired a unique
The guest acquired a unique antique.

Type each line once. At end of each line, return carriage quickly and immediately begin typing on next line. Then do again.

The squatter
The squatter squandered
The squatter squandered a
The squatter squandered a quarter.

General Guidelines

REJECTING-POSITION LETTER

If you have decided to reject an offer of employment, you must send a letter detailing your decision as soon as possible. Follow the guidelines listed below; an example of the rejecting-a-position letter is illustrated.

1. The format of the letter can be the block or modified block style.
2. Be certain that your letter has no typographical, spelling, or grammatical errors. Check to see that correction of errors has been made neatly.
3. The content of your letter can include:
   a. Opening paragraph: make a direct statement rejecting the position; include the title of the position.
   b. Second paragraph: indicate your pleasure at having been selected for the position. If you rejected the offer for a positive reason (accepted another position for more money; better geographical location; personal reason), include it. If you rejected the offer for some negative reason (not enough money; poor working conditions) do ***not*** include it.
   c. Closing paragraph: express your appreciation for the offer.

3103 West Lawn Street
Austin, Texas 41890
(Current Date)

Mr. H. L. Jones
Jones and Smith
7765 Down Street
Dallas, TX 46220

Dear Mr. Jones:

I have reached the decision not to accept your offer to join your firm as an assistant auditor.

As I mentioned to you during the interview, I have always hoped to relocate in some state other than Texas. I have accepted an offer with an auditing firm in Kentucky.

Thank you very much for your offer. I especially appreciate the kindness extended to me during my visit to your office.

Sincerely,

Fred A. Summers

Fred A. Summers

SENTENCES

Lines 1-10 once—speed

Take:
Two 15-sec. timings on Lines 1 through 10.
Then take two 30-sec. timings.

```
1   Go quickly; request the exquisite quartz antique.      10
2   Do that quotient; it is a frequent quiz question.      20
3   Does that quart of liquid quinine quiver quietly?      30
4   Did the squadron eat squab and squash frequently?      40
5   Put thick lacquer on the unique antique aquarium.      50
6   Ducks squirmed and quacked in the squalid quarry.      10
7   Quarantine the queasy squirrel in the square box.      20
8   The quake left queer quagmires in the old square.      30
9   That squad had qualms about the frequent quizzes.      40
10  Does the quitter frequently squabble and quibble?      50
    ----1----2----3----4----5----6----7----8----9---10
```

TIMINGS

Type once at controlled rate.
Take one 1-min. timing.
Take another 1-min. timing.

```
     The quick squad conquered the unique quintet          10
without question.  The quarterback squelched most          20
questions about technique or quality of the team.          30
If they qualify for the trophy, will they quietly          40
squash the next team or will the coach require an          50
extra practice session?                                    53
```

Type once at controlled rate.
Take one 1-min. timing.
Take another 1-min. timing.

```
     Angelique might request a price quotation on          10
an exquisite antique quilt.  She acquired it from          20
a queen in a quaint town near the equator.  Quiet          30
inquiries have arisen from qualified buyers.  The          40
question is, should she keep the quality quilt or          50
sell it quickly as requested?                              56
```

Type once at controlled rate.
Take one 1-min. timing.
Take another 1-min. timing.

```
     The quaint quill is only a quarter.  Is it a          10
unique antique?  Inquire quickly and acquire that          20
exquisite pen.  The tip makes queer squibbles and          30
squirts ink.  It requires a queer technique for a          40
quality work.  Quaint old squires always used the          50
antique quill pens in all inquiries.                       57
----1----2----3----4----5----6----7----8----9---10
```

Thinking Drill

LOOK
SELECT
TYPE

Look at these words:

equator *quality* *Queen* *quarrel* *quarterback* *quiet*

Now—type each sentence below, inserting the appropriate word.

1. The King and ________ were on tour.
2. The _______ ran with the ball.
3. It is very hot at the _______ .
4. ________ , not quantity, is most important.

General Guidelines

ACCEPTING-POSITION LETTER

An accepting-position letter should be sent immediately if you have decided to accept the position. Follow the guidelines below; an example of an accepting-position letter is illustrated.

1. Be sure that your letter has no typographical, spelling, or grammatical errors. Check to see that correction of errors has been made neatly.
2. The content of your letter may include:
   a. Opening paragraph: make a direct statement accepting the position; include the title of the position, salary, and the date you will report to work.
   b. Second paragraph: relate your enthusiasm in accepting the position; include any additional information pertaining to the existing circumstances.
   c. Closing paragraph: express your feelings about working for the individual or organization. Indicate that if the person wishes to contact you before you report to work, he or she may do so. Include where you may be reached (telephone number).

3103 West Lawn Street
Austin, Texas 41890
(Current Date)

Mr. Robert Davis
Director of Personnel
American Auditing Company
124 South Third Street
Louisville, KY 40201

Dear Mr. Davis:

I am pleased to accept your offer of employment as an assistant auditor for the American Auditing Company at a salary of $14,000 a year. The date you wish me to begin, June 1, is satisfactory.

I plan to move to Louisville on May 25 and will report to your personnel division at 8:00 a.m. on June 1. I will begin searching for a place in which to live this weekend.

I am looking forward to the opportunity of working with you and your staff at American Auditing Company. If you should wish to contact me before I leave Austin, my phone number is 816-732-7865. I can be reached before 7:30 a.m. and after 3:30 p.m. on weekdays.

Sincerely,

Fred A. Summers

Fred A. Summers

Number Keys

Numbers Are Important. Whether you are learning to type for personal or vocational use, the number portion of the keyboard is certainly as important as the alphabetic one. Numbers used by people on a personal basis include social security, telephone, address/zip code/postal zone, age, weight, height, serial, and driver's license numbers, to name a few.

There are countless ways in which numbers are used in typewritten form on business documents. Some examples include: current date, business address and telephone, price of goods and/or services, salaries, insurance policy numbers, and meeting and conference dates.

Numbers and the Keyboard. Look at your typewriter keyboard. Notice that the numbers are placed in numerical order on the top row. Numbers will be easier for you to touch operate than alphabetic characters because there are only 10 of them, compared with 26 letters of the alphabet. And the numbers are in order, as compared to the letters, which are randomly placed on the keyboard.

Hands. Place your fingers on the home row (*a s d f j k l ;*) as shown here:

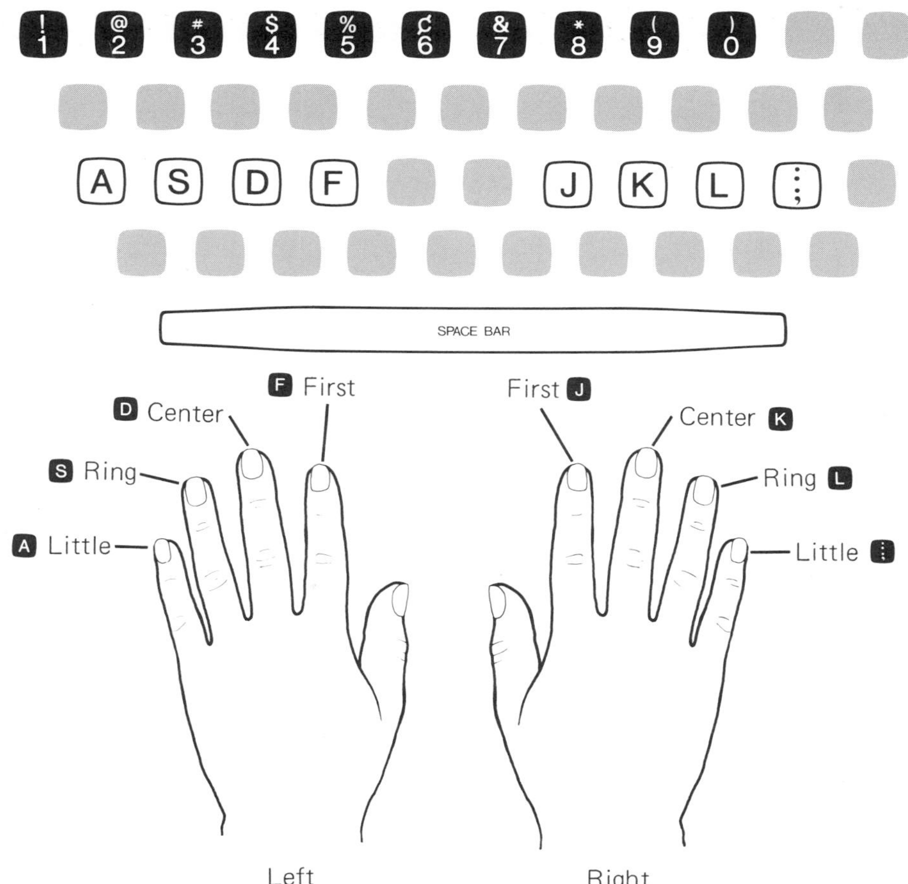

How to Type Numbers. As numbers appear most frequently with alphabetic characters, you will learn the home-row method of typing numbers. You will work from the home row in developing locational security. To help you stay close to the home-row keys, the letter *a* will be used as an anchor key. Since commas and decimals are used frequently with numbers, these keys will also be introduced. The reaches to the decimal (period) and comma keys will bring your right hand back to the home position.

General Guidelines

THE FOLLOW-UP LETTER

Sending a follow-up letter after being interviewed for a position may give you an advantage over other candidates for the same job. The follow-up letter will indicate that you are sincere about the position and would really like to have the job. An example of a follow-up letter is illustrated on this page. The letter should contain:

1. Opening paragraph: a "thank you" for the interview and an expression of appreciation for the courtesy and consideration extended to you. Mention the position for which you were interviewed and the date and place of the interview.
2. Second paragraph: reaffirm your interest in the position and the organization. Mention anything that you have done since the interview which demonstrates your interest in the job (additional research on the company or conversations with local representatives). Submit any information you wish to add to your original application. Express a willingness to provide additional data if needed.
3. Closing paragraph: close with a suggestion for further action, such as your availability for additional interviews at the employer's convenience.

3103 West Lawn Street
Austin, Texas 41890
(Current Date)

Mr. Robert Davis
Director of Personnel
American Auditing Company
124 South Third Street
Louisville, KY 40201

Dear Mr. Davis:

Thank you for granting me an interview last Friday, April 16, 1977, for the position in your auditing department. I certainly appreciate the courtesy and consideration extended by you and your staff.

I would like you to know that my interest in your organization has grown even more after visiting your home office. The auditing staff members, as well as your administrative staff, seem to be warm, considerate people with whom I would like to be associated. If you need additional information to assist you in making a decision regarding my qualifications for the position, please contact me.

I would be most pleased to come to Louisville for a second interview at your convenience. You may contact me at 816-432-7865 before 7:30 a.m. and after 3:30 p.m. on weekdays.

Sincerely,

Fred A. Summers

Fred A. Summers

Margins:
Elite: 25 and 75
Pica: 17 and 67

IMPORTANT: Use the same margins for the entire number section.

The Space Bar and the Letter A

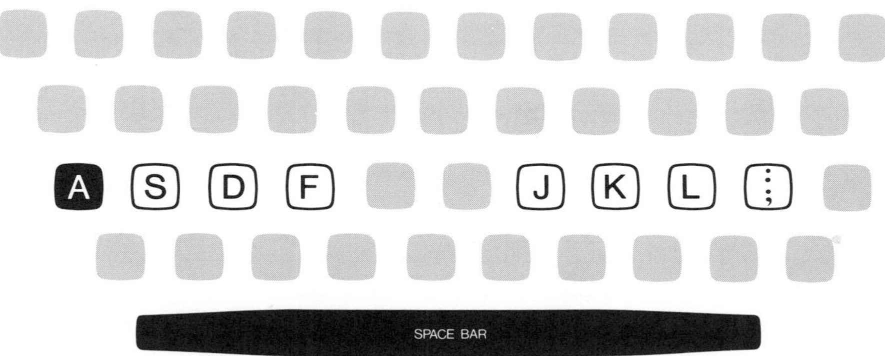

Left little finger (home row) strikes the letter ***a***. The right thumb strikes the space bar.

Type each line twice.

a a a a aa aa aa a a a aa aa a a aa a aa aa a a a

aa aaa a a aa a aaa aa a aaa a a aa aa aaa a aa a

The Number 1

The left little finger strikes the number 1. Some individuals use the lower-case L; however, this will cause problems on electronic keyboards. To input the number 1, you must use the 1 key on electronic keyboards.

As you type the number one, think ***one*** to yourself. As you type 11, think ***eleven.*** As you type 111, think ***one eleven.*** This procedure will help increase your typing speed as you begin typing numbers in units of two and three digits.
When letters and numbers are combined, use the following technique for reading the copy. For the combination ***a1***, think *ay-one*. For the combination ***a111***, think *ay/one-eleven*.

Type each line once.
Then repeat, for speed.

al lal alll al al all alll al llall al lal all al

all alll lla al lal all llla lll lla ll al lla la

FORMER EMPLOYERS (List Below Last Four Employers, Starting With Last One First)

Date Month and Year	Name and Address of Employer	Salary	Position	Reason for Leaving
From Summers To 1977-76-75	Jones and Smith 7765 Down Street Dallas, Texas 46220	$3.00/hr	Auditing Trainee	Return to school
From May, 1974 To Aug., 1974	Continental Engineering Co. 7761 Down Street Pumona, Texas 40160	$3.00/hr	Traffic Rate Clerk	Attend school
From To				
From To				

REFERENCES: Give Below the Names of Three Persons Not Related To You, Whom You Have Known At Least One Year.

	Name	Address	Business	Years Acquainted
1	Dr. Lawrence Jamison Chairman	Dept. of Accountancy TSU, Austin, TX 41890	Education	4
2	Ms. Joanne Davis	Continental Engineering 7761 Down St./Pumona TX	Supervisor Traffic Deparment	5
3	Mr. H. L. Jones	Jones and Smith 2350 Lariat Rd/Dallas TX	President	4

PHYSICAL RECORD:

List Any Physical Defects None

Were You Ever Injured? No Give Details

Have You Any Defects In Hearing? No In Vision? No In Speech? No

In Case of Emergency Notify R. A. Summers (Name) 2115 Sherwood/New London, TX (Address) 815-745-6154 (Phone No.)

I authorize investigation of all statements contained in this application. I understand that misrepresentation or omission of facts called for is cause for dismissal. Further, I understand and agree that my employment is for no definite period and may, regardless of the date of payment of my wages and salary, be terminated at any time without any previous notice.

Date 5/1/78 Signature Fred A. Summers

DO NOT WRITE BELOW THIS LINE

Interviewed By Date

REMARKS:

Neatness		Character	
Personality		Ability	

Hired For Dept. Position Will Report Salary Wages

Approved: 1. Employment Manager 2. Dept. Head 3. General Manager

The Number 2

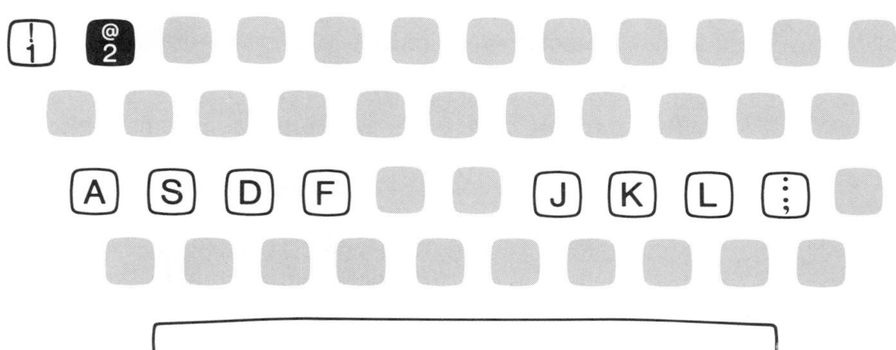

Home-row *s* finger moves up and to the left to the number *2*. Place both hands on the home row and practice the move from *s* to *2*. Look at your hands and watch your finger make the motion. Do this several times; then look away and try the same motion. Continue this procedure until you can make the motion correctly without looking at the keyboard.

Type each line once.
Then repeat, typing faster.

```
2 2 22 22 222 222 2 2 22 222 222 2 222 22 222 222
1 2 1 21 221 122 121 221 2 1 212 112 1 12 21 21 2
a12 2a1 112a 12a12 21a1 122a a11 a2a 12a 1a2a 122
```

Note: Did you think of 221 as ***two-twenty-one***? Did you think of 112a as ***one-twelve/ay***?

When working with groups of numbers having four digits and no natural break, think of the numbers as two pairs.

Type each line once.

```
1221 1112 1221 1112 2112 2112 1122 1122 1221 222
a1122 a1221 1112a 1212a a1112 a2112 a1212 a1221a
```

When typing number groups that have more than four digits and no natural breaks such as a space, comma, or decimal, use a 2-3-2 reading pattern. The number 21221 would be ***twenty-one/two twenty-one***. The number 2121221 would be ***twenty-one/two-twelve/twenty-one***.

Type each line once.

```
21 221 21 221 21 221 a21 212a 12 11a 2121 a121 a2
21221 21121 21221 a21112 a12212 a12121 21212 a122
a2112121 22 1 21a 2122121 12221 a212a 1221a 12221
12 12 12 12 121 121 121 121 a2a a221 a221 2a211 1
212a1 121221a 12122a1 22221a 12212a 221221a 21a22
```

General Guidelines

THE APPLICATION-FOR-EMPLOYMENT FORM

Some companies require that all applicants complete an application-for-employment form. Some of the information requested on the application form will be the same as that which you have included on your personal-data sheet. Application forms may require additional information such as car ownership, arrest record, health details, special skills, and licenses. The important differences between the application form and the personal data sheet are:

1. The application form is employer-initiated; the data sheet is employee-initiated. As such, the company controls the information generated from an application form, whereas the potential employee is able to decide which information to include on the data sheet.
2. An application must be filled in as presented. A data sheet can be creatively designed by the applicant and arranged to highlight the positive qualifications and downplay weak or negative aspects.
3. An application form is usable only by the issuing company. A data sheet can be designed for use with many companies with little or no changes made.

Follow the guidelines below; an example of an application form is illustrated.

1. Be sure that the information you typed on the form contains no typographical errors. Check to see that correction of errors has been made neatly.
2. Attempt to furnish as much information as possible. It is better to insert *no*, *none*, or *not appropriate (NA)* than to leave blanks.
3. You may have to abbreviate some words because of a lack of space.

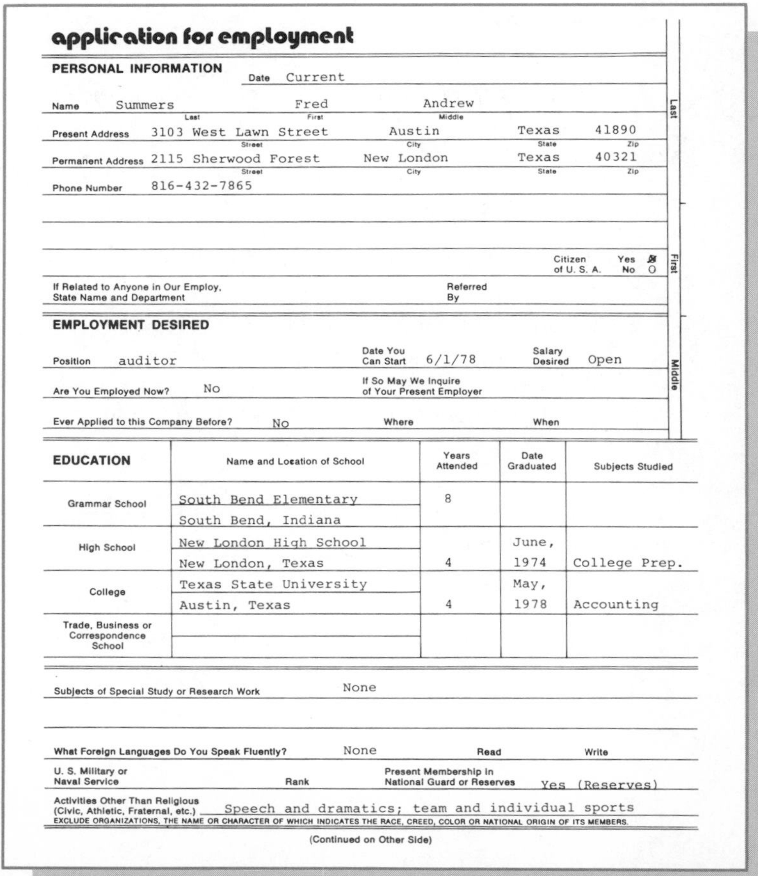

application for employment

PERSONAL INFORMATION Date Current

Name Summers (Last) Fred (First) Andrew (Middle)

Present Address 3103 West Lawn Street (Street) Austin (City) Texas (State) 41890 (Zip)

Permanent Address 2115 Sherwood Forest (Street) New London (City) Texas (State) 40321 (Zip)

Phone Number 816-432-7865

Citizen of U. S. A. Yes ☒ No ○

If Related to Anyone in Our Employ, State Name and Department — Referred By

EMPLOYMENT DESIRED

Position auditor — Date You Can Start 6/1/78 — Salary Desired Open

Are You Employed Now? No — If So May We Inquire of Your Present Employer

Ever Applied to this Company Before? No — Where — When

Last / First / Middle

EDUCATION	Name and Location of School	Years Attended	Date Graduated	Subjects Studied
Grammar School	South Bend Elementary South Bend, Indiana	8		
High School	New London High School New London, Texas	4	June, 1974	College Prep.
College	Texas State University Austin, Texas	4	May, 1978	Accounting
Trade, Business or Correspondence School				

Subjects of Special Study or Research Work None

What Foreign Languages Do You Speak Fluently? None — Read — Write

U. S. Military or Naval Service — Rank — Present Membership in National Guard or Reserves Yes (Reserves)

Activities Other Than Religious (Civic, Athletic, Fraternal, etc.) Speech and dramatics; team and individual sports

EXCLUDE ORGANIZATIONS, THE NAME OR CHARACTER OF WHICH INDICATES THE RACE, CREED, COLOR OR NATIONAL ORIGIN OF ITS MEMBERS.

(Continued on Other Side)

The Number 3

Home-row *d* finger moves up and to the left to the number *3*. Place both hands on the home row and practice the move from *d* to *3*. Look at your hands and watch your finger make the motion. Do this several times; then look away and try the same motion. Continue this procedure until you can make the motion correctly without looking at the keyboard.

Remember: return your hands to the home-row position after striking a number.

Type each line once.

3 3 3 33 33 33 3 3 3 33 33 333 33 33 33 33 33 3 3

332 32 213 231 12 1321 231 32 231 2312 232 1213 3

a33 a3 a32 a321 a233 a3232 a132 13232 3223212 a23

a323 a3212321 a1323la al 231a a123 232 32 332 a13

3 233 13 231 23 233 323321 33212 13 321 3323 1231

323132112 231132a 22312a 2a 2331 a21321 a22132213

TIMED WRITINGS

How many "words" of numbers can you type in 30 seconds and in one minute? The material below is marked as "words" (see the end of each line). A word in typewriting is made up of five letters/digits and/or spaces.

Take two 30-second timings on line 1. If you finish the line before time is up, repeat it. Since you typed for only 30 seconds, double your rate to compute your "word-a-minute" rate. Repeat the drill on line 2.

Now take two 1-minute writings on lines 3 and 4. If you finish, begin over on line 3. Your goal for the 1-minute writing is to equal or better the "word-a-minute" rate you make on the 30-second timings.

1 1233 1223 3221 3222 1312 3122 2311 3321 1232 3112 10

2 12 31131 221312 12131 32 233 121 123 2231 3231 23 10

3 21 1132 132 32 3112 321233 123 133132 123212 3123 10

4 311132 1223 12 1122331 23222123 3 12 33312 321 32 10

----1----2----3----4----5----6----7----8----9---10

Set your margins for a 50-space line (review pages ix-x). Concentrate on keeping your eyes on the copy.

Type each line twice.

1233 1213 1223 1223 1133 3311 2211 2211 1132 2211

a12 31131 231321 211312 a12132 32233 a121 123 233

1233 1222 1333 1221 1331 3331 2222 2221 1112 1113

General Guidelines

THE APPLICATION LETTER

Your application letter is important. Follow the guidelines below; an example of an application letter using the guidelines is illustrated.

1. Your letter should not exceed one typewritten page.
2. Be certain that your letter has no typographical, spelling, or grammatical errors. Check to see that the correction of errors has been made neatly.
3. The content of your letter can include:
   a. Opening paragraph: make a direct statement as to why you are writing: which position you are interested in, how you heard of the vacancy (if one exists), and/or why you are interested in this particular position and company.
   b. Second paragraph: tell the reader what you are currently doing. Explain why your background is particularly appropriate for this position. If you feel your educational background is stronger, discuss it; if you have strength in work experience, discuss it. Highlight your achievements and qualifications through education or previous experience, but do not repeat everything on your data sheet.
   c. Third paragraph: if previous paragraph was used for explanation of education, devote this one to experience, or vice versa. Emphasize how your background fits this position. Refer reader to further information on the personal-data sheet which is enclosed.
   d. Fourth paragraph: use this one to really sell yourself; be creative. Show how you are different and more qualified for the position than others who would be applying. You might wish to include honors, participation in organizations, offices held, and so on. If you have your credentials on file with some type of placement service, tell the reader how to obtain them.
   e. Closing paragraph: make it easy for the reader to take action. Show interest in coming for an interview at the reader's convenience. Facilitate an immediate reply by giving your complete phone number.

3103 West Lawn Street
Austin, Texas 41890
(Current Date)

Mr. Robert Davis
Director of Personnel
American Auditing Company
124 South Third Street
Louisville, KY 40201

Dear Mr. Davis:

Please consider me as an applicant for the accounting position which your firm has announced is vacant. Your advertisement, which appeared in the March 18, 1977 issue of the Los Angeles Times, was most impressive.

I am a full-time student at Texas State University, Austin, Texas, majoring in accounting and minoring in data processing. The accounting program at Texas State meets all state CPA requirements and gives me the educational background required for your vacancy.

On-the-job experience has played a major role in my career decision. This experience includes working for the past three summers as an auditing trainee for Jones and Smith in Dallas. The experience has given me a wide perception of an auditing firm. Additional information relating to past educational and work experience is detailed on the enclosed personal data sheet.

I am positive I can "do the job for you." In addition to possessing the necessary educational background and work experience, my ability to get along with people will provide your firm with a valuable asset.

I am available for a personal interview at your convenience. You may contact me at 816-732-7865 before 7:30 a.m. and after 3:30 p.m. on weekdays.

Sincerely,

Fred A. Summers

Fred A. Summers

Attachment

The Number 4

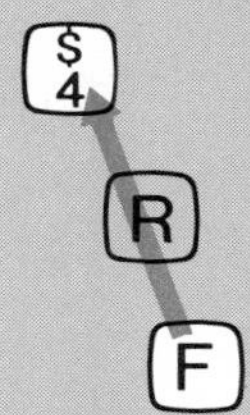

Home-row *f* finger moves up and to the left to the number *4*. Place both hands on the home row and practice the move from *f* to *4*. Look at your hands and watch your finger make the motion. Do this several times; then look away and try the same motion. Continue this procedure until you can make the motion correctly without looking at the keyboard.

Be sure to concentrate on the number combinations as you type.

Type each line once.

```
4 4 44 44 444 444 4 4 44 4444 4 44 44 44 444 44 44
14 134 1431 2343 343123 43 334 3 3421 23214 432442
al4 a4231 24 4a24 1432a 34 a4321 a4323 a431 a342 a
4 43 344 343 4321 3422 23423 3443 22343 343 44 334
4343213413 34343213311 4323412341 3431233 44342 43
```

Type the lines at your own rate—but remember, type as rapidly as possible.

Type each line once.

```
333 333 333 444 444 444 333 333 444 444 222 222 22
333 333 333 444 444 444 333 333 444 444 222 222 22
12221 12221 13331 13331 14441 14441 12221 12221 13
12221 12221 13331 13331 14441 14441 12221 12221 13
```

The Number 5

Home-row *f* finger moves up and to the right to the number *5*. Place both hands on the home row and practice the move from *f* to *5*. Look at your hands and watch your finger make the motion. Do this several times; then look away and try the same motion. Continue this procedure until you can make the motion correctly without looking at the keyboard.

General Guidelines

REFERENCE-REQUEST LETTER

You *must* secure permission from a person before listing that person as a reference on your data sheet. Although you may obtain the permission orally, common courtesy dictates that you request permission in written form. Follow the guidelines below; an example of the reference-request letter is illustrated.

1. The format of the letter can be the block or modified block style.
2. Be certain that your letter has no typographical, spelling, or grammatical errors. Check to see that the correction of errors has been made neatly.
3. The content of your letter can include:
   a. Opening paragraph: make a direct statement as to why you are writing, and why you are requesting his/her assistance.
   b. Second paragraph: tell the reader what you are currently doing. It may have been some time since you and he/she have been associated.
   c. Third paragraph: mention any personal items that you feel are appropriate. This is especially critical if there has been a lapse of time since you have been associated with the person. It may be necessary to "jog" the individual's memory.
   d. Closing paragraph: express your appreciation for the individual's assistance. Indicate that if the person wishes to contact you to clarify any information to please do so. Also include where you may be reached (telephone number).

3103 West Lawn Street
Austin, Texas 41890
(Current Date)

Ms. Joanne Davis, Supervisor
Traffic Department
Continental Engineering Company
7761 Down Street
Pumona, TX 40160

Dear Ms. Davis:

I am seeking your permission to use your name as a reference to include in my credential file. I am requesting that you serve as a reference, as you were my direct supervisor while I was employed at Continental during the summer of 1974.

Since we saw each other last, I have been pursuing a degree in accounting at The University of Texas at Austin. I will be graduating at the conclusion of the current semester and am beginning the process of interviewing for an auditing position in several auditing firms. I majored in accounting and minored in data processing at UT and have enjoyed my studies very much. I was fortunate to be able to work for three summers at a large auditing firm in Dallas. The experience will be a definite asset in my search for a permanent position.

The time spent in your department is another positive experience in my background. Not only have the various job duties and tasks in which I was involved been quite important to me, but the sharing of your ideas of personnel management were invaluable. I shall always remember the many times you were gracious enough to take time from your busy schedule to discuss your philosophy of working with people.

I shall certainly appreciate your serving as a reference for me. If you wish to contact me for clarification of any item, you may reach me at 816-732-7865 before 7:30 a.m. and after 3:30 p.m. on weekdays.

Sincerely,

Fred A. Summers

Fred A. Summers

Type each line once.
Then do again.

```
5 5 55 55 55 5 5 5 15 15 15 51 15 55 51 55 51 151
11 55 a55 11 55 a55 11 55 55 11 51 a51 15 15 15 5
55 44 a45 54 14 15 24 25 34 35 53 43 52 42 51 41a
```

Remember to read the number combinations correctly.

Type each line once.
Then do again.

```
15115 15115 55151 55151 15 51511 151 155 15115 51
15115 15115 a55151 a55151 15 5151 151 a155 a51151
```

TIMINGS

Use the following lines for speed practice. Use the same procedure that you did earlier. Remember? Take two 30-second writings on line 1. If you finish before time is up, begin again. Since you typed for only 30 seconds, double your rate to compute your "word-a-minute" rate. Repeat the drill on line number 2. Then take two 1-minute timings on lines 3 and 4. If you finish both before time is up, begin again on line 3. Your goal for the 1-minute writing is to equal or better the "word-a-minute" rate you made on the 30-second timings.

```
1   25 35 a45 34 45 15 251 a342 235 325 325 a451 5141        10
2   4241 4521 31442 51431 51431 4251 4251 5421 5421 2        10
3   12 41 41 31 31 31 a55 55 15 51 a544 a344 a233 a12        10
4   12 51 31 21 31 31 55 55 51 15 455 344 233 1231 15        10
    ----1----2----3----4----5----6----7----8----9---10
```

The Number 6

Home-row *j* finger moves up and to the left to the number *6*. Place both hands on the home row and practice the move from *j* to *6*. Look at your hands and watch your finger make the motion. Do this several times; then look away and try the same motion. Continue this procedure until you can make the motion correctly without looking at the keyboard.

Type each line once.
Then do again.

```
6 6 6 66 66 66 66 6 6 6 6 66 666 61 61 61 61 61 6
11 a66 11 66 11 66 11 66 11 66 a66 11 66 11 66 61
166 166 a661 661 161 161 a611 661 661 116 11 a666
11666 16661 61 66 66 111 666 661 1166 16661 61 61
```

General Guidelines

PERSONAL-DATA SHEET

Your personal-data sheet should "sell" you. There are many different formats that can be used in the typing of the data sheet. An example that is popular is illustrated on this page. Regardless of the exact format, the same categories of information are usually found on a data sheet. These include:

1. Location Information: Your full name, home and/or school addresses, telephone number, and job interest.
2. Personal Data: There is some general disagreement on what information should be included in this section. An employer may not discriminate against any applicant because of race, creed, color, physical characteristics, age, marital status, or sex. Use your common sense—the idea is to "sell" yourself.

   Many data-sheet examples show this section moved to the area directly preceding the reference section. There is no set order for items 2-7. You should arrange the data sheet to accentuate your positive traits and downplay your weaker areas.
3. Education: The first entry should be the most current. Show college, university, and high school from which graduated or attended; include any honors received. Give names, addresses, and dates of all institutions attended, program, degree/diploma received. Include a list of courses completed if you wish. Show other positive information such as honors, rank in class, and so on.
4. Experience. First entry should be the most current. Be selective but show any type of experience that you feel should be considered by the prospective employer. Give past employer's name, dates, job title, and responsibilities.
5. Activities and Interests: Divide into clubs—high school and post-secondary levels—and hobbies. Again, be selective. This area may be omitted if there is sufficient material in other categories.
6. References: Include at least three references. ALWAYS ask an individual if she/he will serve as a reference for you before listing. Include: past employers, teachers, and others who will be able to vouch for your qualities as an employee. Gives names, titles, complete addresses, and telephone numbers.
7. If you have a complete set of credentials on file at an organization, include where they may be obtained.

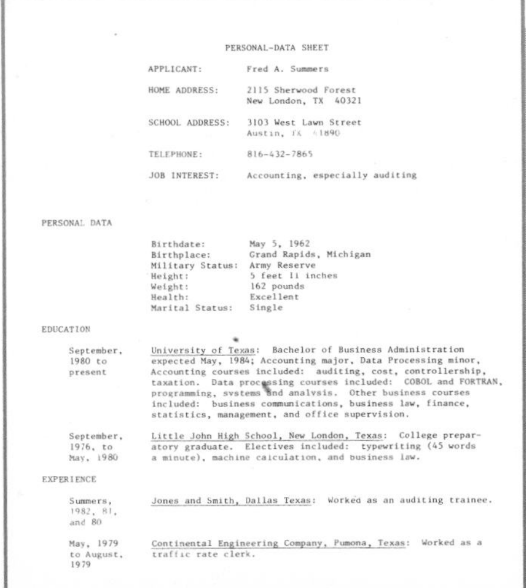

PERSONAL-DATA SHEET

APPLICANT: Fred A. Summers

HOME ADDRESS: 2115 Sherwood Forest
New London, TX 40321

SCHOOL ADDRESS: 3103 West Lawn Street
Austin, TX 41890

TELEPHONE: 816-432-7865

JOB INTEREST: Accounting, especially auditing

PERSONAL DATA

Birthdate: May 5, 1962
Birthplace: Grand Rapids, Michigan
Military Status: Army Reserve
Height: 5 feet 11 inches
Weight: 162 pounds
Health: Excellent
Marital Status: Single

EDUCATION

September, 1980 to present — University of Texas: Bachelor of Business Administration expected May, 1984; Accounting major, Data Processing minor, Accounting courses included: auditing, cost, controllership, taxation. Data processing courses included: COBOL and FORTRAN, programming, systems and analysis. Other business courses included: business communications, business law, finance, statistics, management, and office supervision.

September, 1976, to May, 1980 — Little John High School, New London, Texas: College preparatory graduate. Electives included: typewriting (45 words a minute), machine calculation, and business law.

EXPERIENCE

Summers, 1982, 81, and 80 — Jones and Smith, Dallas Texas: Worked as an auditing trainee.

May, 1979 to August, 1979 — Continental Engineering Company, Pumona, Texas: Worked as a traffic rate clerk.

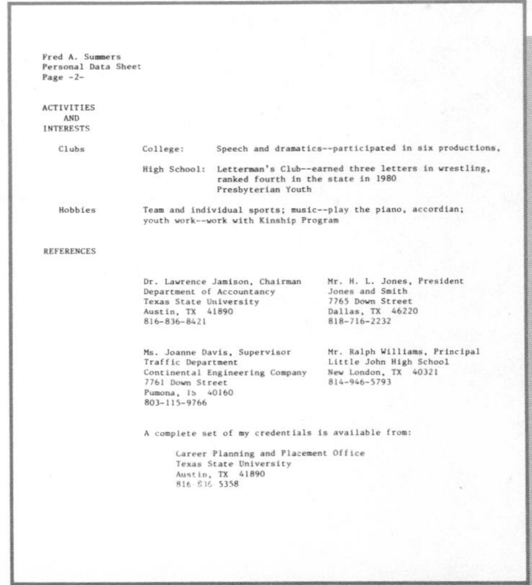

Fred A. Summers
Personal Data Sheet
Page -2-

ACTIVITIES AND INTERESTS

Clubs

College: Speech and dramatics--participated in six productions,

High School: Letterman's Club--earned three letters in wrestling, ranked fourth in the state in 1980
Presbyterian Youth

Hobbies

Team and individual sports; music--play the piano, accordian; youth work--work with Kinship Program

REFERENCES

Dr. Lawrence Jamison, Chairman
Department of Accountancy
Texas State University
Austin, TX 41890
816-836-8421

Mr. H. L. Jones, President
Jones and Smith
7765 Down Street
Dallas, TX 46220
818-716-2232

Ms. Joanne Davis, Supervisor
Traffic Department
Continental Engineering Company
7761 Down Street
Pumona, TS 40160
803-115-9766

Mr. Ralph Williams, Principal
Little John High School
New London, TX 40321
814-946-5793

A complete set of my credentials is available from:

Career Planning and Placement Office
Texas State University
Austin, TX 41890
816-836-5358

The Number 7

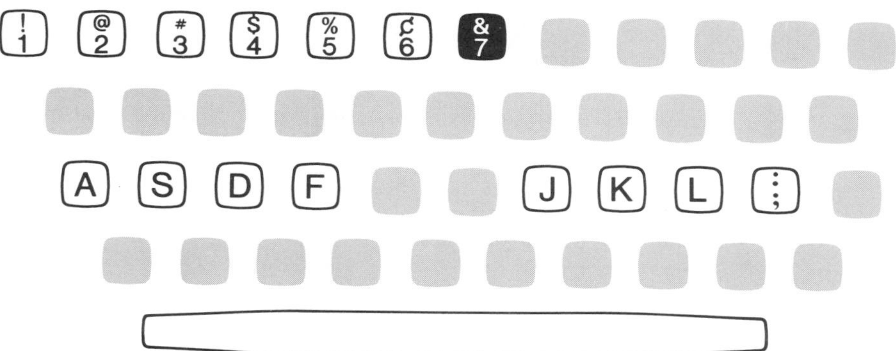

Home-row *j* finger moves up and to the left to the number *7*. Notice the difference between the reaches to the number *6* and the number *7*. Place both hands on the home row and practice the move from *j* to *7*. Look at your hands and watch your finger make the motion. Do this several times; then look away and try the same motion. Continue this procedure until you can make the motion correctly without looking at the keyboard.

Type each line once.
Then do again.

```
7 7 7 77 77 7 7 7 77 7 7 77 77 7 77 7 7 77 77 777
7 77 777 7777 7 7 77 77 777 777 7777 7777 7 77 77
76 76 67 77 66 776 776 77 777 6776 76 76 67 66 77
75 75 a55 77 66 76 57 57 a76 77 777 677 a555 76 6
```

NUMBER-CONCENTRATION DRILL

See how quickly you can complete the following:

1. Type the numbers 1 through 7 three times. Space once after each number.
2. Type the numbers 1 through 7 three times. Space twice after each number.
3. Reverse the order, type from 7 down to 1. Space once after each number.
4. Type from 7 down to 1. Space twice after each number.

SPEED-DEVELOPMENT DRILL

How many "words" a minute can you type now that the numbers 6 and 7 have been added? Take two 30-second timings on line 1. If you finish before time is up, begin again. Because you typed for only 30 seconds, double your rate to compute your "word-a-minute" rate. Repeat the drill on line 2. Then take two 1-minute timings on lines 3 and 4. If you finish both before time is up, begin again on line 3. Your goal for the minute writing is to equal or better the "word-a-minute" rate you made on the 30-second timings.

```
1  a1234 5671 a2345 a6712 3457 a61234 3467 1234 4651     10
2  6771 4323 1612 5661 6675 a1267 5672 4216 5437 a43     10
3  5734273 5743216 a1276516 a25123 67 7113 6711 6 67     10
4  5421 4375 16 2367 5 672 51 61742 6611317 16 767 5     10
   ----1----2----3----4----5----6----7----8----9---10
```

The Job-Campaign Module

The most important communication you will compose and type as an individual will be the items related to your application for employment. The written communication you prepare will make the first impression on your prospective employer. From the letter of application and data sheet, the prospective employer will determine if you are to have an interview.

Additional correspondence with which you should be familiar includes:

1. Reference-request letter
2. Application form
3. Follow-up letter
4. Accepting-position letter
5. Rejecting-position letter

(Examples and guidelines for preparation of all the related job-seeking correspondence items are included in this section.)

Carefully read the general guidelines for the preparation and compare the guidelines with the illustrated examples. Then complete the following.

INSTRUCTIONS

1. Prepare a copy of your personal data sheet.
2. Prepare a reference-request letter that could be sent to each of the individuals listed as references on your data sheet.
3. Select a position for which you would like to apply and prepare an application letter.
4. Assume the company to which you have written the application letter has invited you for an interview. They have sent you an application for employment form that you are to complete and bring with you to the interview. (You do not have to fill one out at this time.)
5. Assume you have had an interview with the organization. Prepare a follow-up letter.
6. Assume you have been offered the position and wish to accept. Prepare an acceptance letter.
7. Assume you have been offered the position and wish to decline. Prepare the rejection letter.

The Number 8

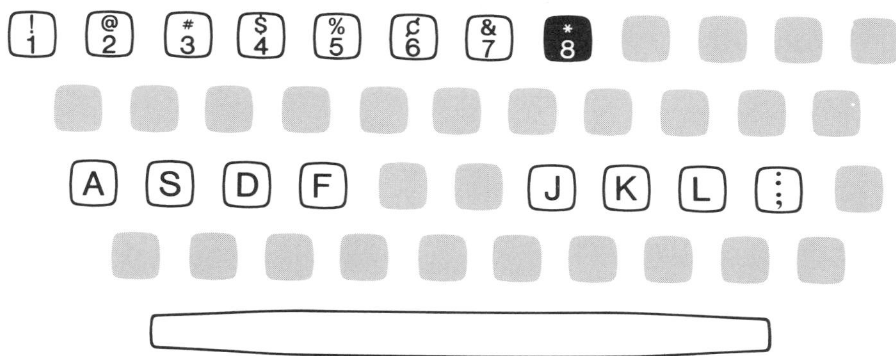

Home-row *k* finger moves up and to the left to the number *8*. Place both hands on the home row and practice the move from *k* to *8*. Look at your hands and watch your finger make the motion. Do this several times; then look away and try the same motion. Continue this procedure until you can make the motion correctly without looking at the keyboard.

Type each line once.
Then do again.

```
8 8 8 88 88 88 8 8 8 88 88 888 888 88 88 88 88 88
87 a8 6876 287 a248 836 872 347 288a 6788 8 82678
all 88 ll a88 ll 88 ll 88 ll 88 ll a88 ll 88 ll 8
83 83 38 a33 88 8a a8 88 a83 83 38 33 a88 81 al88
```

NUMBER-CONCENTRATION DRILL

See how quickly you can complete the following:

1. Type the numbers 1 through 8 as many times as you can in 30 seconds. Space once between numbers.
2. Reverse the order; type from 8 back to 1 as many times as you can in 30 seconds. Space once between numbers.

The Number 9

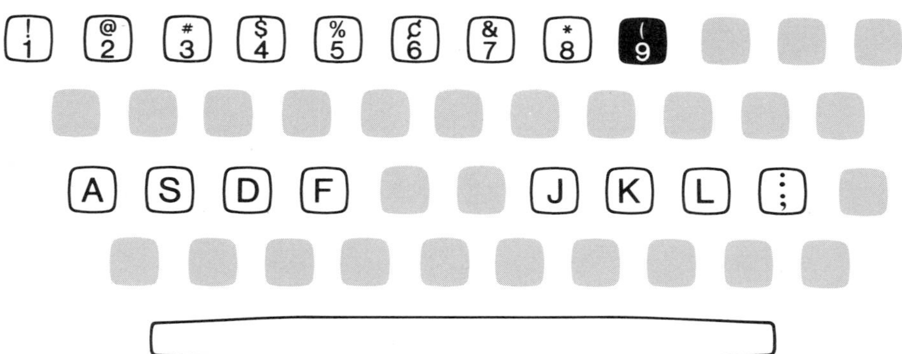

Home-row *l* finger moves up and to the left to the number *9*. Place both hands on the home row and practice the move from *l* to *9*. Look at your hands and watch your finger make the motion. Do this several times; then look away and try the same motion. Continue this procedure until you can make the motion correctly without looking at the keyboard.

CORPORATE-RESOLUTION FORM

This is to Certify That at a meeting of the Board of Directors of the ________ DeLuxe Paint Company ________ a corporation existing under the laws of the State of Minnesota, duly called and held (1st day of current month) 19____, at which a quorum of said Board was present and voting, the following resolution was adopted:

Be It Resolved: That the Federal Bank and Trust Company, Minneapolis, Minn., is hereby designated as the depository of the funds of this Company.

AND BE IT FURTHER RESOLVED: That checks of this corporation drawn on the Federal Bank and Trust Company, Minneapolis, Minn., and orders for transfer or withdrawal of the funds of this corporation on deposit on said bank, in whatever form, shall be signed by any of the following officers:

Gordon Rome ________ Pres. ________ Secy.

Karen Hutchinson ________ Vice Pres. Kevin McLeroy ________ Treas.

and countersigned by any one of the following:

Cy Clemenson, Chairman ________

____

And that said officers, or any ________ of them are hereby authorized for and on behalf of this corporation, to borrow money of the Federal Bank and Trust Company, Minneapolis, Minn., and to sign, execute and deliver the notes of this corporation therefor in such amounts, for such times, such rate of interest and upon such terms as they may see fit and are hereby authorized to pledge to said bank the bills receivable, stocks, bonds or other property of this corporation as security for any money so borrowed and to offer the bills receivable of this corporation to said bank for re-discount.

AND BE IT FURTHER RESOLVED, that the said Federal Bank and Trust Company, Minneapolis, Minn., is hereby authorized and directed to honor and pay any checks drawn as above set forth, whether such checks be payable to the order of any officer signing or countersigning said checks, or any of said officers in their individual capacities or not, and whether such checks are deposited to the individual credit of the officer signing or countersigning said checks or to the individual credit of any of the other officers or not.

IN WITNESS WHEREOF, I have hereunto affixed my name as Secretary, and have caused the corporate seal of said corporation to be hereto affixed, this (current date) day of ________, 19____.

(SEAL) J. Clauson
Secretary

I, Gordon Rome ________, a Director of said corporation, do hereby certify that the foregoing is a true and correct copy of a resolution passed as therein set forth.

Gordon Rome
Director

Task 25

Working Papers, p. 213

Prepare a corporate-resolution form from the following:

Klauson Manufacturing Co.
(first day of current month)
Claude Klauson (pres.)
Jane Wilson (V-P) Kam Wilson (Treas.)
countersigned by: J. L. Winston
. . . . two . . . . . they . . . . . are
Claude Klauson (current date)

Type each line once.
Then do again.

99 9 999 9 99 91 91 91 99 99 99 9 999 9 99 999 91
989 a489 19891 1919 1891 a981 1986a 183218 189 19

a98 98 99 88 a89 998 998 888 991 999 a98 98 99 88
94 a2989 a923 a989 a239 a9a23 a9891 123 a98 a2919

NUMBER-CONCENTRATION DRILL

1. Type 1 through 9 as many times as you can in 30 seconds. Space once between numbers.
2. Reverse the order, type from 9 back to 1 as many times as you can in 30 seconds. Space once between numbers.

The Number 0

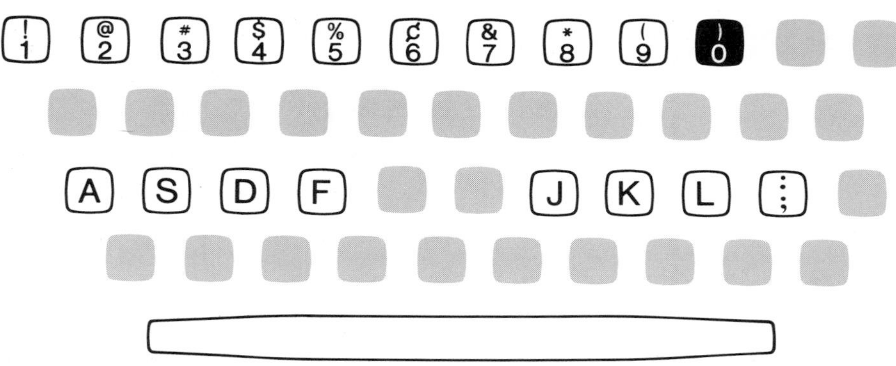

Home-row *;* finger moves up and to the left to the number *0*. Place both hands on the home row and practice the move from *;* to *0*. Look at your hands and watch your finger make the motion. Do this several times; then look away and try the same motion. Continue this procedure until you can make the motion correctly without looking at the keyboard.

Note: Be sure to use the *zero* key, not the capital *o*.

Type each line once.
Then do again.

0 00 0 000 0 000 0 00 0 0 00 0 000 00 0 00 000 00
10 20 30 40 50 60 70 80 90 a10 a20 a30 240 250 10

NUMBER-CONCENTRATION DRILL

1. Type the numbers from 1 on as far as you can in 30 seconds; space once after each number.
2. Type the numbers from 2 on as far as you can go in 30 seconds increasing by two's (2 4 6 8 10 12 etc.). Space once after each number.

REVIEW AND MASTERY

Set your machine for a 70-space line (review page x). Concentrate on keeping your eyes on the copy as you type the material below.

Type each line once.

a1201 1316 1403 a2304 3405 4506 a5607 6708 7809 a8910 1011 2112 a3313
1415 6816 a2317 a3218 2219 3220 a7821 9222 9023 a1524 3852 a5426 1927
1929 3030 4531 a7932 3433 2134 a9535 8736 9137 a2938 5739 23270 a3341
1743 a7744 7645 a6746 5647 a6748 4859 4750 a5151 4552 7853 7654 77449

MESSAGE/REPLY FORM

Many organizations have adopted some type of *message/reply form*. This form is usually carbonized and allows the receiver of the message to send back the reply at the bottom of the original message.

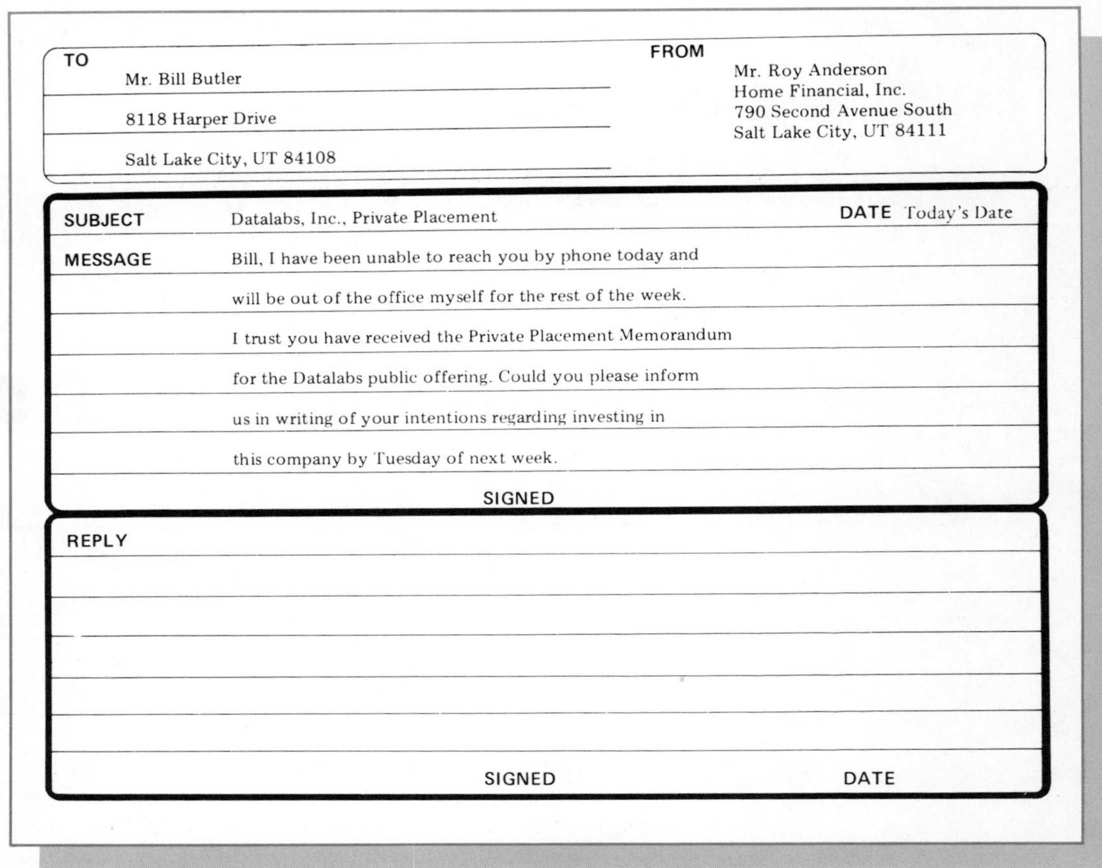

TO
Mr. Bill Butler
8118 Harper Drive
Salt Lake City, UT 84108

FROM
Mr. Roy Anderson
Home Financial, Inc.
790 Second Avenue South
Salt Lake City, UT 84111

SUBJECT Datalabs, Inc., Private Placement DATE Today's Date

MESSAGE Bill, I have been unable to reach you by phone today and will be out of the office myself for the rest of the week. I trust you have received the Private Placement Memorandum for the Datalabs public offering. Could you please inform us in writing of your intentions regarding investing in this company by Tuesday of next week.

SIGNED

REPLY

SIGNED DATE

Task 24

Working Papers, p. 211

Type the following information on a message/reply form.

To: Mr. Raymond Karlson / Karlson Supply Company / 134 East Rommina Drive/ Los Angeles, CA 91234 From: Ralph Johnson / Johnson Construction Company/ 16 Emma Avenue / San Jose, CA 90302. SUBJECT: Clear Lake Project. Ray, there seems to be some type of mix-up on the Contract Bid for the Clear Lake Project. According to our records we established a Bid number of CL-101-Qa. The local authorities indicate to us that is not the number recorded by the state. PLEASE—check this out and let me know the correct number as soon as possible.

Legal Forms

It is common to prepare legal information on a printed form in those states that have granted permission to do so. Examples of printed legal forms include wills, contracts, and corporate resolutions. The guidelines for their preparation are similar; therefore, examples will not be given here of all the varying types of legal forms.

SPEED-DEVELOPMENT DRILL

Take two 1-minute timed writings on lines 1 through 3. If you finish all three lines before the time is up, begin again on line 1. Then take two 1-minute timings on lines 4 through 6. If you finish all three lines, begin again on line 4.

```
1   27 821 59361 40352 89734 92035 64019 9356 693 958        10
2   3177 50 6512 96 8742 56034 56832 85923 780 847 91        10
3   6409 7483 9467 3520 5945 2635 5705 8932 6485 1956        10
4   23670 81251800 165 908125635 69312 9871 6017340 2        10
5   716941 83201933 516386143 5113818 8542001 88490 1        10
6   236115432 11621618 1123419051 33991668 45441 4091        10
    ----1----2----3----4----5----6----7----8----9---10
```

The Comma

You have now mastered all ten digits and are ready to move into other areas of the keyboard. There are two symbols used frequently with numbers—the *comma* and the *decimal point*. The next new key is the *comma*.

Home-row *k* finger moves down and to the right to the *comma*. Place both hands on the home row and practice the move from *k* to *comma*. Look at your hands and watch your finger make the motion. Do this several times; then look away and try the same motion. Continue this procedure until you can make the motion correctly without looking at the keyboard.

When numbers are separated by commas, periods, spaces, letters, or other symbols, use these division points to read numbers. For example: 5,134 would be read "five/one thirty-four."

Type each line once. Then do again.

```
45,134 38,751 7,893 5,313 4,497 1,438 6,719 6,151
7,361 1,368 1,434 9,860 5,167 34,511 76,924 6,331
21,468 38,107 48,243 1,509 5,114 15,816 6,184,336
```

Task 21
Working Papers, p. 209

Prepare "while you were out" form.

TO: Alice White
Airline called (9:30 am) your flight cancelled at NOON due to fog. Do you want to drive to Minneapolis + leave from there. Can get you on flight leaving at 3:30 this aft. Call Joan at 414-6673

Task 22
Working Papers, p. 209

Prepare "while you were out" form.

TO: Jim Been
Jack called at 3:30 Please pick him up at Hendersons on your way home.

Task 23
Working Papers, p. 209

Prepare "while you were out" form.

TO: Leslie Garrison
Fred Summers called at 2:00p.m. call him back as soon as possible regarding contract (413-6987)

The Decimal Point

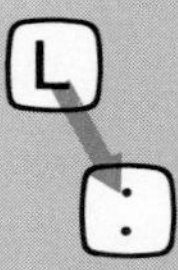

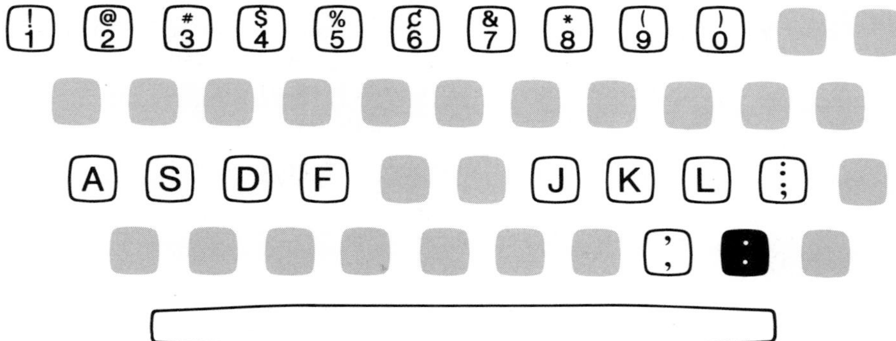

Home-row *l* finger moves down and to the right to the *decimal*. Place both hands on the home row and practice the move from *l* to *decimal*. Look at your hands and watch your finger make the motion. Do this several times; then look away and try the same motion. Continue this procedure until you can make the motion correctly without looking at the keyboard.

Type each line once.
Then do again.

41,345.51 15,378.78 31,428.27 89,261,500.68 59.63

61.34 91,007.23 851,267.18 109.01 13.17 8.43 4.40

596.27 990.85 67,349.34 23,265.08 186.84 4.23 .87

NUMBER-CONCENTRATION DRILL

See how quickly you can complete the following:

1. Type from number 1 on as fast as you can in one minute. Type a comma and then space once between each digit (1, 2, 3, 4, etc.).
2. Type from 1 on as far as you can in one minute. Type a decimal and then space once between each digit (1. 2. 3. 4. etc.).

TABULATION

Turn back to the illustration of your machine and review the location of the tabulation mechanisms (tab key or bar, tab-clear key, and tab-set key). Then read the explanation on pages 19 and 20 carefully.

Set four tabs, ten spaces apart. Count from the left margin. As you are typing the numbers, keep your eyes on the copy. Remember—you want to move from the left to the right across the page typing each column entry.

3901	3802	4703	5604	10051
9306	8207	7508	6509	10108
5211	0412	1913	0714	28147
3016	2617	1718	4819	57203
9021	7822	9023	7624	15242
1926	2427	3328	4229	14305
9731	2632	5833	4034	43354
0936	1837	1338	8539	67409

Task 18
Working Papers, p. 207

Prepare a copying report for the following:

The Research Department (counter number 166) has the counter reading of 19,673. Reported by Alan Larsen. Comments: We have had some trouble this month. The copier is "burning" every other copy. Please contact repairman at once.

Task 19
Working Papers, p. 207

Prepare a copying report for the following:

Payroll Office, Counter # - 1

Reading 143,611
by L. Jameson

Comments: our machine was due for checkup 3 weeks ago. What is the problem?

Miscellaneous Communicative Forms

Many offices use varying types of forms for communication—especially within the confines of the organization.

TELEPHONE MESSAGE FORM

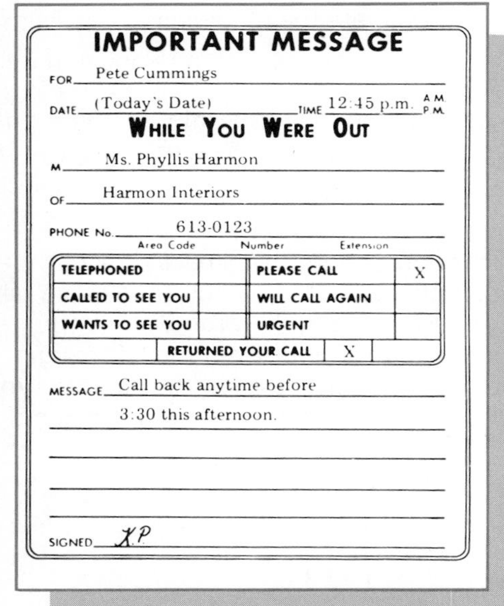

IMPORTANT MESSAGE

FOR Pete Cummings

DATE (Today's Date) TIME 12:45 p.m. A.M. P.M.

WHILE YOU WERE OUT

M Ms. Phyllis Harmon

OF Harmon Interiors

PHONE No. 613-0123
Area Code Number Extension

TELEPHONED		PLEASE CALL	X
CALLED TO SEE YOU		WILL CALL AGAIN	
WANTS TO SEE YOU		URGENT	
	RETURNED YOUR CALL	X	

MESSAGE Call back anytime before
3:30 this afternoon.

SIGNED XP

IMPORTANT MESSAGE

FOR Pete Cummings

DATE (Today's Date) TIME 1:10 p.m. A.M. P.M.

WHILE YOU WERE OUT

M Mr. Ken Byrd

OF The United Way

PHONE No.
Area Code Number Extension

TELEPHONED	X	PLEASE CALL	
CALLED TO SEE YOU		WILL CALL AGAIN	
WANTS TO SEE YOU		URGENT	
	RETURNED YOUR CALL		

MESSAGE Mr. Byrd will not be able to make
tomorrow's meeting. Has rescheduled the
appointment for next week Thursday, (Date),
at 9:30 a.m. to discuss our company's U.W.
campaign efforts.

SIGNED XP

Task 20
Working Papers, p. 209

Prepare a "while you were out" telephone form for:

James Wenner 1:45 pm
Ms. Helen Wilson called of Wilson Manufacturing
493-8974 — Please call back today before 4:30 pm
VERY IMPORTANT!!

Two 1-minute timings on Lines 1 and 2.

Two 1-minute timings Lines 3, 4, and 5.

NATURAL NUMBER PATTERNS

When numbers are grouped naturally by commas, spaces, and decimals, read the number by divisions. For example 1,676,352.17 is read *one/comma/six seventy-six/comma/three fifty-two/decimal/seventeen*.

1 1,676,352.17 3,131 2.24 a36,342 101.31 166,801 89 10
2 236,731 831,643 534.67 4,091,867 a458,713 501,316 10
3 61,301.04 .36 89,341.76 31,700.73 151,317 416,319 10
4 6,117.08 7.43 a98 634,513.77 3,397.13 811,543,024 10
5 76,244.83 7.43 98 634,413.77 5,397.13 a811,543 21 10

Take two 1-minute timings for speed.

Then take two 1-minute timings for accuracy.

REVIEW OF TABULATION

Set four tab stops at 10-space intervals across the page.

4901	8702	3303	3904	7205	5
6106	8307	9408	2709	3710	5
1511	5712	2613	9114	1515	5
5716	9117	5618	6619	3820	5
2621	3122	4523	2324	3125	5
6726	3528	8528	3529	4130	5
7731	6932	8533	7434	9935	5
8836	2337	6138	1639	5840	5

Take two 1-minute timings on Lines 1-4 for speed.

Then take two 1-minute timings for accuracy on Lines 1-4.

Then take two 1-minute timings on Lines 5-9, combining speed and accuracy.

REVIEW OF PATTERNIZING NUMBERS

Remember to read numbers in 2-3-2 combinations. If the number group is separated by a letter, space, comma, decimal, or some other symbol, use those points as divisions for reading.

1 7371130 91368840 1534986003 51673455189 963310931 10
2 45134157 386005138 789 5133459 1 38886190 34141 2 10
3 21468159 515113 6873931 438761 223026501 89340013 10
4 6135910 619822385 3676 1090101 3948131 1788434341 10
5 161,761 36,017 a8,131 2,924 361,342 101,431 2,699 10
6 2,361,731 a31,464 55,565,577 39,913,867 9,586,713 10
7 61,201,304 a36 932,341,176 700,318,173 57,318,923 10
8 63,116 10.81 5.87 34.238 a098 11.151 69.138 15.38 10
9 76.924 40.83 78.431 .98 63,485 13.667 a9.39 4,131 10

Task 17

Working Papers, p. 205

Prepare a time-report form for the information below.

EMPLOYEE NO. 17 NAME (PRINT) Lottie Holechek

COST CENTER Schofield 400-A PERIOD ENDING DATE Current

Proj./Acct. No. Base	Sub.	Description	M	T	W	T	F	S	S	Total Hours
9110		Duplicating	2	1	1		2			6
9163		Personal Development					4			4
9165		Vacation				8				8
9110		Typewriting	6	7	7		2			22
		Total Hours	8	8	8	8	8			40
		Supervisor Signature								

(Enter Time in Whole Hrs.: M–S columns)

COPYING REPORT

A copying report is submitted to Duplicating Services at the end of each month (or some other time) as a record of the number of copies made to date on a copying machine. Each department is given an electronic device that is inserted into the copier and serves as a counter.

DUPLICATING SERVICES

MONTHLY COPYING REPORT

Department/Office Marketing

Counter Number 54002

Counter Reading 156,209

Person Reporting (Your Name)

Comments: The new machine is making fantastic copies!

Please Return To Duplicating Services by the First Day of Each Month.

Type Line 1 once.

Take a 1-minute timing on Lines 2-5. Goal: 3 or fewer errors.

Take a 1-minute timing on Lines 6-10. Goal: 3 or fewer errors.

Take a 2-minute timing on Lines 1-10. Goal: 5 or fewer errors.

1	161176 36017 38131 2924 361.42 101431 166,810 895	10
2	236,731 831464 55565577 3,013.67 4586713 50131672	10
3	51201304 436 892341176 31,700.73 15183.7 415531 1	10
4	631171081 587 34238 10989115 15 5,148.01 538.32 7	10
5	6,924,083 7834 98 634,413.77 69397413 81145438571	10
6	7361130 9,368.40 153,986.03 51673455189 9655151 5	10
7	45134145 387005138 .89 5313459 14,887.09 53151557	10
8	2146859 381076 48,331.90 41133590 1518614 1610720	10
9	413451 51513 6783931 529761 22,026.01 89376003183	10
10	613591031 71,833.85 1090101 3948131 17,843,244.11	10

BUILDING SUSTAINED SKILL ON NUMBER COPY

Take two 3-minute timings. Compute "word-a-minute" rate by dividing total words typed by three.

2634 10485 10.90 a64781 2.89 11,584,609 449345125	10
656.98 11,067 14 48067015 28 842 550.18 56,679 23	10
12 4954 50,874 280 796,416.83 92645 15,041 550914	10
4 284 96175 2.95 59,602.88 15281 23 741 681104 47	10
99 84.22 903 571.28 67,832,523.15 82 904 56451089	10
80 106 29.15 61700 281,401,282.00 67414451 510 15	10
224 50 4605141•489,753 4.86 21 8674005 71.26 4559	10
667101 8.26 5,410 49724301 9,454.89 556 78911 531	10
46 82 96.48 4457004 33216 5436 434215 61780 2,466	10
510 196.02 10,815.90 32 4489 221 734.59 4483765 2	10
---1----2----3----4----5----6----7----8----9---10	

Report Forms

TIME REPORT

WEEKLY PROJECT TIME REPORT

EMPLOYEE NO. 3562 NAME (PRINT) Ralph Howard

COST CENTER P1012 PERIOD ENDING DATE* September 26, 19__

Proj./Acct. No. Base	Sub.	Description	M	T	W	T	F	S	S	Total Hours
D05998	203	Field-Effect Transistor Analysis	9			4				13
D10062	203	Production Support			5					5
E91222	705	Research Support			2	5				7
9161		Illness		7						7
9169		Doctor		2						2
9163		Personal Development (Seminar)			2					2
		Total Hours	9	9	9	9				36
		Supervisor Signature								

(Enter Time in Whole Hrs.)

Indirect Account Numbers**

9110 - Clerical - Supervision & Work Not Assigned Project Numbers
9161 - Illness
9163 - Personal Development
9164 - Personal Absence
** Fill in Base No Field

9165 - Vacation
9166 - Holiday
9167 - Budgeting/Planning
9168 - Miscellaneous
9169 - Doctor/Dentist

*Period ending date should always be a Sunday except when the month ends on a day other than Sunday. When this occurs, the period ending date should be the last day of the month.

Specialized Punctuation-Mark Keys

Certain punctuation marks may be used to set apart or to distinguish a word or words. Because of the varying rules regarding the use of these marks, they are presented in this separate section.

Introduction to the Hyphen

Margins
Elite: 25 and 75
Pica: 17 and 67

IMPORTANT: Use the same margins for the entire specialized punctuation section.

Type Lines 1 and 2 once—speed.
Type Line 2 again.
Type Line 3 and the following partial line once.

Home-row *;* finger moves up and to the right to the *hyphen* key. Place both hands on the home row and practice the move from *;* to *hyphen*. Look at your hands and watch your finger make the motion. Do this several times; then look away and try the same motion.

DRILL

```
1   ;- ;- ;- ;-; ;-; -;-; ;- ;- ;-;- ;-; ;-; ;-; ;-;-
2   two-thirds, high-level, soft-spoken, high-ranking
3   Dan said that the paper had at least fifteen mis-
    takes in it.
```

A hyphen is a mark of punctuation used to divide words that must be carried over to the next line of typewriting. Care must be taken to divide words correctly. Listed below are some of the more common rules. There is an exception to every rule—if in doubt, consult a good dictionary. (Numerous word divisions in a manuscript should be avoided.)

General Guidelines

PREFERABLE PRACTICES

1. Leave at least three letters on the end of a line and carry over at least three letters on the next line.
2. Never divide a word that is the last word on a page or paragraph.

General Guidelines

A FEW DO'S

WORD DIVISION

YOU MAY DIVIDE:

1. Between syllables according to pronunciation	provoke	MAY BE DIVIDED	pro-voke

Task 13

Working Papers, p. 199

Prepare a work-request form for Susan Fields in the Research Department, phone #344-1163. Account #166-193A. The request is for repair work to be completed in the Schneider Wing, Room 113 (Conference Room). The work to be done is: replace present center light fixture with one that will hang directly over conference table. Refinish inside of door. Resurface entire floor.

Task 14

Working Papers, p. 201

Prepare a work-request form for:

James Waterman (President's Office), Telephone 732-6143 Presidents Building, Room #1

Repairs: (1.) replace ceiling tile (all) (2.) panel North + South walls (check with Mr. Alberts for paneling sample.

DUPLICATING REQUEST

DUPLICATING SERVICES REQUEST				JOB NO.
FROM Mark Nelson	COST CENTER B317	MAIL STOP NO. 4400	DATE (Today's Date)	EXT. 6973
QUANTITY NEEDED 100	NO. OF MASTERS 6		DATE REQUESTED (Three Days from Today)	
PAPER COLOR Buff	DISTRIBUTE TO		DELIVER TO Mark Nelson	
PRINTING: Offset; Copy Process; One Side Only; Head to Head; Head to Foot	SPECIAL INSTRUCTIONS			
ASSEMBLY: As Paged; Do Not Assemble; Padding	OFFICE SERVICES USE ONLY			
	MACHINE	TIME	MATERIAL COST	
STAPLING: Top Left; Top Center; Left Side; Special				
BINDING: 2 Holes; 3 Holes; Left Side; Top; GBC; Tape Binding; Special				

Task 15

Working Papers, p. 203

Prepare a duplicating request for: Dr. Larry Schnack/Cost Center: President's Hall/Mail Stop #1/Extension #1. Have 10 masters that we must have by tomorrow. Please deliver to Schnack. Use Copy Process on blue paper. Need 300 copies. Run as paged; please staple on top left.

Task 16

Working Papers, p. 203

Prepare a duplicating request for:

Jane L. Dalton / Cost Center: Office 406. 17/Ex 7 117. Needs ASAP—deliver to her. Has 1 master—Needs 600 copies (offset) on buff paper. Do not assemble but need 3 holes on left side.

2. Between two consonants UNLESS	napkin	MAY BE DIVIDED	nap-kin
a root word would be destroyed	billing	MAY BE DIVIDED	bill-ing (not bil-ling)
3. Between two vowels that are pronounced separately	continuation	MAY BE DIVIDED	continu-ation
4. *After* a one-syllable vowel rather than ***before*** (preferable) UNLESS	benefactor	MAY BE DIVIDED	bene-factor
the vowel is a part of a suffix	acceptable	MAY BE DIVIDED	accept-able
5. Between two parts of a compound	salesperson	MAY BE DIVIDED	sales-person

A FEW DON'TS

DO NOT DIVIDE:

A. Words of one syllable	which storm	NEVER NEVER	wh-ich sto-rm
B. If one or two letters in a word are to be separated	along enough almost	NOT NOT NOT	a-long e-nough al-most
C. A syllable with a silent vowel sound	yelled strained	NEVER NEVER	yel-led strain-ed
D. Proper nouns, abbreviations, contractions, or number combinations	Barbara March 14 NSA 31 Oak Lane couldn't	NOT NOT NOT NOT NOT	Bar-bara March 1-4 N-SA 3-1 Oak Lane could-n't

DRILL

Type each word below and show how it is to be divided:

1. letter — let-ter
2. March — March
3. compose
4. enough
5. anyplace
6. perpetrator
7. wouldn't
8. walked
9. homerun
10. important
11. Delaware
12. almost
13. stenographer
14. technique
15. introduce

Task 12
Working Papers, p. 197

Prepare an expense report for Mr. Ed. Freidman, Accounting Department.

Dates – April 14 + 15 (Mon + Tues)
Expenses: airline ticket $277.85

	Monday	Tuesday
(1.) meals:		
lunch	= 6.20	7.00
dinner	= 17.50	0
(2.) lodging	= 41.50	0
(3.) parking	= 5.75	5.00
(4.) transp.	= 16.00	16.00
(5.) telephone	= 1.80	0
(6.) tips	= 7.75	4.00

Be sure to total across + down on expense report.

Work/Service Request Forms

In any type of business organization there are numerous forms relating to varying requests that must be prepared. These requests may stay "in-house" or may be of the type that are sent outside the organization.

WORK REQUEST

WORK REQUEST

This work order must be filled out for all work requested of the Division of Physical Plant, except for emergencies. Please report emergencies to the Physical Plant Office, Room 103, Maintenance & Stores Building, Extension 3411.

REQUESTED BY Penny Waterman DEPARTMENT Geology PHONE 836-1184

BUILDING Shea Science Building ROOM NO. OR AREA 409

APPROVED BY ______ (Department Chairman) ACCOUNT NO 102-039 DATE (Today's Date)

DESCRIPTION OF WORK (USE SEPARATE REQUEST FOR EACH PROJECT)

Replace damaged ceiling panels and repair roof to prevent water seepage.

ESTIMATE REQUIRED YES ______ NO ______ LABOR $ ______

MATERIAL $ ______

ESTIMATE APPROVED ______ (Department Chairman) TOTAL $ ______

PLEASE DO NOT WRITE BELOW THIS LINE

WORK ORDER NO ______ LABOR COST $ ______

ASSIGNED ______ DATE ______ MATERIAL COST $ ______

BUILDING NO ______ OUTSIDE SERVICES $ ______

UWEC EQUIPMENT NO ______ TOTAL CHARGE $ ______

DATE COMPLETED ______ CHARGED TO ABOVE ACCOUNT $ ______

APPROVED ______ (Supervisor) CREDIT ACCOUNT NO ______

Date	Name	Rate	Hours	Total
				$
				$
				$
				$
		TOTAL		$

MATERIALS USED

General Guidelines

COMPOUND WORDS AND NUMBERS

A hyphen is sometimes used to separate a compound word and spelled-out numbers.

1. A hyphen is used as a "combining" mark. Not all authorities agree on which combinations should or should not be hyphenated. If in doubt, consult a reference book or dictionary.
   A. As a general rule, use a hyphen between two or more word combinations used as a unit ***before*** a noun.

      fifteen-story building
      tax-free proposal
      hard-working person

   B. If the word combinations used as a unit appear ***after*** a noun, do not hyphenate.

      a building fifteen stories high
      a proposal that is tax free
      a person who is hard working

   C. Words beginning with ***ex***, ***self***, and ***vice*** are usually hyphenated.

      ex-roommate
      self-taught

2. Hyphenate ***spelled-out*** numbers between 21 and 99 if they stand alone or if they are used with numbers over 100. Never hyphenate digits.

   sixty-six
   one hundred sixty-six (***and*** can be omitted)
   one and one-third

DRILL

Retype the statements below, inserting hyphens where appropriate.

eight cylinder engine
an engine that has eight cylinders

an effort at the last minute
a last minute effort

the man was self employed
a self employed man

twenty six
thirty four
one hundred
one hundred fifty six

General Guidelines

THE DASH

A dash is formed by typing two hyphens with no space before, between, or after. The dash is often used in place of quotation marks or parentheses and to avoid confusion of too many commas. It is also used for special emphasis.

```
There is a flaw in the plan--a fatal one.
All books--fiction, poetry, and drama--will be on sale.
I cooked the meal--but they got the credit for it.
I said once--and I will say it again--I disagree.
```

EXPENSE REPORT

After returning from a business trip, it is necessary for the executive to file the amount of expenses incurred in order to be reimbursed.

EXPENSE REPORT

NAME Jill Stuart	DEPARTMENT Research	WEEK ENDING October 11

IMPORTANT: To be reimbursed for expenses, report must be turned in by Thursday of following week.

	SUNDAY	MONDAY	TUESDAY	WEDNESDAY	THURSDAY	FRIDAY	SATURDAY	TOTAL
DATE		Oct. 7	Oct. 8	Oct. 9	Oct. 10	Oct. 11		
BREAKFAST		4 50	5 75	5 50	4 25	5 00		25 00
LUNCH		8 95	7 25	8 50	6 75	7 50		38 95
DINNER		21 50	17 00	16 95	17 50			72 95
*LODGING		42 75	42 75	42 75	42 75			171 00
*AIR OR RAIL TRANSPORTATION		563 00						563 00
PARKING			4 50	4 50	4 50			13 50
LOCAL TRANSPORTATION			12 50	12 50	12 50			37 50
LOCAL TELEPHONE		1 25						1 25
*LAUNDRY & VALET								
TIPS, ETC.		9 50	7 00	7 00	8 00	4 00		35 50
TOTAL		650 70	96 75	97 70	96 25	16 50		958 65

**round trip

SPEEDOMETER FINISH								
SPEEDOMETER START								
AUTO MILES TRAVELED								

CASH ACCOUNTING

TOTAL EXPENDITURES $ ______

ADVANCE CASH ☐ CHECK ☐ $ ______ (check one)

BALANCE DUE ME $ ______

BALANCE DUE $ ______

MILEAGE ALLOWANCE: ______ PER MILE

TOTAL AUTO MILES TRAVELED ______ AT ______ PER MILE

TOTAL EXPENSES 958 65

*ENCLOSE RECEIPT SEE INSTRUCTIONS ON REVERSE

I CERTIFY THAT THE ABOVE EXPENSES WERE INCURRED BY ME AS NECESSARY BUSINESS EXPENSES AND ARE TRUE AND CORRECT

SIGNATURE J. Stuart APPROVAL ______

Task 11

Working Papers, p. 195

Prepare a travel itinerary for Mr. Ed Freidman, Accounting Department, for his trip to Atlanta, Georgia from our home office (Los Angeles). He is leaving on April 14 from LA to Atlanta on Flight 606 Western Airlines. Departure time is 9:45 am; arrival time is 10:15 am. He is to pick up a rental car (reservation has been made) at Ames Car Rentals. The following day (April 15) he is to drive to Sherman, Georgia, to meet with our branch officials. He is to leave from the airport in Sherman that evening for LA on Flight 545, Western Airlines; departure time is 6:30 pm; arrival at Los Angeles International Airport at 11:19 pm.

DRILL

Type each sentence below, inserting the dash(es) where appropriate.

Send that order to the fourth floor not the third.
Next year, Mary with the help of her mother, her father, and her uncle will be able to make a trip to Europe.
Dawn ordered chili not tomato soup.
Send that order today not tomorrow.
Whenever he gets that look on his face look out.

Introduction to the Underscore

OR

The *underscore* key may be located on the *6* or the *hyphen* key. Check to determine where it is on your machine. If shift of *6*, reach to top row with home-row *j* finger up and to the left. REMEMBER—you must depress the left shift key. If on the hyphen key, home-row *;* finger moves up and to the right to the hyphen key. REMEMBER: you must depress the left shift key. Place both hands on the home row and practice the correct motion. Look at your hands and watch your finger make the motion. Do this several times; then look away and try the same motion.

Important: Type just one set of drill material below. Select whichever is appropriate for your machine.

SHIFT OF *6* KEY

Lines 1-3 once—speed
Lines 2 and 3 again—speed

1 j j6 j6 j_ j_ j_j _j_ jj __ j_ j_ _j_ _j_ j6 j6j_
2 Look at this. The book title is, Slow Down Soon.
3 I read Changing Times, American Home, and Sports.

SHIFT OF *HYPHEN* KEY

Lines 1-3 once—speed
Lines 2 and 3 again—speed

1 ; ;- ;- ;_ ;_ ;_; _;_ ;; __ ;_ ;_ _;_ _;_ ;- ;-;_
2 Look at this. The book title is, Slow Down Soon.
3 I read Changing Times, American Home, and Sports.

General Guidelines

THE UNDERSCORE

Some words are italicized when set in type; italics are shown in typewritten material by underlining the word.

1. Underscore titles of books, magazines, and newspapers.
   Gone with the Wind   Harper's Bazaar   New York Times

Executive Travel Forms

Several forms may be required for business executives while traveling. Two of the most common are the *travel itinerary* and the *expense report*.

TRAVEL ITINERARY

The itinerary printed form can be simple or complex. It may include only the necessary travel information; in addition, it may include the actual business that will be conducted (where and when) and other details.

TRAVEL ITINERARY

ADVICE OF TRAVEL CONFIRMATION FOR DR. JILL STUART
NAME

DATE	FROM	TO	AIRLINE OR TRAIN	LVS.	ARVS.
10/7	New York City	Montreal, Quebec	Eastern #741	8:25 am	9:35 am
10/8	Montreal, Quebec	Los Angeles	Air Can #793	5:30 pm	9:25 am
10/11	Los Angeles	New York City	American #431	1:45 pm	9:40 pm

CONFIRMED BY Pat – 604-3118

REMARKS: Mr. Mark Henderson is meeting you at the airport in Montreal.
A car has been reserved in L.A. to be picked up at the airport.

APPROVED BY ____ ACCEPTED BY ____

TICKETS IN BOX NO. N/A AT ____ AIRPORT ____

2. Underscore the names (not makes or models) of ships, trains, and aircraft.
   the ocean liner Queen Mary
   the zephyr Chicago Sun Streak
   the aircraft Silver Eagle One
3. Underscore technical words that are not a part of our normal language.
   The coast redwood, or Sequoia sempervirens
4. Underscore for special emphasis of a word, or words, in a sentence.
   He said there were too many problems involved in the contract agreement.

DRILL

Type each of the statements below, concentrating on the use of the underscore.

Quality of Roses by Juan L. Cordoba — a book
He Ran Alone by Barbara Whitter — a book
San Francisco Examiner — a newspaper
Popular Mechanics — a magazine
Chicago Zephyr — a train
the Nautilus — a ship
Air Force One — a jet
panettone — an Italian bread

Introduction to the Apostrophe

OR

The *apostrophe* key may be located on the *8* or beside the *semicolon* key. Check to determine where it is on your machine. If shift of *8*, reach to top row with home-row *k* finger up and to the left. REMEMBER—you must depress the left shift key. If beside *semi* key, home-row *;* finger moves to the right to the *apostrophe* key. Place both hands on the home row and practice the correct motion. Look at your hands and watch your finger make the motion. Do this several times; then look away and try the same motion.

Important: Type just one set of drill material. Select whichever is appropriate for your machine.

SHIFT OF *8* KEY

Lines 1 and 2 once—speed
Line 2 again—speed

```
1   k' k' k' k'k k'k 'k'k k' k' k'k' k'k k'k k'k k'k'
2   Al's Dad's Ted's Allen's Jane's Jan's Ken's Len's
```

Task 8
Working Papers, p. 191

Prepare an invoice from the Nelson Supply Co. for the following:

Send invoice to Able Mfg. Co. for:
white 16# bond paper (50 reams / $5.75 ream)
bus envelopes (50 pkg. / $6.15 pkg.)
yellow 2nd sheet paper (10 reams / $1.15 ream)
"Please determine extensions + total"
Their order #177 Our order #: 1-17-2376, terms 2/10, net 30, shipped UPS.

STATEMENT OF ACCOUNT

The company who sold and delivered the order will prepare and send to the purchaser some type of "statement of account," which will inform the purchaser of the amount due. Three copies of the statement are usually prepared (an original and two copies).

Statement of Account

Date Current

To Able Manufacturing Company
1678 East Wilson Avenue
Winston, NC 31456

NELSON SUPPLY COMPANY
132 Main Street
Palo Alto, California 94303
(315) 436-1778

Date	Items	Debits	Credits	Balance Due
1/16/78	Office Supplies (your order #7-1100)	772.50		772.50

Task 9
Working Papers, p. 193

Prepare a statement of account for the following:

To: The Able Mfg. Co. for their order #145-Za. Total amount due: $5,800.

Task 10
Working Papers, p. 193

Prepare a statement of account for the following:

To: The Able Mfg. Co.
Their order #177 for $606.50

BESIDE *SEMI* KEY

Lines 1 and 2 once—speed
Line 2 again—speed

```
1   ;' ;' ;' ;'; ;'; ';'; ;' ;' ;';' ;'; ;'; ;'; ;';'
2   Al's Dad's Ted's Allen's Jane's Jan's Ken's Len's
```

DRILL

Lines 1 and 2 once—speed

```
1   Alfie's neat sedan hasn't had a dent; he's tense.
2   Dale's latest theft hadn't shaken Jeanne's faith.
```

General Guidelines

THE APOSTROPHE

1. An apostrophe is used in a contraction (shortened spelling of a word, substituting an apostrophe for the missing letter).

cannot	can't
could not	couldn't

2. An apostrophe can be used to show possession. Add an *'s* to show possession.

a hat belonging to John	John's hat
the voices of the people	people's voices
the guess of anybody	anybody's guess

If a noun ends in ***s***, add the apostrophe only.

the sonnets of Keats	Keats' sonnets
the clothes of the girls	girls' clothes

3. An apostrophe can also be used as a symbol for feet.

100 feet	100'
255 feet	255'

SPECIAL NOTE: some individuals have trouble deciding if a word is a personal pronoun or a contraction. Example: their they're

Remember: THE APOSTROPHE INDICATES A MISSING LETTER.

They're, therefore, has to indicate ***they are***.

Additional examples:

They're taking their own sleeping bags.	(NOT: taking they are sleeping bags.)
Give the dog its bone.	(NOT: dog it is bone)

DRILL

Type each entry in the left column. Tab over and type showing possession, dimension, or contraction.

boat that belongs to Don	Don's boat
the attorney for the ladies	ladies' attorney
the house Billy lives in	
car belonging to Mavis and Ed	
a luncheon of businessmen	
it is	
are not	
he is	
we are	
do not	
does not	
100 feet	

Task 6
Working Papers, p. 189

Complete a purchase order for the Able Mfg. Co.:

Please order 50 reams of white bond paper -- 16# @ $5.75 per ream (cat. #16); 50 packages of large bus. envelopes @ $6.15 per package (cat. #117); 10 reams second sheet yellow paper @ $1.15 per ream (#223)

Order #177, terms 2/10, net 30, UPS

Order from: Nelson Supply Co.
132 Main St.
Palo Alto, CA 94303

INVOICES

Upon receiving an order, a company fills it and prepares an invoice. Three copies of the invoice are usually prepared (an original and two copies).

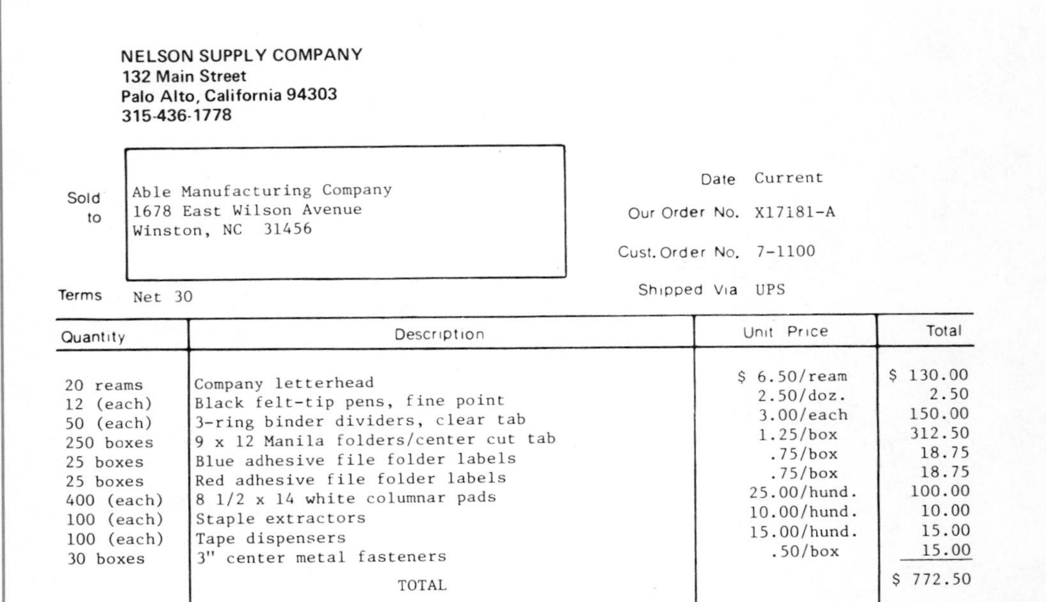

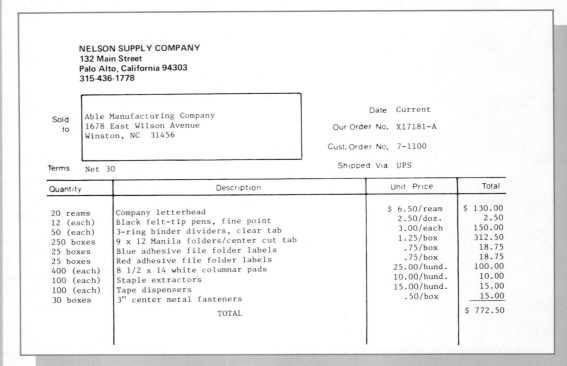

NELSON SUPPLY COMPANY
132 Main Street
Palo Alto, California 94303
315-436-1778

Sold to: Able Manufacturing Company
1678 East Wilson Avenue
Winston, NC 31456

Date: Current
Our Order No.: X17181-A
Cust. Order No.: 7-1100
Shipped Via: UPS

Terms: Net 30

Quantity	Description	Unit Price	Total
20 reams	Company letterhead	$ 6.50/ream	$ 130.00
12 (each)	Black felt-tip pens, fine point	2.50/doz.	2.50
50 (each)	3-ring binder dividers, clear tab	3.00/each	150.00
250 boxes	9 x 12 Manila folders/center cut tab	1.25/box	312.50
25 boxes	Blue adhesive file folder labels	.75/box	18.75
25 boxes	Red adhesive file folder labels	.75/box	18.75
400 (each)	8 1/2 x 14 white columnar pads	25.00/hund.	100.00
100 (each)	Staple extractors	10.00/hund.	10.00
100 (each)	Tape dispensers	15.00/hund.	15.00
30 boxes	3" center metal fasteners	.50/box	15.00
	TOTAL		$ 772.50

Task 7
Working Papers, p. 191

Prepare an invoice from the Nelson Supply Co.:

Sold to: The Able Mfg. Co. / 1678 East Wilson Ave. / Winston, NC 31456 / 50 packages company printed checks @ $16 per package / 250 boxes of window envelopes @ $20 per box. (Determine extensions and total.) Their order #145-Za; our number 1-16-2375; terms net 30, shipped UPS.

DRILL

Type each of the following sentences inserting the correct word. REMEMBER: AN APOSTROPHE STANDS FOR A MISSING LETTER.

its	it's	1. _____ clear, the dog buried _______ bone.
they	their	2. There are twenty-one dents in _______ car.
whose	who's	3. _____ coat is that?
whose	who's	4. _____ going to the picnic next week?
your	you're	5. _____ going to regret _______ rash action.

Introduction to the Quotation Mark

OR

The *quotation-mark* key may be located on the *2* or the *apostrophe* key. Check to determine where it is on your machine. If shift of *2*, reach to the top row with home-row *s* finger up and to the left. REMEMBER—you must depress the right shift key. If beside the *semi* key, home-row *;* finger moves to the right to the *quote* key. REMEMBER—you must depress the left shift key. Place both hands on the home row and practice the correct motion. Look at your hands and watch your finger make the motion. Do this several times; then look away and try the same motion.

Important: Type just one set of drill material below. Select whichever is appropriate for your machine.

SHIFT OF *2* KEY

Lines 1 and 2 once—speed
Line 2 again—speed

```
1   s2 s" s" s" s"s s"s s"s s" s" s" s"s s"s" s" s"s"
2   "hello" "Help" "gasp" "Fiddle" "Ha" "Hi" "splash"
```

SHIFT OF ′ KEY

Lines 1 and 2 once—speed
Line 2 again—speed

```
1   ;' ;" ;" ;" ;"; ;"; ;"; ;" ;" ;" ;"; ;";" ;" ;";"
2   "hello" "Help" "gasp" "Fiddle" "Ha" "Hi" "splash"
```

DRILL

Lines 1 and 2 once—speed

```
1   "At last," said Sal, "is that lad's knee healed?"
2   "At least," said Al, "Jake ate the jelled salad."
```

Task 3

Working Papers, p. 185

Complete a requisition for the following:

Frank James (location: third floor) in the Payroll Department (Account Code 102-043) has exhausted his supply of company printed checks. The stock number is C101. The checks come in packages—he needs 50 packages. He would also like to order 1000 window envelopes, our stock number E07. The envelopes are packaged in boxes of 250.

Task 4

Working Papers, p. 187

Complete a requisition for the following:

Edna Popsal, Word Processing Dept. (basement, Acct. Code 102-049) needs:
50 reams 16# bond paper (white) #BW16
50 packages large bus. envelopes — #BE01
10 reams second-sheet paper (yellow) #SPY01

PURCHASE ORDERS

After the individual or department responsible for placing orders receives a requisition, the source from which to order is identified. A purchase order is then prepared. Three copies (an original and two copies) of the order are usually typed.

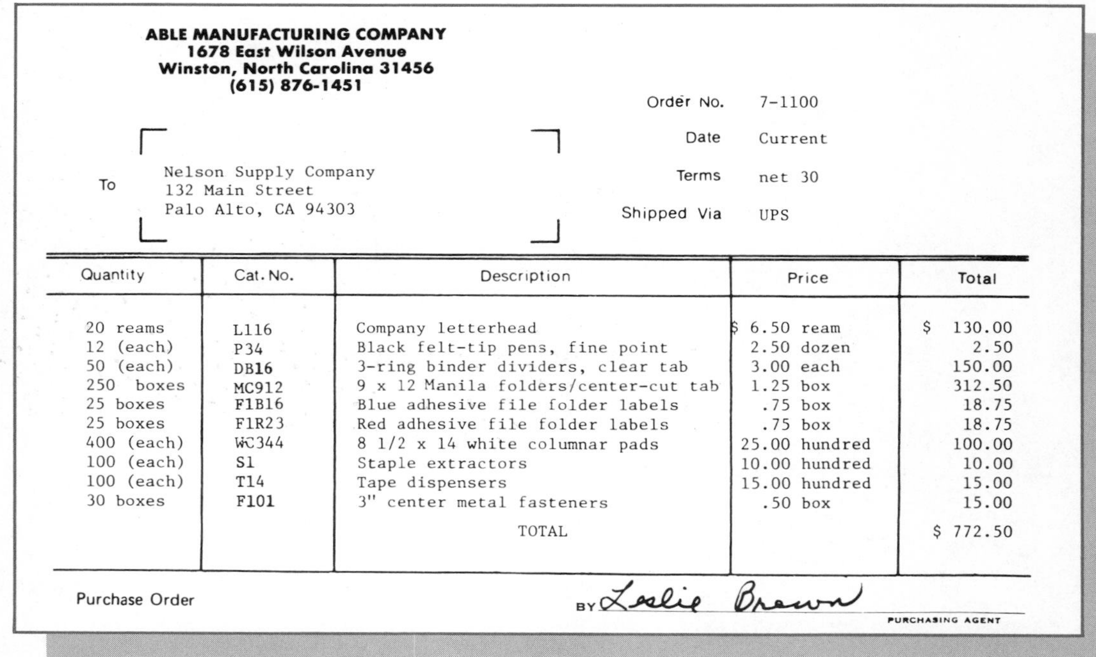

ABLE MANUFACTURING COMPANY
1678 East Wilson Avenue
Winston, North Carolina 31456
(615) 876-1451

Order No. 7-1100
Date Current
Terms net 30
Shipped Via UPS

To
Nelson Supply Company
132 Main Street
Palo Alto, CA 94303

Quantity	Cat. No.	Description	Price	Total
20 reams	L116	Company letterhead	$ 6.50 ream	$ 130.00
12 (each)	P34	Black felt-tip pens, fine point	2.50 dozen	2.50
50 (each)	DB16	3-ring binder dividers, clear tab	3.00 each	150.00
250 boxes	MC912	9 x 12 Manila folders/center-cut tab	1.25 box	312.50
25 boxes	F1B16	Blue adhesive file folder labels	.75 box	18.75
25 boxes	F1R23	Red adhesive file folder labels	.75 box	18.75
400 (each)	WC344	8 1/2 x 14 white columnar pads	25.00 hundred	100.00
100 (each)	S1	Staple extractors	10.00 hundred	10.00
100 (each)	T14	Tape dispensers	15.00 hundred	15.00
30 boxes	F101	3" center metal fasteners	.50 box	15.00
		TOTAL		$ 772.50

Purchase Order

BY *Leslie Brown*
PURCHASING AGENT

Task 5

Working Papers, p. 189

Complete a purchase order for the following:

The Able Manufacturing Co. wants to order from The Nelson Supply Co., 132 Main St, Palo Alto, CA 94303, terms net 30, UPS.

#101-4A—50 packages of company printed checks ($16/package)
#614-Z—250 boxes window envelopes ($20/box)
Order #145-Za

General Guidelines

QUOTATION MARKS (WRITTEN CONVERSATION)

1. Quotation marks are used as guideposts in written conversation to avoid difficulty in reading. When each new speaker says something, the material begins on a new line and is indented.

   "The weather is really nasty," said Nancy.

   Relaxed, Jan yawned and said, "Oh, I really hadn't noticed."

   "That's because you have been sleeping all morning," murmured Nancy with a slight sneer in her voice.

2. The comma and period are customarily placed inside the quotation marks. See above examples.

3. The question mark can be placed either inside or outside the end quotation mark—depending on the sentence logic.

   A. Place outside if the entire sentence is a question.

      When did he say, "I shall not return"?
      Did he say, "I saw ten paintings at the exhibit"?

   B. Place inside if the quotation only is a question.

      The owner shouted, "Why don't you just leave?"
      She asked, "Do you know if the train is late?"

4. The semicolon and colon ***always*** go outside the end quotation mark.

   Last week she announced, "recreation time will be lengthened"; however, we have not experienced it yet.

DRILL

Type each of the following sentences, placing quotation marks in appropriate places.

The typewriter is old, stated Mr. Barlow, and must be replaced.
Why did the pilot say, We'll be thirty minutes late?
Catherine sleepily said, Why don't you just be quiet?

Type the following three sentences as conversation.

We will be landing thirty minutes late, announced the pilot. Deanna muttered, I suppose that means we miss dinner. The flight attendant smiled and said, Perhaps we'll be on time after all.

General Guidelines

TITLES AND WORD EMPHASIS

1. Quotation marks are used to enclose titles, such as poems, short stories, chapters or essays or articles in magazines and other larger works, radio and television programs, and short musical works.

   "The Midnight Ride of Paul Revere" is a good poem.
   The last episode of "Star Trek" was really interesting.
   The plot of "Last Rays of Daylight" was dull for a short story.
   Did the band perform "Stardust" last evening?
   I read the article "Thirty Ways to Avoid Work" in the magazine.

2. Quotation marks may be used within a sentence to give a word or words special emphasis, such as a technical word used in a nontechnical sentence, slang expressions, humorous expressions, or defined words. (In type, defined words are usually set in italics.) Be careful not to overuse the quotation mark in this manner.

   The "aglaonema" is commonly called the Chinese Evergreen.
   Marvin thought the concert was "far out" and enjoyable.
   Their idea of "fast" service is serving one customer at a time.
   According to Webster's dictionary, a wren is a "brown singing bird."

The Ordering Process

An ordering process will vary among organizations. It may be quite simple, requiring a minimum number of forms, or quite complex, requiring a large number of forms. Illustrated below is an example of an ordering process and the forms that must be completed on the part of the company placing the order and also on the part of the company filling the order.

Company Placing Order	*Company Filling Order*
Requisition	
↓	
Purchase Order ——————▷	Invoice
	↓
	Account Statement

REQUISITIONS

Reference pp. 324-325

A requisition is completed by the individual or department who needs the items. An original and one file copy are usually prepared. The original is sent to the person or department who has the authority to place the order.

REQUISITION

Department ____Accounting____ Date ____(Today's Date)____

Account Code Number ____103-4459____ Requested by ____Mary Opitz____

Location ____Box 2380____ Approved by ________

Stock No.	Quantity Requested	Unit	Item Description	Quan. Issued	Unit Cost	Total Price
XXXXX	XXXXXXX	XXXXX	XXXXXXXXXXXXXXXXXXXX	FOR STOCKROOM USE ONLY, DO NOT FILL IN.		
C63	2	Reams	Company letterhead			
K16	1	box	Black felt-tip pens, fine point			
D08	50	each	3-ring binder dividers, clear tab Manila folders, center-cut tabs,			
D30	2	boxes	9" x 12"			
G38	2	boxes	Adhesive file folder labels, blue			
G39	2	boxes	Adhesive file folder labels, red			
C40	4	boxes	Columnar pads, 8½" x 14", white			
F11	1	each	Staple extractor			
F13	1	each	Tape dispenser			
M67	3	boxes	Metal fasteners, 3" center			

Received by ________ Date ________

Filled by ________ Posted by ________

DRILL

Type each of the following sentences, inserting quotation marks to enclose titles or special words of emphasis.

That story was a real corker.
The gemot was used largely in early English government.
With friends like you, who needs enemies?
A narrow path or ledge is sometimes called a berm.
The poem entitled Barney's Revenge is not very long.
At midnight, Joan saw The Night of Laughter on television.
The author's last short story, Bars on the Doors, was a mystery.
Her favorite song is Thunder Serenade by Marlo Zahn.

General Guidelines

THE EXCLAMATION POINT

1. If your typewriter does not have an exclamation point key, it is necessary to construct it. Type the apostrophe, backspace once, and type a period.
2. The exclamation point is used to express a high degree of emotion or strong feeling.
3. The exclamation point may be used in:
   a. One word
      What! You mean the flight has been delayed for six hours?
   b. A phrase
      How frightening! The fire broke out only ten minutes after we had left.
   c. A clause
      The date of the meeting—mark it on your calendar!—is November 10.
   d. A sentence
      So there you are, you rascal!
   e. A quotation that is exclamatory
      My brother yelled, "Run for your life!"
   f. A complete sentence that is exclamatory
      I simply do not believe the fiscal report that states, "The absentee rate was increasing by 500 percent"!

DRILL

Type each sentence, inserting appropriate ending punctuation.

1. Congratulations You won the first prize
2. Jan shouted What a mess
3. I emphatically restate my position, I will not resort to underhanded tactics
4. Help Help I'm locked in
5. Oh, how ridiculous He's never even seen the inside of a bank

Task 2

Look at the filled-in check illustrated below.

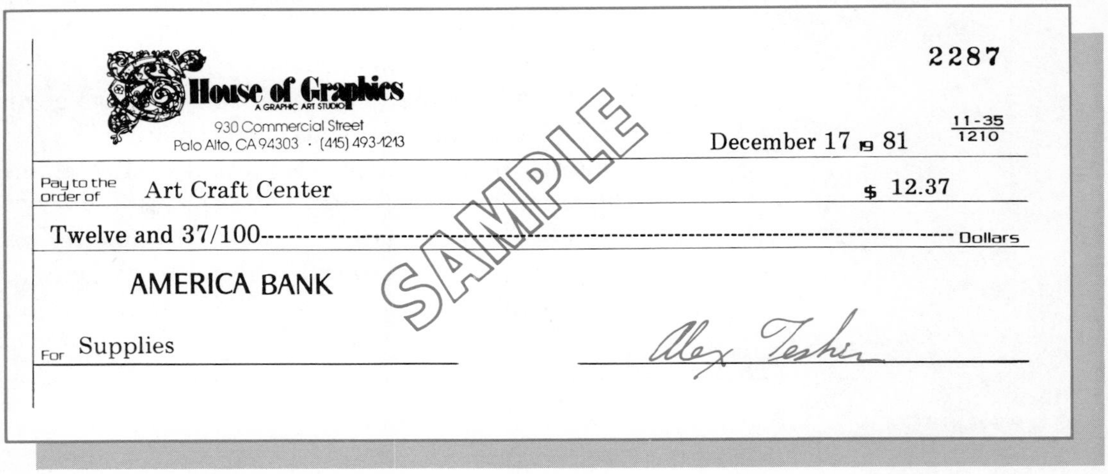

House of Graphics
A GRAPHIC ART STUDIO
930 Commercial Street
Palo Alto, CA 94303 · (415) 493-1213

2287

December 17 19 81 11-35/1210

Pay to the order of Art Craft Center $ 12.37

Twelve and 37/100-- Dollars

AMERICA BANK

For Supplies

Alex Tesher

SAMPLE

Type checks (Working Papers, pages 181-83) for each of the individuals below. Sign your name on each check.

Ruby L. Maggnusen	$ 89.26	Salary
Karen Jones	141.44	Salary
Bob Klein	206.10	Salary
Elmer Roubinek	14.89	Postage
Joe S. Barns	6.68	Supplies
Jane L. Dalton	119.23	Salary

Symbol Keys

Margins
Elite: 25 and 75
Pica: 17 and 67

IMPORTANT: Use the same margins for the entire symbol section.

Symbols are located on the number keys that you already have learned. You have already mastered the necessary reaches; now all you have to do is learn the location of each symbol. REMEMBER: be sure to depress the shift key firmly.

On some kinds and models of machines, certain symbols may be on different keys. The book will call your attention to these differences. But when you change machines, be sure to check to determine if the machine has the symbols in a different place. Also, not all symbols are on all machines; it may be necessary that you "create" them.

SHIFT OF *4* KEY

$/4

f4 f4 f$ f$ f4 f$ f$ $$$ f4f4 ff ff f4f fff
444 ff $4 $4 44 $$44 $4.00 $$44 $4.00 4$ $40.00
$1 $2 $3 $4 $5 $6 $7 $8 $9 $10 $11 $120 $16.00 f$

$1.44 $26.80 $17.31 $689.33 $1,640.68 $143,789.00
Add $1.16, $28.96, $17.44, $18.00, $21.13, $4.26.
The gifts cost $1.10, $6.90, $19.89, and $101.13.

SHIFT OF *6* KEY

¢/6 OR @/¢

The ¢ key may be located on the *6* key *or* beside the *semicolon* key. Check to see where it is on your machine. Do only *one* of the drill sections.

j6 j6 j¢ j¢ j6 j¢ j¢ ¢¢¢ j¢j¢ j¢j¢ j¢j¢ j6j j¢j¢j
666 6¢6¢ ¢6 ¢6 66 ¢¢66 6¢ 66¢ 6¢ ¢¢ 6¢6 6¢ 66¢ 6¢
6¢ 16¢ 13¢ 89¢ 42¢ 99¢ 6¢ 14¢ 62¢ 80¢ 21¢ 89¢ 11¢

Add 6¢, 36¢, 96¢, 68¢, 1¢, 43¢, 71¢, 31¢ and 21¢.
The gifts cost 12¢, 9¢, 5¢, 7¢, 29¢, 45¢ and 87¢.
The boy spent 29¢, 6¢, 8¢, 46¢, 71¢, 78¢ and 91¢.

BESIDE *SEMI* KEY

;¢ ;¢ ;¢ ;¢ ¢¢ ;¢ ;¢ ¢ ¢¢ ;¢ ¢;¢; ;¢;¢ ;; ;¢;¢;¢;
1¢ 1¢ 2¢ 2¢ 3¢3¢ 4¢4¢ 1¢, 2¢, 3¢, 2¢, ;¢; ;¢; ;¢;
6¢ 16¢ 13¢ 89¢ 42¢ 99¢ 6¢ 14¢ 62¢ 80¢ 21¢ 89¢ 11¢

Add 6¢, 36¢ 96¢ 68¢ 1¢, 43¢, 71¢, 65¢, 1¢ and 1¢.
The gifts cost 12¢, 9¢, 5¢, 7¢, 29¢, 45¢ and 87¢.
The boy spent 29¢, 6¢, 8¢, 46¢, 71¢, 78¢ and 91¢.

SHIFT OF *3* KEY

before number = NUMBER

after number = POUND

#/3

d3 d3 d# d# d3 d# d# ### d3d3 d#d# d#d# d3d# d#d
333 3#3# #3 #3 33 ##33 #3 3# ##33 3# #3 d3#d d#d
#33 33# 39 9# #168 168# #106 106# #3 3#3 21# #12

If not the same, you must realign the paper: push in on the Platen Variable (Left Platen Knob) and turn until the amount of space looks correct.

E
E Edward J. Sampson

5. Continue practicing this exercise (type any words) until you are able to make the adjustment correctly.

Task 1

DRILL—TYPING ON FORMS

Review the filled-in *Application for Employment* shown below.

application for employment

PERSONAL INFORMATION Date Current

Name Summers (Last) Fred (First) Andrew (Middle)

Present Address 3103 West Lawn Street (Street) Austin (City) Texas (State) 41890 (Zip)

Permanent Address 2115 Sherwood Forest (Street) New London (City) Texas (State) 40321 (Zip)

Phone Number 816-432-7865

Citizen of U. S. A. Yes ☒ No ○

If Related to Anyone in Our Employ, State Name and Department — Referred By

EMPLOYMENT DESIRED

Position auditor — Date You Can Start 6/1/78 — Salary Desired Open

Are You Employed Now? No — If So May We Inquire of Your Present Employer

Ever Applied to this Company Before? No — Where — When

Last — First — Middle

EDUCATION	Name and Location of School	Years Attended	Date Graduated	Subjects Studied
Grammar School	South Bend Elementary South Bend, Indiana	8		
High School	New London High School New London, Texas	4	June, 1974	College Prep.
College	Texas State University Austin, Texas	4	May, 1978	Accounting
Trade, Business or Correspondence School				

Subjects of Special Study or Research Work None

What Foreign Languages Do You Speak Fluently? None — Read — Write

U. S. Military or Naval Service — Rank — Present Membership in National Guard or Reserves Yes (Reserves)

Activities Other Than Religious (Civic, Athletic, Fraternal, etc.) Speech and dramatics; team and individual sports

EXCLUDE ORGANIZATIONS, THE NAME OR CHARACTER OF WHICH INDICATES THE RACE, CREED, COLOR OR NATIONAL ORIGIN OF ITS MEMBERS.

Fill out an application form (Working Papers, page 179) using your personal information.

Buy 6#, 21#, 13#, 41#, 8#, 3#, 71#, 23# and 14#.
Items #10, #7, #3, #6, #4, #1, and #19 are mine.
Get #6 weighing 10# and #2299 weighing 189,756#.

SHIFT OF *7* KEY

&

j7 j7 j& j& j7 j& j& &&& j7j7 j&j& j&j& j7j& j7j
777 7&7& &7 &7 77 &&77 j7& j7j& && j&j& j7j& &j&
17 & 60 & 9 & 16 & 14 & 71 & 77 & 45 & 61 & 9891

Buy gifts from the J & K store and the R & Sons.
Jim & Steve & Arlen & Robert were tired & dirty.
Sally & Donald went to Smithetsers & Sons today.

TIMED WRITING

How fast and accurately can you type these symbols, numbers, and words?

Leslie and Sharmon went to Libby & Kern to see if 10
they could buy items #17 weighing 4# for $211.50, 20
#89 weighing 10# for 63¢, and #6, #123, and #6773 30
all weighing 15# for 99¢. Later they went to the 40
R & L Store to attempt to buy items #292 weighing 50
5# for $1.16, #1788 weighing 100# for $11.89, and 60
#23221 weighing 50# for $11.25. 66

----1----2----3----4----5----6----7----8----9---10

SHIFT OF *5* KEY

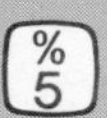

%

f5f f5f f5f f5f f5f f%f F%F f5f F%F5 f%f5 f%f f%f
555 5%5 5%5 5%5f f5%f f5%f f5%f f5%f f%f f5%f f%f
55% 555% 5% 5%5% 555% 55% 5% 5% 55% 555% 5%, 555%

Did you know that 5% of 3,000 equals 150% of 100?
A 6% discount and a 10% reduction will equal 16%.
They made 55% of their shots and 8% of the fouls.

SHIFT OF *2* KEY

@ OR @

The @ key may be located on the *2* key *or* beside the *semicolon* key. Check to see where it is on your machine. Do only *one* of the drill sections.

s2s s2s s2s s2s s2ws sw2s sw2s s@s s@s s2@s sw2@s
S@S s2s s@s sw@s S@S S@WS SW@S S@S s2s s@2s sw2@s
14 @ $2.00, 16 @ $55.00, 1 @ $17.59, 13 @ $124.66

It is better to buy 9 @ 18¢ rather than 18 @ 10¢.
I will take 4 @ 6¢, 14 @ 2¢, 17 @ 5¢, and 1 @ 3¢.
If you add 1 @ 5¢ and 1 @ 3¢ it will cost you 8¢.

Task 1

Plain paper

Type in narrative format

Reference: p. 323

Meeting of the C & I Committee. January 12, 1982. Meet in the Royal Building at 7:30 p.m. Les Schneider, president, began the meeting. No one was absent. There was a visitor present: C. Larson. The secretary, J. L. Kadmas, read the minutes of the last meeting, Dec. 18, and they were approved. K. Root (treasurer) said we have a balance on hand of $56.78.

The business conducted included the following:

Guest speaker--Leonard Haas: spoke to us on three items. (1. Benefits 2. Absenteeism 3. Vacation policy)

C. Larson (visitor) also spoke to us regarding the problems of that the plant administration was having in regards to sick-leave for all employees.

Requests for new parking permits for the handicapped were discussed. Decision was made to have the security force screen all requested.

Tabled--request that when holidays fall on Monday, third-shift workers would not work on Sunday before.

Report from legal department that at present time not possible to have more than one kind of annuity on payroll-deduction plan.

Next meeting will be held on February 11, 19__.

Meeting was adjourned at 9:35pm.

Reports from:
nominating committee — received & filed

General Guidelines

TYPING ON LINES

Being able to type neatly on a line is very important when completing printed forms. The bottom edge of all letters should be a little above the line. To practice typing on a line:

1. Insert a sheet of paper. Using the Underscore Key, type a continuous line about 4 inches long.

   ____

2. Return the Carrier and reposition your machine so that you will type on the same line. Type your name.

   Edward J. Sampson

3. Look at the amount of space between the bottom of the letters and the horizontal line toward the bottom of the Cardholder.

   This is the amount of space there should be between a line and the letters above it.

4. Type another line. Remove your paper. Reinsert the paper and space down to the typed line. Type the first letter of your first name. Compare the space between the bottom of the letter and line with the correct spacing of your first attempt.

   If approximately the same, continue typing your name.

   E

(cont'd. on next page)

BESIDE *SEMI* KEY

;@; ;@; ;@; ;@;@ ;@;; ;@;; ;@; ;@; ;@;; ;@;@ @;@;
;;@: :@; ;@; ;:@; :@:; ;:@; ;:@: ;@; ;;@@ @;@; ;@
14 @ $2.00, 16 @ $55.00, 1 @ %17.59, 13 @ $124.66

It is better to buy 9 @ 18¢ rather than 18 @ 10¢.
I will take 4 @ 6¢, 14 @ 2¢, 17 @ 5¢, and 1 @ 3¢.
If you add 1 @ 5¢ and 1 @ 3¢ it will cost you 8¢.

TIMED WRITING

How fast and accurately can you type these symbols, numbers, and words?

If you were to get a discount of 10% and paid the 10
bill early giving you an additional 2%, you would 20
be able to save almost 12% on each purchase. The 30
4 @ $5.63 will probably give you 200% better work 40
performance. However, the 3 @ $4.89 will give an 50
additional discount of 13% if paid now. The best 60
buy will be giving you at least a 5% savings when 70
you buy 2 or more @ $4.00. 75

----1----2----3----4----5----6----7----8----9---10

SHIFT OF *8* KEY

k8k k8k k8k ki8k ki8k ki8*k k*k K*K k*k k*k *ki*k
k*k K*K k*k k8*k k8*k k*k*k k8k*k k8*k k*k K*K k*
8*8 8*8 8*8 k8*k ki8*k k*k 8*8*8 *** 8*8 ki8* k*k

The check was for $***4.65 and it should be $.46.
The asterisk symbol * is used to footnote tables.
The table had the following note: *Source table.

SHIFT OF *9* KEY

l9l l9l l9l l9l lo9l lo9l lo9(l l(l l(l lo(l lo9(
l(l l(l l9l l(l l9(l lo9(l lo(l lo9(l l9(l l(l l(
9(9 9(9 9(9 9(9 l9(l (l9l (l9l l9l (l9l (l9l (l9l

SHIFT OF *0* KEY

;0; ;0; ;0; ;0; ;p0; ;p0; ;p0; ;p0; ;p); ;p); ;0;
;); ;); ;); ;); ;); ;0); ;); ;0); ;p0); ;p0); ;);
0)0 0)0 00) 00) 00) 00) ;;) ;) ;) ;) ;0); ;0; ;);

The price ($1.95) was more (5¢ more) than I paid.
Most of the teams (at least 6) won all six games.
Mary (the wife) and George (the husband) like it.

Specialized Production Tasks

There are many kinds of production typing tasks in addition to those you have completed up to this point. By using good judgment, you will be able to master most kinds of production tasks.

In this section, you will gain experience in some rather specialized typewriting tasks which will include:

Meeting Minutes. You may be called upon to take minutes at a meeting. After recording the proceedings, usually in longhand, you will want to type, duplicate, and distribute the information. There are many different formats for typing meeting minutes. Following is an illustration of one commonly used format.

Forms. Typing on a printed or duplicated form is not difficult; you must, however, be certain that your machine is adjusted correctly so that the information you type is aligned properly.

After practicing aligning your machine to type on printed lines, you will be ready to begin typing on printed forms. This section contains examples of forms frequently used by business organizations. A completed example is shown for each type of form. After carefully looking over the example, you are to complete the task(s). Obtain the blank forms from your Working Papers. Your instructor will inform you how many of each kind of form you are to complete.

6-9 lines top margin

COLORADO RURAL TRAINING PROGRAM
COMMUNITY TRAINING AND DEVELOPMENT, INC.

ds

Minutes of Meeting, September 15, 1978

ts

A regular meeting of the Colorado Rural Training program, Community Training and Development, Inc. was held on Monday, September 15, 1978, in Schneider Hall at 8 p.m. Mr. Ray Wagoner, president called the meeting to order. Roll call was taken and a quorum was present. ss

ds

The secretary, Ms. Leslie Bronson, read the minutes of the August 18 meeting. The minutes were approved as read.

The treasurer reported a balance on hand of $597.42. The report was placed on file for audit.

Mr. Clyde Johnson reported on behalf of the Membership Committee. He moved that Mr. Wayne Gibbs be admitted to membership in the organization. The motion was seconded and carried.

The report of the Program Committee was received and placed on file.

right and left margins at least one inch

Mrs. Clara Atkins, chairman of the special committee appointed to investigate parking facilities near Schneider Hall, reported that members of the organization will receive permits to place on their cars while attending meetings on Monday nights.

The resolution relating to the use of the library by nonmembers, which was postponed from the last meeting, was then taken up. The motion and a pending amendment were laid on the table after the chair announced that the guest speaker had received a phone message which would require his early departure.

The president introduced the guest speaker, Mr. James Coen, whose subject was "How to Be a Better You."

At the conclusion of Mr. Coen's talk, the resolution relating to the use of the library by nonmembers was taken from the table. After amendment and further debate, the resolution was adopted as follows: "Resolved, That all nonmembers of the organization be permitted to use the library at any time during regularly scheduled library hours."

Mr. William Gordon moved that the organization undertake the establishment of a summer camp for boys and girls on its lakefront property. Mrs. Rae Thomas moved to amend the motion by inserting the word "underpriviliged" before boys and girls. Mr. Clem Dorsey moved the matter be referred to a committee of three to be appointed by the chair with instructions to report at the regular October meeting. The chair appointed Mr. Clem Dorsey, Mrs. Anna Flynn, and Mr. George Fine to the committee.

It was announced that preparations have begun for the annual Winter Social scheduled for January 18, 1979.

The meeting adjourned at 10:05 p.m.

4 lines

Leslie Bronson

Leslie Bronson, Secretary

6-9 lines bottom margin

Type each line as shown, creating the symbols.

TIMED WRITING

It is easy to write a check for any amount when a 10
check suppression symbol is used. An example may 20
be $******7.63. The amount ($****7.63) cannot be 30
altered. If she (Joan) does not write the checks 40
carefully, he (Tom) may alter the amount to read, 50
look, and be $**5.43. A special check may have a 60
special surface (special ink) which will help you 70
eliminate the possibility of changing the amount. 80
However, be careful when you write your checks or 90
cash any checks. 93

----1----2----3----4----5----6----7----8----9---10

THE / KEY

```
;;; ;/; ;/; ;/; ;/; /; /; /; ;/; /// ;//; /// ;/;
;?; ;?; ;/; ;/; ;/; ;/; ;/?; ;/; ;/?; /// // ////
Tom/Mary/George/Sue; 123/456; 502/46/6312; 8/6/79
```

The current trend is up/down every minute/second.
You may take the dog and/or the cat with you now.
Which will you select? Cash/a trip/a new outfit.

Created Fractions

Many fractions must be created on the typewriter. The / symbol is used to create the fraction.

1/2 2/3 3/4 4/5 6/7 7/8 9/10 9/8 7/6 5/43/2 1/10
10 1/2; 25 1/8; 92 1/6; 14 5/8; 50 1/2; 82 28/33;
Hat size 6 5/8; sleeve 33 1/9; shoe size 9 1/2 D.

How fast and accurately can you type these symbols, numbers, and words?

TIMED WRITING

The measurements in the new office complex are to 10
be completed today. The main room may be larger, 20
longer, and wider. It may be 17 1/8 feet long or 30
nearly 5 1/2 feet longer than our present one. I 40
believe it may be 14 1/10 feet wide or 8 7/8 feet 50
wider than our present office. I would like that 60
room to be 20 1/4 x 24 1/5 feet, but it costs too 70
much to build such a room. Therefore, I can save 80
almost 1/3 on the cost of construction this year. 90

----1----2----3----4----5----6----7----8----9---10

Task 8

Use of leaders in tables: Full sheet; 10 spaces between longest entries

Reference: p. 299

Note: This is one of the few times when the right edge of words is justified.

WEDDING ANNIVERSARIES

leave 2 blanks on all lines

First	Clocks
Second	China
Third	Crystal and Glass
Fourth	Electrical Appliances
Fifth	Silverware
Sixth	Wood
Seventh	Desk Sets-Pen & Pencil Sets
Eighth	Linens and Laces
Ninth	Leather
Tenth	Diamond Jewelry
Eleventh	Fashion Jewelry and Accessories
Twelfth	Pearls or Colored Gems
Thirteenth	Textiles and Furs
Fourteenth	Gold Jewelry
Fifteenth	Watches
Sixteenth	Silver Holloware-Sterling or Plate
Seventeenth	Furniture
Eighteenth	Porcelain
Nineteenth.	Bronze
Twentieth	Platinum
Twenty-fifth	Sterling Silver Jubilee
Thirtieth	Diamond
Fortieth	Ruby
Forty-fifth	Sapphire
Fiftieth	Golden Jubilee
Fifty-fifth	Emerald
Sixtieth	Diamond Jubilee

THE ½ KEY

;½; ;½; ;½; ;½; ;½½; ;½½; ;½; ;½; ;½; ;½½; ;½; ;½
;½; ;½; ;½; ;½½; ½½½ ;;½½ ;½; ;½½; ;½; ;½½; ;½ ;½
10½; 8½; 16; 15½; 123½; 456½; 789½; 20½; ½; ½; ½;

Tom gave ½ to Bill and ½ to Andy; I got a big 00;
This week I worked 5½ days; I got paid for ½ day.
Add ½ to ½ and you have 1; this amount is ½ of 2.

SHIFT OF ½ KEY

;½; ;½; ;½; ;½; :¼: :¼: ;½¼; ;½¼; ;¼; ;¼; ;¼; ;¼;
;½; ;½; ;¼; ;¼; ;½¼; ;½¼; ;½¼; ;¼; ;¼; ;½¼; ;¼;¼;
2¼; 3½; 4¼; 5½: 6¼; 7½: 8¼; 9½; 10¼; 11½; 12¼; ¼;

He gave ¼ to Tim, ¼ to Jo, ¼ to Ben, and ¼ to me.
The show is ¼ over and I am ¼ hour from the show.
Nearly ¼ had colds; the ¼ did not; ¼ felt sickly.

TIMED WRITING

How fast and accurately can you type these symbols, numbers, and words?

The company changed the policy and now we will be 10
paid for ½ hour of overtime. This policy was in- 20
valid until yesterday when over ½ of the members, 30
administrators, and staff voted to approve it. A 40
vote of ½ was needed. It is surprising that ¼ of 50
us felt we should be paid for ¼ of that overtime. 60
Perhaps if we would have spent ½ month working on 70
the campaign, the other ¼ would have agreed also. 80

----1----2----3----4----5----6----7----8----9---10

Created Symbols

Sometimes typists must create symbols that do not appear on the keyboard. Common symbols that must be created are shown below.

Symbol Names	*How to Create It*	*Example*
Caret (insertion)	Insert a diagonal; type insertion above	school The current/election
Multiply (times; by)	Type the small x	The value of 12 x 12
Equals	Type a hyphen slightly raised; backspace; type a hyphen slightly below (use cylinder knob to raise and lower hyphen)	The value of 12 x 12 = 144
Divide (into)	Type a colon; backspace; type the hyphen	12 ÷ 12 = 1

Task 7

Type as a financial table.

Reference:
p. 298

Cleveland State University

BUDGET COMPARISON

	1979-80	1980-81
State General Purpose Revenue	($313,016,800)	($342,149,254)
General program appropriations	242,578,800	242,502,797
Pay Plan Suppl (GPR portion)	16,083,600	30,783,157
Teaching hospitals	5,772,700	5,088,200
Utilities	15,366,600	23,508,700
Debt service	33,215,100	40,266,400
Student fee income	81,929,960	92,647,977
Federal programs & projects	110,939,998	123,040,359
Gifts & trust fund income	20,748,500	22,048,500
University Hospitals revenue	30,130,500	37,108,800
Auxiliary Operations	82,010,868	90,144,188
Operational receipts	22,842,579	25,156,894
	$661,619,205	$732,295,972

Add (plus)	Type the hyphen; back-space; type the diagonal	A + B = C
Subtract (minus)	Type the hyphen	A — B = C
Exclamation Point	Type the apostrophe; backspace; type the period	!

DRILL

Type each line as shown, creating the symbols.

NBEA
The professional/convention is to be held Monday.

nearest long distance
He ran to the/telephone to make the/call to Mary.

Uncle
Hurry to the phone, it might be/Bill calling you.

The value of 6 x 6 is larger than 5 1/3 x 6 1/25.

Mary made the 2 x 4 board slide through the lake.

The dimensions are 123 x 144 x 142 inches inside.

If A = B and D = F, the value of A and F = total.

The values of A and B are X and Y. Could C = XY?

A + B = C; A + D = C; Does B = D? If so, A = 16!

If 6 ÷ 6 = A, does 12 ÷ 12 = A? If not, why not?

The test grades 8, 9, and 7 ÷ 3 average out at 8!

Mary had 4 ÷ 2; John has 6 ÷ 3; they each have 2.

A + B and C + D = F. If 8 + D = F, should A = C?

The value of A and B = 5; as a result A + B = 10.

The total is equal to A + B + C ÷ F + GG ÷ H + J.

Task 6

Boxed table: Full sheet; 5 spaces between columns, type body as illustrated.

RESULTS OF ENVIRONMENTAL PROTECTION AGENCY
GASOLINE-CONSUMPTION TEST

Small Sporty Cars	Engine	Transmission	EPA Estimates	
			Highway	City
Chevrolet Monza 2 + 2	140-cu.-in. 4-cyl. 2-bbl.	Manual	30	19
Chevrolet Monza Towne Coupe	140-cu.-in. 4-cyl. 2-bbl.	Manual	30	19
Pontiac Sunbird 2-Door Coupe	140-cu.-in. 4-cyl. 2-bbl.	Manual	30	19
Oldsmobile Starfire Sport Coupe	140-cu.-in. 4-cyl. 2-bbl.	Manual	30	19
Buick Skyhawk "S" Coupe	231-cu.-in. V-6 2-bbl.	Manual	26	17
Datsun 280 Z Sport Coupe	168-cu.-in. 6-cyl. F.I.	Manual	25	17
Toyota Celica ST & GT Sport Coupes	133.6-cu.-in. 4-cyl. 2-bbl.	Manual	32	19
VW Scirocco Sport Coupe	97-cu.-in. 4-cyl. 2-bbl.	Manual	38	26
Fiat XL/9 Coupe	78.7-cu.-in. 4-cyl. 2-bbl.	Manual	31	21
Audi Fox 2-door Sedan	97-cu.-in. 4-cyl. F.I.	Manual	36	24
BMW 2002 2-Door Sedan	121-cu.-in. 4-cyl. 2-bbl.	Manual	30	20
Mazda Cosmo Coupe	80-cu.-in. Rotary 4-bbl.	Manual	28	17
Porsche 914 Coupe	120-cu.-in. 4-cyl. F.I.	Manual	31	20
Triumph TR-7 Coupe	122-cu.-in. 4-cyl. 1-bbl.	Manual	27	19

Horizontal and Vertical Centering

Horizontal Centering

To center a word, phrase, or sentence horizontally on a page:

1. Move carriage or element to center point of page (Elite: 50; Pica: 42).

BACK SPACE

Back—1 for 2

2. Backspace ONCE for each TWO strokes or spaces in the information to be centered. Example:

```
Ca|li|fo|rn|ia
```

Important—Remember to backspace ***once*** for every ***two*** strokes.

If there is a single character left, drop it (do not backspace for one remaining character). Example:

```
op|ti|on|al| a|ct|iv|it|ie|s
```

4. Efficiency Guideline

Keep your little finger on the Backspace Key; mentally say each two characters and spaces; backspace ***once*** after saying each ***two***. Example:

(to be centered)	`Horizontal Centering`
(mentally say)	`Ho ri zo nt al  C en te ri ng`

DRILL

Insert a sheet of paper and practice horizontally centering each of the following lines:

```
Getting a Job

Vertical Centering

Review and Check

Betty Allen

Frank Bestemore
```

Compare your copy to the example. Does it look the same? Now type the problem again; attempt to complete it in a shorter amount of time. How does your second attempt compare to the example?

Task 4

Ruled table: Full sheet; 5 spaces between columns, double space body

Set up as a ruled table with a double line before column heads.

CLASS LIST OF GIRLS
W.R. MANZ ELEMENTARY SCHOOL

Name	Address	Father's Name	Phone No.	Birth Date
Bennett, Jean	3423 Riley St.	Roy	832-8970	6/19/69
Brehm, Kathleen	1206 E. Hamilton	Richard	834-9036	5/12/69
Butros, Linda	1227 Collins Ct.	Raeef	832-5375	12/18/69
Egan, Jodi	3446 Trimble St.	John	834-3935	6/20/69
Egan, Katherine	1004 E. Fillmore Av.	James	834-9423	5/25/69
Hanson, Cristin	3436 Rudolph Road	Wayne	832-5119	1/30/69
Ives, Kelly	1506 Taft Av.	Gary	834-4654	12/20/69
Johnson, Jennifer	1334 Cummings	Arthur	834-5527	10/9/69
LaBarre, Patricia	223 E. Tyler	James	834-9931	4/29/69
Orth, Phyllis	712 E. Grant	Marlo	832-6961	11/6/68
Sattem, Susan	1104 Cummings	David	835-3017	10/22/68

Task 5

Boxed table: Full sheet; 10 spaces between columns, type body as illustrated.

Reference: p. 297

EPA CALIFORNIA GAS MILEAGE GUIDE FOR NEW CAR BUYERS

Small Economy cars	Engine	Transmission	EPA Estimates Highway	City
Chevrolet Vega Sport Coupe	140-cu.-in. 4-cyl. 2-bbl.	Manual	30	19
Pontiac Astre 2-Door Coupe	140-cu.-in. 4-cyl. 2-bbl.	Manual	30	19
Toyota Corona 2-Door Sedan	133.6-cu.-in. 4-cyl. 2-bbl.	Manual	32	19
Datsun 710 2-Door Sedan	119-cu.in. 4-cyl. 2-bbl.	Manual	33	22
Fiat 131 2-Door Sedan	107-cu.-in. 4-cyl. 2-bbl.	Manual	30	19
Mazda RX-3 Coupe	70-cu.-in. Rotary 4-bbl.	Manual	29	19
VW Dasher 2-Door Sedan	97-cu.-in. 4-cyl. F.I.	Manual	36	24
Volvo 242 2-Door Sedan	130-cu.-in. 4-cyl. F.I.	Manual	27	18

Task 1

Practice centering the following tasks:

```
Invited to Attend
the First Annual
Student Forensics Follies
Student Theatre
October 17, 19--
8:00 p.m.
```

Task 2

```
Plan to Attend
the
Pre-game Pep Rally
Tomorrow (October 190
3:00 p.m.
Football Field
```

LOCK

SHIFT

For emphasis you may wish to capitalize a whole word or whole line. To capitalize more than one consecutive letter, use the Shift Lock Key. It is located above the Left Shift Key. Depress the Shift Lock Key, and the machine will only print upper-case (capital) letters. To unlock, tap the Shift Lock Key.

Task 3

```
YOU
are Invited
to Attend the
First Annual
STUDENT FORENSICS FOLLIES
STUDENT THEATRE
October 17, 19--
8:00 p.m.
```

Task 4

PARTICIPANTS

James Wong
Betty Lee
Roman Shipek
Joe Leipsel
Jack Johnson
Miguel Ortega
Jim Barton

Task 3

Ruled table: Full sheet; 5 spaces between, single space body with double between groups

CENTRAL BANK RATES FOR DISCOUNTS AND ADVANCES TO COMMERCIAL BANKS (Type title on two lines)

(Percent per annum)

Country	Rate as of October 31, 1980	
	Percent	Date effective
Argentina	18.0	Feb. 1972
Austria	6.0	Apr. 1975
Belgium	6.0	Aug. 1975
Brazil	18.0	Feb. 1972
Canada	9.0	Sept. 1975
Denmark	7.5	Aug. 1975
France	8.0	Sept. 1975
Germany, Fed. Rep. (spell out) of	3.5	Sept. 1975
Italy	6.0	Sept. 1975
Japan	6.5	Oct. 1975
Mexico	4.5	June 1942
Netherlands	4.5	Sept. 1975
Norway	5.0	Oct. 1975
Sweden	6.0	Aug. 1975
Switzerland	3.0	Oct. 1975
United Kingdom	12.0	Oct. 1975
Venezuela	5.0	Oct. 1970

Vertical Centering

To center something vertically on a page, you must determine how far to space down on the page before typing the first line. To determine this, follow this procedure:

Lines available

6 lines equal 1"

1. Determine how many lines are available on the paper on which you will be typing. A typewriter is calibrated so that 6 lines equal 1 inch:

   ```
   xxxxxxxxxxxx
   xxxxxxxxxxxx
   xxxxxxxxxxxx   } 1"
   xxxxxxxxxxxx
   xxxxxxxxxxxx
   xxxxxxxxxxxx
   ```

   8½"

   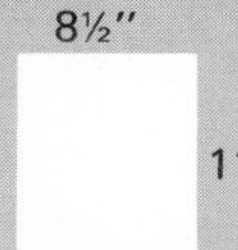

   11

   If you will be using a full sheet of paper (8½ inches wide; 11 inches long), there are 66 lines available (11 inches times 6 lines equals 66). If you are going to use a half sheet of paper, there are 33 lines available (5½ inches times 6 lines equals 33).

Lines used

2. Determine the number of lines the information you are going to place on the page will occupy (in other words, how many lines will be used). Assume you want to horizontally and vertically center the following:

   ```
            Welcome!
          Texas Tech's
          Fifth Annual
     Homecoming Activities
       October 21, 19--
   ```

   The number of lines the information would occupy depends on the spacing used:

Single Spacing	*Double Spacing*	*Triple Spacing*
1 Welcome!	1 Welcome!	1 Welcome!
2 Texas Tech's	2	2
3 Fifth Annual	3 Texas Tech's	3
4 Homecoming Activities	4	4 Texas Tech's
5 October 21, 19--	5 Fifth Annual	5
	6	6
	7 Homecoming Activities	7 Fifth Annual
	8	8
	9 October 21, 19--	9
		10 Homecoming Activities
		11
		12
		13 October 21, 19--

Lines not used

3. Determine the number of lines that will not be used (subtract the lines to be used from the lines available). Using the same example:

Single Spacing		*Double Spacing*		*Triple Spacing*	
Full Sheet	Half Sheet	Full Sheet	Half Sheet	Full Sheet	Half Sheet
66	33	66	33	66	33
−5	−5	−9	−9	−13	−13
61	28	57	24	53	20

Task 2

Ruled table: Full sheet; 5 spaces between, single space body

center headings

Alumni Development Fund
Contributions From
States with more than 200 Alumni

all caps

State	Number of Alumni	Contributors	Goal	% of Alumni Contributing
1. Virginia	299	128	40	42.81
2. Maryland	242	85	30	34.71
3. Pennsylvania	231	48	27	20.78
4. Ohio	318	59	38	18.55
5. New York	371	68	44	18.33
6. Colorado	770	129	91	16.75
7. Missouri	246	39	29	15.85
8. Oregon	577	90	68	15.60
9. Florida	426	66	50	15.49
10. Michigan	458	69	54	15.06
11. Illinois	892	129	106	14.46
12. California	3,240	433	383	13.67
13. Nebraska	289	39	34	13.50
14. Indiana	245	33	29	13.47
15. Arizona	468	60	55	12.82
16. Washington	1,134	140	134	12.35
17. Iowa	429	53	51	12.35
18. Wisconsin	764	94	90	12.30
19. Texas	551	57	65	10.34
20. Montana	643	65	76	10.11
21. South Dakota	494	49	59	9.92
22. Canada	768	71	91	9.24
23. Minnesota	6,918	591	818	8.54
24. Foreign Countries	551	43	65	7.80
25. North Dakota	13,617	1,008	1,610	7.40

"Split" lines not used

4. Determine how far to space down from the top of page (divide "lines not used" by two.)

Single Spacing		*Double Spacing*		*Triple Spacing*	
Full Sheet	Half Sheet	Full Sheet	Half Sheet	Full Sheet	Half Sheet
2⟌61 = 30½ = 30	2⟌28 = 14	2⟌57 = 28½ = 28	2⟌24 = 12	2⟌53 = 26½ = 26	2⟌20 = 10

If fraction

Note: If fraction occurs from division by two, drop it.
Note: Always advance the paper one additional line.

SUMMARY

Lines available ——▶ 66
Subtract lines to be used ——▶ 28
Lines not used ——▶ 38
"Split": half on top; half on bottom. ——▶ 2⟌38 = 19 = begin on line 20!

Counting down

BEGINNING TO COUNT DOWN

All typewriters have a point from which to begin counting down to the line on which you want to begin typing. Check your machine to determine how far you should roll the paper before beginning to count.

TYPING TASKS

Center each of the following problems both vertically and horizontally. Each task will indicate the size paper and the line spacing to be used.

Task 5

Half sheet; double spacing

```
Atlanta Christian College
Central University
Danbury State College
Foothills College
Kilgore College
McGill University
Northern Illinois University
Seneca College
```

Task 6

Full sheet; single spacing

```
Calgary, Alberta
Toledo, Ohio
Salem, Massachusetts
Monmouth, Illinois
Rochester, New York
Moncton, New Brunswick
Oxford, Ohio
Livonia, Michigan
Kentfield, California
Minneapolis, Minnesota
Wakefield, Rhode Island
Coral Gables, Florida
Middlebury, Vermont
Glenville, West Virginia
Omaha, Nebraska
Phoenix, Arizona
Huron, South Dakota
Big Spring, Texas
Bangor, Maine
Winnepeg, Manitoba
```

Task 1

Ruled table: Full sheet; 10 spaces between, double space body

Reference: p. 296

Type in all caps

Importance of Factors in Evaluating Applications for Managerial Positions

Factor	Very Important	Important	Minor Importance	Not Considered
Communication skills	88.3%	11.7%	0.0%	0.0%
College grades	8.0	70.5	18.9	2.7
Prestige of college attended	0.4	18.6	53.4	27.7
Recommendations of teachers	7.2	36.0	47.3	9.5
Major field of study	30.3	58.3	11.4	0.0
Personal appearance	43.4	50.6	6.0	0.0
Degree received or years of college	24.2	57.4	17.0	1.5
Previous work experience	49.1	39.6	10.6	0.8
Impression of personality	50.8	46.6	2.3	0.4
Career goals	49.2	43.9	6.4	0.4
Familiarity with company	14.8	29.5	45.1	10.6
Extracurricular activities	4.2	32.6	49.2	14.0
Recommendations of former employers	43.0	43.8	10.9	2.3

Prepared from a recent study by the Indiana Commission for Higher Education

Task 7

Half sheet; triple spacing

Rodney Schmidt
Robert Talmage
Agnes Salzer
Gladys McCabe
Connley Hartman
Ted Faravelli
Manasseh Manoukian

Headings

If it is desirable or necessary to center a heading over a listing, always type in all capitals and triple space before beginning the next line.

Task 8

Half sheet; single spacing

MAJOR CITIES OF THE WORLD

Athens, Greece
Cairo, Egypt
Lisbon, Portugal
London, England
Madrid, Spain
Montreal, Quebec
Moscow, Russia
New York, New York
Paris, France
Rome, Italy

Task 9

Full sheet; double spacing

AVERAGE TEMPERATURE/DAYS WITH RAIN FOR MARCH

New York 40°/12
Athens 53°/11
Barcelona 54°/7
Cairo 63°/2
Casablanca 58°/2
Dublin 42°/19
Geneva 38°/13
Lisbon 55°/14
London 44°/20
Madrid 48°/10
Milan 47°/6
Paris 44°/14
Rome 52°/19
San Francisco 53°/9
Tel Aviv 58°/9
Vienna 40°/7
Zurich 42°/14

Task 36

Type in attractive format.

COMPUTER SCIENCE
CLASS LIST

Name	Year	Major
Josephine Petrushki	Jr.	International Studies
Morgan Sutherland	Sr.	Political Science, Journalism
Helen Rechzepiejewski	So.	Art, Foreign Languages
Geraldine May Anderson	Fr.	Computer Science, Accounting
Hartley Jonathan Smith	Jr.	Library Science, History
Helen Magdelina Sabrina	Sr.	Geography, Geology
Charles Robert Tremain	So.	Computer Science
Robert John Rooney	Sr.	History, Sociology
Patricia Ann Rooney	Sr.	History, Sociology
Merrill Davis Prissel	Fr.	Business Administration

Task 37

Full sheet; 10 spaces between columns, double space body

APPLICANTS FOR SECRETARIAL POSITION IN
OFFICE ADMINISTRATION DEPARTMENT
> single space

arrange in alphabetic order

Name	Phone Number	Timed Writing Gross w.p.m.
Kim Benik	834-0467	77
Peggy Hollister	835-0718	69
Jean Kruegar	836-5202	67
Sandy Callahan	836-4594	76
Susan Behnke	836-5318	65
Nancy Haas	836-2618	69
Virginia Sneen	832-4595	89
Becky Waldusky	835-2306	64

Composition Module

Now that you have learned the keyboard, it is time to further develop your skills to think and compose at the machine. While learning the keyboard, you were given the opportunity to Think and Type. This section of the book will give you the opportunity for additional practice in composing.

There are four stages, or levels, in building compositional skill. These four levels include the:

1. Word-response level (You have already begun working at this level.)
2. Phrase-response level
3. Sentence-response level
4. Paragraph or "complete" stage

One-Word and Phrase Response

One-Word Response (Yes or No)

Read a question and answer it by typing either *yes* or *no*. REMEMBER: do not hesitate. Type your answer as quickly as possible.

1. Do you like animals?
2. Do you like the weather today?
3. Are you satisfied with the courses in which you are presently enrolled?
4. Would you like to go into politics?
5. Does your school publish a newspaper?
6. Do you participate in any sport?
7. Do you like to watch television?
8. Do you own a car?
9. Is the community in which your school is located your "hometown"?
10. Does your school have "homecoming" activities?
11. Are you married?
12. Do you have any brothers or sisters?
13. Are you graduating this year?
14. Are you going to work next summer?
15. Are you a "good" speller?
16. Are you going home during the next vacation break?
17. Do you like school?
18. Do you like coffee?
19. Would you like to become President of the United States?
20. Do you like to cook?
21. Do you like to dance?
22. Would you like to become a millionaire?
23. Do you like hot weather?
24. Do you like music?
25. Do you like to type?
26. Do you have a roommate?
27. Is today Wednesday?
28. Did you get up early this morning?
29. Do you like pizza?
30. Have you read a newspaper today?
31. Did you work last summer?
32. Were you satisfied with your grades last term?

Task 34

Type in attractive format.

THE REASONS WHY BUSINESS USES TEMPORARY SECRETARIAL HELP*

Reasons	Frequent Users	Occasional Users
Peakload Periods	86.5%	43.3%
Temporary Replacement	48.6%	46.7%
Vacation Replacement	70.3%	40.5%
One-time Projects	54.1%	40.0%
Specialized Work	27.0%	13.5%
Possible Permanent Recruitment	18.9%	8.4%
Lower Employee Cost	10.8%	3.4%
Less Paperwork	2.7%	1.7%

*The Office, August 1982

Task 35

Type in attractive format.

CURRENT TARGET CASHIERS

Name	Date Hired	Salary
Dejewski, Jill	12-12-80	$4.79
Gifford, Mary	01-29-82	4.40
Jasinski, Debbie	04-02-80	4.65
Ludka, Linda	10-03-79	4.85
Marino, Dani	09-03-80	3.02
Miller, Lori	03-20-81	4.40
Patane, Cheryl	06-10-81	4.79
Pike, Jodie	05-16-82	4.40
Riley, Kathy	05-26-81	5.09
Sherlock, Karen	03-18-81	4.56
Stawicki, Karen	07-11-81	4.81
Zanoni, Cindy	09-18-82	4.40
Zawicki, Mary	05-30-82	4.40

One-Word Response (Which One?)

Read a question and answer it by typing one of the two responses. REMEMBER: do not hesitate. Type your answer as quickly as possible.

1. Are you a female or male?
2. Are you married or single?
3. Is your typing instructor male or female?
4. Would you rather drink coffee or tea?
5. Would you rather dance or read?
6. Would you rather ski or swim?
7. Would you rather drive or ride?
8. Would you rather eat or cook?
9. Would you rather walk or talk?
10. Would you rather hike or bike?
11. Would you rather dance or sing?
12. Would you rather eat pizza or steak?
13. Would you rather write or type?
14. Would you rather study or play?
15. Would you rather own a dog or cat?

One-Word Response (Opposites)

Read a word and type the opposite of it. REMEMBER: do not hesitate. Type your answer as quickly as possible.

1. day
2. salt
3. Mother
4. Uncle
5. Grandmother
6. rich
7. war
8. young
9. love
10. hot
11. clean
12. male
13. minus
14. seldom
15. floor
16. here
17. no
18. winter
19. sick
20. true
21. high
22. up
23. over
24. few
25. wrong
26. beginning
27. forget
28. stand
29. give
30. short
31. new
32. win
33. negative
34. good
35. open
36. come
37. child
38. wet
39. all
40. fast

Task 32

Full sheet; 5 spaces between columns, double space body

INCOMING SALES BY PRODUCT

Division	Plumbing Supp.	Bldg. Hdwr.	Ind. Hdwr.	Total
Atlanta	$ 67748.30	$ 81260.60	$ 87773.50	$ 236782.40
Baltimore	91355.40	103176.60	12006.90	206538.90
Boise	44672.50	54293.80	79823.80	178790.10
Boston	85563.60	52055.10	103990.20	241608.90
Chicago	73913.90	99639.80	165997.70	339551.40
Dallas	73189.50	65219.90	90415.30	228824.70
Denver	90054.20	90337.60	56229.50	236621.30
Indianapolis	66681.70	24479.40	62422.40	153583.50
Kansas City	82158.80	145423.40	63273.80	290856.00
Los Angeles	136515.50	115307.80	142831.90	394655.20
New York	118891.40	138424.90	158627.40	415943.70
TOTALS	$930744.80	$969618.90	$1131452.40	$2923756.10

Insert Commas
eg., $67,748.30

Task 33

Full sheet; 10 spaces between columns, double space body

GREFSHEIM SHOPPING MALL
SERVICE CENTER EMPLOYEES

Name	Code	Telephone
Shannon Herold	28	835-6946
Kelly Brueggmann	45	835-4839
Chuck Rumpel	1	836-2275
Sharon Talbott	38	835-5222
Lynn Gardner	54	834-4608
Mary Grefsheim	46	835-6946
Phil Krueger	52	835-5792
Veronica Smith	37	834-8244

Phrase Response

Read a question and answer it by typing several words. Do not make complete sentences—just answer the question. REMEMBER: do not hesitate. Type your answer as quickly as possible.

1. What are your first and last names?
2. What are your first, middle, and last names?
3. What is the title of your favorite song?
4. What is the name of the last movie you saw?
5. What is the name of the last television show you saw?
6. What is the name of the town in which your school is located?
7. What is the name of the town in which you were born?
8. What are your father's first and last names?
9. What are your mother's first and last names?
10. What is the complete name of this course?

Task 30

Full sheet; 10 spaces between columns, double space body

MARINE MIDLAND BANKS, INC.,

~~Head~~ Office Location	Total Domestic Offices	Total ~~Domestic Offices~~ Holdings (In millions of dollars)
New York City	26	$3,133
Buffalo	91	1.497
Syracuse	45	638
Rochester	36	537
Poughkeepsie	38	313
Elmira	25	306
Troy	25	208
East Setauket	27	177
Watertown	19	168
Jamestown	10	137

Task 31

Full sheet; 5 spaces between columns, double space body

Note: when one heading is positioned over two columns, find center point between 2 columns and backspace once for each 2 spaces required for the multi-column heading; then type it.

EPA G/CAS MILEAGE ESTIMATES FOR FULL-SIZE CARS

Model	Standard Engine	Standard Transmission	EPA Estimates Highway	City
Chevrolet Impala	250 cu.-in. 6cyl. 1-bbl.	Automatic	22	17
Pontiac Bonneville	301 cu.-in.* V-8, 2-bbl.	Automatic	23	17
Oldsmobile 98	350 cu.-in. V-8, 4-bbl.	Automatic	21	15
Buick LeSabre	231 cu.-in. V-6, 2-bbl. 2.73 Rear Axle	Automatic	25	18
Cadillac DeVille	425 cu.-in. V-8, 4-bbl.	Automatic	18	14

*Not Available in California

Choosing the Right Word

One of the most common problems a writer faces is how to choose the exact word to convey a certain thought or idea to the reader. Writing must be precise; vague words or unacceptable usage of words may obscure the author's meaning.

General Guidelines

CORRECT WORD USAGE

1. Use concrete nouns, descriptive adjectives, adverbs, and phrases; do not use vague or abstract words.

   Some words are vague; they can mean many different things. Words such as ***nice***, ***good***, ***bad***, ***thing***, ***work***, and so forth, do not give the reader much information.

   Examples:

   Vague: The lecture was good and I learned a lot.
   Better: The lecture solved two problems for me. I learned how to balance a checkbook and how to calculate interest.
   Vague: a nice color
   Better: an emerald green, a vivid scarlet, a dull black
   Vague: he said
   Better: he shouted defiantly, he muttered, he demanded

2. Use English idioms correctly.

   An idiom is an expression peculiar to a language and is perfectly acceptable if used correctly.

   Examples:

Correct	*Incorrect*
acquitted of	acquitted from
aim to prove	aim at proving
can't help feeling	can't help but feel
comply with	comply to
independent of	independent from
in search of	in search for
kind of (+ noun)	kind of a (+ noun)
aloud	out loud
try to	try and
different from	different than

3. Use the correct word; some words are often misused.

   Examples:

   accept *to take or receive*
   advice *an opinion*
   biannual *twice a year*
   council *a governing body*
   fewer *(use with nouns that can be counted: fewer apples)*
   good *modifies a noun or pronoun*
   angry at (*things and animals*)
   angry with (*people*)
   angry about (*occasions or situations*)
   except *to leave out*; *aside from*
   advise *to recommend*
   biennial *once every two years*
   counsel *to give advice*
   less *(use with nouns that cannot be counted: less noise)*
   well *modifies a verb or adverb*

Task 28

Full sheet; 10 spaces between columns, double space body

OVERSEAS LONG-DISTANCE TELEPHONE RATES* > single space

Country	~~Station-to-Station~~ Direct Dial	~~Person-to-Person~~ Collect
Australia	$9.00	$12.00
France	6.75	12.00
Germany	6.75	12.00
Italy	6.75	12.00
Japan	9.00	12.00
Philippines	9.00	12.00
United Kingdom	5.40	9.60

← ss

← ds

~~*Rates quoted~~ *Rates are ^for 3-minutes ^during daytime. ~~rates~~.

Task 29

Full sheet; 5 spaces between columns, double space body

DAIRYLAND ALL-CONFERENCE > single space
Basketball Team 1981-1982 (all caps)

Player	School	Height	Class
Darwin Durst	Osseo-Fairchild	5-10	Senior
Mike Gilbertson	~~E-S~~ Elena Strum	6-0	Junior
Todd Horel	Augusta	5-10	Senior
Randy Janke	Lincoln	~~6-0~~ 5-9	Junior
Doug Lee	Augusta	5-11	Senior
Steve Lyga	Whitehall	6-2	Junior
Greg Pronschinski	Independence	5-8	Senior
Darrell Sather	~~E-S~~ Elena Strum	6-4	Senior
Keith ~~Sexe~~ Dexel	~~Blair~~ Fall Creek	6-1	Senior
Mark Sosalla	Whitehall	5-10	Senior
Randy Symicek	Independence	6-0	~~Senior~~ Junior
Mark Ward	Blair	5-10	Senior

Sentence Response

1. Drawing from your experience and observations, try to think of descriptive adjectives, adverbs, or phrases to make the sentences below more interesting. Type the revised sentences.
   1. The last book I read was good.
   2. Today is a nice day.
   3. My favorite sport is fun.
   4. My favorite color is a nice color.
   5. My best friend is nice.
2. Select the correct idiom from the sentences below and type each sentence as it should be written.
   1. (Try to, Try and) type the data without any errors.
   2. Juan went (in search for, in search of) a new typewriter ribbon.
   3. My book is (different from, different than) Harriet's book.
   4. I will try to (comply with, comply to) your wishes.
   5. This (kind of a, kind of) paper is easier to store.
3. Select the correct word from the sentences below and type each sentence as it should be written.
   1. (Accept, Except) for Henry, the entire class went on the trip.
   2. Our teacher strongly (adviced, advised) us to study for the exam.
   3. There have been (fewer, less) absences this winter than last winter.
   4. We have (fewer, less) flour than we need.
   5. He is a (good, well) student.
   6. Martha doesn't feel (good, well) today.
   7. Sean plays the violin (good, well).
   8. I am angry (at, about, with) my best friend.
   9. I am angry (at, about, with) the rising costs of the textbooks.
   10. I am angry (at, about, with) Whiskers, my cat.

Task 26

Full sheet; 8 spaces between columns, double space body

DEPARTMENT HEADS OF MIDELFORT CLINIC

Name	Department	Extension
Florence B.	Pediatrics	5220
Helen B.	Internal Medicine	5325
Diane C.	Surgery	5631
Jerry L.	Dermatology	5630
Jane F.	OB-Gyn	5547
Bonnie C.	Medical Records	5224
Dennis O.	Business Office	5837
Florence H.	Secretaries	5230

Task 27

Full sheet; 8 spaces between columns, double space body

DEPARTMENT SUPERVISORS
OF CLAIRMONT STORES

Current Date

Name	Department	Extension
Lynn Anderson	Personnel	382
Jim Elliot	Treasurer	256
Don Graffe	Shop	371
Lisa Orton	Data Processing	416
Mike Pankratz	Accounting	555
Joan Rosen	Operations	450
Sarah Strauss	Payroll	265
Steve VandenLangen	Safety	370

Composing Paragraphs

A paragraph is a group of related sentences—an organized and meaningful unit in a piece of writing.

General Guidelines

COMPOSING PARAGRAPHS

A paragraph should contain a topic sentence and several supporting sentences. The sentences should be organized in a logical manner and should flow into each other. Transitional words are used to connect one sentence to another.

a. A ***topic sentence*** expresses the main idea or subject of the paragraph. The topic sentence usually opens the paragraph since most readers like to know what the paragraph is about before they read on. The example below shows the topic sentence underscored.

b. ***Supporting sentences*** describe, explain, or further develop the topic sentence.

Example: In a small office, the receptionist has a wide variety of duties. Answering the telephone and receiving callers is a primary responsibility of any receptionist. Sometimes an employer will ask a receptionist to take an important client to lunch or to contact a business customer. The correspondence in a small office varies from simple letters to complicated reports, and so the receptionist handles many types of communication.

DRILL

Step 1

Compose a short paragraph using the following topic sentence. Concentrate on content; you will revise the material later.

"A shortage of quality paper causes problems."

Step 2

Proofread—watch for spelling, punctuation, and grammatical errors.

Step 3

Retype, correcting all errors.

DRILL

Compose a paragraph consisting of three or more sentences for each of the situations given below. Follow the three steps outlined above.

1. Describe what you like about your school.
2. If you were elected President of the United States, what would be the first thing you would attempt to change after taking office?
3. After you finish your education, what do you want to do, and why?
4. Do you believe that everyone is prepared to vote on every issue at the age of 18?
5. If you had the opportunity to travel next summer, all expenses paid, would you rather travel to Europe or tour the United States? Why?
6. Do you believe that everyone should have the opportunity to obtain 14-16 years of free education? Why or why not?
7. If you had an opportunity to help with conservation of our natural resources, which resource would you select? What would you do?
8. Do you think there is too much emphasis on sports in our schools? Why or why not?
9. If you had the opportunity to serve as a teacher in your school next year, what courses would you teach? Why?
10. Do you believe that there is too much violence shown on television? Why or why not?

Task 24

Full sheet; 5 spaces between columns, double space body

AUTOMOTIVE EXPORTS FROM U.S.

(Total Value in Millions)

Year	Vehicles	Automotive
1950	$ 147	$ 259
1955	406	746
1960	747	1,276
1965	634	1,266
1970	739	1,929
1975	1,397	3,652
1980	4,580	9,450

Task 25

Full sheet; 5 spaces between columns, double space body

SATURDAY SPECIALS

Item	Regular Price	Sale Price
Pierced Earrings	$ 1.76	$ 1.26
Photo Albums	2.97	1.97
Shoulder Bag	6.97	4.97
Pre-washed Jeans	11.96	9.22
Men's Sport Jacket	7.96	6.88
Nylon Panty Hose	1.00	.58
Self-cleaning Iron	23.97	19.84
Oven-broiler	31.87	25.97
Sabre Jigsaw	11.88	8.88
Orbital Sander	16.97	13.88

Short Composition and Informal Writing

When preparing short compositions or informal writing, you must pay careful attention to grammar, punctuation, spelling, and overall construction. You must also be concerned with organizing your material so that it is presented in a logical manner. The major stages involved in the process of writing a short composition are: preparing to write, writing the rough draft, revising the rough draft, and proofreading the final copy.

General Guidelines

PREPARING TO WRITE

1. *Choose a subject that is familiar to you.*
   Most beginning writers find that it is easier to write about familiar things. Search your experiences for interesting subjects, look through newspapers for ideas, or look around you for an interesting topic.
2. ***Organize your thoughts by making an informal outline.***
   Example:

TACOS

I. Ingredients needed:
   A. Tortillas
   B. Meat
   C. Cheese
   D. Lettuce and tomatoes
   E. Onions
   F. Sauce

II. Procedure for making:
   A. Cook and season meat.
   B. Chop other ingredients.
   C. Fill tortillas.
   D. Heat tacos.
   E. Add other ingredients.

III. How to eat:
   A. Atmosphere
   B. No utensils

DRILL

Choose a subject or topic about which you would like to write, drawing from your own experiences and knowledge. Some possibilities are: hobbies, pets, vacations, interesting buildings, peculiar customs, superstitions, or any other topic that interests you.

Prepare and type an informal outline on the subject you have chosen. Save the outline; you will need it throughout the section on composition.

General Guidelines

COMPOSING A ROUGH DRAFT

1. *Compose or type quickly*; put your thoughts on paper from your outline.
2. *Concentrate on content*; at this point, don't worry about grammar, punctuation, or mechanics. Let the thoughts flow. Concentrate entirely on converting the outline to sentences and paragraphs. Occasionally you may find that you have failed to include an important point in the outline. If this happens, by all means add it to the composition.

Task 21

Half sheet; 10 spaces between columns, double space body

Reference: p. 295

METRIC CONVERSION TABLE

T.S.

Fluid Ounces	Milliliters
D.S. 1 oz	30 ml
4 oz	120 ml
6 oz	180 ml
8 oz	240 ml
10 oz	300 ml
15 oz	450 ml

Task 22

Full sheet; 10 spaces between columns, double space body

AVERAGE CLASS GRADES

Class	Grade
Accounting	A
Shorthand	A
Typing	A
Geography	A
Biology	B
English	B
Chemistry	C
Music Theory	C
Home Economics	D

Task 23

Full sheet; 10 spaces between columns, double space body

CLASSES AND PROFESSORS

Course	Name
Beginning Shorthand	Dr. ~~Missel~~ missling
Economics 111	Dr. Ellickson
Advanced Typing	Dr. ~~Lambert~~ Johnson
Physical Education	Dr. Wigglesworth
Accounting	Dr. ~~Ozzello~~ Ozello
Psychology	Professor Manning
Statistics	Professor Graine

arrange courses in alphabetic order

3. ***Keep potential readers in mind.*** As you type, try to visualize your reader(s) and keep the level of language geared to them.
   Example:

   TACOS

   Tacos are a lot of fun to make and eat. They are easy to make at home and do not take a lot of work. The tortillas can be purchased . . .

   * * *

   When you have eaten your first taco, you will agree that tacos are good.

   As you can see, the sentences are not structured; the thoughts and content are more important in a rough draft.

DRILL

From the outline that you composed in section 1, type a rough draft. Remember—do not worry about mechanics. Concentrate on ***content and converting your outline into sentences***. When you have finished your rough draft, set it aside for a couple of days.

General Guidelines

REVISING THE ROUGH DRAFT

1. *Evaluate the material carefully*. Read the composition several times. Examine every word and sentence. Sometimes it helps if you read it aloud; you will be amazed at how errors and offending phrases come to light. Mark any changes you wish to make.
2. *Every word should pertain to the topic.* In a short composition, there is no room for irrelevant sentences.
3. *Checklist for revision*:
   a. Is the introductory paragraph interesting and useful?
   b. Are the sentences and paragraphs coherent and clear?
   c. Do the sentences and paragraphs flow with smooth transitions?
   d. Is the sequence a logical one?
   e. Do your sentences provide some variety?
   f. Are the word choices precise and descriptive?
   g. Is every comma justified?
   h. Do the verb tenses correspond to each other properly?
   i. Is every word spelled correctly?
   j. Are words capitalized correctly?
   k. Are there any misplaced modifiers?

DRILL

Evaluate your rough draft carefully, using the revision checklist. Mark the necessary corrections on your rough draft. If you are in doubt about something, consult a dictionary or an English grammar handbook.

General Guidelines

PREPARING THE FINAL COPY

1. *Typing the final copy*
   a. Use white paper of good quality.
   b. Type on one side only.
   c. Double space between lines of text.
   d. Indent the first line of paragraphs.
   e. Set margins for a 6-inch line.
   f. Center the title.

Task 19

Half sheet; 5 spaces between columns, double space body

SPORT ACTIVITIES BY SEASONS

Spring	Summer	Autumn	Winter
Baseball	Car Racing	Duck Hunting	Basketball
Bowling	Fishing	Grouse Hunting	Handball
Fishing	Golf	Football	Hockey
Swimming	Softball	Soccer	Swimming
Tennis	Swimming	Softball	Trapping
Track	Tennis	Swimming	Wrestling

Task 20

Full sheet; 5 spaces between columns, double space body

DELTA ZETA SORORITY
MEMBERSHIP LIST

NAME	MAJOR	YEAR	GPA
Dianne Deering	Office Administration	Junior	3.4
Cathy Brown	Marketing	Junior	2.7
Mary Swehla	~~Undecided~~ Biology	Sophomore	3.0
Denise Rogney	Marketing	Junior	2.8
Kathy Kluesner	Management	Junior	2.8
Mary Millot	Elementary Education	Sophomore ~~Junior~~	2.9
Margaret Minsloff	Special Education	Junior	2.3
Lori Pues	Special Education	Senior ~~Junior~~	2.2
Kathy Mason	Business Education	Junior	2.5
Cory Coonen	Special Education	Junior	2.9
Sally Fruend	Secondary ~~Elementary~~ Education	Junior	2.8

2. *Proofreading the final copy*
   a. Proofread the copy carefully ***before*** you remove it from the typewriter.
   b. Check for mechanics, spelling, and typographical errors.
   c. Read slowly.

DRILL

Type the final copy of your rough draft. Be sure to proofread it before you take it out of the typewriter.

Task 17

Full sheet; 5 spaces between columns, double space body

Reference: p. 293

ANNUAL FIELD AND STREAM FISHING-CONTEST WINNERS

← T.S.

Species	Angler	Location
Largemouth Bass	Wallace Barnhoeft	Green Lake, WI
Florida Bass	Betty Rucker	New Port, FL
Redeye Bass	Jimmy Rogers	Lager Creek, GA
Rock Bass	Emmitt Robinson	Jacobson, KY
Smallmouth Bass	Tom Justice	Danawha, WV
White Bass	Ted McLaughlin	Nacimiento, CA
Crappie	Kenneth Gentry	Marshall, IL
White Crappie	Glen Fletcher	Glendale, IL

← D.S.

Task 18

Half sheet; 5 spaces between columns, double space body

FAMOUS SCULPTURES

Sculpture	Location
The Great Sphinx	Giza, Egypt
Charioteer of Delphi	Delphi, Greece
Michelangelo Buonarroti	St. Peter's, Rome
Virgin of Paris	Notre Dame Cathedral, Paris
Amida Buddha	Kamakura, Japan
Mask of Horns	Tervuren, Belgium
Auguste Rodin: The Thinker	New York, New York
Marine Corps War Memorial	Arlington, Virginia

Straight-Copy Skill Building Module

One of your goals for this course is to improve your straight-copy speed and accuracy. This module contains four types of material:

1. Alphabetic review
2. Timed short-drill material
3. One-, three-, and five-minute straight-copy timed writings.

Now that you have mastered the keyboard, your instructor may have you spend the next few class periods building your speed and accuracy. You will probably be directed to this module frequently throughout the course.

Alphabetic Review. Sixteen sentences and one timed writing are presented for each letter of the alphabet. You may use this material both for developing speed and for developing accuracy:

1. Accuracy development—if a particular letter of the alphabet causes you problems (you consistently type another letter instead of the one you want), use this material for reinforcement practice in eliminating the error.
2. Speed development—words in the English language are composed of ***digraphs*** (two-letter combinations) and ***trigraphs*** (three-letter combinations). The more fluently you can type these combinations, the faster you will type. Use this material to develop your speed to higher levels.

The procedure you should use when using this material is to:

1. Take a one-minute timing on the paragraph. Determine the total number of words and the total number of errors.
2. Determine your practice goal. Concentrate on:
   SPEED—if you had no more than one error
   or
   ACCURACY—if you had two or more errors
3. Type the ten sentences ***concentrating*** on your individual practice goal.
4. Take another one-minute timing on the paragraph. Determine speed and accuracy. Compare with your first timing. If you improved according to your goal, proceed to another section emphasizing another letter. If you did not improve according to your practice goal, type the sentences again. Remember—concentrate on your individual goal. Take another timing on the paragraph. Compute the words and errors. In either situation—either you improved or you did not—move on to another section. (Return to the section emphasizing this particular letter tomorrow.)

Timed Short-Drill Material. The material in this section may be used for either 15-, 30-, or 60-second timings. You may use it for either speed or accuracy development.

Determine the amount of time you will be typing (15, 30, or 60 seconds). Move to the right-hand side of the page and identify the particular column of the time you will be typing. Proceed ***down*** that row of figures to the one that represents the "words-a-minute" rate you think you can average a minute. Type the material to the left of the figure. If you complete the selection before time is called, it means that you averaged at ***least*** that many words a

Task 14

Full sheet; 5 spaces between columns, double space body

LEGAL TERMS RELATED TO SELLING

contract	essential elements	competent parties
enforceable agreement	mutual assent	legal agreement
consideration	cooling-off period	sale of goods
contract to sell	conditional sale	consignment
bailment	bailor	bailee
express warranty	implied warranty	full warranty
agent	principal	agency
express authority	implied authority	apparent authority
liability	misbranding	monopoly
unit pricing	fair-trade laws	endorsement

Task 15

Half sheet; 5 spaces between columns, single space body

WORDS INDICATING HAPPINESS

prosperous	favorable	fortunate	successful
bright	wealthy	optimistic	healthy
refreshing	victorious	triumphant	secure
nice	pleasant	charming	elated
cheerful	satisfied	joyous	peaceful
gleeful	content	appreciate	attractive
beneficial	jovial	delighted	exhilarated

Task 16

Full sheet; 5 spaces between columns, triple space body

American Male Painters

Audubon, John	Hart, George	Pierce, Waldo
Cole, Thomas	Henri, Robert	Pyle, Howard
Davis, Stuart	Hicks, Thomas	Shahn, Ben
Earle, Ralph	Kuhn, Walt	Sloan, John
Fuller, George	Marin, John	Stella, Joseph
Grosz, George	Melchers, Gari	Tiffany, Louis
Harding, Chester	Moran, Edward	Weber, Max

minute. Next go to the following material (which is longer) and attempt to complete it before time is called. Keep progressing down until you cannot complete the selection in the given time.

If you are using the material for SPEED development, don't worry about errors—make your fingers fly. If you are using the material for ACCURACY development, concentrate on accuracy; attempt to finish the selection, but do not proceed down to the next selection until you can finish the selection within the time allotment ***with no more than one error***.

One-, Three-, and Five-Minute Straight-Copy Timed Writings. These selections are to be used for 1-, 3-, and 5-minute timed writings. They are placed in order from the easier to type to the more difficult, according to ***Syllabic Intensity***. Syllabic Intensity (S.I.) is an approximate indication of how difficult material is to type. The lower the S.I., the easier the material is to type; the higher the S.I., the more difficult it is to type. The S.I. indication is illustrated on each timing directly beneath the timing number. You may find this S.I. indication helpful in your skill-building process in several ways:

1. If you are on a typing "plateau" (just can't seem to type any faster), select lower S.I. material. It will help your fingers move faster.
2. If you are typing "out of control" (lots of errors), select higher S.I. material. It will help your fingers slow down.

When taking timings, your goal will be to improve either your speed OR your accuracy. REMEMBER—you must concentrate on one or the other. Your goal will probably change daily—or even several times during a particular class period. You may wish to use the procedure outlined below for your daily routine for speed or accuracy development:

1. Take a timing, typing at a "comfortable" rate. A comfortable rate is when you are typing at your normal rate, not pushing for speed or driving for accuracy.
2. Determine your words-a-minute (*wam*) rate and number of errors.
3. Take another timing. But before you do, set a specific goal:

   If the number of errors you made on the first timing was not over the maximum set by your instructor for an "acceptable" timing, concentrate on SPEED.

   If the number of errors you made on the first timing was over the maximum set by your instructor for an "acceptable" timing, concentrate on ACCURACY.
4. Continue this procedure, readjusting your goal or keeping the same one when taking each timing.
5. Remember—the secret to building ***both*** speed and accuracy is concentration.

Task 12

Full sheet; 5 spaces between columns, double space body

COMMON BUSINESS TERMS

accounting	advertisement	agenda
air freight	appointment	data processing
bailment	barter	brand
broker	capital	commission
consumer	consumption	credit
discount	ethics	form letter
human relations	income	merchandise
money	organization	personnel
quota	retail	salary
textile	verification	warehouse

Task 13

Full sheet; 5 spaces between columns, double space body

CITIES WITH OVER 100,000 TELEPHONES

Akron	Albuquerque	Amarillo	Atlanta
Austin	Baltimore	Boston	Calgary
Canton	Charlotte	Chicago	Cleveland
Dallas	Dayton	Detroit	El Paso
Flint	Gary	Halifax	Houston
Indianapolis	Las Vegas	London	New York
Omaha	St. Louis	Seattle	Tampa

Straight-Copy Skill Building

Now that you have mastered the keyboard, it is time for you to improve your basic speed and accuracy. The next section of the book contains three types of materials:

1. Alphabetic review
2. Timed short-drill material
3. 1-, 3-, and 5-minute straight-copy timed writings

You will want to build your straight copy speed and accuracy as high as possible before moving on to production typewriting; therefore, you must concentrate while completing the drill work. Be relaxed, and don't worry; you will be able to build your speed and accuracy quite easily with the right mental attitude.

Your instructor will inform you what type of drills and timings you will be doing in this phase of the course. After moving on to production typewriting, there will be times when your instructor will have you return to this section of the book to refine your straight-copy skills.

Alphabetic Review

Words in the English language are composed of "digraphs" (two-letter combinations) and "trigraphs" (three-letter combinations). An example of a very common digraph would be the combination of the letters ***t*** and ***h***. You want to be able to type the ***th*** combination as quickly and smoothly as possible. If you type the word ***the***, you will find it quite easy to type, and you probably typed it quite quickly. You also want to be able to type the ***th*** combination rapidly when you type ***them***, ***those***, ***that***, and other words with ***th***.

In this section of the book, each letter has been paired with the other letters in the alphabet. You will find a series of words, several sentences, and a timed writing emphasizing each combination for each letter.

Do not attempt to type too long on the material in this section. It should be used for a limited amount of time each day. You may also find the material an excellent aid if you are having trouble with a "consistent" type of error—one that you keep making over and over. An example of a consistent error would be when you type ***n*** for the ***m*** most of the time. If you have any consistent errors, turn to the page(s) devoted to the letter(s) causing your problem and type through the material. IMPORTANT—concentrate while typing the material, and you will find the error being eliminated.

Margins
Elite: 20 and 80
Pica: 12 and 72

IMPORTANT: Use the same margins for the entire straight-copy skill building section.

EMPHASIS ON

A

1 abide absorb slab babbly jab act actor race bacon react ace
2 adapt adult lead stead lead affect affirm leaf crafty rafts
3 again agony cage eagle image aisle aim airport pairs praise
4 all along alarm goal coal ballast amble among clamps flames
5 ant annex angel annoy angle divan scan apple apply apes man
6 The actor felt he could adapt to the lead in the first act.
7 All hangars at this airport are leased from a crafty agent.
8 Jac's amazing kayak, with ample ballast, will always align.

----1----2----3----4----5----6----7----8----9---10---11---12

Task 10

Half sheet; 10 spaces between columns, double space body

Actors in
Well-Known Movies

Gregory Peck	The Omen
Burt Reynolds	The Longest Yard
Richard Dreyfuss	Jaws
Jack Nicholson	One Flew Over the Cuckoo's Nest
Al Pacino	The Godfather
Woody Allen	Love and Death

General Guidelines

THREE OR MORE COLUMN TABLES

Typing a table with three or more columns follows the same procedure as typing a table with just two columns. Select the guide line (longest line) in all columns; count the blank spaces between all columns.

Task 11

Full sheet; 5 spaces between columns, double space body

DATA PROCESSING TERMINOLOGY

Keypunch	Printer	Magnetic
File	Disk	Card
Blocking	Address	Tape
Computer	Access	Data
Program	Symbolic	Random
Source	Object	Sort
Read	Write	Sequential
Density	Flowcharting	Punch

5 5

opaque aquarium arrive arise earth glare stark aspen feasts
atlas attack path float watch audit author caulk fraud haul
avail avoid avert cave pave gawk drawer straw hacksaw borax
waxen axle relax galaxy climax flax pray pay say day hazard
blaze amaze raze gaze crazy lazy faze someday straw betrays
An annoying, angry ant ran at an angle around the aquarium.
The author asked his arch rival why he hated autumn feasts.

That happy play has an amazing climax. It affects all 12
watchers. The absorbing last act is majestic with an array 24
of blazing ideas. Any apt actor who speaks well may apply, 36
and qualify for a part. The author is apt and adept; he is 48
ascending toward a lavish share of awards. He is aware and 60
now aims to avoid mistakes in reaching goals ahead. He had 72
to fire an agent who made absurd demands and squandered all 84
the cash on large purchases. He is a fraud and a hoax. 95

EMPHASIS ON 

bag bar bat bake back batch battle urban debar combat cabin
be bet bed beg beam bean bear tribe robe probe globe lumber
big bit bird bike bias birth cabin cubic debit robin mobile
object subject objectives objects subjects subjected object
blow blab blur blob bleak block able cable noble blur amble
A big black bear lumbered about a cabin begging for a bite.
The mobile beam on the bike probed the biased urban battle.
Bo scrambles and climbs to noble objectives; he is capable.

----

lamb limb dumb numb tomb bamboo climb amber combo scrambles
boy box bow boat boil bolt bomb hobo slob robe about abound
bran brat brig brag brim brace derby zebra arbor orbit herb
bombs gabs rubs grabs lambs slabs swabs bombs climbs scrubs
bug bus but buy bulb bulk bump abuse rebut album doubt bugs
That amber blob is blurred; it is about a block away or so.
That bragging boy is a brat when he grabs and climbs lamps.

While the boys scrambled about, Barb baked a big batch 12
of bars. The bleak cabin needed a good scrubbing. She had 24
been able to buy a bulb for the amber lamp. The bright and 36
probing beam chased the gloom away. A cheery robin sitting 48
on a limb called to other birds. The tasty leg of lamb and 60
herb dressing would soon be ready. The slight haze of that 72
day made the family feel an abounding sense of peace. Soon 84
they would climb aboard the boat and return to urban life. 96

----1----2----3----4----5----6----7----8----9---10---11---12

Task 7

Half sheet; 10 spaces between columns, double space body

Distribution of Migratory Waterfowl

Pintail	437,300
Shoveler	240,300
Green-winged teal	123,800
Gadwall	58,200
Widgeon	50,700
Redhead	23,100
Canvasback	8,000
Lesser Scaup	6,700
Ruddy	2,100

Task 8

Half sheet; 10 spaces between columns, double space body

Names and Ages ← single space
of the Leonard Wild Family

Leonard	48
Mary	46
Thomas	26
John	19
Rosemary	18
Karen	16
Robert	14
Shirley	13
Kenneth	11

Task 9

Half sheet; 10 spaces between columns, double space body

Care Units at
Sacred Heart Hospital

2nd Floor — Neurological	6 " — Surgical
3rd " — Maternity	7 " — Pediatrics
4th " — Psychiatry	8 " — Orthopedics
5 " — Medical	9 " — Rehab/Medical

EMPHASIS ON

1 chew chat chief change choice ache much each ditch anchored
2 tack pick lick flock crackle beckon bucket sticky reckoning
3 city cinch cider civic civil acid sack beach grace city can
4 claw clip club claim climb clause muscle declined enclosing
5 coil comb coin coast cough column scope scold discover acid
6 The scarred cedar canoe is wrecked and anchored on a beach.
7 It is a cinch that the sticky civil clause needs reckoning.
8 Pick up the tacks and the bucket, and climb into the attic.

9 acquitted acquire lacquered acquaint acquittal acquisitions
10 cram crib crop crash crawl cruise acre scrap scrub scrolled
11 fact tract actor edict eject elect erect actual cactus duct
12 cub cult curb curse curve curfew acute scuff focus occurred
13 cyst cycle cider cymbal cypress cyclone agency saucy policy
14 I discovered the lacquered comb on a beach along the coast.
15 Carlo scans the scenic acres of cactus as he cruises along.

The chief and the crew did concur. That ocean cruiser 12
could be launched at once. It was a fact, the cursed cruel 24
pirates had discovered their recent acquisition of sacks of 36
gold coins. As the panic arose, the excited crew scanned a 48
curving cedar grove along the coast. Those ancient cypress 60
boards crackled as the excess load caused the boat to crawl 72
and cease almost all movement. The acute crisis excluded a 84
quick chance at a complete escape. 91

EMPHASIS ON

1 day dare date dance soda sedan sandbar roadbed sedan adapts
2 den deal deaf dense tide cadet handful wilder handcuff date
3 edge hedge ledge badge judge pledge adhesive withdraw wedge
4 did dish audit media radio candid idle madly candle bundles
5 kidney sadness midnight kindness abundant boundary lavender
6 An aide can adapt those new sandbags to deal with the tide.
7 The steadfast judge pledged his badge to the stodgy widows.
8 In the bedlam, did that spindly windmill fall in the ditch?

9 doe done dorm doubt adorn ardor widows windpipes headpieces
10 dry drape draw drop adrift bedrock odd adores handsome drag
11 dual duck dunce adult undue advises adverse adjust adjourns
12 dwarfs dwindles roadways headway goodwill hardware sandwich
13 dynamic dynamo dynamite tidies body bandy candy handy cedar
14 The stampede at midnight had the doe in a state of sadness.
15 A handsome adult cannot have a dull wardrobe or drab shoes.

----1----2----3----4----5----6----7----8----9---10---11---12

Eau Claire State, Wisconsin	6
Pikeville State, Kentucky	7
Marymount, Kansas	8
St. Mary's, Texas	9
Shepherd College, West Virginia	10

Task 5

Full sheet; 10 spaces between columns, double space body

single space < The First Ten Presidents of the United States } all caps

triple space <

George Washington	1
John Adams	2
Thomas Jefferson	3
James Madison	4
James Monroe	5
John Quincy Adams	6
Andrew Jackson	7
Martin Van Buren	8
William Henry Harrison	9
John Tyler	10

Task 6

Half sheet; 5 spaces between columns, double space body

CLASSIFICATION OF TELEVISION PROGRAMS

1. Adventure	2. Children's movies (ts)
3. Comedy	4. Documentary
5. Drama	6. Featured films
7. Game shows	8. News, daytime
9. News, evening	10. Public affairs
11. Religious	12. Sports
13. Variety	14. Specials

Even the steadfast must agree some birthdays are dandy 12
with abundant kindness and others seem to be dark and dull. 24
Adults have undue qualms when adjusting to growing older; a 36
child stampedes through the days with wild abandonment. No 48
doubt a small child full of daring and dynamic energy deals 60
with life in a candid way. All the bedlam and wild dashing 72
dispels any dim attitudes of dour adults. To avoid adverse 84
thoughts on birthdays, spend them with children. 94

EMPHASIS ON

1 each earn ease east easy earth steak swear sweat knead seal
2 fence farce dances places hordes prudes tired timed devotes
3 effect effort effective efficient eggplant eggshell egghead
4 eight either eject reject sleek else elder elbow elect else
5 emit ember empty emery embark item enact endow enjoy endows
6 It is easy to earn a good economic way of life by each one.
7 The barge is wedged under the bridge; it's eight feet high.
8 The elder clerk objected to the sleek jeweler's empty case.

9 enact endow enjoy enter entry blend scent epic creeps peeps
10 equal equip equalizes requires erase erect erode erase epic
11 essay escape escort pressed etch ether etching sheet ethics
12 even ever evades shrewd chew few drew threw exam chew every
13 eye exact exert honey money chimney antifreeze index freeze
14 To enact that epic opera, one is required to erect scenery.
15 Did either team argue at a league event about vague ethics?

That eccentric thief scares me. He swears that he did 12
not steal the wealthy lady's jewels. He is either embarked 24
on an evil route of crime, or else he is a cheap cheat. At 36
best, he knows how to effect an illegal entry. Each of his 48
creeping moves suggests a false value. He prizes money and 60
exerts extra effort to obtain it. In any event, it appears 72
that he has the stolen jewelry. He is edgy and down. Does 84
he wish to change the tale? 89

EMPHASIS ON

1 fad fan far fat fact fade fail daft taffy affect safe graft
2 fee few fear feat feed feel chafe safe defray deface defeat
3 fir fit files fir fills films life lifts swift edify strife
4 flag flap flat flaw flog flop self half wolfs rifles shelfs
5 influxes infant infects infield inflames inflates infringes
6 It is a fact, Fannie is fat; she feeds her face with taffy.
7 File all the facts and filled films in that fireproof safe.
8 Before the fox infects the folks, get a rifle from a shelf.

----1----2----3----4----5----6----7----8----9---10---11---12

Task 2

Full sheet; 10 spaces between columns, double space body

all caps

CAPITALS OF SELECTED STATES

T.S.

Montana	Helena
Arizona	Phoenix
South Dakota	Pierre
Kansas	Topeka
New Mexico	Santa Fe
Minnesota	St. Paul
Wisconsin	Madison
Tennessee	Nashville
Pennsylvania	Harrisburg
Hawaii	Honolulu

D.S.

10 blank spaces between

Task 3

Half sheet; 10 spaces between columns, double space body

COST OF MAINTAINING AN OFFICE

Rent of Space	$2,400
Lighting	210
Heat	240
Water	28
Janitorial Service	900

Task 4

Full sheet; 10 spaces between columns, double space body

NATIONAL ASSOCIATION OF INTERCOLLEGIATE
ATHLETIC RANKINGS

Single space when main heading requires more than 1 line

Alcorn State, Mississippi	1
Grand Canyon, Arizona	2
Kentucky State, Kentucky	3
Gardner-Webb, North Carolina	4
Fairmont State, West Virginia	5

(cont'd. on next page)

9 for fox foam foil fold folk sofa offers enfold often before
10 fry from frog fret fresh fruit surf turf dwarf wharf defray
11 chefs fumes reefs calfs puffs leaps golfs leafs huffs cuffs
12 left daft loft aft deft raft lifts soft sifts adrift drafts
13 fun fur funds fuse fusses fudge bluffs scuffs buffet fluffy
14 That flag flapped in the infield before that football game.
15 The chefs fumed as the fresh fruit on that buffet softened.

Often, before we face all the facts, our own fears may 12
begin to defeat us. Life seems filled with deep strife and 24
failure. We become inflamed at the self and fuss in small, 36
futile ways. This is the time to stop fretting and inflate 48
our ego with a firm, fresh start. Swiftly, our spirits are 60
lifted. We have a fine feeling of being free from cares or 72
defeat. 73

EMPHASIS ON  **G**

1 gain gait gale game gang gave cigar vague agree again agent
2 badge ledge fudge judge wedge badges sledge gadgets pledges
3 ghost thigh coughing might eight fright slighted background
4 glad glee glow glue glare glass beagle gargle toggle vulgar
5 gnaw gnash signs goals goats gold golf gone gowns bingo gin
6 Gail agrees with that judge; vague pledges are not genuine.
7 The legal agents will get the genuine badges for all games.
8 Eight glad beagles glared at the slight girl on the ground.

---

9 goals goats gold golf gone gowns bingo grab gray grid gowns
10 length outgrowth shotgun nightgown outgoing bagful tagboard
11 gulf gust guess guest guides gauge ought laughs rough sugar
12 foggy dingy clergy zigzags gangway ragweed wigwam quagmires
13 baggy energy oxygen hygiene bodyguard gym dingy edgy stingy
14 The grim golfers merged on the driving range by the lagoon.
15 The large gray barge surges and swings against the bridges.

The gang is going to get a bag of hamburgers after the 12
game. That last game was grim. The team's energy ought to 24
be higher, as the rough gripping coughs are gone. The last 36
germs have given way to good health through better hygiene. 48
It is my guess, that the girls will get eight goals. Those 60
grounds are genuinely great. The eighty dingy lights which 72
were illegal, glow brighter. When the gala bash is in full 84
swing, the manager will give the guest a grand gift. 95

----1----2----3----4----5----6----7----8----9---10---11---12

General Guidelines

LEADERS

A *leader* is a row of periods that helps the eye travel from one column in a table to another. Leaders permit reading from one column to another without moving the eyes up or down. Leaders are usually used when there is a considerable amount of blank space between columns. To insert leaders:

1. Leave one blank space after the first entry. Check to see if the first period will begin on an "even" or an "odd" space.
2. Type periods, leaving a blank space between each.
3. Stop periods two or three blank spaces in front of the next column.
4. On each succeeding line after typing the left-hand entry, space once and:
   a. Determine if the periods will "line up." In other words, are you on the same type space (even or odd) as the first line?
      (1) If so, begin typing the row of leaders.
      (2) If not, space once and then begin typing leaders.

```
First . . . . . . . . . . . . . . . . . . . . . . .    $100.00
Second  . . . . . . . . . . . . . . . . . . . . . .    $ 75.00
Third . . . . . . . . . . . . . . . . . . . . . . .    $ 50.00
Fourth  . . . . . . . . . . . . . . . . . . . . . .    $ 25.00
```

Notice that on some lines there will be one blank space before the leaders begin, and on other lines there will be two blank spaces. Remember—you must always have at least one blank space. Never begin the leaders without spacing at least once.

Following is a series of tasks to be typed. Notice that in this section there are reference pages indicated to the left of each task.

1. If this is the first time you have typed this particular kind of task, turn to the reference pages(s) and:
   a. Read the information.
   b. Complete the drill material section (if any is provided). The drill will give you practice before typing the task.
2. If you have already typed this kind of task before (and consequently have already read the information and completed the drills), refer to the reference page only if you need help in completing the task.

Task 1

Full sheet; 8 spaces between columns, double space body

Reference: p.289

JOSEPH I. SOWINSKI FAMILY >all caps

ds

Birthdays

ts

Joseph	November 18
Geraldine	April 2
Michael	January 6
James	February 26
Paula	October 4
John	February 25
King	February 18

ds

8 blank spaces between

EMPHASIS ON

hair hail hard harm harp hash hatch haste harsh happy haven
chap chin chip char chat chef inch each bench latch notches
head heals hear here herb herds health hearth height hectic
hide high hike hilt hint hire hitch hinder thigh thing whip
hock hold home hook hope hour shoot shore chokes shot chore
The hardwood benches are chipped; have Herb haul them here.
A head chef is happy when he chops herbs into healthy hash.
Hide that thing; it has harsh hooks that hinder his chores.

---

bash dish gush mash lash mesh bush fresh harsh shall shines
bath math both lashing booths filth tenth tight death south
wheat wheels whales wharfs where while sighs wholes wheezes
withhold hill hinge inhibit orchid thief thirst whip within
shower howl hostile hole hone shrimp threw thread throws ha
Shall Holly hire Hal to chop those high bushes at her home?
A white whale wheezed and was near death in the south tank.

Those happy chaps hope to hike to the rough shore. It 12
is eighty miles from their homes. If harsh weather hinders 24
them, each has a small tight tent. While they are enroute, 36
the head chef can prepare wholesome meals. Breakfast might 48
be ham and eggs or hotcakes. A hearty lunch of milk, fresh 60
fruit and sandwiches will be eaten in haste. The plans for 72
night meals include meat, mashed potatoes and other things. 84
They are healthy and hearty. They may catch fresh fish. 95

EMPHASIS ON

I

aid aim air aide bail hail hair bribes tribes fibers libels
ice icing icicle iceberg click crick price thick voice dice
did die dig dim brief sieve grief thief wield spiels yields
igloo ignite ignore ignorant eight light tight cigar slight
alike spike strikes likely ill illegal illusions child oils
Big pieces of ice on the bridge made it slick and slippery.
Did that guide brief the alien aide in detail about fibers?
Ignore that ignorant person; he is a drifter or a criminal.

---

ill illusion bilk broil child frail inch index inept brings
prior audio radio onion strip swipe script cipher ship snip
ire ironic birth weird wired itch itself ditch trait writes
drive alive divan diver waive civil strive river viva fixes
sixty dizzy seizes sizzles quiz mixture prefixes sixty itch
Equip the ship's cabin with a radio and wire the islanders.
Rich had an itch to fix a pizza; he's a genius in kitchens.

----1----2----3----4----5----6----7----8----9---10---11---12

General Guidelines

FINANCIAL TABLES

Financial tables are similar to other tables and are typed in column form. A financial table usually contains one column (describing various items) that is much longer than the other columns. As a result, the spacing between columns differs from that of other types of tables. In a financial table:

1. Leave six to eight spaces between the largest column and the following column.
2. Leave two to three spaces between all "money" columns.
3. Align dollar signs and decimals.

Financial statements are usually dated

American Institute of Certified Public Accountants Foundation

STATEMENTS OF CHANGES IN FUND BALANCE

Years Ended August 31, 19 , and 19

	1981	1980
Income:		
Income from securities, less custodian fees	$ 27,677	$ 26,616
Gain (loss) on sale of securities	7,742	(946)
Contributions received for support of accounting research program	6,795	119,233
Total	$ 42,214	$144,902
Disbursements:		
Contributions to American Institute of Certified Public Accountants:		
For library expense	$ 4,000	$ 4,000
For costs of accounting research program	276,885	215,189
Stationary, postage, and other expenses	27	361
Total	$280,912	$219,550
Net (decrease) in Fund	$238,698	$(74,648)
Fund balance, beginning of year	643,039	717,687
Fund balance, end of year	$404,341	$643,039

2-3 spaces

align $ signs and decimals

6-8 spaces

That stadium by the river isn't immune to crime. Last 12
night a thief seized an expensive radio from a taxi driver, 24
who was picking up a rider. The thief ditched the radio in 36
the river. A diver fished it out quickly. The weird irony 48
is that the thief is out of jail on bail. It's likely that 60
he bribed an ignorant civil aide. In spite of this, he has 72
been identified. His alibi is nullified. Irate voices are 84
being raised to swiftly close the issue. 92

EMPHASIS ON

1 jab jam jar jaw jay Jack jade jail jazz ajar jaunt majority
2 adjourn adjacent adjustments adjournments adjusts adjusting
3 jet jeep jeers jerks jests jeans ejecting jelly jerky jewel
4 jig jilt jinxing jigger jigsawing jingle lockjaw disjointed
5 enjoy inject injure injury conjure enjoyment object subject
6 Jack adjusted the jerky jeep by ejecting the jammed object.
7 Jane's jewel is a jade; she just lost it on the jaunty jet.
8 That jumpy jigsaw is jinxed and could injure Jean; junk it.

----

9 enjoy inject injure injury conjure enjoyment object subject
10 job jog joy join joke joint banjo enjoy jokers jolly jockey
11 jug jumps junks just jury judges juices juicy jumpy juggles
12 deject projection reject inject jingle journey enjoy joyful
13 majority enjoin disjointed joggle joker job juice junk just
14 Mix a jug of juice with that jelly and pour it in jam jars.
15 John and Jonas enjoy jogging on the journeys to their jobs.

The object of the jury is to judge that subject and to 12
be just. The adjacent jail adjoins the courtroom. A jaunt 24
to the jail is not enjoyable. The judge's job is to remain 36
judicious when the final judgment must be made. All jurors 48
must be adults; juveniles are not allowed on the jury. The 60
jokers who jeer and jest will be ejected. Adjournment will 72
take place after justice has been resolved. 81

EMPHASIS ON

1 karat kayak polka linkage packages alkali stockade workable
2 inkblot backboards cheekbone workbooks whiskbrooms backbone
3 keen keeps kettle keeper kennel kernel speaker baker marked
4 kill kick kiln kind king kiss skid skill skimp skirt asking
5 fickle pickles sickly inkle buckles tinkles cackles tackles
6 Kevin marked the package of workbooks for the keen speaker.
7 Karl keeps the workable kayak near a kettle by the kennels.
8 Hector needs a checkup; his skull was kicked as he skidded.

----1----2----3----4----5----6----7----8----9---10---11---12

General Guidelines

BOXED TABLES

Tables containing an unusually large amount of data may require the typist to leave only a few blank spaces between columns. When this occurs, it is a common procedure to type the table in "boxed" form. The only difference between the "ruled" and "boxed" forms is the addition of vertical lines. These lines help the reader to differentiate between columns.

The vertical lines may be inserted using either of the following two procedures:

1. After typing the entire table, position the notch of the cardholder in the center between a column. Insert the tip of a pen into the notch. Hold firmly. Turn platen so paper moves upward. Repeat for each blank between columns. (See page 165.)

2. After typing the entire table, remove paper from machine. Turn paper sideways and insert. Position paper so the center of two columns is on the line of writing. Insert the line using the underscore key.

HIGH SCHOOL COURSES COMPLETED BY CPS CANDIDATES

Name of Course	Numbers of Semesters Completed						
	0	1	2	3	4	5 or more	Average Number of Semesters
Accounting	432	102	376	9	83	12	1.265
Business Arithmetic	604	80	238	18	69	5	.903
Business English	699	70	161	6	71	7	.728
Business Law	853	87	69	0	5	0	.242
Clerical and Office Practice	528	97	230	18	117	24	1.213
Data Processing	979	23	9	0	0	3	.067
Economics	774	132	96	1	8	3	.376
General Business	691	58	168	8	71	18	.811
Shorthand	252	37	267	25	380	53	2.458
Typewriting	95	72	333	29	426	59	2.858

milkman bookmobile workman checkmate lockjaw folktales skid
knee knit knob know knew knack knife knock knights weakness
reckon beckon hickory reckoning backgrounds backhand markup
awkward backward clockwise silkworms buckwheat weekday ward
husky sticky whacky skyline milky risky hockey jerky cranky
The markup of the bookmobile's stockpile will be a jackpot.
The husky boy is awkward and jerky in the hockey workshops.

That old workman knows his work is risky. His kind of 12
weakness is in his knees. He checks the skyline stockpiles 24
from an airplane cockpit. It is awkward to go backwards or 36
clockwise and keep a keen eye out for cracking walls. When 48
he has checked the skyline, he has breakfast. His business 60
is on the edge of bankruptcy. He needs a workable new plan 72
for a husky bankroll. Perhaps he will hit a jackpot soon. 84

EMPHASIS ON L

lad lag lap law lay lack lake latch blame clash blaze clank
elbows albino toolboxes welcome ulcer falcon alcove welcome
bald fold mild builds field child leads less lest plea leaf
blends calf golfs myself behalf engulfs shelf itself golfer
indulges algebra bellhop railheads pilgrim lid lie lip lien
A lad squelched the blaze as the sailboat lay in an alcove.
Lay the toolbox by the mailbox and latch the balcony doors.
Aldo pleaded with the child to leave the calf in the field.

---

blind slim bliss folk chalk stalk balky silky milky polkas
helm film balmy almost almond salmon lob logs loafs blonds
slow gulps helps scalps helper false pulse impulse bolster
halt jilts belt bolt hilt silt lube luck lurk lumps lunges
salve solves valve shelves calves lymph imply hilly twelve
The blond culprit's impulse was false; he lost the jewelry.
A lone helper bolstered a slow cavalry by loaning a helmet.

Long ago, pilgrims loved to indulge in blunt folklore. 12
Tales, sometimes false, were told with glee daily. One old 24
tale included a blazing clash of sailors in balky sailboats 36
on a bottomless lake. The last sailor alive was a lad that 48
was blind. As he lay clinging to a slim balsa log in filth 60
and slimy silt, the leader's falcon led help to him. Balmy 72
days followed as the lad's leg healed slowly and the salves 84
applied to his eyes let the light in. 91

----1----2----3----4----5----6----7----8----9---10---11---12

5. Type the following five columns of words; determine how far to tab over for each column so the layout will look attractive.

book	eggs	seem	less	need
wall	food	cuff	full	toss
sees	fill	tool	hood	door
skill	apple	petty	sleep	shall

Repeat the drill if the layout is not attractive. Typing tables using a tab grid takes some practice.

General Guidelines

RULED TABLES

There are certain situations when tables are included on a page with other typewritten information. When this occurs, the tabled information looks better if presented in "ruled" form. The rulings also set the table apart from the other material on the page.

A ruled table contains a line before and after the column headings. Another line appears after the last entry. To insert the lines:

1. Use the underscore to type the line.
2. Single space before typing the line and double space after it.
3. The line begins at the left margin and extends to the right as far as the last letter of the longest entry in the last column.

GAMMA LAMBDA CHAPTER OF SIGMA SIGMA SIGMA

ts

ds

Name	Office	Class
Caron Hollingsworth	President	Senior
Peggy Peterson	Vice President	Junior
Pam Snyder	Treasurer	Sophomore
Linda Shelly	Secretary	Junior
Chris Erheart	Education Director	Senior

ss ds ss

Note: some style manuals recommend using a double underscore the first time a ruled line appears.

Name	Office	Class

EMPHASIS ON 

1 mail make made mast math meet melts mess match smash images

2 dumb limbs bombs lamb combs tombs gumbo bamboo climbs amber

3 me merge melon medal mercy meter member amends smear farmer

4 mike mint mind mist might merge mixed smile admire famished

5 hymn column autumn chimney amnesty remnant amnesia comforts

6 Thelma and Mel may land a medal at the member's math match.

7 He made amends for smashing the melons and making the mess.

8 Mike might mope more if the campus merger is in the autumn.

9 mode mopes moon more moist months mouse among smooth amount

10 damp jump camp lump romp dump limp champ campus dampen hemp

11 ramrods comrades stemware teamwork bantam warmth stormdoors

12 clumsy flimsy whimsy hamster steamship whimsical bottomless

13 much must munch smudge amuse may anatomy enemy roomy steamy

14 Cam camped among the remnants of an old chimney for months.

15 The warmth and teamwork of the comrades might make enemies.

The merger of an academy and the campus may take place 12
in the autumn. It might bring mixed emotions from some men 24
and women. The stormy economic issue might make an anatomy 36
class impossible at the academy. Some who must commute for 48
months are not amused; they feel that the merger is clumsy 60
and dumb. There is not much warmth among the enemies. The 72
teamwork is not smooth. The amount of stormy mass meetings 84
must be diminished. An amendment must be made. 93

EMPHASIS ON 

1 nag nap nail name nasal nasty naval snag canal gnash annals

2 inch fence munch winch since lunch bench dunce hence concur

3 bend fend fund bind ponds gland net new next cane lane nine

4 confer enfolds informs infects unfolds lung sang lunge song

5 nice niece night knits knife units banjo enjoys injury nine

6 Nancy and Andy concur; nail the fence to the round benches.

7 An unfair king informed the next landlord of the needy men.

8 Cranky Nina's nice pink banjo is nicked; she plans revenge.

9 pink wink lank brink plank enlist unless inboards unlatched

10 nod not now none noun know snort censor inside ransom knobs

11 went cent ninth agent absent nurses numbers snub menu notes

12 anvil invade invert converts inward unwind jinx invite jinx

13 anyway deny penny ebony vinyl bronze stanza conquer unbolts

----1----2----3----4----5----6----7----8----9---10---11---12

Tab Grids

To increase your production skill in typing tables, you should master the use of ***tab grids***. A tab grid is created by presetting tab stops (usually four or five spaces apart) between the Left and Right Margin Stops.

Tab grids are used to reduce the time spent determining the space between columns in tables. For a six-column table, you simply "eye" the layout and tab to a preset stop for the column. If the next document consists of only four columns, it is not necessary to clear previous tabs and set new ones. You simply tab to preset stops in the grid that will provide an acceptable layout for these columns. Example of a four-column table using a tab grid:

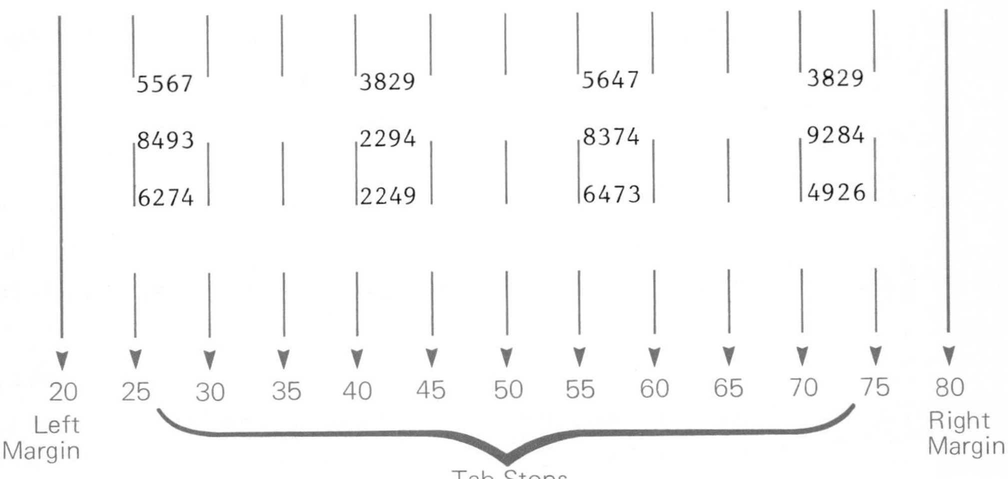

Example of a six-column table using the same tab grid:

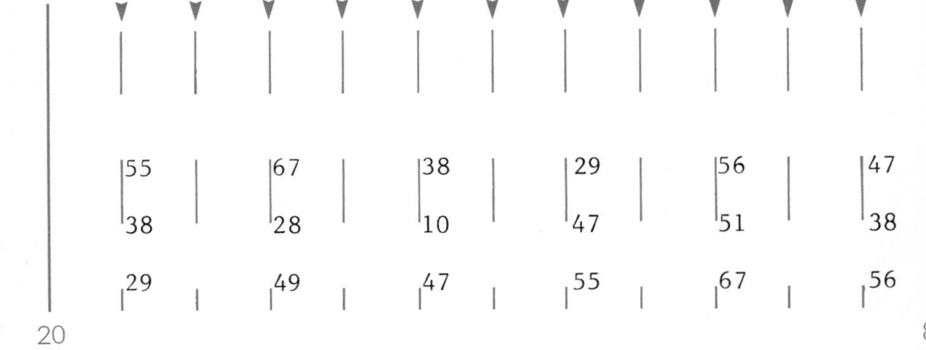

DRILL

1. Move margins to edge of paper.
2. Clear all tab stops.
3. Preset tab stops every 5 spaces.
4. Type the following three columns of numbers; determine how far to tab over for each column so the layout will look attractive.

4567	6319	7865
3218	4769	3290
4118	3901	2129

(cont'd. on next page)

At sunset, it is nice to enjoy dining out on a bank of 12
a river. Unless uninvited insects and lots of ants come to 24
the picnic, you will certainly unwind. As those soft night 36
sounds enfold you, frenzied inward nerves and the decisions 48
that haunt you drain from your mind. You may enjoy napping 60
on a nearby bench. Next, swing into action, after your nap 72
and inhale much air into your lungs. Unpack the nice lunch 84
and munch away. Don't deny yourself this experience. 95

EMPHASIS ON O

1 oak boat coal loaded coach toasted oboes obey obtains globe
2 occurred ocean occasional clock odd odor dock dodge octopus
3 of off often office offense proof offer clogs logical clogs
4 oil ointment coils boils coin join book cook evokes strokes
5 old olive cool bolts scolds color omit only omission commas
6 An oblong clock was loaded on the odd boat at the old dock.
7 That lofty cook knows that soggy cookies are moist or oily.
8 Omit the olives and onions from the omelet and let it cool.

9 one once onward bond bonus snoop open optic opera cop troop
10 orbit order ornate orange bore forge cost frost chose ghost
11 others dot froth quote cloth scoot our out ought tour broth
12 oval ovens over coves remove proven own owe bow crow drowns
13 ox box toxic fox oyster decoy enjoy cozy doze frozen nozzle
14 Ora ordered an ornate organ for her house; it's not costly.
15 The boss chose the boring quotes from a book of poor prose.

An oldtime cowboy often chose a lonely life out on the 12
open range. Hoards of prowling foxes snooped among the old 24
cows and their young ones. Owls often hooted as an obscure 36
and occasional sound annoyed them. The food was often cold 48
and soggy. Cooking his food and boiling his coffee over an 60
orange-hot fire offered some enjoyment, however. Through a 72
long night his mournful songs poured out. He was a proven, 84
loyal worker who overcame obstacles or coped with problems. 96

EMPHASIS ON

1 pan paw pay park paved pail palm pauses spaces spades spare
2 topcoat upcoming soapbox lapful cupful helpful upgrade plea
3 peg pen pep peer peck peak peel peeve cape type mope drapes
4 nymph lymph graph cipher hyphen orphan phoned nephew gopher
5 pin pit pine pier pipe pile pill pinched spill spicy impish
6 Peg's helpful nephew peered into the topcoat for a pet pen.
7 Phyllis can spare a cupful of soap and a pail if Pa phones.
8 Peter spoke with poise as the spring prom plans progressed.

----1----2----3----4----5----6----7----8----9---10---11---12

General Guidelines

LONG HEADINGS

To center a column head that is longer than the guide line in a column:

1. When backspacing to set the left margin and the column head is longer than the longest item in the column, the heading becomes the guide line.

METRIC CONVERSION TABLE

Fluid Ounces	Milliliters
4 oz	120 ml
6 oz	180 ml
8 oz	240 ml

Guide line (longest item in column) — Guide line (longest item in column)

2. Set the left margin and space forward ONCE for each character and space in the guide line and the blank spaces between the columns. Set the tab stop. Return, type the first heading, tab, and type the second column heading.

```
Fluid Ounces      Milliliters
            123456
```

3. Return to the left margin. It will now be necessary to move the left margin so that the column entries will be centered under the typed column heading. Use the same process that you learned for short headings of spacing into the guide line to find the center. (Space forward ONE for every TWO).

```
Fl ui d_ Ou nc es →
```

Your machine is now positioned at the exact center of the guide line.

4. Backspace ONCE for each TWO characters and spaces in the longest item in the column.

```
← 4_ oz
```

5. Move the left margin to this point.
6. Tab to the first stop. Space in to the center of the guide line.

```
Mi ll il it er →
```

7. Backspace ONCE for each TWO characters and spaces in the longest item in the column.

```
← 12 9_ ml
```

8. Set a new tab stop at this point. (Remember to remove the "old" stop.)

DRILL

Practice centering each of the following:

Residence	Condition
City	New

Surname	Position
Smith	3

9 ply plea plum plot plan plow plug plane splint employ maple
10 pool post poke pore pole port pond price spree spring sprig
11 lapse elapses upset glimpsed slipshod depth adopts slipshod
12 punt pull push sports output upward sleepwalk spurts inputs
13 stopwatch equipment lumpy occupy zippy sloppy choppy snippy
14 Skippy, the snippy pup pulled and pushed the floppy puppet.
15 Push the pulsing pump upward and stop the ship's equipment.

If the plan for upgrading the park in the spring would 12
be accepted, the plot could be plowed now. Adept employees 24
can plant the maple and pine trees by the pond with the new 36
equipment. Those sprigs of spindly aspens should be pulled 48
up, or snipped off. The spaces for pleasant picnics should 60
be paved, as well as the paths to the ponds. The chipmunks 72
and other park pets won't be upset and peevish if the plans 84
are to plant all spots with pleasant posies. 93

EMPHASIS ON

1 acquits acquire lacquer acquire acquaint acquittal question
2 equal equip equity equate require request equator equipment
3 liquid unique antique tourniquet technique earthquakes quid
4 inquiry inquire conquer delinquent conquest aquarium quells
5 squad squat squaw squid squab squash squashy squadron quake
6 The queen questioned the unique request for that equipment.
7 Quentin acquired the liquid lacquer for the quaint antique.
8 The squad questioned and quizzed the quiet delinquent lads.

9 quip quit quiz quack quilt quire quest quick quiet question
10 quadrangle quadruple quaff quagmire quail quake qualitative
11 qualification quarantine quarrel quarry quarters quickening
12 quiet quill quiver quorum quota quotation quote quintuplets
13 quilt quinine quintuple quiz quizzical quorum quench quiets
14 The squadron ate squab and squash after the quick conquest.
15 The inquisitive delinquent inquired about the antique vase.

At the request of an old acquaintance from the Equator 12
city, quotations for equipment will be sent quickly. These 24
earthquakes ruined her unique antique aquariums. The eight 36
techniques of restoring them require liquid lacquer and the 48
equipment in question. Answer her inquiry and quote a good 60
price to her. Ask her to reply quickly as to the quantity. 72
The question of her delinquent account must be settled when 84
the equipment is ordered. 89

----1----2----3----4----5----6----7----8----9---10---11---12

General Guidelines

COLUMN HEADINGS

A heading above a column identifies what is contained in that column. To make the heading appear attractive within the table, it is centered over the column. In some cases the heading may be shorter than the longest line in the column; in other cases it may be longer than the longest line in the column.

Short Heading	Long Heading
Washington, D.C.	Johnny

General Guidelines

SHORT HEADINGS

To center a short heading over a column:

1. Set the left margin and tab stops for columns as usual.
2. Type the title; triple space.
3. Beginning at the left margin, space forward ONCE for each TWO characters and spaces in the guide line.

   Wa sh in gt on ,_ D. C.

   Your machine is now positioned at the exact "center" of the first column. Consider this position to be the "centering point" of that column.
4. Backspace ONCE for each TWO characters and spaces in the heading.

   Sh or t_He ad in g

5. Type the heading and underscore it. You have now centered the heading over the guide line of the first column.
6. Tab to the next column and repeat the process. Continue until you have centered a heading over each column.
7. Return to the left margin and begin typing the body of the table.

DRILL

Practice centering each of the following illustrations.

City	State
Los Angeles	Minnesota

Name	Sex
William	Female

EMPHASIS ON

1 rap ran race rave raise cram fray curbs herbs carbon adverb
2 arch marches mercy pierces arcade card bird board hard lard
3 red reel rein rent rested reach bore turf surf dwarf whales
4 urge barge large forge merge purge rip rig rich ridge organ
5 cork dark hark perk shirk fork curls twirl early snarl fork
6 Did he crash into the boards in the arch or the hard rails?
7 The risky merger of those rich firms raises grim arguments.
8 The large barge surged in the surf to reach the coral reef.

---

9 dorm firm warm army swarm storms barn burn worn torn kernel
10 rot row roof rove room roast crooks carp harp corps carpets
11 burst first harsh marsh horse worst dirt berth birth quarts
12 nerves served surveys serving curving rut ruler drug shrubs
13 vary weary spry vary bury jury wary berry curry entry marry
14 Shirley really should burn that pair of torn burlap drapes.
15 The heartless crooks robbed the poor farmer at the airport.

A rapid rise in industrial prices is normally absorbed 12
by the consumers. Large firms that need raw materials work 24
hard to realize a profit. It is a marvel that the poor and 36
weary customer can afford to purchase services or products. 48
The grim race to raise prices must be curbed early. Scores 60
of workers who earn small salaries find no mirth in fierce, 72
sharp rises in the market. 77

EMPHASIS ON

1 sad safe salt same assay disarm disbar obscure disband scat
2 scan scald scorn disc essay ascend wisdom misdeals misdoubt
3 see seat self served tensed those misfit satisfy misfortune
4 disgust disguise disgorge misguide she shy sing shale trash
5 sin sir sit six since basis visit music ski skin skill husk
6 The flashy salesroom she visited was a disgraceful mistake.
7 That obscure essay serves no purpose and scorns all wisdom.
8 The dismal aspects of some prisons are a dismay to newsmen.

---

9 sly slam slim slang measles smug smart dismal dismay smells
10 snag snow snug snares parsnips snicker sob soak some solved
11 spy spins star stay speak aspens squat squad squash squeaks
12 step stew stir most chest taste subs sues sums usury absurd
13 swab swap swim sweat answer daisy fussy flimsy glassy swats
14 Speak to that smug spy and ask if the cameras were smashed.
15 That squad of unusual skaters has an absurd and lousy star.

----1----2----3----4----5----6----7----8----9---10---11---12

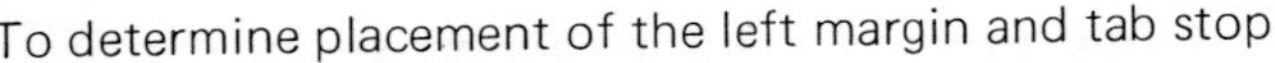

To determine placement of the left margin and tab stop:

1. Select the ***guide line*** in each column. The guide line is the longest entry in the column. In the example on the previous page, the guide lines would be:

   `LTD Landau      Continental`

2. Determine the amount of blank spaces to leave between columns (remember—it is usually best to leave between 5 and 10 blank spaces.) In this example, use 6.

   `LTD Landau      Continental`
   `          [123456]`

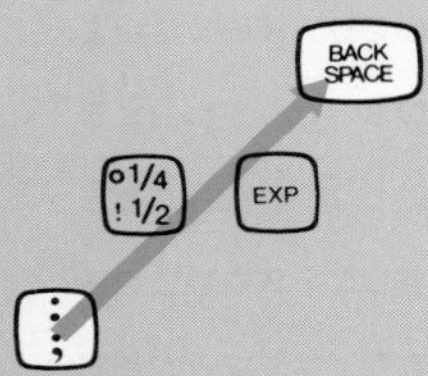

3. Move to the center point of the paper.
4. Using the guide lines and 6 blank spaces, backspace ONCE for every TWO characters and spaces in the material.

   ← LT D La nd au 12 34 56 Co nt in en ta l

5. Set the left margin at this point.
6. To set the tab stop in the proper location, space forward ONCE for each character or space in the first column and the blank spaces between columns.

   LTD Landau123456 →

7. Depress the Tab Set Key.
8. Return to the left margin and begin typing the first line.

DRILL

Practice determining the location of the left margin and tab sets for the illustrations below. Each illustration shows you the longest line of each column and the number of spaces to leave between the columns. Follow the general guidelines for horizontal centering that you have just learned.

`Washington, D.C.      Seattle, Washington`
`                [123456]`

`President        Leslie Sorenson`
`         [12345678]`

`Scottish Terrier      Poodle`
`                [123456]`

`Janie          William`
`     [12345678910]`

A sulky, sad loser is scorned by most of us. A dismal 12
loss or misfortune doesn't have to end in disgrace. Surely 24
most folks in such spots show disgust at a loss. But, such 36
persons briskly squelch those feelings and smile, as living 48
goes on. There is always a lesson to be learned from every 60
mistake or loss. Stay in the driver's seat and see all the 72
good things that come along. Solving basic problems easily 84
is necessary to reduce tensions. 90

EMPHASIS ON 

1 tag tan tab tale talking tall tame taste stains stamp fatal
2 catch wretch blotch clutch watch witch sketch switch stitch
3 tee tea teen tell tend tent tear tense baste skate foretell
4 the them then than that thing earth tie tin tip tilt sticks
5 atlases antler costly settles bottles cattle gentle battles
6 Catch that tall, thin teen and tell her to watch the store.
7 The wretched witch tended to foretell fortunes in tea cups.
8 The gentle cattle are too thin; the earth's thaw is timely.

- -

9 toes too top toads toils tomb tone tooth stole stone actors
10 try trot true trek track tribe tub tug turf turn tutor tusk
11 two twig twin twice twine twirl twisting between bewitching
12 type typewriter typical typewriting rusty nasty witty dusty
13 waltz quartz nutmeg catnip catsup itself stool still guilty
14 The strutting entry of the actor stumped the top two stars.
15 The toiling tutor might try trimming the time of a student.

- -

Tenseness while typing causes costly mistakes. Take a 12
gentle tip or two and practice them as you type. Watch out 24
for fatigue--a tired typist tends to clutch at the keys and 36
doesn't tap them with a gentle touch. Twirling or twisting 48
in your seat is a fatal trick at the typewriter. Talking a 60
lot as you type is first on the list of bad techniques. Do 72
not try too hard, as this often turns those keys into some- 84
thing terrible. Don't let the typing mistakes continue. 91

EMPHASIS ON 

1 quails squaw quakes equals squab usual square squash actual
2 scrubs doubts chubby public submitting double subtle rubber
3 chuck pouch truce plucks lucky cloud crude judge audio ugly
4 cruel guess undue value query squeak squealed tongue accrue
5 bluff stuff fluff scuff snuff stuffy muffin suffered fluffy
6 Chuck is lucky; that subtle judge is too grouchy in public.
7 The quiet guy is suffering as that ugly cough gets rougher.
8 I quess that tough guide has taught thousands about values.

----1----2----3----4----5----6----7----8----9---10---11---12

DRILL

Practice the roll-back method of vertical centering on the material below. Do not worry about horizontal placement; this is a drill for you to perfect your skill in vertically centering. Use a full sheet of paper for each. After typing each one, remove the paper and look at the typed copy. Does it look vertically centered? If you have followed the correct procedure, it will be centered on the page.

Single space	Double space	Triple space
one	one	one
two	two	two
three	three	three
four	four	four
five	five	five
six	six	six
seven	seven	seven
eight	eight	eight
nine	nine	nine
ten	ten	ten

General Guidelines

HORIZONTAL CENTERING

After determining the vertical placement of the table, center the heading in all capital letters and triple space. You are now ready to determine where the left margin and tab stop must be set for horizontal placement. Assume you are going to type the following problem:

MAJOR AUTOMOBILES

Chevelle	Torino
Nova	Mustang
Firebird	Sunbird
Seville	Continental
Fury	Camaro
Monaco	Duster
LTD Landau	Impala
Gremlin	Hornet

9 ugly gouge tough laugh taught build quiet juice quire quirt
10 ulcer caulk pulse tulip vault adults faulty results helpful
11 umpire umbrella clump mumps gummy serum humans humid summer
12 undo union unite unity uncle until count undue blunt bounce
13 urges used utility puzzle author buzz ukulele furrow spouts
14 The faulty vault caused undue upheaval at that institution.
15 Count that adult's pulse; he has a clump in his upper lung.

The impulse to judge individuals quickly causes faulty 12
results. It is unwise and unfair to jump to conclusions in 24
a hurry. Actually, a useful guide to a sound understanding 36
of humans is to quietly assess the situation. A subtle and 48
thorough query can subdue doubts and evaluate behavior. An 60
ugly and cruel deduction about another's values could cause 72
undue suffering. 75

EMPHASIS ON 

1 van vat valid value vapor vacant valley rival canvas invade
2 vex very veto venue verbal veneer versus lively invent live
3 vie vim via visa vigor visit virus victor divide vivid evil
4 vow vocal volume voyage savory volatile flavor evoke convoy
5 salve chevron vulgar vulcanize vying heavy anchovy invading
6 The evil virus invaded the valley of very lively villagers.
7 Is it valid if Van vetoes the valuable division of travels?
8 A savory flavor is evoked in veal by serving anchovies too.

---

9 convoy evoke favorite provoke vocation volley devote flavor
10 avoidance devoted favor flavorful ivory revoke voile volume
11 favorable havoc voluntary vow divorce favored invoice vocal
12 activity civil evidence living provide revival serving vise
13 preview provided revive shaving video vigil novice shelving
14 Violet vows to avoid the vocalist, as his volume is vulgar.
15 Victor moved Vera's valuable vases to an attractive alcove.

A visit to a village in a quiet valley gives vitality, 12
vim, and vigor to the tired individual. Nothing rivals the 24
valuable voyage to revive the spirits. Heavy problems seem 36
to vanish and vexing tribulations evaporate. Vivid visions 48
of a diverse way of living evoke valuable impressive vistas 60
of rest. Save those fevered nerves and prevent grievous or 72
adverse tribulations. Endeavor to take advantage of events 84
which elevate the spirits; you deserve the very best. 91

----1----2----3----4----5----6----7----8----9---10---11---12

General Guidelines

TYPEWRITER PREPARATION

To prepare the machine for typing of a table using a standard sheet of paper 8½ inches wide:

1. Move the Left Margin Stop to the left as far as it will go.
2. Move the Right Margin Stop to the right as far as it will go.
3. Clear all Tab Stops.

General Guidelines

VERTICAL CENTERING

There are two popular methods of determining vertical placement: (1) the counting method, and (2) the roll-back method.

1. Counting Method. This is the method of vertical centering that you have already learned. Review pages 81-82.
2. Roll-back Method. The roll-back method of vertical centering is much faster to complete than the counting method. It is based on the same principle as horizontal centering: back ONE for every TWO. In using this method you go to the vertical center of the paper (line 33) and come back up the paper one line for each two lines in the information to be centered.

To vertically center using the roll-back method:

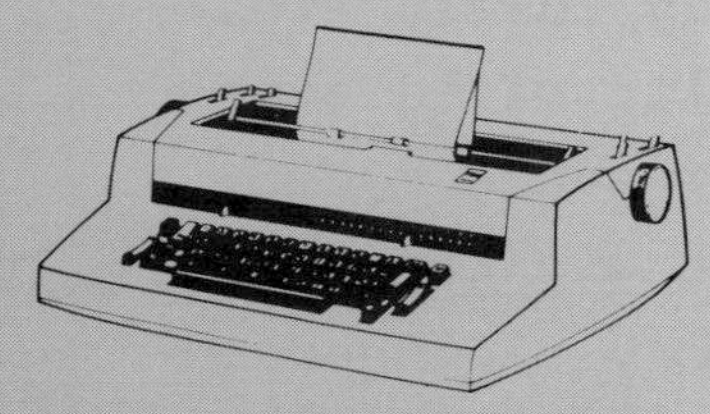

1. Insert a sheet of paper.
2. Insert the paper so that both ends of it meet (the paper bail must be against the paper).

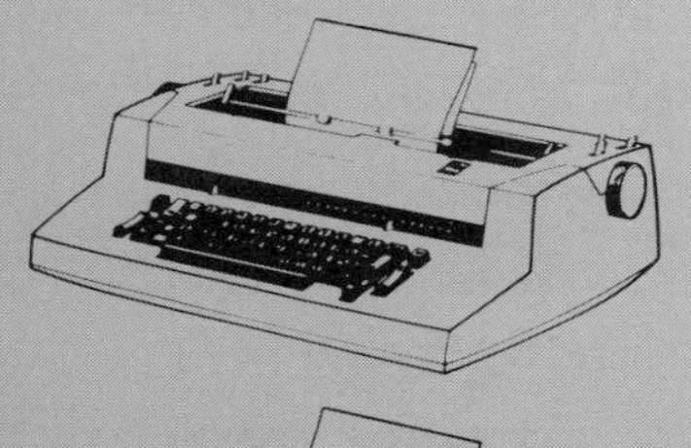

3. Advance the paper three more lines. This is line 33, the vertical center of the paper.

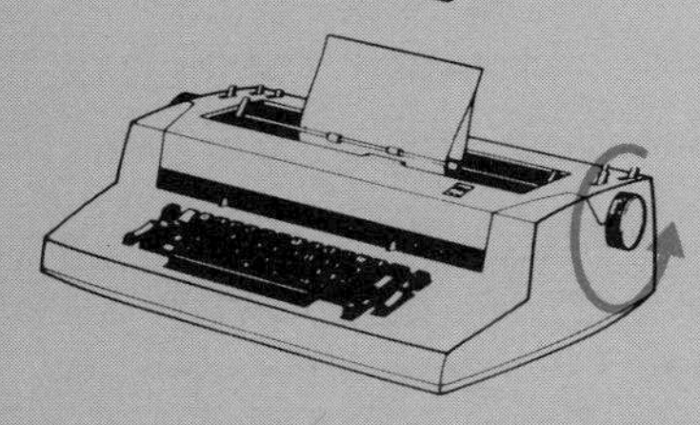

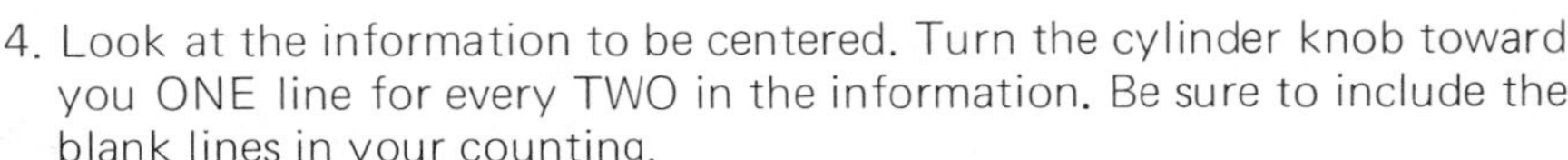

4. Look at the information to be centered. Turn the cylinder knob toward you ONE line for every TWO in the information. Be sure to include the blank lines in your counting.

EMPHASIS ON 

1 was war ward wave wash wary warp waste swarm reward freeway
2 cowboys cowbirds cowbell crowbars snowbell awful endowments
3 crowd rowdy dowdy chowder powder dawdle slowdown fellowship
4 wet week went weld were well west wedge sweat flower unwind
5 who why whom whim when whip whales cowhide nowhere cowhands
6 That rowdy crowd swarmed on the west freeway and went wild.
7 Wes was awarded with twelve weeks of rest as a wise reward.
8 Who wired the winch to that warship and prowled in the bow?

9 wit wig win wild wine wish winch wired twice swift swindles
10 drawl growl crawl prowl lowly scowl bowl acknowledge lawful
11 clown spawn drown blown crown brown frowning disown yawning
12 woe won wow wood worn word work worst sword plywood sawmill
13 wry wrap wrist wretch wreck browse newsprint newscast words
14 The swift cowhand will win the lawful crown on the weekend.
15 The wry newsman writes wretched words on the wrecked wagon.

The news on the network newscast might spawn a winning 12
wealth of followers. If the newsman can draw a wider range 24
of viewers, his rewards are power and wealth. Watchers and 36
followers of a witty newscaster are won when the daily news 48
is written well. It is not a waste to rewrite the worst of 60
interviews when witless words can wreck a well-planned show 72
or review. He who dawdles in the newsroom will not work or 84
write very long. His award will be awful reviews. 94

EMPHASIS ON 

1 exam example vexation examine exacting exalt exact exacting
2 excel excess exhibit excavate exceed excuse exclude excites
3 axes vixen exerts fixed waxen mixed boxer relaxing executed
4 exhale exhaust foxhole exhibit exhaustion exhibition exhort
5 axis taxi toxic exiles pyxie anxious anxiety flexible exits
6 Examine the exhaust on the taxi and fix that vexation soon.
7 The excellent boxer put on an exciting exhibition at least.
8 The sixteen extra oxygen mixtures exploded next to an exit.

9 expire expenses express explored expanses exploded expended
10 next text mixtures sixteen extent extended extreme textures
11 luxury luxuriant exuberant exult oxygen xylophone exquisite
12 mixed execute vixen exert relaxed deluxe exhibits auxiliary
13 toxic pyxie approximate anxious exile peroxide axle extreme
14 exacting examination vexation example exclusion excise exam
15 boxer deluxe relaxed axe executive fixed vixen waxen fixing

----1----2----3----4----5----6----7----8----9---10---11---12

Tables

A large amount of the information processed in business consists of enumerated data. Because of the very nature of this type of data, it is often difficult and impractical to present in sentence and paragraph form. Most typists and readers prefer numerical data presented in table form. A table is a combination of centering and tabulation. An attractive and readable table is usually centered vertically as well as horizontally on either a full or a half sheet of paper.

General Guidelines

SIMPLE TABLES

1. Tables may be typed with single, double, or triple spacing.
2. A simple table consists of a heading(s) and two or more columns of material.
3. There is a triple space between the title and body.
4. There are usually 5 to 10 blank spaces between columns.
5. In a column consisting of words, the left edge is justified; for a column of numbers, the right edge is justified.
6. The width of each column is determined by the widest item in the column.

Title: the title identifies the table and is typed in all CAPITAL LETTERS.

Spacing (triple space after title) (Body usually double spaced)

MAJOR AUTOMOBILES

TS

Columns: the listing of data in two or more columns. The column is as wide as the widest item, usually separated by 5 to 10 spaces

Chevelle	Torino
Nova	Mustang
Firebird	Sunbird
Seville	Continental
Fury	Camaro
Monaco	Duster
LTD Landau	Impala
Gremlin	Hornet
Dasher	Audi Fox
Aspen	Caprice

ds

5 to 10 Blank spaces

Body: the horizontally centered columns.

An example of relaxing exercises is the flexing of lax 12
muscles daily. Excess anxieties are exhausting to all that 24
are under extreme pressure. Programs of extensive, complex 36
exercises are a vexation. Most experts agree that exertion 48
to exhaustion is wrong. A flexible, yet exuberant exercise 60
involves exhaling noxious air and inhaling oxygen. 70

EMPHASIS ON 

yap yard yarn yawn yacht yardage yardarm kayak royal voyage
hybrid daybed keyboard playback honeybee bodyguard crayfish
bicycle cyclone boycott gaudy hydrant honeydew rhythm royal
yea yes yet year yelp yearly yellow yearbooks layers dryers
joyful boyfriend oxygen zephyr hyphens anyhow yuletide yule
That shy bodyguard daydreams in the yard about motorcycles.
Yes, buy the layers of yellow nylon for the sunny skylight.
A yearbook is a joyful memory of happy years and busy days.

- -

nymph rhyme symbol enzyme payment symptom anymore syrup wry
yipping drying prying style asylum nylon payload nylon very
cynic lynx canyon dynamic dynamite gyrates pyramids hayrack
type typical flypaper cysts always myself systems analyzing
byword everywhere eyewitness pyxie analyze paralyze plywood
That lynx is in that broken shanty beyond the rocky canyon.
A systems analyst is typical as he analyzes all efficiency.

- -

A hobby is healthy for nearly everyone. A typical and 12
unhealthy symptom of an extremely busy employer is anxiety. 24
You may enjoy skydiving or flying as an activity. Yet, you 36
might fill joyful and happy days by playing the rhythm of a 48
song on a piano keyboard. Analyze your daydreams and style 60
your life to trying entirely new ways of doing. I, myself 72
have always enjoyed a foray into the dynamic joy of geology 84
as a hobby. Prying through mystical layers of dirt is fun. 96

EMPHASIS ON 

czar zany pizza hazards wizards lizards bazaars stanza ooze
zest zebras zesty zeppelins gazes dazes zeal hazel pretzels
zig zip zinc zing zippy zigzag zipper zither zillions sizes
guzzle nuzzle frazzle puzzle muzzle sizzles dazzles nozzles
zoo zone zoom zombi zoology razors zodiac rezone horizontal
A dozen zesty spices are drizzling and oozing from a pizza.
The dazed czar gazed at the zillions of lizards and zebras.
The zodiac puzzle makes the dazzled wizard dizzy and woozy.

----1----2----3----4----5----6----7----8----9---10---11---12

Financing. The cost of the rebuilding project is estimated to be approximately 1.1 million dollars. Federal funding is available. As the major expense will be involved with the removal of dirt so that the roadway goes under the railroad tracks, it may be possible that the railroad can be persuaded to cooperate to the extent of providing a part of the money required for such a rebuilding project.

EXHIBIT B

Traffic Counts

Date	Time	Mad. W of X	Mad. E of X	Dewey S of X	Dewey N of X
10/13	3:00-3:10 P	83	97	29	6
10/13	3:20-3:30 P	84	108	35	9
10/24	12:00-12:10 A	19	13	3	2
10/24	8:45-8:55 A	48	91	6	9
10/24	1:10-1:30 P	50	68	20	5
10/25	10:25-10:35 P	50	23	13	1
10/25	10:45-10:55 P	27	21	8	1
10/29	10:15-10:25 P	48	31	6	5
11/09	1:00-1:10 P	58	61	13	2
11/09	1:20-1:30 P	47	62	15	4
11/15	10:00-10:10 P	38	33	11	6
11/15	10:15-10:25 P	52	21	11	6
11/15	10:40-10:50 P	41	25	7	17
11/16	8:20-8:30 P	37	79	5	3
11/20	2:30-2:40 P	104	102	26	9
11/21	1:10-1:20 P	64	86	10	4
11/24	9:50-10:00 A	41	70	8	4
11/24	10:40-10:50 A	62	85	10	4
11/24	2:10-2:20 P	73	84	24	1

9 **cozy hazy lazy crazy woozy tizzy fuzzy dizzy jazzy zucchini**
10 **antifreeze bronze craze dozer frozen graze penalize baptize**
11 **magazine zinc zippered zing zinnia zip zither zillion dozes**
12 **pretzel recognize snooze zealot horizontal zoom razors lazy**
13 **cozy crazy hazy zombi horizon zoology zodiac magazine zings**
14 **A fuzzy buzzard zoomed crazily on that horizon with a zest.**
15 **Did Buzzy and Hazel realize the prized magazine was seized?**

That wizard of zoology amazes zillions of zoo visitors 12
daily. The dazzling display of puzzling zebras daze people 24
of all sizes. Lazy lizards zigzag into a dizzy speed on an 36
oozing pond. Monkeys puzzle many folks by the crazy antics 48
on the hazardous horizontal bars. The graceful gazelles in 60
brown graze in the park plazas. After a day at the zoo, it 72
is fun to stop at a bazaar and have a zesty pizza. 82

----1----2----3----4----5----6----7----8----9---10---11---12

Timed Short-Drill Material

The material contained in the next section is to be used for building your straight-copy speed and accuracy under timed conditions. You have used similar material and procedures while learning the alphabetic keyboard.

Procedure: Identify the column heading of the time that you will be typing. Go down the list of figures at the right of the material to the figure that represents the word-a-minute rate you think you can average a minute. Type the material to the left of the figure. If you complete the selection before time is called, it means that you averaged ***at least*** that many words a minute. Next, go to the following sentence (which is longer) and attempt to complete it before time is called. Keep progressing down until you cannot complete the selection in the time given. REMEMBER—for speed: don't worry about errors; make your fingers fly. For speed ***and*** accuracy: attempt to finish, but do not progress down until you can finish the selection with no more than one error.

	Seconds		
	15	30	60
Use a handy airline pocket flight guide.	32	16	
Place those big tickets in the long envelope.	36	18	
The legal people do not want to disagree with him.	40	20	
The trouble with those animals is that they need water.	44	22	
Staple four sheets of paper together in the lefthand corner.	48	24	
Send the second element over to him. I believe he needs it soon.	52	26	
Do not wait to phone me. My major responsibility now is to help them.	56	28	
This magazine is fairly good. It would be better if it had a harder cover.	60	30	15
Please invite both of them. I need to have them determine if they are eligible.	64	32	16

Only short segments of two other city streets approach this volume. Traffic volume is fairly well distributed, however, with the largest volumes being recorded early in the morning and later in the afternoon, corresponding to local industrial shift changes.

Congestion. In addition to peak hour capacities, congestion is caused by four existing conditions:

1. A major delay is created by the at-grade level crossing of the railroad. Heavy vehicular traffic and 15 regular trains and several locals and switching movements each day make it quite evident that the railroad represents a significant disruption to traffic flow.

2. Due to reasons previously mentioned, sharp turns at the Birch Street/ Germania and Germania/East Madison intersections cause a general slowdown of traffic, which often affects traffic flow at the crossing.

3. The combination of steep grades and the at-grade roadway causes congestion, as normal traffic is not able to pass slow-moving traffic. This problem is compounded on East Madison Street where a steep grade is encountered (See Exhibit C).

4. As shown in Exhibit A, Madison Street east of the intersection and Madison Street west of the intersection does not line up. A sharp right turn is also required from Dewey Street northeast onto East Madison Street. As motorists traveling east on Madison Street assume they have the right-of-way, they do not hesitate to cross over the dividing line into the right eastbound lane, often creating potential accidents with Dewey Street motorists.

Accidents. During the past six months there have been 25 accidents recorded at the intersection. With three exceptions, these accidents were all attributed to the at-grade railroad crossing. In one instance a motorist collided with a train traveling on the southbound track.

Proposal

Recommendation. This committee recommends that the intersection be rebuilt as shown in Exhibit D. The grade of Madison Street is considerable in a relatively short distance--an 11% grade (See Exhibit C).

East of the intersection the situation is somewhat improved. The rise over the distance is somewhat less (a 6% grade). Dewey Street is presently extremely steep north of the intersection, and after construction of an underpass (which would lower Madison Street), the slope would be far too steep. It will be necessary, therefore, to complete quite a large amount of dirt removal.

Dewey Street north of the intersection would be blocked off and a turnaround area would be constructed for traffic to park, turn around and go back up the hill (north). Dewey Street is often heavily traveled south of the intersection, and it is a convenient way of merging onto Madison Street going east; therefore it is recommended that Dewey Street remain open at the crossing.

(cont'd. on next page)

	Seconds		
	15	30	60
That tape dispenser is missing. I believe I know who the low person is that took it.	68	34	17
Oil paintings, in many cases, have proven very good investments. We should buy more, now.	72	36	18
The typewriter is broken. Have Dick call the repairman as soon as he returns from the meeting.	76	38	19
There are many fine job openings in the business world. A person seeking one must have good talent.	80	40	20
The doctor is quite busy. If you can, be sure to arrange for our appointment in the very near future.	84	42	21
Going to a meeting can be an enjoyable experience. We might go by car or by plane. Try to go to the meeting.	88	44	22
Vacation time can be exciting. You can either travel or stay at home. Whichever is done, plan to have loads of fun.	92	46	23
The electrical wiring in the house is worn out. We must get an electrician to give us an estimate to repair it at once.	96	48	24
Target shooting is great fun. It is exciting to become active in a sport that one can enjoy. Young and old can participate.	100	50	25
In many towns it is difficult to locate a place to rent. You can usually find something, but it may not be exactly what you want.		52	26
The airport is closed because of poor visibility. We had to land at another city quite a distance away. I hope we can get there soon.		54	27
The owner is doing a study on revising the furniture in our office. I certainly hope that we will be able to purchase some new desks soon.		56	28
The city youths charted their national tour on the map. They plan very carefully and in great detail. Each stop is timed exactly for ten hours.		58	29
Staplers are a necessity in an office. They come in all kinds of sizes, shapes, and forms, designed for all jobs. They also are in different colors.		60	30
The typewriters in the typing room at the school are about worn out. I sincerely hope that there will be enough money to trade them for new ones.		62	31
After turning right at the third corner, you will see the site. Spend enough time analyzing the location so that you will be able to give us a logical report.		64	32
A shy person tends to stay in the background of social activities. This type doesn't make new friends easily. He or she should try very hard to relax in any crowd.		66	33

The objective of the recommendation is to relieve traffic congestion that affects the business and industrial portions of the city, while also providing for safe and more efficient travel.

The Problem

Existing Conditions. Topography and the location of commercial business have primarily determined the character and location of the street network in the immediate area. Because of the steep grades in certain areas, several industries are located on the plateau of the river. As a result, access roads have tended to be located in valleys, where lesser slopes are available. Such locations, however, limit the continuity which results in many jogs and offsets in the street system. For instance, when traveling up the hill on Madison Street motorists must travel in a northeast direction (See Exhibit A).

Immediately after crossing the railroad tracks--which cannot be seen until the motorist is directly upon them--a seven-degree jog to the right must be made. Right turns onto Dewey Street are permitted, but the effort involved to make such a turn is such that many motorists make it improperly and dangerously. The net result is often confusion, danger to both motorists and pedestrian traffic, and generally bad feelings.

Train traffic, which at this point is the main double-track line (main-line) of the CP&W Railroad Line, with several side tracks south of Madison Street, is a serious barrier to automobile traffic and has long been recognized as bad. A separation of grades was planned by the railroad more than 30 years ago, but the expense involved was so great that no steps have ever been taken to carry out the needed reconstruction.

Traffic. The route including Birch Street, Germania Street, and East Madison Street is the only east/west arterial serving the northern half of the city. The use of this particular route has developed due to the industry in the northern part of the city and highway traffic to and from the principally rural areas to the north and east.

Studies have shown travel patterns in the city to be of three basic types: local traffic within the city, travel from outlying regions into the city and returning, and external traffic passing through the city. Industry located in the northern part of the city probably is responsible for the largest part of the traffic. The greatest proportion of traffic to and from these industries originates to the north and east.

There are three routes serving the northeast section of the city from Starr Avenue/Birch Street, Highway 73/Birch Street, and C.T. Highway Q/Birch Street. Of these, because of the construction of a major interchange and viaduct now in progress, the majority of the traffic naturally travels west on Birch Street from Highway 73. A good arterial street connection between this route and the downtown area is therefore vitally important. Traffic studies conducted have revealed the overall average daily traffic using this route is one automobile every 4.5 seconds during the daytime hours, making it one of the highest volume routes serving the central city (See Exhibit B).

(cont'd. on next page)

SECONDS 30 60

He thought he would like a beef hamburger for lunch. However, the roast beef looked better. Unable to decide between the two, he finally took the fried chicken special. 68 34

That lovely song is a smash hit. Although the lyrics are sad, the haunting melody is easy to remember. Maybe the composer will win an award or a grand prize for that talent. 70 35

The old photograph is faded and worn. Can it be restored? It would take an artist many days to fix it. The cost might be expensive. Perhaps that museum curator will restore it. 72 36

The winter skating party was a huge success. The roaring bonfire helped ward off the cold. The children enjoyed the hot chocolate and the roasted weiners. A good time was had by all. 74 37

Take a dose of that medicine every five hours. Also, rest as much as possible. It is a good idea to drink a lot of liquids and eat plenty of fruit. Your cold symptoms should disappear quickly. 76 38

John is fixing up that old cabin. He expects the project to take at least six months. If he shingles the roof and paints the exterior, the results will be amazing. That hillside site is delightful. 78 39

Poor Paul was stranded in the airport lounge all night. The plane he intended to take was grounded because of heavy fog. He was not very comfortable. He was not only cold, but was very hungry and weary. 80 40

Hopefully, the child will not have to stay there much longer. A large hospital can be frightening to such a tiny baby. Although the staff of nurses and doctors are quite friendly, she really wants to go home. 82 41

A good health insurance should be a part of our life plans. One is never prepared for a major illness. But if one should occur, good insurance will ease tensions. Money worries are not a problem when getting well. 84 42

That fine old estate is elegant. Huge trees surround the entire house. The lush green grass is highlighted by masses of brilliant flowers. Inside, there is a huge collection of antiques. Indeed, it is a unique house. 86 43

Because of a severe ice storm, most city residents were without electric power. Many homes had little or no heat. Some people found they were not able to cook meals. The power was restored in most homes by the third night. 88 44

That expert pianist has performed in public for fifty years. Critics have said that she plays as well as ever. Few others have duplicated or attempted the feat. The concert next week, however, will be her last. Be sure you go. 90 45

TABLE OF CONTENTS

Reference: p. 245-46

List of Exhibits

RECOMMENDATIONS FOR THE MADISON STREET CROSSING

This report contains the basic data gathered and analyzed to make recommendations regarding the Madison Street crossing. The recommendation made by this committee strongly supports the rebuilding of the crossing as soon as possible.

Purpose

The purpose of this committee was to study possible alternatives to the traffic problem as it now exists at the Madison Street crossing, make recommendations for an arterial street improvement which would serve the central part of the city, provide access to the downtown area and to major industry, link Highway 73 with the east/west arterial street system across the Chippewa River, and eliminate the serious and chronic problem with the CP&W Railroad traffic.

(cont'd. on next page)

	SECONDS 30	SECONDS 60
Eat three balanced meals each day. Include fresh vegetables, fruit, milk, and meat. Be sure to begin the day be eating a hearty breakfast. Those who skip breakfast usually run out of energy. Be sensible in eating wisely every meal.	92	46
More and more people are beginning to learn about the delights of taking a trip and camping out. The different types and kinds of camping equipment are almost endless. The cost can be quite low or quite high. Select your camp gear soon.	94	47
An automobile can be costly to own. Just to run it requires a tank of gasoline. Other costs such as tires, oil, valves, and minor repairs add to the total bill. Insurance is an added expense. Perhaps it would be wise to take the bus or taxi.	96	48
The design in that fabric is unique. Geometric shapes can be seen as the focal point. Tiny circles add to the stunning work of art. Blues and browns blend in harmony. The hues and tints are a marvel. It is truly a fine example of a great artist.	98	49
A good secretary must be skilled in answering the telphone. A calm and friendly voice puts most callers at ease. Learning to handle calls quickly and efficiently will add to the firm's image. Practice each day on personal calls at home. You can learn.		50
On a bright day when you are bored, make a visit to the local library. You will find exciting books on varied subjects. Hours of leisure time can be spent among those interesting shelves. You might enjoy browsing among the magazines. Get in a reading habit.		51
Many students have great difficulty when taking a test. They simply can't relax. Sometimes a student's mind just goes blank. Studying for a test helps. A good night's sleep is an aid. Just before taking the exam, walk briskly in the outdoors, for a good start.		52
Good manners are a must every moment of the day. A polite person thinks of others, first. A thank you can brighten the gloomiest day. Please should be used automatically. Excuse me is a phrase that should always be on the tip of your tongue. Concentrate on manners.		53
What you want and get out of life depends largely on planning. If you have goals that you want to achieve, you are on the right track. Too many people wander through daily living. Many have no idea of what they really desire or how to achieve. Plan ahead and succeed now.		54
Gestures and facial expressions can tell others a lot about you. This silent language has been ignored in the past. People all over are paying more attention to this new and fun subject. Watch the faces of others with whom you converse. You can start to see all those signals.		55

Task 5

This multipage report illustrates the "left-bound traditional business report." Type all pages.

Reference: p. 245

SPECIAL NOTE: Exhibits A, C, and D are in Working Papers.

RECOMMENDATIONS

FOR THE

MADISON STREET CLOSING

Prepared by:

R. Decker
J. Parsons
L. Kolstad

Distributed to:

R. Long
W. Edgar
L. G. Arnold
K. Robinson

Distribution Date:

(Current Date)

(cont'd. on next page)

Seconds
60

A good worker always finishes what he or she starts. Leaving many small duties undone presents a problem. Soon, they will grow and become a huge mountain. If you do a job thoroughly, you will feel a real satisfaction. Get into this habit right now. You might have a surprise soon. 56

Many folks enjoy a camping trip in the wilds. Today gear and equipment used for camping is varied and quite useful. From sleeping in a tent to relaxing in an elegant motor home, the range of choices is wide. What type of person you are will dictate the kind of equipment you will want. 57

Finding a cure for a common cold has eluded scientists for decades. The symptoms can be relieved in a variety of ways, but there is simply no cure available. One would think that a world that sends men to the moon could surely find a quick cold remedy. The only answer is to rest as you wait. 58

A career in nursing can be a rewarding experience. The joy of helping the sick get well is a special feeling. The work is hard and the days get long, but the effort is worth the end result. An efficient and kind nurse will go a long way. Both men and women alike are discovering this great field. 59

Good dental habits are a must for every person. A thorough brushing at least once a day is vital. If brushing is neglected, plaque and tartar will build on the teeth. This leads to serious dental disease. Your family dentist can show you how to brush properly. Healthy gums and teeth are a necessity. 60

Going to the circus is always exciting. The artists who perform provide thrills and chills in their acts. The trained animal acts are fun to watch. Another funny part of the circus is the many clowns who do all sorts of hilarious antics. Along with the acts in the ring, some like to eat good cotton candy. 61

Bird watching has become an exciting hobby to a lot of people. To be an avid watcher, you must first study many species. You have to learn how to know the various birds. Early morning is a good quiet time to observe the birds in their natural surroundings. Your own fine interest in bird watching can be joyful. 62

In the olden days, there were no streetlights like we enjoy today. The streets were lighted each evening by a person. He lit each individual lamp one by one. As he walked around, he would call out the hour and tell the citizens that all was well. Although the system was not too efficient, many said it was romantic. 63

Choosing a painting for your home can be quite frustrating. First, you must have some knowledge about the world of art. Study various artists and their subjects. Choose a quality painting that appeals to you, not one that someone else says is beautiful. Try to pick one that has varied colors which are enjoyable and airy. 64

cities and it is only a 9-hole course. The other course open to the general public is only a par three course.

Supply vs. Demand. To compare the supply and demand in golf, it is necessary to base all projections on the amount of play a course can handle. The National Golf Foundation has determined this maximum potential; upon reviewing user statistics provided by the four local courses, it has been determined that there are approximately 550 golfers per day (six months only) who wish to play but are unable to secure reservations.

Costs. A survey was conducted to determine the average construction costs for our area and the four surrounding districts. Actual construction costs will vary from the estimate depending upon the site of the proposed golf course, amount of earth moving necessary, the type of watering system used and the size of the club house. For a golf course in our city the site should be approximately 225 acres or larger. Of these 225 acres, 175 acres would be used for an 18-hole course, club house and parking lot. The remaining 75 acres should be used for an additional 9-hole course when the demand equals the supply in the future.

The estimated golf course cost is projected as:

Land purchase (250 acres @ $5000)	=	$ 1,250,000
Construction	=	750,000
Club house	=	300,000
		$ 2,300,000

Recommendation. It is recommended by the committee that the board seriously consider the development of a course in our city. They may wish to obtain additional data on:

1. Availability of 250 acres of unimproved land in a suitable location
2. Availability of experienced personnel
3. Amount of capital available at this time

Distribution Copies: S. Harder
W. Simmonson
J. Cotton

Straight-Copy Timings

One-Minute Timings

Timing 1-1

S.I. 1.30

As you learn to type, you also must learn to set goals for your- 14
self. If your goal is to improve the rate of speed you have attained 28
on any one-minute timed writing, then it is important for you to know 42
the previous typing speed. When you type the one-minute timing, keep 56
your previous speed in mind. You will find that you will really want 70
to improve a word or two each time. Don't set your goals higher than 84
that which is reasonable to achieve in one timing. Increasing by one 98
or two words per day will result in a substantial gain for you during 112
the semester. 115

Timing 1-2

S.I. 1.32

Learning to type rapidly is probably the most exciting thing you 14
can do. When you build your rate to at least your handwriting speed, 28
the skill will be very valuable. If you learn to type 75 or 80 gross 42
words a minute, you will see that typewriting can be fun. An ability 56
such as typewriting should be highly developed, if it is to be of the 70
best advantage. If you can type at least three times faster than you 84
write, you will have more time to work on many other projects. After 98
you become an outstanding wizard on the typewriter, you can find ways 112
of earning money with your skill. 119

Timing 1-3

S.I. 1.35

Prepare for your career now. If you select a career field which 14
interests you now, you can continue to study and prepare yourself for 28
your future work. Getting a desired kind of job simply does not just 42
happen by accident. Each individual must make a plan. Those courses 56
that you take while in a formal school setting will have a bearing on 70
the kind of job for which you will be qualified. You must strive and 84
work hard to acquire the skills needed in your chosen career. 96

Timing 1-4

S.I. 1.37

Many people have imitated a number of different kinds of animals 14
which are very expert gliders and fliers. The flying squirrel glides 28
gracefully through the air going from branch to branch. Man tries to 42
glide from high cliffs in an object that appears like a huge kite. A 56
glider plane will fly soundlessly and smoothly for many miles. A bat 70
with its broad membranous wings and elongated fingers can soar as the 84
birds do. A huge jet airplane with big rigid wings will soar through 98
the air with the grace of a large bird. There is truly a resemblance 112
between man and nature in the skies. 119

----1----2----3----4----5----6----7----8----9---10---11---12---13---14

Task 4

Type as memo report.

Current Date

TO: Esther Ramell, Chairman
Board of Directors

Proposal Development Committee (James, LaMaster, Ryan, Akola, Barber)

RECOMMENDATIONS REGARDING THE DEVELOPMENT OF A PUBLIC GOLF COURSE

This committee was given a charge at the last board meeting to develop a basic proposal regarding the need and cost for constructing a new public golf course in our city. Accordingly the committee gathered the data and presents this report.

Summary. The city presently has four golf courses--two courses are open entirely to the general public; one course is open to the public only one day per week; and, one course is private and not open to the public. User statistics reveal that this area could profitably support another 18-hole golf course. Construction costs could be returned within five or six years of beginning the operation.

Background. The remarkable growth of the number of golf courses has been due primarily to the promotion of the game on a national basis. The insistent demand by golfers for additional facilities and the possibilities that these would prove self-sustaining have caused many cities and private organizations such as ours to make adequate provisions for golf. Studies have revealed that income has exceeded operating expenses by a considerable margin at every course which has been opened during the past fifteen years.

In our area, golfing demand is expected to increse about 22 percent between the years 1985 and 1995. The golfing demand in the year 2000 has been projected to be 58 percent greater than it was in 1980. Estimates for our area indicate a need for an additional 10 equivalent 9-hole courses by the year 2000.

Current Status. At the present time our city has four golf courses. These include two country clubs and two privately owned courses. Each of the four courses has undesirable features for the citizens and visitors of our city. One country club is private and not open to the public; another country club is open only one day a week to the general public. One of the privately owned courses, because of its location, is used by golfers from two

(cont'd. on next page)

Timing 1-5

S.I. 1.40

Skiing is a sport that can be enjoyed in summer and winter. The 14
two seasons offer two different kinds of skiing. Water skiing can be 28
done in the summer; snow skiing can be done in the winter. Equipment 42
needed for the two sports is quite varied. For the snow season, warm 56
clothing and a good pair of skis are necessary. For the summer sport 70
of water skiing, a swim suit and skis will provide the skier with all 84
the necessary items. 88

Timing 1-6

S.I. 1.42

When making all future plans, you should consider an aspect that 14
some persons forget. There are many roles or functions in your daily 28
living which make up your character. For example, you are a son or a 42
daughter, a brother or a sister, and maybe an employee. As your life 56
progresses, you will become more involved, and your roles will become 70
more complex. Career demands and financial plans will place you in a 84
variety of roles. How you handle these roles and blend them together 98
will determine your success in life. 105

----1----2----3----4----5----6----7----8----9---10---11---12---13---14

Timing 1-7

S.I. 1.43

The ceiling fixtures which were standard equipment in many older 14
homes do nothing more than flood the rooms with a harsh, unflattering 28
light. The glaring effect can be greatly softened by bringing lights 42
down to the areas in which they will be used. The direction and also 56
the intensity of the lights can be controlled. The older fixture can 70
be replaced with a newer style such as a hanging swag lamp or a floor 84
lamp. Table lamps can be purchased in a wide variety of sizes, style 98
choices, and colors which blend and harmonize with any decor. 111

Timing 1-8

S.I. 1.44

Roller skating can provide hours of exciting fun. If there is a 14
nearby rink, the rest is simple. A pair of roller skates is the only 28
equipment needed. Most modern roller skating rinks are equipped with 42
rental skates at a nominal price. Skating requires lots of energy or 56
zest to keep skating for a long period of time. The beginning skater 70
should only skate for a short time and not get too tired. After some 84
time has passed, the skater should be able to skate for hours without 98
ever getting tired. 102

----1----2----3----4----5----6----7----8----9---10---11---12---12---14

before the date was checked for accuracy in the edit run. Errors were time consuming and had to be returned to the user fr correction before they could be inputed again. Using CRT entry the initial keying of data is not accepted if editing displays an error on the CRT. The source document needs only to be referenced once and it never leaves the user's hands until the entry takes place successfully. Much reference reporting can take place on CRT screen displays that formerly required bulky printouts / (Para.) / User Reques. Mr. David E. Burnsteen, Director of Computing Services at Rookes, Inc. is asking for bids and/or suggestions for improved computing service by January 1 of next year. Specifically, they are interested in replacement of present fixed disk for the Maxon Z-4700 to the more efficient removable disk. This will increase kisk capabilities with a minimum increase in cost. He also wishes to look at suggested plans for the addition of more remote terminals such as CRT's or teletypes for potential departmnet users. No definite company policy for these additional terminals is in effect. / (New Para.) / Recommendation. It is recommended that our organization consider the preperation of a bid for the contract for the expansion of computing services at Roodes, Inc. We have successfully bid for this type of contract before and there should be no great difficult or expense in bydding for the Roodes, Inc., contract. Suggested Procedures. A team of three (3) individuals should spend at least five days at Roodes, Inc. , doing a comprehensive user survey. In addition, a computer technician should contact Mr. Burnsteen and spend some time at the computer installation sigt to determine the type of removable disk which we would suggest. Upon gathering the data the team can develop the actual proposal. It will not be difficult to develop the bid cost factor nor the justification.

Distribution Copies:

D. Mandix
S. Skahaug
W. Grambo

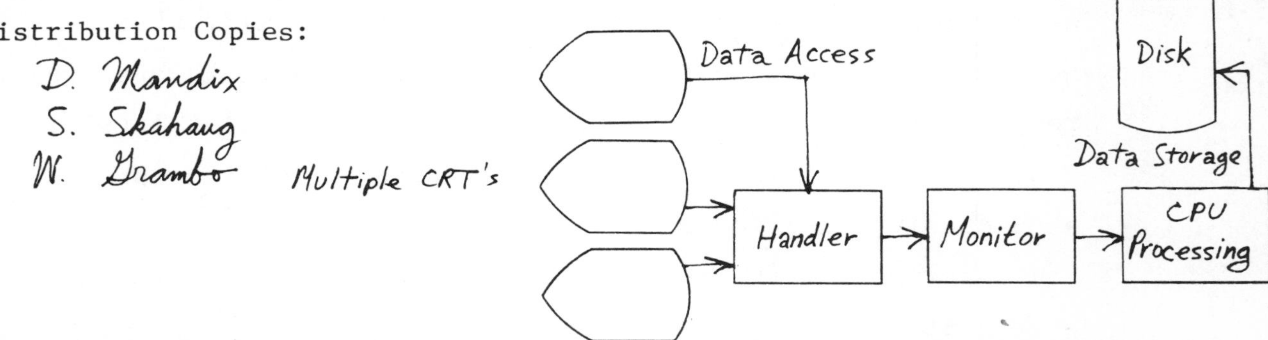

Figure 1 -- REMOTE DATA ENTRY

Timing 1-9

S.I. 1.45

To use your spare time effectively, you must have a plan. Every 14
successful person knows how to utilize spare hours. Plans with goals 28
are a must to enjoying leisure time. Many folks waste precious hours 42
trying to decide what to do for recreation. By the time they decide, 56
the leisure time has vanished. You must plan ahead for activities or 70
relaxing times. Forget your own problems while you focus on enjoying 84
those games, books, and vacations. 91

Timing 1-10

S.I. 1.46

When considering the purchase of any article of clothing, do not 14
let any sales person convince you to take a garment that does not fit 28
well. If you decide to buy something that does not fit, be sure that 42
the store from which you buy the clothing has an excellent alteration 56
department. Make sure that they understand that the clothing must be 70
altered to fit before you make the final arrangements to purchase the 84
item. To be completely assured and satisfied, take a friend along to 98
give you another opinion on how you look. 106

----1----2----3----4----5----6----7----8----9---10---11---12---13---14

Timing 1-11

S.I. 1.47

If you enjoy observing the many species of birds, there are many 14
ways of attracting them. A bird requires a shelter, food, and water. 28
Provide fresh, clean drinking and bathing water each day. Some fresh 42
seeds and fruit placed in accessible feeders are necessary. The bird 56
shelters should be quite durable and waterproof. All baths, feeders, 70
and shelters should be kept out of the reach of other animals. Those 84
birds need all the security and safety that you can provide for them. 98
Your new friends will appreciate your efforts. 107

Timing 1-12

S.I. 1.48

Recreation is becoming more and more popular among people of all 14
ages. One particular sport which is growing rapidly is cross-country 28
skiing. If a person makes an effort to get out of the house and puts 42
on a pair of skis, cross-country skiing can be a great enjoyment. No 56
specialized skills are needed to learn to ski cross-country. The few 70
basic beginning instructions are simple to master. The excitement of 84
gliding over that snowy countryside, through the magnificent forests, 98
and over the hills is a thrill that no one should miss. 109

----1----2----3----4----5----6----7----8----9---10---11---12---13---14

and processing services as a basis for departmental decision making. / (Para.) / History. Previous to 1975, all of the coputing services centered around a Maxon Z-3500 located in the main administrative building. Programming was carried on through a Maxon CD-110 remote terminal in an adjoining building. The terminal included a line printer, card reader, and several teletypes. Computer related work was carried on simultaneously during the day using a priority basis in running concurrent jobs. / (Para.) / In October, 1975, a changoever took place from the Maxon Z-3500 to two ~~additional~~ computers. A Z-4700 was placed in the main administrative building and a Z-5000 was placed in ~~the~~ an adjoining building. The changge-over allowed much more flexibility, as advantage could be taken of direct on-line terminal access at department locations with cathode ray tubes (CRT's) as an alternative to printed report referencing. Through a service bureau computer output, microfiche is used as another alternative to printed reports. (Para.) / ~~Currently eight CRT's are conte~~ Present Situation. currently eight CRT's are connected through one access terminal to the Z-4700. An extra CRT is available in case of breakdown. The multiple CRT connections meet at the handler for common entry to the CPU. The handler acts as a traffic controller keeping track of where inputed messages come ~~from~~ and where outputed messages go. From the handler the message passes through the monitor. The monitor permanently records when the message arrives, which CRT it arrived from, and whether it was an inquiry for a display of information or an update. From the monitor a program picks up the message and pulls the correct program from a disk file as specified by the message. With this sytem, all eight CRT's may be in use simultaneously. Eight messages could call in eight different programs to process data adn return it to the CRT's. Ony one message at a time, however, can pass through the handler and monitor. ONly one link exists between the CPU and disk files. Some waiting may then occur for one program while ~~antoehr~~ another is obaineing information from the disk.

* (draw display -- located next page. Be sure and make exact size as shown... type lettering and words.

In comparing traditional data entry and reporting with CRT data entry and reporting, the number of manual operations in each system can be seen. In the traditional entry system, keying took place at teast twice

(cont'd. on next page)

Timing 1-13

S.I. 1.49

A good typist soon learns how to proofread. Glaring errors will 14
mar the neatness and quality of a good report. Find all the mistakes 28
before you type the final copy. Learn to watch for correct spelling, 42
grammar, and typing. You might wish to examine your typewritten work 56
two or three times and make quite certain it is without mistakes. In 70
the long run, you will be pleased that you have carefully prepared an 84
excellent typewritten copy. The person who reads your copy will have 98
much respect for your ability as a typist. Learn to proofread. 111

Timing 1-14

S.I. 1.50

To honor a deserving person in the community is a fine thing. A 14
most interesting factor becomes apparent many times, in the ugly form 28
of jealousy for another's accomplishments. Most people can take high 42
honor quite graciously--that is, if they were the ones to win. Those 56
individuals who did not win may begin to hold a grudge against anyone 70
who was a winner. When something like a community honor causes deep, 84
hard feelings on the part of some people, it becomes an empty prize-- 98
the winner may be the loser. The spirit of honors and awards must be 112
one of generous and living happiness. 119

----1----2----3----4----5----6----7----8----9---10---11---12---13---14

Timing 1-15

S.I. 1.51

Our world is composed of many colors. The primary colors can be 14
observed in many places. The various tints and shades which comprise 28
the secondary colors are mixtures of primary colors. For example, if 42
red and yellow are mixed together, the result will be orange. Yellow 56
and blue mixed would produce some shade of green. If all the primary 70
colors were mixed together, the results would be black. As you drift 84
along through life, concentrate on the marvelous shading which nature 98
has devised for your enjoyment. 104

Timing 1-16

S.I. 1.52

You are a consumer. Without you and millions of other consumers 14
in the nation, businesses would have to close. There would be nobody 28
to buy those goods and services which businesses produce. The impact 42
of ceasing all operations would quickly affect every person. Workers 56
would have no jobs and would have no money to continue living. There 70
would be no hustle and bustle of daily life. Every family would have 84
to supply all the necessities in life for themselves. Each family or 98
group would have to grow food, produce clothing, and provide shelter. 112

----1----2----3----4----5----6----7----8----9---10---11---12---13---14

vote in a city-wide referendum on the location for the new bridge. / (Para.) / Recommendations. It is recommended that our organization present the results of the preliminary survey to the city council. In addition, a proposal should be prepared to present to the council recommending that a complete city survey be conducted relating to the bridge construction site. / (Para.) / Future. If, after reviewing the data in this report, the council wishes to conduct the city survey, it will be necessary we have the following information available:

1. possible items to be included on questionnaire.
2. time table for completion of the project.
3. cost plan, profit margin and bid cost to city.

/ (Para.) / If you wish us to begin gathering data on the three items, please respond as soon as possible so that department personnel may be assigned to the project.

Distribution copies: S. Savalino
W. Lewis

Task 3

Type as memo report.

Note to student: Be sure to correct any errors overlooked in editing.

TO: Kenneth A. Chopp, research assistant Current Date

FROM: Estel Mattini

COMPUTER HARDWARE ANALYZATION AT ROODES, INC.

Rdes, Inc., requested that we perform a pliminary analyzation of their present computer installation. They are comtenplating a change in hardware and their director of computing srvices asked that we consider bidding our equipment and services for their consideation. / (Para.) / Background. At the present time the function of the computer at Roodes, Inc., is to store and retrieve vast amounts of information and to make calculations that formerly took peope tremendous time periods ot calculate. The computing service does not take on the decision making functions of the various departments, nor does it exercise control over them. The present function is basically to provice common filing, data classification

(cont'd. on next page)

Timing 1-17

S.I. 1.53

An old pocket watch is an object of beauty. Many people collect 14
good antique watches because they contain some of the finest artistic 28
engraving that was so common years ago. The better watches were made 42
of gold or silver and had ornate and intricate symbols, scenes, or an 56
initial or two engraved on the surface. A watch fob was also common. 70
It was attached to the watch chain and represented companies, groups, 84
and other popular renderings of that time. Many watches, chains, and 98
fobs are priceless family possessions today. 107

Timing 1-18

S.I. 1.54

Old pictures are fascinating. Looking at photos that were taken 14
long ago can provide many hours of enjoyment. The methods of living, 28
clothing, and quaint objects are captured forever in old photographs. 42
Who are the individuals in the picture? In what location was the old 56
picture taken? These are some of the factors that will lead to hours 70
of enjoyment in the attempt to provide answers. It is really too bad 84
that more photographs are not available for people to view. Everyone 98
should have the opportunity to look at old pictures. 109

----1----2----3----4----5----6----7----8----9---10---11---12---13---14

Timing 1-19

S.I. 1.55

Costs of building a woodburning furnace are very low. Materials 14
may be purchased through your local salvage dealer, or for a somewhat 28
higher price, you could have a sheet metal contractor fabricate parts 42
to your specifications. Regardless of which method you should select 56
to build your furnace, be sure and follow all safety suggestions when 70
you put it together. After it is completed you will surely enjoy the 84
lovely warmth of the woodburning furnace. Treat it properly and soon 98
you will wonder how you ever got along without it. 108

Timing 1-20

S.I. 1.56

Gain more confidence in yourself. In many instances, we are too 14
critical of ourselves. Each of us identifies our very own individual 28
weaknesses and strengths. The main problem, however, is that we tend 42
to pay more attention to those weaknesses than to the strengths. The 56
moment you find yourself dwelling on some negative aspect, you should 70
stop and think. You should remind yourself that all people have both 84
positive and negative traits. Learn to stress the positive and cease 98
accenting the negative. Developing confidence is not difficult. 111

----1----2----3----4----5----6----7----8----9---10---11---12---13---14

Task 2

Type as memo report.

Current Date / TO: Donald A. Almanson, President / K. S. Snider, Research Coordinator / PRELIMINARY REPORT ON LAKE-JONES STREET BRIDGE / As per your instructions, the Research Department has investigated the Lake-Jones Bridge project. In obtaining data for this report, the department personnel assigned to the project followed the guidelines as set forth in the company policy book. / (Para.) / Summary. A majority of the public sampled are definitely against the bridge being constructed at the Lake and Jones Streets location. In addition, the majority feel that the city council has disregarded taxpayer rights and has mandated the bridge be built at this location for the financial gain of downtown businessmen. / (Para.) / Background. The Lake-Jones Bridge project is included in the city overall "701 Comprehensive Traffic Plan." Present plans by the city government dictate that the bridge project will begin next September, with completion expected eighteen months later. Solicitation for construction bids have already been advertised and will be opened on the fifteenth of next month. / (Para.) / The Problem. Our organization was charged by the city council to undertake a sample survey to determine public reaction to the bridge project. Accordingly, the research department selected a sample of 500 city residents and administered an oral interview. The individuals selected for the sample included a complete cross section and representative numbers according to sex, age, geographic location within the city, and net income. All individuals in the sample were homeowners, and consequently, paid city property tax. / (Para.) / Procedure. The individuals selected for the sample were drawn in a systematic random manner. The questions which were to be asked were developed by the department staff and tested in a field situation to obtain validity. A schedule was set up for the interviews and the investigators gathered the data. The data ~~was~~ were tabulated, analyzed and included in this report. / (Para.) / Findings. Eighty-nine percent (445) of the people surveyed are against the building of the bridge at the Lake and Jones Streets location. Ninety-four percent (470) indicated that the downtown merchants, not the general public, will receive the most benefit ~~of~~ from a Lake-Jones Bridge. Ninety-nine percent (490) feel the taxpayers should have an opportunity to

Timing 1-21

S.I. 1.58

Credit buying plays an important role in our economy. The major 14
portion of credit buying involves installment plans. Buying items on 28
the installment plan allows the customer to pay for items over a time 42
period, usually monthly. For the more expensive items, such as a car 56
or a boat, the installment plan works quite well. A consumer must be 70
prudent when buying items on the installment plan. Too many debts at 84
one time will result in financial disaster. 93

Timing 1-22

S.I. 1.59

Some people find the study of migrations of many birds extremely 14
interesting. Most birds fly southward for the cold winter months and 28
northward for the warm summer months. No one is really certain why a 42
particular flock returns year after year to that same locality. Many 56
persons enjoy numerous hours during the year watching their feathered 70
friends. Bird watching is indeed a rewarding hobby. For the serious 84
bird-watcher, there are many clubs and books to aid in the activity. 98

----1----2----3----4----5----6----7----8----9---10---11---12---13---14

Timing 1-23

S.I. 1.60

Our planet earth is indeed a world ravaged by humans. Pollution 14
and destruction of natural resources are taking place at a dangerous, 28
frightening rate. Cautious hopes are being raised by individuals who 42
see some signs of concern for wildlife and environment. Perhaps this 56
very concern can be turned into everyday action. The world will then 70
be a better, happier, and cleaner place in which to live. All people 84
must do their part to cooperate in this effort. Without this cooper- 98
ation of everyone, the world will surely become more polluted. 111

Timing 1-24

S.I. 1.61

For many people, the variety of the changing seasons is the high 14
point of their lives. Young and old look forward to the temperatures 28
which change every few months. In the winter, the snow provides much 42
entertainment through skiing, sledding, and skating. As the pleasant 56
activities come to an end with the nearing of spring and summer, many 70
new activities will be enjoyed. Swimming, boating, camping, fishing, 84
and tennis are a few sports that are summertime favorites. Gardening 98
is also a spring and summer hobby for many. 107

----1----2----3----4----5----6----7----8----9---10---11---12---13---14

Reference:
p. 211

TYPES OF ADVERTISING MEDIA*

Nationwide	Old London Square Mall
newspaper	newspaper
television	radio
radio	television
direct mail	direct mail
magazines	magazines

*Ranked according to frequency of utilization

Conclusion. The use of advertising media by merchants at the Old London Square Mall closely follows what is being done on a national scale. The only difference found was in the ranking of television and radio. Television is second in popularity nationwide, and radio is third. At the Old London Square Mall, radio is second in popularity and television is third.

Recommendations. Our agreement called for both a written report and an oral presentation of the findings. This information was given to the merchants at their last monthly meeting. A recommendation was made that the merchants utilize television more than radio in the future. After discussion, it was decided by the members in attendance to follow this recommendation for the next six months. Accordingly, the mall manager was instructed to change the mall cooperative advertising campaign. We were given another agreement to provide a research follow-up report at the conclusion of the trial period.

Follow-up. Jim Lane will be in charge of the follow-up research project. Alice Barnes, June Folton, Bob Arterburn, and Leslie Barth will work with him.

Timing 1-25

S.I. 1.62

Early man was forced to do most of his calculations mentally. A 14
method for counting was devised, using fingers or objects. Later, an 28
abacus was introduced. The abacus is a simple apparatus that is made 42
of beads and strings. Every string of beads represents the number of 56
fingers on a pair of hands. The positions of the strings represent a 70
certain decimal value. Addition and other calculations can be easily 84
performed on the abacus. It is, however, quite unusual to locate any 98
person still using the ancient abacus. 106

----1----2----3----4----5----6----7----8----9---10---11---12---13---14

Timing 1-26

S.I. 1.63

Giving a formal speech or presentation can be an embarrassing or 14
awkward moment in time. Sometimes, when an audience does not respond 28
to the speaker, it is next to impossible to communicate main thoughts 42
and points to the audience. The use of audio-visual materials is one 56
helpful technique for stressing major ideas. The speaker who uses an 70
overhead or film projector usually finds that an audience listens and 84
responds quickly. Another good aid is to use good charts and graphs. 98
If a speaker is experienced, a combination of audio-visual aids could 112
be very effective and interesting. 119

Timing 1-27

S.I. 1.65

More and more individuals are attempting to handle many problems 14
that arise regarding home repairs. Many years ago, most families did 28
not attempt to make any home repairs--they merely called a repairman. 42
Today, with the tremendous rise in the price of labor and material, a 56
wise home owner will quickly learn how to make minor repairs. Makers 70
of tools have helped considerably; the wide choice of tools gives the 84
amateur repairperson unlimited possibilities. These unique tools are 98
quite easy for all amateurs to use. 104

----1----2----3----4----5----6----7----8----9---10---11---12---13---14

Task 1

Type as memo report.

Reference: p. 224

Current Date

TO: You, the Student

Business People of America

MEMORANDUM REPORT PREPARATION

Reports in business are frequently prepared in different forms from those in education. You are looking at a very popular example, the memo report. Rather than prepare both a report and an accompanying letter or memo, the two are combined. This method is usually used for reports that are fairly short--fewer than three pages. You will notice that the style is the same as shown in the memorandum section of this text.

Many times you will find that the report content lends itself to the use of subheadings as shown below.

Summary. The findings of the survey of advertising at Old London Square Mall are similar to the national trends. All the mall stores use, in addition to local cooperative advertising, some type of outside media. The choice of outside media compares quite closely with national trends, since newspapers are listed most effective and used most frequently, followed by radio, television, direct mailing, and magazines.

Background. Our organization entered into an agreement three months ago with the merchants of the Old London Square Mall to investigate avenues of approach to effective advertising. We assigned methods currently in use throughout the nation, and especially those methods utilized by businesses in some type of physical location arrangement (shopping centers, malls, and so on). After gathering the evidence used throughout the country, a questionnaire was prepared and administered to all the merchants located in the Old London Square Mall. The results of both the nationwide survey and the mall survey were then compared.

Findings. Nationwide merchants agree that individual firms must do more advertising than the cooperative efforts the mall association makes. Cooperative efforts seem to be quite effective when the entire mall conducts some type of sale (usually seasonal), but for the remainder of the time it is the individual firm that must generate sales by individual advertising efforts. The Old London Square Mall merchants agree with this 100%. The national use and popularity of various types of advertising media is somewhat different from what the Old London Square Mall merchants now use.

(cont'd. on next page)

Three-Minute Timings

Timing 3-1

S.I. 1.38

Rain is quite welcome when the land is dry. The earth's surface 14
holds quite a bit of water but in times of very dry weather it always 28
seems to be in the wrong place--or it is of the type that it can't be 42
used. Normally, the U.S. receives adequate amounts of rain; however, 56
there are particular periods when clouds don't release their moisture 70
for long amounts of time. Most clouds usually move from west to east 84
across the nation. If there should be a high pressure system holding 98
near the west coast, it will divert the clouds and moisture northward 112
into Canada. Many experts feel that the climate over the whole earth 126
is becoming warmer and drier. These experts state that the supply of 140
water we now have in the nation will not be enough for us to continue 154
wasting our water in the future as we have done in the past. To most 170
people, the warning might go unheeded; some will help to conserve our 184
water supply. New ways of obtaining water will have to be developed; 198
we cannot afford to depend entirely on rain for all our water source. 212

----1----2----3----4----5----6----7----8----9---10---11---12---13---14

Timing 3-2

S.I. 1.41

Since the first moment in time when two people traveled beyond a 14
shouting distance of each other, humans have searched for a method of 28
talking over a long distance. Earlier cultures tried drums and smoke 42
signals for messages. Today, the traffic noises in most places would 56
cover the sounds of a drum; fire engines would arrive on the scene to 70
drown the fire. People communicate easily today with our telephones. 84
Most of us don't realize how advanced the technology of phone service 98
has now become. Old photos show endless miles of phone wires hung on 112
poles; today we would find the wire buried. The switchboard operator 126
has been replaced by automatic dialing handled by a big computer with 140
the sound waves being relayed across the world by one satellite. The 154
repair person has now been replaced by a trained service person. The 168
changes that have taken place are numerous; however, the objective of 182
the service is still the same--allowing people to talk with the other 196
people. The next time you have a chance, look for other changes; you 210
will be amazed with what you will find. 218

----1----2----3----4----5----6----7----8----9---10---11---12---13----14

DRILL

Construct a line graph and a bar graph using the following information for both:

Number of telephone calls for Illian Industries on Monday, June 1

8:00	40
9:00	15
10:00	25
11:00	35
1:00	5
2:00	45
3:00	25

DRILL

Construct a pie graph showing the following information:

Results of an opinion poll on the question: "Should a new park be built on Bay Street?"

No opinion:	20%
Strongly favor:	25%
Strongly against:	30%
Mildly in favor:	15%
Mildly against:	10%

DRILL

Construct a picture graph showing the following information.

Number of households using Niagara Products

Region 1:	250,000
Region 2:	400,000
Region 3:	300,000
Region 4:	150,000
Region 5:	350,000

Each symbol, a house, represents 50,000 households.

Timing 3-3

S.I. 1.42

Today, the costs of food are increasing at an alarming rate. At 14
the same time, the quantity of produce, vegetables, and fruits is not 28
meeting the demands of consumers. The major problem lies in the fact 42
that at certain times produce is quite plentiful and at other times a 56
shortage exists due to growing seasons in certain regions. All of us 70
know it is a good practice to save money for the future; but how many 84
of us realize that it is a good idea to save food for the future? An 98
excellent and thrifty practice is to preserve food for later use. It 112
is a good feeling to see row upon row of canned vegetables and fruits 126
which have been preserved. Another good method of preserving produce 140
is by freezing in meal-sized quantities. The latter method is a very 154
easy one; but does require the use of a deep freeze unit. Many great 168
books and pamphlets are available on the topic of the home preserving 182
of many vegetables and fruits. The joy of eating out-of-season foods 196
is boundless--the money saved is endless. 204

----1----2----3----4----5----6----7----8----9---10---11---12---13---14

Timing 3-4

S.I. 1.43

Many people are growing herb gardens. The herb plants provide a 14
variety of new seasonings, fragrances, and flavorings. Growing herbs 28
is quite similar to growing a vegetable garden. You should select an 42
area for your herb garden that is sunny, as herbs demand an abundance 56
of sunlight to make them sweet and flavorful. To supply enough herbs 70
for a family of four, you would need a garden space about ten to fif- 84
teen feet square. If you do not have enough room, it is very easy to 98
grow an abundance of herbs in an ordinary window box or in small clay 112
flower pots. If grown inside, the herbs should be placed in a window 126
which receives full sunlight at least one half of the day. In a case 140
where sunlight is not available, a fluorescent-light garden will give 154
you an abundant harvest of herbs. To promote a compact growth, it is 168
a good idea to snip the plants back on a regular basis. Herbs placed 182
with other plants add charm and grace with the rich foliage. Freshly 196
picked herbs can either be dried or frozen for future use. Many good 210
cookbooks will give directions for using a variety of herbs. 222

----1----2----3----4----5----6----7----8----9---10---11---12---13---14

3. ***Drawings*** are usually prepared in permanent India ink.

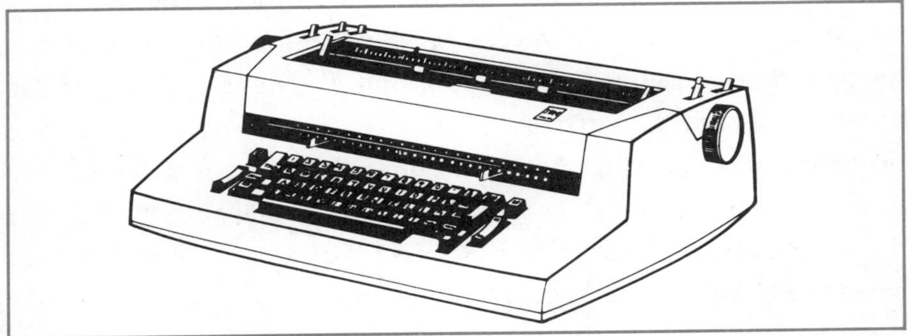

4. ***Miscellaneous***: flow charts, maps, organizational charts, schematic drawings, and computer printouts are used in many types of business reports.

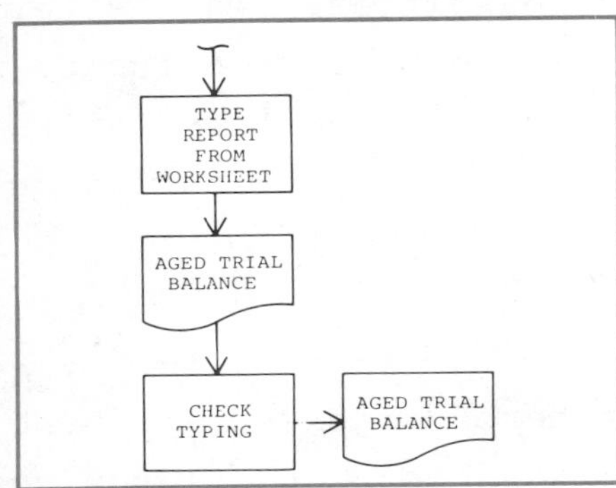

Flow Chart

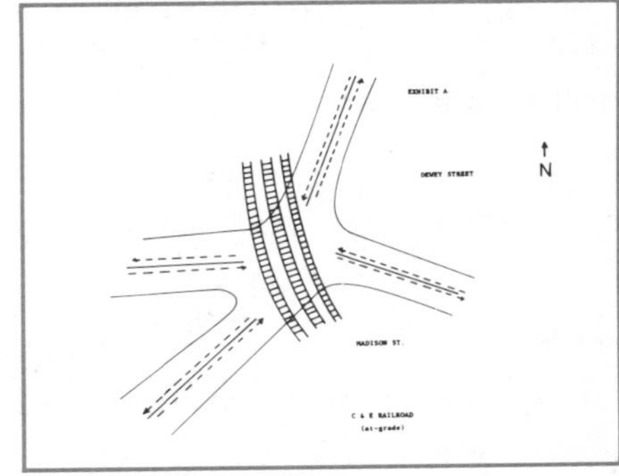

Map

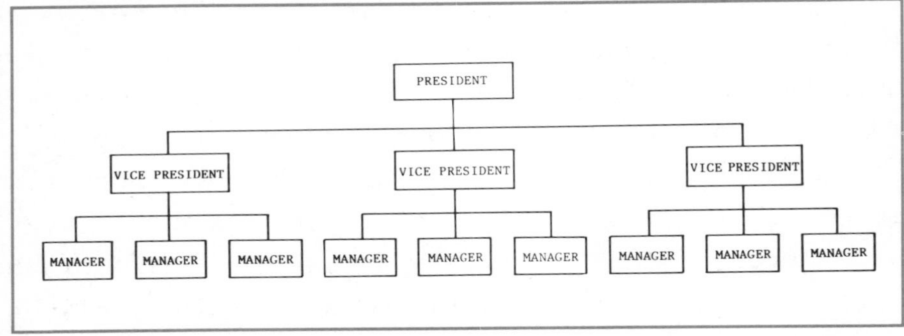

Organizational Chart

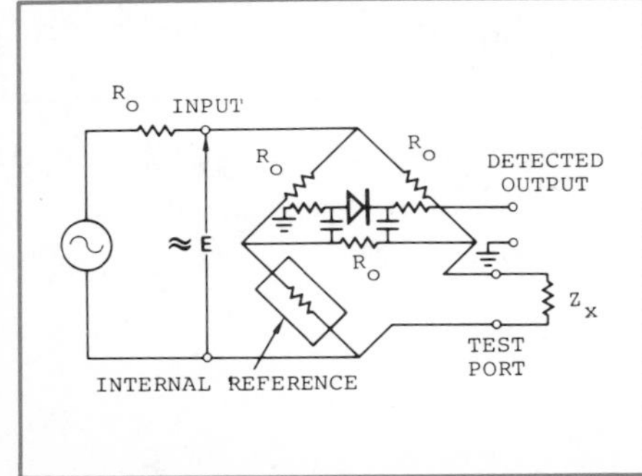

Schematic Drawing

```
C PRINT AVERAGE RATE
       RTEAVE=RTESUM/24.
       WRITE (3,6) RTEAVE
     6 FORMAT (1,7HOAVERAGE RATE IS ,F5.2)

C PRINT RATE ARRAY
       WRITE (3,7) ((RATE(I,J),J-1,4),I=1,6)
     7 FORMAT (1X,4F10.2)

C END OF JOB ROUTINE
       WRITE (3,8)
     8 FORMAT (11HOEND OF JOB)
       STOP
       END
```

Computer Printout

Timing 3-5

S.I. 1.44

There is nothing more gorgeous than a butterfly in flight. That 14
gentle flutter of wings is like a whisper. The colors in the fragile 28
creature are truly a gift of nature. It is a marvel that an ugly and 42
wormlike creature could become such a lovely work of art. The entire 56
life cycle of many butterflies is quite short; as the cold weather or 70
snows begin to arrive, most life ends for these insects. One certain 84
species, the Monarch, migrates to the mountains of Mexico and the far 98
shores of the Pacific Ocean. The Monarch is a symbol for one town on 112
the coast. Each year in the fall, the colorful Monarchs fly for many 126
hundreds of miles to winter in a tiny grove of trees fondly named the 140
"Butterfly Trees." After the butterflies have arrived in the fall, a 154
huge parade announces their return. No one realizes just what causes 168
the Monarch migration. Expert scientists study this interesting fact 182
of nature year after year in hopes of finding new clues. An instinct 196
for survival is quite apparent in the fragile Monarch. 207

----1----2----3----4----5----6----7----8----9---10---11---12---13---14

Timing 3-6

S.I. 1.46

New statistics show that every year twelve thousand persons will 14
lose their lives in home fires. Another thirty thousand could suffer 28
serious injuries because of fire. Experts agree that as many as half 42
of those lives might have been spared if each homeowner had taken one 56
simple safety measure. A simple device, the smoke detector, has been 70
in production for many years. In the past, the fire alarms have been 84
sold mostly to a few building contractors who installed them in homes 98
that were being built. Recently, the alarms have been advertised and 112
offered for sale to all consumers. Yet, very few homes have an alarm 126
system. Why aren't all homes equipped with these lifesaving devices? 140
The major reason seems to be much apathy and lack of awareness. Many 154
people feel that a fire just could not happen to them. Sadly enough, 168
records show that no one is safe from a dangerous fire. A good smoke 182
detector, which can be installed in minutes, is needed for each home. 196
A consumer should shop carefully for an alarm and compare the quality 210
and purchase price of several smoke detectors. 219

----1----2----3----4----5----6----7----8----9---10---11---12---13---14

c. Pie graphs are used to present simple data such as percentages of total amounts, days, time, and so on.

1. The first and largest section of the "pie" is usually begun at the twelve o'clock position. Other sections are then presented in the order of descending size.
2. If desired, each section can be shaded or colored differently to draw the reader's attention to the various sections.
3. All typing should be in one position; the reader should not have to adjust the paper to read captions.

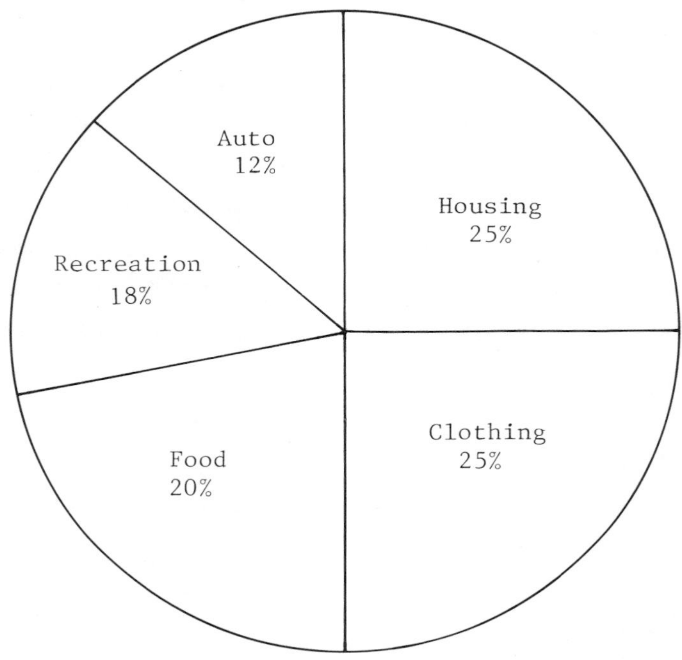

SPENDING PATTERNS OF LATHROP RESIDENTS

d. Picture graphs are similar to bar graphs, but use symbols or pictures.

year										
2005	$	$	$	$	$	$	$	$	$	$
2000	$	$	$	$	$	$	$	$		
1995	$	$	$	$	$	$				
1990	$	$	$	$	$					
1985	$	$	$	$						

PREDICTED SALES FOR TWENTY YEAR PERIOD

$ = one million dollars

Timing 3-7

S.I. 1.48

The lowly gourd is an ornamental vegetable that grows on a vine. 14
The vines have long, trailing stems with large leaves which sometimes 28
measure over a foot wide. In many places of the country, gourds grow 42
wild. The plant can be grown very easily from seeds, in places which 56
have adequate sunlight. The outer part, or rind, of a gourd is quite 70
hard and very tough. Many earlier pioneers depended upon gourds very 84
heavily. They used the shells for jugs, bottles, cups, and sometimes 98
for cooking pots and pans. Many people, however, do not realize that 112
inside that outer shell is a tough, stringy fibrous mass. The inside 126
masses, when dried, make useful sponges. A few varieties are edible, 140
if picked while young and tender. Most gourds, however, are used for 154
decorative purposes only. The strange and quite unusual colorings of 170
gourds range from delicate yellows to verdant greens; the patterns of 184
stripes are very different. The sizes of gourds can differ from very 198
tiny ones to extremely large ones. 205

----1----2----3----4----5----6----7----8----9---10---11---12---13---14

Timing 3-8

S.I. 1.50

Most students are eager for the answer to the question of how to 14
get a job the first time. Sadly enough, there is no single answer to 28
this question. There are many sources to tap when searching for that 42
new job. Schools usually employ counselors who will help many first- 56
time workers decide on a new job or even a career choice. Some large 70
schools also have a job referral service which brings an employer and 84
an employee together. Most cities have local employment services for 98
the person seeking a new position. The services are a good indicator 112
of job openings in the local region. Civil Service Offices will also 126
yield job information about government jobs and careers. The student 140
who is determined to find that very first job will surely learn quite 154
fast that there are many kinds of new career choices available in the 168
world today. The student must be prepared, however, to have patience 182
and determination. Another fact to keep in mind is that most persons 198
have started at the bottom rung of the ladder, not the top. 210

----1----2----3----4----5----6----7----8----9---10---11---12---13---14

b. Bar graphs are used to show relationships between two sets of data. Bar graphs can be constructed either vertically or horizontally depending upon the amount of space available in the report and the amount of space required for the graph. The bars should all be of the same width and wider than the space between any two of the bars.

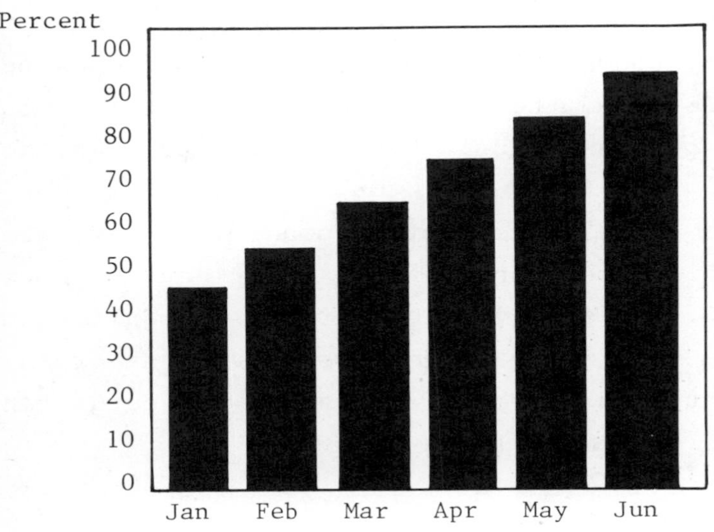

OCCUPANCY RATE FOR
MIDLAND HOTEL
FIRST SIX MONTHS OF OPERATION

Vertical Bar Graph

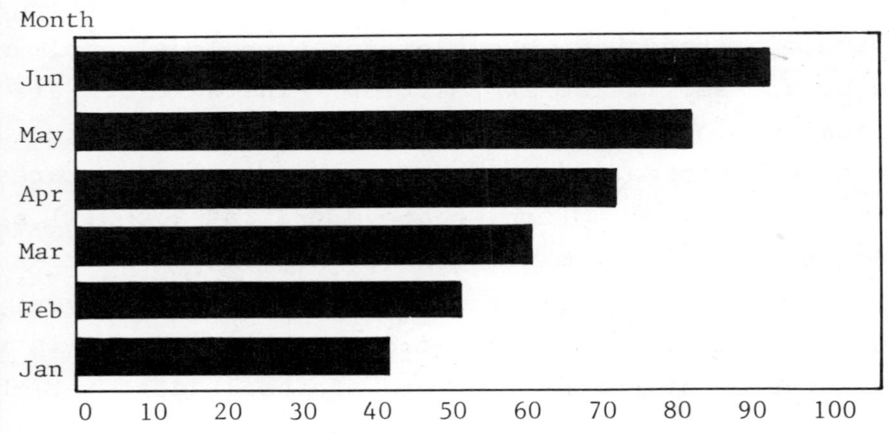

OCCUPANCY RATE FOR MIDLAND HOTEL
FIRST SIX MONTHS OF OPERATION

Horizontal Bar Graph

Timing 3-9

S.I. 1.52

The United States Postal Department developed the system of area 14
ZIP codes. Use of the new modern code was to be a time-saving method 28
to improve postal service. The zip code numbers are read by machines 42
at fast rates. The first digit indicates one of ten geographic areas 56
in the nation. The second digit shows a state or a heavily populated 70
area. The third digit indicates a major destination place within the 84
state. The final two numbers indicate either a delivery station in a 98
large town or a sectional post office. Some persons, however, do not 112
always write the proper numbers on an envelope. Others simply forget 126
to write the zip code number. The postal workers are forced to spend 140
an excessive amount of time sorting the mail by hand, which increases 154
the cost of handling mail. Perhaps a penalty should be levied on the 168
people who either forget the numbers or write them incorrectly. If a 182
system of fines was begun, perhaps zip codes would begin to appear on 196
most, if not all, letters and parcels. 204

----1----2----3----4----5----6----7----8----9---10---11---12---13---14

Timing 3-10

S.I. 1.53

Everyone, at some time or other, experiences a puzzling lapse of 14
memory. A name or a date, or the details of an experience, vanish in 28
the dark recesses of the mind. Strange as it may seem, the forgotten 42
detail will just pop right back into our conscious thought an hour, a 56
day, a week, and even months later. If we were never conscious of an 70
annoying lapse of memory, we would probably not be curious about that 84
process of remembering data and facts. What is it that makes a human 98
memory function or disfunction? Many medical experts have devoted an 112
enormous amount of time studying the mystery of human memory. In the 126
past, there have been many successful studies done which prove that a 140
person's memory can be improved. Many people are able to improve the 154
ability to remember by associating new names, facts, dates, and faces 168
with simple objects. Learning to file facts and data in the mind may 182
be a process of concentrating for a few moments on a specific object. 196
Experts are just beginning to unlock the secrets of a human mind. 209

----1----2----3----4----5----6----7----8----9---10---11---12---13---14

play to facilitate easy viewing. You should always place the display AFTER reference has been made to it in the text, not before. If you should have more than six displays or exhibits, you may wish to prepare a "List of Displays" or "List of Exhibits" page that includes the page number where each is located. This separate page would follow the "Table of Contents" page in the report.

Types of Displays/Exhibits.

1. *Photographs.* In some instances photographs may be affixed to the report pages(s). You must know the exact size of each photo and leave enough room for it.
2. *Graphs.* Graphs are frequently used in business reports since they illustrate relationships more clearly than do words. The titles on all graphs are centered BELOW the graph. Types of graphs include the following:
   a. Line graphs show the relationship between two sets of information plotted in relation to two axes drawn at right angles. The information usually has a range, such as time, age, distance, weight, height, dollar amounts, and so on.
      1. Line graphs may be drawn in ink on cross-ruled paper or on paper of the same quality as the business report.
      2. The bottom portion of the graph usually should represent time (days, weeks, months, hours, years, and so on). The side portion should represent other measures or items.

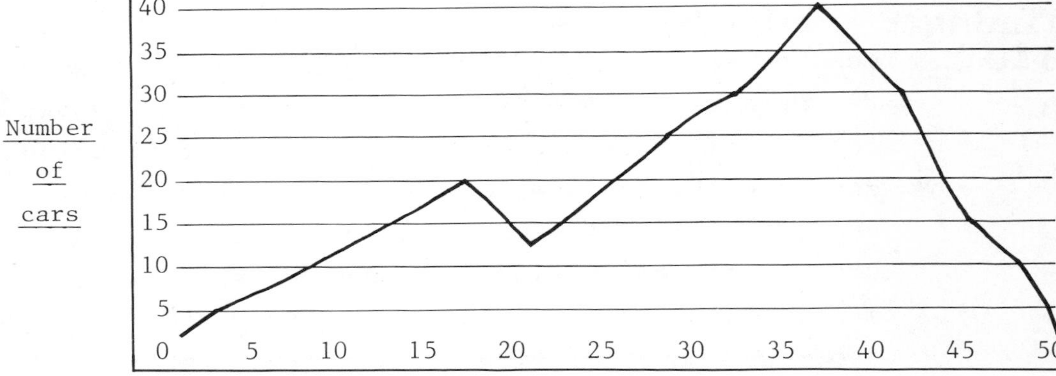

NUMBER OF CARS CROSSING LAKE INTERSECTION IN A FIFTY-DAY PERIOD

Timing 3-11

S.I. 1.54

Have you tried skiing on water? If you have enjoyed any type of 14
water activities, you could certainly have considerable fun skiing on 28
the water. Some people own boats which are used entirely for pulling 42
water skiers. Large boats and motors are required for pulling either 56
adults or youngsters. A boat owner normally provides an ample supply 70
of safety equipment for water skiers. Learning to water ski is not a 84
difficult problem. Your first venture around the lake might be quite 98
short if you lose your balance. You may, however, whiz over the lake 112
and remain upright the entire time. Your ability to balance yourself 126
on the skis plays a major role in your success as a water skier. Any 140
expert water skier can perform a wide variety of tricks on the water. 154
Experts ski on only one ski, while others have learned to ski without 168
any skis at all. Water shows, which are now quite popular, offer the 182
viewer a variety of maneuvers on water skis. A quite unique event is 196
watching a skier "soar" through the air on a kite and land gracefully 210
on skis. Water skiing is an exciting experience for almost anyone. 224

----1----2----3----4----5----6----7----8----9---10---11---12---13---14

Timing 3-12

S.I. 1.55

When guests visit our homes, most of us enjoy the experience. A 14
preparation period preceding a visit is not so enjoyable. Usually, a 28
thorough cleaning and polishing is in order, along with planning good 42
meals for the guests. The entire family labors to prepare their home 56
for the expected guests. Excitement mounts as the magic time for the 70
arrival of the guests draws nearer. Sometimes, the waiting will seem 84
like an eternity. After the guests have arrived, there is usually an 98
excited hustle and bustle as the unpacking chores are done. Everyone 112
can then settle down for a friendly chat and to catch up on events at 126
a leisurely pace. A welcome guest is one who tries not to intrude in 140
established family routines. Guests might assist, whenever possible, 154
with the burden of routine chores such as cooking, cleaning, or other 168
duties. If a visit is lengthy, it is traditional to send a gift or a 182
small token of thanks to the host family after the visit is over. An 196
accompanying personal note is needed to thank the host family. 208

----1----2----3----4----5----6----7----8----9---10---11---12---13---14

Business Reports

Preparation of business reports is somewhat different from preparation of educational manuscripts (term papers). There are a variety of styles and procedures used by various organizations. The major differences are explained here, and you will use these procedures for the typing of the business reports contained in this section of the text.

Form. Business reports usually are prepared in two basic formats: the memorandum business report (see example, pages 276-77), and the more traditional, formal "left-bound business report" (see example, pages 284-85).

Format. The content of business reports will vary considerably. You will usually find, however, that the sequence of the parts of a business report will differ somewhat from educational reports. The major difference is that the first section of a business report may be the ***summary*** section, which you would normally expect to find as the last section in an educational report.

Style. Business reports are usually single spaced, blocked paragraph, with double spacing between paragraphs. The memorandum business report follows the preparation guidelines for a regular memo. The "left-bound business report" normally follows the same guidelines that are used in preparation of a left-bound educational manuscript.

References. The most common style of reference notation in a business report is the ***endnote*** system of placing all complete reference information at the back of the report.

Displays. Business reports commonly contain some type(s) of visual displays. They may include actual photographs, typed tables, graphs, inked drawings, illustrations, and so on. The typist normally does not have to actually prepare the display, except for the typed table, but does have to allow room on the typed page so that the display may be affixed. In some situations the typist may be required to actually draw various graphs and illustrations. (The general types of graphs and the preparation of them are listed on pages 271-74.)

Exhibits. Because of the nature of the business report, it is quite common to include various types of exhibits in the report (see display information above). When the displays are too long and/or too large to illustrate within the body of the report, they are usually placed on the last pages of the report and identified as "Exhibits."

Supportive Parts. The business report may contain some or all of the supportive parts you find in the educational report. One important addition is the "preparation and distribution information." This information includes the name(s) of the individual(s) involved in the preparation of the report and also the name(s) of the individual(s) who are receiving a copy of it. This information is sometimes placed on the cover sheet or on a separate page immediately following the cover sheet. On memorandum reports the preparation and distribution information is usually found in one of three locations: (1) in the opening informational lines, (2) in the first paragraph of the body, or (3) as the last entry on the last page.

Preparation of Displays and Exhibits. Typists are usually responsible for the preparation of display tables and may be asked to prepare simple graphs and drawings. When planning for the space to be left for an affixed display and/or exhibit, be sure to allow enough white space before, after, and around the dis-

Timing 3-13

S.I. 1.56

The common cattail is a wild plant which grows in marshy places. 14
Although the tall plants are rooted underwater in the mud, they raise 28
their long, slender leaves and fuzzy brown flowers to heights of over 42
seven feet. Birds seek shelter among the cattails, as the very dense 56
foliage and growth provides security. Early Indians used the cattail 70
for food, mattress stuffing, and material for basket weaving. People 84
today like to arrange cattails in an attractive container for display 98
in their homes. Other common names for the cattail are bulrushes and 112
tule-reeds. Gathering cattails can be fun and also interesting. The 126
cattails can be sprayed with various types of material to make a most 140
interesting display for the home or office. It is not difficult, for 154
most people, to create the various displays. A hobby and crafts shop 168
will be able to furnish many varities of spray materials which can be 182
applied by anyone. The next time you wish to prepare an interesting, 196
different creation, attempt cattail displays. 205

----1----2----3----4----5----6----7----8----9---10---11---12---13---14

Timing 3-14

S.I. 1.57

Interest in amateur tennis during the past ten years has been on 14
the increase. The popularity of the newer type of steel and aluminum 28
rackets skyrocketed. In cold climates where outdoor tennis cannot be 42
played all year, many buildings were turned into indoor courts. Some 56
of the newer indoor courts have restaurants and saunas. Today, there 70
are great opportunities for boys and girls, as well as men and women. 84
The professional tennis world needs players and teachers. Even for a 98
player who does not make the professional status, playing tennis just 112
for the exercise and fun is still a very exciting sport. The results 126
of playing tennis, whether professional or amateur, would be pleasing 140
to most people. A new physical fitness which comes with the exertion 154
of playing tennis is superb. Muscle tone is excellent, excess weight 168
goes away, and in general, the total health of the individual will be 182
greatly improved. Tennis is a rather inexpensive activity. A charge 196
for the court and the buying of tennis balls will add to the cost. 210

----1----2----3----4----5----6----7----8----9---10---11---12---13---14

Task 35

Type as a contents page.

CONTENTS / I. The Challenge of Teaching-page 1 / A. Today-page 5 / B. Tomorrow-page 10 / II. Public School Structure-page 19 / A. Pre-school-page 24 / B. Lower Elementary-page 29 / C. Middle School-page 35 / D. Junior High-page 41 / E. Senior High-page 49 / III. Post-Secondary Education-page 54 / A. Vocational-Technical School-page 60 / B. Community College-page 64 / C. Junior College-page 72 / D. Four-Year College/University-page 77 / E. Graduate School-page 84

Task 36

Type as a contents page.

I. Our Economic Society 1
A. Our Needs + Wants 3
B. Producing Goods 6
C. Providing Services 10

II. Society + Business 11
A. What is "business"? 13
B. How business is organized 16

III. Your Relationship with Business 18
A. As a Consumer 21
B. As a Producer 25

Task 37

Prepare a contents page for Task 22 (the manuscript on pages 265+266).

Timing 3-15

S.I. 1.58

Employee evaluation is one of the most important tasks of any of 14
today's modern managers. The work of employees must be evaluated and 28
assessed from time to time. A good evaluation is needed to determine 42
whether or not an employee should be promoted and receive an increase 56
in salary. The system of evaluating workers also pinpoints any signs 70
of future problems if the employee simply is not doing his or her job 84
well. The modern manager has to devise some sort of system that will 98
be fair and, at the same time, very comprehensive. Devising the sole 112
instrument to be used is not an easy task and requires much time. An 126
efficient procedure might be to gather and review the instruments and 140
programs in use by similar organizations. There are consultant firms 154
who, for a small charge, can help the manager develop a comprehensive 168
evaluation program. The new system must undergo a thorough period of 182
testing before full implementation. The length of the testing period 196
should always be determined by the structure of a particular business 210
and the number of persons who are involved in the testing project. 223

----1----2----3----4----5----6----7----8----9---10---11---12---13---14

Timing 3-16

S.I. 1.59

The wise use of energy is becoming more and more important every 14
day. Until recently, most persons weren't aware of actually how much 28
energy was being wasted daily. The wise use of energy also saves the 42
consumer considerable amounts of money. Each degree over sixty-eight 56
on the thermostat adds three percent to the required amount of energy, 70
and adds the same amount to a fuel bill. A hundred-watt bulb burning 84
for ten hours uses about one pound of coal--costing the consumer more 98
money for wasting electricity. If that faucet leaks just one drop of 112
water each second, it can waste seven hundred gallons of precious and 126
needed water each year. There are many ways to conserve our nation's 140
energy. Each person must make conservation practice a habit. People 156
often have a mistaken thought that conserving is a problem of someone 170
else. This train of thinking could only hamper all efforts of energy 184
conservation. To save scarce resources for some future use, each one 196
must do his or her part to conserve precious energy. 207

----1----2----3----4----5----6----7----8----9---10---11---12---13---14

Task 29

Type as cover sheet.

MEAL PLANS FOR STUDENTS, a report for Business Communications, by yourself. Instructor is Mrs. Andersen. The class meets on Monday, and Wednesday from 10:45 to noon.

Task 30

Type as cover sheet.

A NEW WAY TO TRAVEL is the title of a short paper you have prepared for Dr. Fox in your Monday evening Literature 118 class (meets from 7 to 9 o'clock)

Task 31

Type as cover sheet.

Selecting a Post-Secondary Institution, by Jane L. Dalton for B.E. 714 (Introduction to Research Methods) Section 01. The course is taught by Dr. Seymour.

Task 32

Type as cover sheet.

READING ABILITY / By / Raymond Shepek / L.E. 690, Section 07 / Improvement of Reading / M/W/F/, 7:00 p.m. / Mrs. Leslman / Current Date

Task 33

Type as cover sheet.

HUNTING ANCESTORS CAN BE FUN / By / Mrs. Darlene Morton / History 330, Section 16 / History of Early America / Saturday, 9:00 a.m. / Dr. Mays / Current Date

Task 34

Type as contents page.

Reference: p.246

CONTENTS

Five-Minute Timings

Timing 5-1
S.I. 1.44

Wise managers of money seem to have the ability or the foresight 14
make their earnings stretch a long way. Others spend haphazardly and 28
always seem to be short of money long before the next salary check is 42
due. What factors do the wise managers follow? 52

Food buying takes a large part of the salary check. In the area 66
of buying groceries, one can save a large amount of money by wise and 80
careful buying. There are many fine guides that a shopper can follow 94
to economize and save money. 99

Probably the one best rule to attempt, at the outset, is to plan 113
ahead. Plan all your meals in detail for a certain period--a week, a 127
month--but never day by day. After making the complete plan for your 141
groceries, you are then ready to prepare your shopping list. Be cer- 155
tain that you have included all items necessary for cooking the meals 169
to come. Many people forget to include the small items such as salt, 183
pepper, and needed condiments. Once you have made a list, additional 197
guides are very useful and helpful. 204

After making the major shopping list, you should compare prices. 218
You should look at all the local advertisements in newspapers. Quite 231
often, you will save considerable amounts of your money by comparison 245
shopping. One caution--do not waste time or money for gas by driving 259
your car from store to store. If you do this, you are defeating your 273
purpose. After deciding where to do your shopping, your next step is 287
that of doing the actual shopping. 294

Several tips apply when you are actually in the store. First of 308
all, do not deviate from your basic list, unless you happen to locate 322
some exceptional bargains. Next, compare all the prices according to 336
size: calculate the cost for each ounce, or pound, and then compare. 350
Remember to take the cents-off coupons that you may have clipped from 364
magazines and newspaper ads. Do avoid impulse buying. Experts agree 378
that impulse and unplanned buying accounts for a large portion of the 392
family's grocery bill. Another good tip is to not go shopping if you 406
are hungry. The best time to go shopping is after eating a big meal. 420
You will not be tempted to buy things you really do not want or need. 434

If you will follow the shopping guides discussed here you should 448
find that your weekly shopping trip will be less expensive. The trip 462
should also be much easier and enjoyable for you to complete. 474

----1----2----3----4----5----6----7----8----9---10---11---12---13---14

Task 25

Type as bibliography.

Bibliography--------One hundred Ideas for Living. Published by Washington Editors, Inc., N.Y., Zee, Inc., A. S. Kenney, Editor. "Commandments for Shoppers," p. 16, 1982.--------Wilson Leslie and Sharon Osstres, Consumer Issues and Trends, Mason Publishing Company, New York, 1980, p. 14--------Economic Problems by Wanda Larson, Harold Martin, Kayleen Snyder, and Franklin Thomas, 10th ed., Horizon Pub. Co., New York, 1981, p. 838--------"Braintrust in Washington--Boom or Bust?" U. S. Report, published by Nelson Howard, Editor, March, 13, 1982. Vol. XXXL--No. 9, Washington, DC, page 78. --------Gary Berg, Jack Johnson, Lorraine Missling, and Chet Petersen, American Business Understanding, 4th edition, New York: Advanced Publications, 1982, p. 34-116.

Task 26

Type as bibliography.

BIBLIOGRAPHY / James, Richard J., and Stella Brownson. Data Processing Systems for the Office (Dallas, Texas: Holt and Brown Publishing Company, 1981), p. 91. / Lydell, Arnold, Betty Peterson, and Alice Brown. Procedures in the Modern Office (Chicago, Illinois: Winston Publishing Association, 1982), p. 144-157. / Rice, James. Using Your Skills (New York, New York, 1980) ABC Publishing Co., p. 6. / "The Paperwork Explosion," Today's Modern Office, April, 1982, Vol. 26, No. 1, p. 44. / Hood, Louis. Supervision in the Office (Montreal, Quebec, 1981), p. 414.

Task 27

Type as bibliography.

Bibliography / Wilson's Famous Ideas for Managing Money. Published by the Wilson New York Editors, Inc., LeRoy Wilson, Editor, New York, New York, "Seven Ways to Save Money," p. 16, 1981 ------ Raymond L. Johnson and Lester White, The United States Economy. San Francisco, California: The Jones Publishing Company, 1981, p. 3-7. ------ Consumer Problems by Alvin Shepek, Kenneth Islam, and Jane L. Dalton, 10 ed., Pittsburgh Publishing Company, Pittsburgh, PA, 1977, page 838.------ "Wasting our Nation's Resources," North American Report, published by Edward Mason, Editor, March 1, 1979, Vol. XXXL --- No. 9, page 36.------ James L. Melrose, Ronald S. Puttman, and Gene Blossom, Living Today AND Tomorrow, 4th ed., Lil Rose Publishers, St. Louis, Missouri, 1982, page 121.

Task 28

Type as cover sheet.

Reference: p. 245

COMPETITIVE PRICING AT THE BOOKSTORE / By / Leslie Ryan / English 101 / Report Writing / T/Th, 9 o'clock / Dr. Alderson / Current Date

Timing 5-2
S.I. 1.45

Backpacking in a national forest wilderness may be one method of 14
escaping the crowded conditions of permanent campsites. Backpacking, 28
or hiking with a knapsack, provides dedicated campers with an unusual 42
experience in areas that cannot be reached by car. In planning for a 56
backpacking trip, one should include the entire family. Age seems to 70
be no barrier; young children can carry lighter packs. 81

Experienced backpackers pride themselves on being able to travel 95
light. With some, saving weight is almost a fetish. Backpackers are 109
likely to say that they cut the towels in half and saw the handles of 123
their toothbrushes off to save a few ounces. Hikers measure just the 137
right amount of necessary food and place it in plastic bags. Pads of 151
soap are included, eliminating a bar of soap and a dishcloth. All of 165
these tricks are designed to save the ounces which make up pounds. 179

In addition to traveling light, it is necessary for the hiker to 193
feel comfortable while backpacking in the wilderness. Therefore, the 207
boots that the person selects for the trip should be made of leather, 221
or possibly rubber, if hiking in wet country; shoe soles made of good 235
rubber or a synthetic material are good for hiking. The boots should 249
be comfortable to prevent sore feet on the trip; some hikers prefer a 263
pair of boots that will fit over two pairs of socks, one thin and one 276
thick. The feet are better protected to withstand long mileage on an 290
uneven terrain in the wilderness. 297

There are three major types of packs used today: the packboard, 311
the frame, and the rucksack. The modern versions are the lightweight 325
aluminum packframes, angled at the shoulder and waist to fit the body 339
with nylon bands resting against the back. The frames come in sizes, 353
which vary, to fit different weights and heights. The light frame is 367
secured to the body by light straps from the lower section. The main 381
part of the pack weight is placed on the hips. When the waist straps 395
are released, the frame will hug the back and prevent the walker from 409
losing his or her balance while jumping from rock to rock or climbing 423
along a narrow ledge. 427

Every backpacking person must solve one major problem--whether a 441
tent should be taken. The solution is dependent upon the site or the 455
region to which the person is backpacking. Generally, each person in 469
the hiking group should carry a tent. Lightweight nylon tents do not 483
add much weight to the backpack. 490

----1----2----3----4----5----6----7----8----9---10---11---12---13---14

the price lower. In addition, the consumer is faced with a large variety and type of the same kind of goods, forcing him to make a choice in the area of quality and brand name. / Confusing selling methods. All one has to do is to look at the myriad of advertising techniques used today. From the commercials on television, radio, newspaper pages, and "give-away" gimmicks, one can readily see the confusion that arises. Each advertiser says his product is the best. One consumer expert indicated that a wise consumer looks at advertising by analyzing two points of view: for information about the product and also for deceptive or misleading statements.[3]--------Wanda Larson, Harold Martin, Kayleen Snyder, and Franklin Thomas, Economic Problems, 10th ed., Horizon Publishing Co., New York, 1981, p. 838.--------

Conflict of interests. In the past, there have been many manufacturing groups which have had a tendency to band together to insure higher prices for themselves. In other instances certain groups have worked closely with the government to control prices. Recently, however, many consumer groups have arisen to protect buyers from unfair practices and to give the individual trughful product information. It seems, however, that now the problem is that we have too manys groups involved with protecting the consumer.[4]------------"Braintrust in Washington--Boom or Bust?" U.S. Report, Nelson Howard, Editor, March 13, 1982, Vol. XXL--No. 9, p. 78, Washington, DC.----------

Consumer Rights

Consumers do have certain rights. These include the right to be informed, the right to safety, the right to choose, and the right to be heard.[5] -----------Gary Berg, Jack Johnson, Lorraine Missling, and Chet Petersen, American Business Understanding, 4th edition, Advanced Publications, New York, 1982, p. 34-116.-------------------

(Para.) / You also have the responsibility to be honest and to be reasonable in making complaints. It would seem than, that being a good consumer and buying goods and services wisely is largely an individual matter. The intelligent consumer must study articles, be knowledgeable in analyzing advertising, and also know consumer rights.

Task 24

Type as bibliography.

Reference: p. 243

BIBLIOGRAPHY

Armes, Jane, E. J. James, and Betty Jane Onis. Secretarial Systems Cincinnati, Ohio: Poston, Inc., 1982.

Onie, George. Control in the Office. Chicago, Illinois: Z-Z Publishing Company, 1981.

Prentis, Richard A., and James E. Johnson. Clerical Systems. Dallas, Texas: Weston Publishers, 1982.

"Speed and Quality in Handling Workflow." Office Systems. January, 1981. Vol. 29, No. 3.

Wilson, James. Using Your Skills. New York: Creative Enterprises, 1982.

Timing 5-3
S.I. 1.46

Most of us travel through life eating the same old kinds of dull 14
fruits and vegetables--day after day, week after week, and year after 28
year. For some unknown reason, we seem to be afraid to try something 42
new and different. The exotic fruits and vegetables are beginning to 56
appear in produce markets all over the country. The produce which is 70
termed "exotic" could be **imported from a foreign country** or merely an 82
unusual and different kind of produce. For persons who really desire 96
and like to try new and different foods, exotic produce will bring an 112
awakened sense of taste and will introduce a new eating pattern in an 126
otherwise dull routine of eating. 133

One of the finest fruits on the market today is the mango, which 147
is a fruit from the tropics. Mangos are becoming more and more popu- 161
lar all over the land. The papaya is also a very good tropical fruit 175
that has lots of vitamins and is good to eat. A carambola is quite a 189
strange looking fruit. It has a waxy appearance and contains a solid 203
meat. The cherimoya, or custard apple, is shaped like a large straw- 217
berry and is green in color and oval in shape. The fruit is not very 231
attractive, but has a delicious and delicate flavor. Kiwi fruit, the 245
Chinese gooseberry, is grown in New Zealand; thus the name "Kiwi" has 259
been given to this fruit in honor of the native kiwi bird. The taste 273
is mild and quite enjoyable. 279

The celery root has an ugly appearance. The outside of the root 293
is deceiving; inside the ugly wrapping lies a great surprising flavor 307
treat for vegetable lovers. Fine Jerusalem artichokes, also known as 321
sunchokes, have lots of uses. The crispy, crunchy food has a nutlike 335
flavor and makes a great finger food. A jicama is sometimes known as 349
a Mexican or Chinese potato. The brownish vegetable looks like a raw 363
turnip. The cripsy and crunchy taste treat is quite good when served 377
with a dip of some sort. 382

Although all of us seem to be creatures of habit, there is a new 396
world of eating delights right in the produce bins, waiting for us to 410
discover new taste treats. All it takes is some searching and a very 424
sincere desire to try something new. Maybe a recipe or two would add 436
to the variety of these exotic vegetables and fruits. Many cookbooks 450
contain delightful recipes with which to vary our menus. 461

----1----2----3----4----5----6----7----8----9---10---11---12---13---14

Task 23

Type as left-bound manuscript.

Reference: p. 242

Student note: Be sure to correct errors that were overlooked in editing.

TO PURCHASE--OR NOT TO PURCHASE

Use "endnote" system

I. Wise Buying

This individual

A wise consumer knows how to make a good choice. He is certain that he can save money by knowing how to buy goods and services. Making a choice today is difficult because of the extreme variety of goods and services one can buy. A wise consumer also has to decide if the goods and services that are to be purchases is something that is actually needed of something that is just wanted. Too many persons are caried away by buying something that they just want and don't really need. Debts have a habit of piling up when one buys strictly on the basis of wants. / (Para.) / One recent study of consumer buying habits estimated that a careless shopper--someone with run-of-the-mill luck, buying in a purely random fashion--loses 12%$ to 14% of the total potential buying power. 1-----"Commandments for Shoppers," One Hundred Ideas for Living, Published by Washington Editors, Inc., A.S. Kenney, Editor, Washington, DC, 1982. page 16.--- by using common sense, knowledge, and great care in buying, one can save a great deal of money. / Consumer Problems / The consumer is faced with problems today that haven't existed in the past. One expert stated that these problems were that consumers and producers had conflicting interests, the modern market is terribly complex, there is a variety of goods available, selling methods are confusing, and certain groups have selfish aims and present a conflict of interest. 2-----Wilson Leslie and Sharon Osstres, Consumer Issues and Trends, Mason Publishing Company, New York, 1980, page 14.-----

----- / Conflicting interest. Quite obviously, the problem exists that the buyer wants to pay the lowest price possible, and the seller wants to realize the highest profit possible. Very often there is a conflict between the buyer and the seller. Other factors which have a certain bearing on this conflict are competition between manufacturers making the same type of product. The retail buyer often complicates the problem by sometimes suying and sometimes not buying available supplies and of goods and services. / (Para.) / Complex markets. Many years ago, the buyer and the seller knew each other very well. Because of the population expansion and the large expansion of business rarely do the two have the remotest idea who the other is. This poor relationship can, of course, cause many problems. In aedition, the retailer doesn't know the manufacturer who makes the goods and many--maybe even most times--times deals with the middleman known as a wholesaler. / Goods Available. The law of supply and demand enteres into the consumer situation. If there is a shortage of a certain product and a large number of consumers want to buy that product, then very likely the price will be higher. The reverse of this situation makes

(cont'd. on next page)

Timing 5-4

S.I. 1.47

Each spring thousands of gardeners declare war on one bothersome 14
weed that seems to plague everyone. This weed is the lowly dandelion 28
plant. In earlier times, people savored all the virtues of this many 42
faceted plant. Rather than referring to it as a weed, folks utilized 56
the very fine herbal qualities. Some broths and tonics were made and 70
utilized to restore health to persons who were ill. Even now, modern 84
pharmacies continue to use extracts of this springtime plant in quite 98
a number of medicines on the market for our use. 108

As a food, the dandelion is a big source of nutritious, healthy, 122
and delicious food. It is quite rich in proteins, calcium, and iron. 136
The plant contains more Vitamin A than spinach or green peppers. The 150
durable leaves, which may be used in many delicious salads, should be 164
picked before the first blossoms appear. The tender leaves, although 178
tangy in taste, are very nutritious. If you carefully dry the leaves 192
and boil them correctly, you can make delicious teas. You might wish 206
to consume the new blossoms and make wines, salad garnishes, and some 220
blossoms which have been surrounded by a very tasty batter. You must 234
carefully cut off the stems, as they have a very bitter and offensive 248
flavor. The fine roots of the dandelion plant may be used for coffee 262
extract and some fine broths. You could also make some colorful dyes 276
by utilizing the root systems of the plant. If you are attempting to 290
eliminate this plant from a beautiful lawn, be careful to dig all the 304
root system. If one single portion remains under the ground, chances 318
are, the very next season's crop of dandelions will flourish and will 332
increase in your lawn. Perhaps after trying out the benefits of this 346
misunderstood plant, you will refer to it as a friend and utilize the 360
herbal qualities. Locate a recipe for tea or salad and try this fine 374
plant for a new and exciting taste treat. 382

After you have discovered the treats in store from the dandelion 396
plant, explore other kinds of wild plant life. Most varieties of the 410
world of plants are available in natural states and will provide many 424
treats and supplements. One caution, however, be sure that you study 438
the living plants you are going to consume. There are many poisonous 452
plants which are fatal if eaten. 458

----1----2----3----4----5----6----7----8----9---10---11---12---13---14

that most people already have numerous skills in one degree or another. These skills include talking, listening, reading, writing, using numbers, and using basic office machines. / (Para.) / Many persons have not yet learned effectively how to talk so that others will listen and conversely have not learned how to really listen and comprehend what others are saying. These two skills are probably the most sadly neglected in skill attainment. The skills of writing and using numbers may be developed through practice. The efficient use of office machines enters into an area of specialized technical skills. / Specialized Skills. At beginning level jobs, most of the worker's responsibility lies in the efficient processing of words. The worker may be involved mainly in three areas: typewriting, copying, and duplicating. / (Para.) / The basic electric typewriter is the most important segment of any office system.[4] Of the three skills, skill at the typewriter is the one most in demand. The use of typewriters in offices varies from the small office using a manual typewriter, to electric typewriters, to automated typing systems. The typist who can type accurately and rapidly will have no trouble adjusting to any system. / (Para.) / The world of copying and duplicating records and forms has received increased attention. Because of the need to control copy costs, copy machines are being developed that are much more efficient and can do a variety of work. Duplicating machines which differ from copy machines are also being used. Duplicating machines usually require the preparation of a stencil or master. Some of the newer machines have incorporated both copying and duplicating. / (Para.) / Office Environment / The time has passed when the "office" was thought of as a dull, drab place in which to do business. New ideas and new techniques are being used to make today's office a most pleasant place in which to work. In addition, it has been found that the average office worker will be much more efficient in pleasant surroundings. / (Para.) / Onie, among others, has identified environmental factors that are important to the office environment. They include light, color, music, air, and sound.[5] We will be hearing much more in the future about improving working conditions in the office.

---

[1]Richard A. Prentis and James E. Johnson, Clerical Systems, Weston Publishers, Dallas, Texas, 1982, p. 13, 14.

[2]"Speed and Quality in Handling Workflow," Office Systems, January 1981, Vol. 29, No. 3, p. 60.

[3]James Wilson, Using Your Skills, Creative Enterprises, New York, 1982.

[4]Jane Armes, E. J. James, and Betty Jane Onis, Secretarial Systems, Poston, Inc., Cincinnati, Ohio, 1982.

[5]George Onie, Control in the Office, A-Z Publishing Company, Toronto, Ontario, 1976.

Timing 5-5

S.I. 1.48

Each spring, many gardeners study seed catalogs and garden books 14
hours at a time. After a long winter, most are very anxious to begin 28
the chores of planting colorful flower beds and landscaping their own 42
property. One class of flowers is used very extensively. The garden 56
annuals--flowers that endure for only one year--are probably the most 70
popular of all flowers in the garden. The easier species to grow are 84
the zinnias, marigolds, petunias, and a number of others. Most seeds 98
are planted directly in the ground as soon as the weather warms after 112
the last killing frost. Many gardeners prefer to get a head start by 126
planting seeds inside, in small containers, before the actual growing 140
season. Usually an indoor start is more desirable, especially in the 154
areas which have short growing seasons and long winters. 165

Plants that have been started can also be purchased at all local 179
nursery or garden shops in the spring. Usually, these flowers are in 193
full bloom at the period when they are offered for sale; the gardener 207
can then select the colors and kinds of plants that will look best in 221
the specific garden sites and areas. After the flower garden bed has 235
been prepared, the gardener can simply place the fine blooming plants 249
in the earth and will have an instant garden. 258

Planning flower displays is a time-consuming and rewarding task. 272
For example, a mass of brilliant colors and textures could brighten a 286
dark corner or highlight darker foliage and shrubs. Some annuals are 300
better suited for border planting or edging. Others which grow quite 314
tall can be used for unique backgrounds or screening. There are many 328
annuals that make gorgeous bouquets of cut flowers. The gardener can 342
enjoy the fruits of his or her labor with vases of beautiful blossoms 356
placed all round the house. 361

Growing annuals in containers has become very popular. Creative 375
gardeners will move containers from one place to another to highlight 389
the most beautiful plants in bloom. A movable or mobile green garden 403
allows for the maximum use of color. 410

Most gardeners like to write all the detailed plans on paper. A 424
plan shows them exactly where each new plant is to be located and how 438
many plants should be purchased. 445

----1----2----3----4----5----6----7----8----9---10---11---12---13---14

and Retrieval / The important function of a record storage system is not only that of "putting documents away" but also that of finding and retrieving a document when needed. The method used in record storage is commonly referred to as filing. Filing has been defined as "a system in which records are arranged and stored according to a prescribed system so that they may be located easily and quickly and protected from any type of damage."[3] / (Para.) / Most experts would agree that there are five commonly used methods of storing records efficiently. Although there are many variations to the basic five, most offices use a system in which the filing method is one that is simple and efficient. / Alphabetic filing. This method, although based on a standard set of filing rules, is the simplest and probably the widest used method today in one form or another. / Subject filing. Subject filing is a more complex system requiring the person to be aware of and very familiar with the many subject divisions within a certain company. All materials pertaining to a subject category would be found in one file rather than many. / Geographic filing. Sometimes a business has transactions over a wide area. This type of business would use a system of keeping records by locality of units based on addresses rather than names. The addresses would still be filed in alphabetical order. / Numerical filing. Very often a business will have a tremendous number of individual records. Typical of this would be a hospital. Each client is assigned a number, and all information is filed numerically. / Chronological filing. Some businesses store records according to a date in time. Companies which must contact customers at particular times of the year find this method especially helpful.

----

[3]Ben White and Vera Riles, Filing, Retrieving, and Safekeeping (Denver, Colorado: Mountain Air Printing Company, 1982), p. 4.

Task 22

Type as left-bound manuscript.

JOBS TODAY

The Office / The concept of offices and office work has changed considerably over the past few decades. Businesses have expanded production and services at a rapid pace. The sheer volume of paper work generated by expanding business creates a new job market for workers. One source indicates that since World War II, the employment of office workers in Canada and the United States has grown between 300 and 400 percent.[1] Another publication recently reported that there is an estimated 7,300 miles of paper used daily by business and industry.[2] / (Para.) / Although there is a growing job market, it is a different type of market. The very environment of the office has changed. New ideas and concepts have made most modern offices pleasant places in which to work. The duties of the office worker have also changed. Because of automated equipment, many former routine and manual tasks are now done by machine. The office worker of today and of the future, therefore, has to have highly developed skills in specialized areas. / Needed Skills / There are two areas in which future office workers might well concentrate efforts in order to attain advancement and job satisfaction. They are general skills and technical skills. / (Para.) / General Skills. Wilson[3] indicates

(cont'd. on next page)

Timing 5-6

S.I. 1.49

Becoming a competent writer and spelling words correctly doesn't 14
just happen. Learning to spell words correctly requires great effort 28
and concentration. Ask any good speller which tool is used the most. 42
Usually, he or she will tell you that the dictionary is an indispens- 56
able tool. On the other hand, poorer spellers will probably tell you 70
that they can't or won't use the dictionary regularly. 81

Words which are misspelled cause many serious problems and great 95
difficulties to the writer and to the reader. A writer who is a poor 119
speller is usually much too embarrassed to write business or personal 133
letters, compositions, and reports. There are a few persons who will 147
go to great lengths to avoid all forms of writing because of the fear 161
that the problem in spelling skill will become known. Another disad- 175
vantage the poorer speller faces is that his or her vocabulary is one 189
that is quite limited. Rather than utilize exciting and vivid words, 203
phrases, and sentences, he or she is stuck with old, dull, boring, or 217
over-used words. Worse yet, there are some who use the wrong word in 231
the wrong place. Severe spelling problems and mistakes all add up to 245
a grueling time for the reader. 251

Probably the first step to becoming a better speller is to admit 265
that spelling is not one of your better talents. Then--proceed to do 279
something about the problem--now. You must study words that are very 293
frequently misspelled. Study only a few words at one time; after you 307
have mastered some, begin studying more new words. Another method of 321
improving your spelling technique is to keep a dictionary with you at 335
all times when you are writing. Sure, it takes a few fast moments to 349
use the dictionary--but think of how good you will feel, knowing that 363
the final result is an example of your very best efforts. 375

Studying the common spelling rules is another route to improving 389
your spelling abilities. Learning root words and some of the origins 403
of words will also be another method to improve spelling. Other ways 417
which might help are: learn word syllables, the parts of speech, the 431
prefixes and suffixes, and homonyms and synonyms. If you concentrate 445
on pronouncing words correctly, you will surely improve your spelling 459
ability. You can become a better speller if you really try. 461

----1----2----3----4----5----6----7----8----9---10---11---12---13---14

2 ⟶

information in the manual which pertains to ~~their~~ his/her job. The material should be returned for revision.

TS

Revision.

ds

The writing team's next step is to analyze all suggestions and revise the material. The manual then may be duplicated in final form. Some type of formal presentation should be made to indoctrinate all employees. As time passes, the manual should be examined and revised ~~if~~ when necessary.

Task 21

TRADITIONAL FOOTNOTE METHOD

Type as left-bound manuscript.

Student note: Correct errors that have been overlooked in editing.

OUR PAPER HIGHWAY

Records

The storing of valuable documents and records has had a place in history almost from the beginning of time. Even then, early man sought to find a way to preserve and keep important records of his existence. As buying and selling evolved, the need to keep important records of business transactions also grew. Throughout history, records storage and retrieval has become an exciting and rather new career field.

Importance of Records Storage

Because of added productivity and correspondence of businesses of today, the sheer volume of paperwork has increased beyond one's wildest imagination. Business records take up more space than any other single item. 1 ← Raise number Not only has the need for additional space become critical, but the cost of maintaining the records' system has risen.

One expert indicated that if trends continue, the cost of filing just one document could rise to ten cents.[2] The problemd increase, as one file drawer can hold only a certain amount of items. Not only do the records take up precious space, but the need for higher salaries and equipment soars. Quite obviously, any time or effort spent by office workers or any money spent by a business firm is totally wasted unless the records are really needed and unless those records can be found quickly when needed. / Methods of Storage

ss → ______________ (18 spaces long for elite type, 15 for pica)

ds →

Reference: pp. 238-241

[1]Judy L. Holbreck and Vincent T. Marcus, Problems in Records Storage (Dayton, Ohil: Western Publishing Company, 1981), p. 2: ← ss

← ds

[2]Deborah Dane, "The Rising Cost of Record Storage." Management and Money (April 1982), p. 52.

(cont'd. on next page)

Timing 5-7
S.I. 1.50

Groups of waterfowl fly thousands of miles north every spring to 14
the same breeding ground. During the autumn, as all of their species 28
have done, they fly southward to winter in woody, hot marshes. Is it 42
instinct, habit, or some other unknown mechanism in their brains that 56
forces their flight southward? Whatever the cause, a large number of 70
species do follow the same flight pattern each year during migration. 84
The birds make the exact same stopovers, nesting areas, and winter in 98
warm marshes exactly as did their parent group. This distinct flight 112
pattern can be observed year after year. 120

Routine behavior by birds is actually predictable and may cause 134
some observers to wonder if all birds do have an instinct or merely a 148
habit. Canadian Geese have long-established nesting colonies in many 162
places where they have not nested for years or decades. Perhaps, the 176
changes in nesting areas are chiefly due to the fact that humans have 190
altered and changed nesting grounds to such an extent that many birds 214
are too frightened to return to the familiar grounds. 225

The homing instinct by waterfowl is operated through a female of 239
the species. Younger hens tend to return to the exact nesting ground 253
on which they were reared. The drakes, old or young, are the natural 267
followers; they will wait for the guidance of the hen. 278

Waterfowl have adapted to the changes in habitat. Mallard ducks 292
have demonstrated the unique ability to adapt to change brought on by 306
our civilization. Even in the middle of larger cities, they nest and 320
rear their young on marshes, in catch basins, and in city parks. The 334
mallards often choose quite unusual nesting sites which might include 348
grass, a quiet rose garden, and even the top of a dock piling. Human 362
predations and disturbances can, however, cause a real problem to all 375
waterfowl at one time or another. 482

During the fall and winter, large numbers of the ducks and geese 396
often rest in clear water areas in or near towns and cities which are 410
quite densely populated. The fowl quickly become tamed and willingly 424
accept handouts from all visitors. When the breeding urge and desire 438
to travel northward begins to stir their wild instincts, the initial, 452
natural wariness returns. 457

Many cities and towns are now establishing new wild life refuges 471
for all types of fowl. Perhaps this one new conservation effort will 485
enable the waterfowl to continue on their distinct and unique flights 509
each year. 511

----1----2----3----4----5----6----7----8----9---10---11---12---13---14

Task 20 Office MANUALS ALL CAPS triple space

Type as unbound manuscript.

Student note: Correct errors that may have been overlooked in editing.

Purpose

triple space

More and more offices are preparing and utilizing office manuals. There are many reasons why a firm would develop office manuals.

Information

The manual usually is developed to share pertinent facts and basic information with all employees. Valuable supervisory time is saved due to the fact that initial instructions to new employees need not be repeated. The new worker can read the manual carefully and refer back to it if necessary.

The printed manual is available to all employees at any time. This allows the employees to know exactly the area of his or her responsibilities and duties.

triple space

Advantages and Disadvantages

As with any printed information, the use of office manuals has both advantages and disadvantages.

Advantages

Publicizing the advantages of an office manual will make it much easier for employee acceptance.

Saves money. Using a printed office manual saves money by the fact that the supervisory time is not taken up with endless repetitions of instructions.

Eliminates errors. If an employee has a question about prcedure and the supervisor isn't avaialbe, he can refer to the manual promptly before a costly error is made.

Disadvantages / Costly to produce. In some cases, the manual can be quite costly to produce. There will have to be time spent in the development of the manual and, the time of employees is a financial cost. There is also the printing and binding of the manual to consider.

Reduces worker initiative. The biggest disadvantage could be that the individual worker may regard the manual as specific instructions and make no effort to do anything creatively. The worker may develop a new idea that could be quite cost-saving, but not offer his suggestion because the manual states that it must be done some other day.

PREPARATION

LOWERCASE / SMALL LETTERS

The preparation of an office manual should be completed in a logical, scientific way. First, a committee of workers whould develop a comprehensive out line of the subjects which will be included in the manual.

Writing

The actual writers of the manual should be a good "mix" of experienced and new employees from all levels. The writers must gather and analyze the data for each included subject.

Dubplication and Distribution

The manual should be deuplicated and distributed to all employees. Each employee should be given the responsibility to carefully read and try out the

Timing 5-8

S.I. 1.51

If you have ever visited an art museum, you probably have had an 14
opportunity to view many great sculptures. Talented artists from all 28
over the world have created quite beautiful sculptures. Most people, 42
however, don't realize that many sculptures are available for viewing 56
at any time. The raw earth provides lots of unique and most exciting 70
sights which cannot be found in a museum. The wonderful earth itself 84
has sculptures that may be centuries old and constantly in a state of 98
change. 99

A big waterfall that cascades and flows over the cliffs presents 113
a beautiful sight. Great mountain ranges reaching into the sunny sky 127
produce awe and wonder to most viewers. In any year, tourists travel 141
quite long distances to view the unique landscape or eroded sandstone 155
pillars and arches in dry desert locations. Others travel to see the 169
fantastic sculptures of fine granite slopes, ridges, and peaks in the 183
East. The very gentle contours of a pasture found in the Midwest are 197
most interesting when you pause to question how the landforms of this 211
country, or world, were created. 217

Unlike the surfaces of the moon, our planet is most vibrant with 231
underground activity. Footprints left on the moon could remain there 245
for millions of years. In the warm climate or changing atmosphere of 259
our planet, however, most footprints or any mark would disappear in a 273
matter of days. The earth's surface, unlike the surface of the moon, 287
develops energy from within. Thus, the earth's surface is constantly 301
altered and changed. The winds, rains, and sun are ably aided by the 315
forces of gravity to develop natural sculptures. Sometimes this type 329
of change is not always for the good of the earth. 339

All landforms have a past history and a future course that could 353
develop. The full processes that sculpt the landscape take on direct 367
importance as soon as we try to modify the ground for our own uses or 381
try to protect people from such hazards as floods and mudslides. Man 395
must work with the forces and events of nature to strongly ensure the 409
continuance of the beautiful natural sculptures of our planet. If we 423
continue on an ever-destructive path, the many magnificent sculptures 437
of earth will disappear forever. 444

----1----2----3----4----5----6----7----8----9---10---11---12---13---14

<u>Lack of skills</u>. Until a few years ago, office workers could usually obtain employment directly from high school. Many office positions, however, require more specialized training.

<u>Automated equipment</u>. Because of the development of highly automated equipment, many offices require employees with a background in electronic office systems. The new employee must be highly skilled in the use of automatic equipment and thoroughly understand the techniques and uses of word and data processing.

<u>Career as Office Systems Manager</u>

Because of the changes that have taken place, there is a definite need for offices to use modern techniques and scientific methods. This in turn increases the need for efficient office systems managers. The area of office management as a career can be profitable and productive. Training is available at most post-secondary schools which offer specialized courses in "office systems management."

Task 19

Type as unbound manuscript.

HUNTING ANCESTORS CAN BE FUN / Many people are discovering a new and challenging hobby. This newest pastime is searching for ancestors, or tracing the genealogy of the family. Not only is it fun and rewarding to find out who your ancestors were, but you also learn much about history in the process./ Family Sources / The first place an amateur genealogist must look for information is the immediate family members and any records that may be available. / <u>Immediate Relatives</u> / Of course the first step in tracing a "family tree" is to ask yourself how much and what do you know about your family. By writing those facts on paper, you will be surprised at how much you really know. / <u>Direct interviews.</u> If members of your family are living fairly close, you might want to arrange for interviews with each one. Questions you will want to ask will concern their knowledge of previous family members. Data you will need will consist of dates, exact names, places, and so on. / <u>Letter interviews.</u> Perhaps you know of a relative or relatives that live in distant cities. You will want to compose a letter that states your extent of knowledge about a person and then ask for specific facts that your relative might have concerning that ancestor. Even if that relative doesn't have the exact answer, perhaps she or he can direct you to another source of information. / <u>Family Records</u> / Another source frequently overlooked is the records which a family might have kept over the years. / <u>Bible.</u> The basic source of information in the family is the old "family Bible." Very often, when data was not recorded in any other place, births, deaths, and marriages were frequently recorded in the Bible. / <u>Diaries and letters.</u> Old diaries and letters can be a "treasure-house" of knowledge regarding past family members. Even if they do not give out specific data, you can often learn a lot about the ancestor's life-style and, in general, more about him. / Other Sources / After you have exhausted the sources of your immediate family, there are other places you will want to check. / <u>Printed</u> / Several sources can be searched that may contain printed information regarding your family. / <u>Public library</u>. The library often has a wealth of information concerning early families and history. There are many genealogical periodicals and books written on the subject. / <u>Local records.</u> In searching for printed verification of births, deaths, and marriages, the courthouse in the county in which your ancestor lived can usually provide the full name of your ancestors and other valuable information./<u>State, Province, and Federal records.</u> Other suggested sources for exact information include state/province archives and vital statistics' bureaus. National Archives will also provide a wealth of information, but you must know the dates and place your ancestor resided.

Timing 5-9
S.I. 1.52

Reclining in the cabin of a luxurious airliner gives most people 14
one of the finest experiences in life. Flying is the quickest way to 28
travel a long distance from one location to another. In two or three 42
hours you can travel a distance by air that would require fourteen or 56
more hours of driving via car. You can fly from the Pacific Coast to 70
the Atlantic Coast in a little over five hours. The exact, same trip 84
by car would take you days of exhaustive driving. If your goal is to 98
enjoy the varying scenery that stretches between the coasts, you will 112
definitely want to drive. 117

If you have never had the opportunity to glide through the skies 131
at a very high rate of speed, you might be somewhat nervous or appre- 145
hensive about your very first flight. Rest assured--flying is always 159
safer than driving your own vehicle from your garage to school, work, 173
or on a shopping trip. 177

Traveling via the fantastic jet airplane is the fastest and most 191
economical way to travel for a person, if the distance traveled is at 205
least two hundred miles. If two or more individuals will be covering 219
less than five hundred miles, travel by car will be considerably more 233
economical. If the distance is over one thousand miles, traveling by 247
jet airplane is the fastest way to go and is usually considered to be 261
more economical. The time saved is valuable, especially if your time 275
is limited. 277

Traveling across an entire ocean to another country can be quite 291
an enjoyable experience, especially if traveling in one of the newest 305
wide-bodied jet planes. All seating is quite comfortable and all the 319
aisles are wide. These jumbo jets have a staircase which leads to an 333
upper lounge for the first-class passengers to enjoy. Some airplanes 347
now have a closed-circuit television screen which enables everyone to 361
observe the take-off and landing and the cockpit gauges and controls. 375
On longer flights, you might enjoy a full-length movie in addition to 389
delicious meals and snacks. 394

All experienced air travelers might tell you about all the times 408
they have experienced small inconveniences, such as lost luggage or a 422
delayed flight. Although these things happen, most flights are quite 436
uneventful and very enjoyable. When you hear the roar of jet engines 450
overhead, picture yourself zooming across the big sky in splendor and 464
luxury. 465

----1----2----3----4----5----6----7----8----9---10---11---12---13---14

Task 18

Type as unbound manuscript.

THE OFFICE SYSTEMS MANAGER

Need

The office scene has changed considerably over the past few years. Business has grown, more transactions are taking place, and certain incidents have occurred that require most offices of today to hire a new type of employee--the office systems manager. His or her duties mainly are to see that the office is run as efficiently as possible.

Changes

There are many exciting and new changes that have taken place in the world of offices today. Some of them are inevitable and others have been developed to replace older methods.

Financial Costs

Many businesses have tended to view the cost of operating an office as a necessary, but unproductive, evil. Executives have seen the cost of operating an office rise rapidly.

Increased paperwork. One reason costs have increased is the fact that paperwork in an office has increased dramatically. Unless the flow of paperwork is carefully controlled, costs will skyrocket.

Inflationary times. During the past ten years, the pattern of constantly rising costs has been consistent. Many businesses are forced to cut costs in every conceivable manner. The office systems manager is directly responsible for cost analysis and efficient production.

Change in Employees

There also has been a dramatic change in the characteristics of office personnel throughout the years.

Retiring workers. Many employers feel that there just aren't enough employees to replace older, experienced workers who have retired. New workers are costly to train and sometimes just can't do the job.

(cont'd. on next page)

Timing 5-10

S.I. 1.53

The history of the circus dates back to the early days of Greece 14
and Crete. Evidence and fine paintings have been found by excavators 28
which indicate that the acrobats, tumblers, and jugglers did exist in 42
those early times. During that period known as the Dark Ages, circus 56
tradition was kept alive by unique groups of traveling performers who 70
did acrobatics, tricks, and dances. 77

The forerunner of the circus in our country was the lone trapper 91
or mountaineer, who would come to a settlement with an animal in tow. 105
That creature, usually a tame bear, would then be displayed in return 119
for a few coins or a meal. As years passed, various types of animals 133
were brought to villages for the residents to see. Clowns and daring 147
horseback riders were added to make the shows very exciting. Various 161
small groups of animal acts traveled across our country from ocean to 175
ocean, delighting people of all ages. The groups consisted of two or 189
three wagons and traveled from city to city. The advance agent would 203
go ahead of the wagons and advertise the great coming attractions and 217
acts of the circus. 221

As the years rolled on, the circus became a larger and much more 235
sophisticated organization. The brass bands and colorful wagons were 249
added to the circus. Brave and skillful performers did daring feats, 263
magic tricks, and expert aerial acrobatics which amazed the audiences 277
each time. Instead of three or four shabby wagons, the circus groups 291
traveled with style in beautifully decorated wagons. Some groups did 305
much of their traveling in the splendor of railroad cars. The circus 319
was usually set up in the outdoors under a huge tent. Inside the big 333
tent were two or three rings. Each of the rings featured an act; the 347
audience could see a variety of exciting performances simultaneously. 361
Sometimes it was a problem deciding which ring to watch. 372

The hard times and severe economic problems which were a part of 386
the early thirties affected all circuses. More circuses had to close 400
their doors than ever before. The yearning and the need for exciting 414
entertainment, however, still lingered in the hearts and minds of the 428
people. It is true that the modern circus is usually held in a large 442
arena or building and some of the old atmosphere is missing. But, an 456
element of excitement and fun lives on. The music, the cotton candy, 470
the animals, and the performers carry on a fine tradition. 482

----1----2----3----4----5----6----7----8----9---10---11---12---13---14

<u>Rag dolls</u>. This design was probably the most loved by children. Very often the dolls were constructed at home and were unique.

Mechanical Toys

Old mechanical toys display amazing workmanship. The ingenuity that put them together makes them objects of interest.

<u>Types of Mechanical Toys</u>

Toys, as well as dolls, seem to hold a tremendous attraction for modern-day collectors.

<u>Tin toys</u>. The tin toys were usually painted and were not too durable; because of this fact, they are very rare today.

<u>Iron toys</u>. Some of the more interesting toys were made out of iron. These toys were quite durable and were usually quite detailed in design and workmanship. Vehicles such as trains, cars, and so on, are quite in demand.

<u>Mechanical banks</u>. Usually a mechanical bank would consist of a figure or design that would move when a coin was dropped in. The utter fascination of this type of toy to a child is indescribable. Perhaps this is why collectors are still fascinated with the mechanical bank.

<u>Other toys</u>. Other toys that collectors are quite interested in are wooden, handmade, and hand-carved toys. Sometimes these toys were made out of necessity, and sometimes they were made for the sheer joy of creativity.

Timing 5-11
S.I. 1.54

If you take a stroll on any clear evening, you will experience a 14
breathtaking and awesome example of nature--the stars. Observing the 28
heavens costs nothing. In addition, you are blessed with two natural 42
optical aids with which to enjoy the spectacular starry events. Your 56
eyes are equipped with a natural light-sensitive mechanism. You will 70
be able to see the movements of the constellations month by month, or 84
even better, you can keep a diary of movements of the stars. 96

As you become quite familiar with the heavens, you probably will 110
wish to become better equipped. You can extend your viewing power by 124
adding more optical power of strength. Any good pair of strong field 138
glasses is very helpful. The power quality of any pair of glasses is 152
stated in two numbers. The first number gives the magnifying powers; 166
the second number shows the light gathering power. Another excellent 180
purchase is a telescope, which can be purchased in a large variety of 194
markets. The power of telescopes can be varied by changing lenses to 208
produce greater magnifying power. 214

When using binoculars, it is better to rest the elbows on a firm 228
surface to steady the glasses. A telescope is fairly simple to learn 242
to use. Many telescopes are equipped with a finder. The finder will 256
assist you in focusing on portions of the sky that you wish to study. 270
Adjusting a finder is a quite simple maneuver. With little practice, 284
you will become an expert at using all type of optical equipment. An 298
image will sometimes seem to shimmer. Any shimmering effect could be 312
due to the fact that you jarred the telescope tube or binoculars; the 326
effect may also be due to a turbulence or an atmospheric disturbance. 340
You will soon discover that the best nights for viewing and observing 354
the stars are those nights when the temperatures have remained fairly 368
steady for several nights. 373

Within our own galaxy, you can observe many beautiful sights. A 387
fine domain which you can admire are the satiny stars. It is easy to 401
see all sorts of patterns in the heavens if you simply relax and turn 415
your imagination loose. You can obtain diagrams with which to study, 429
observe, and chart the various star patterns. If you have the equip- 443
ment to look beyond our own galaxy, you will be able to observe stars 457
and galaxies far out into space. An observatory is a marvelous place 471
to observe the heavens. The starry displays and changing seasons are 485
not to be missed by an astronomer. You can develop a very fine hobby 499
through star-gazing, if you care to take the time. 509

----1----2----3----4----5----6----7----8----9---10---11---12---13---14

Task 17

MULTIPLE PAGE WITH HEADINGS

Type as unbound manuscript.

EARLY AMERICAN TOYS

T.S.

Throughout the ages, children have played with toys. However, during the past few years, many people have begun collecting early toys of America.

T.S.

Dolls

Major subhead. Centered, triple before and after.

T.S.

Although dolls come in every size, shape, and description, the earlier dolls tended to be crude and homemade.

T.S.

Patented Dolls

D.S.

Early Pilgrim children played with dolls that came from their "mother" country or were homemade. Later on, after America became industrialized, factories began to manufacture dolls.

T.S.

Paragraph headings. Normal indention, principal words capitalized; underscore and period.

Head only. The earlier makers of dolls usually made only the heads, and the customer added the body. Hence, each doll was unique.

Rubber dolls. Rubber dolls have been in existence for over one hundred years. During this time, doll makers began to design different dolls and take out patents on them.

Wooden dolls. Other dolls were made of wood, usually very crudely jointed and easily broken. Later wooden dolls were made with sturdier ball joints. At this time also, manufacturers made walking dolls and talking dolls.

(cont'd. on next page)

Timing 5-12

S.I. 1.55

Most exciting tales and stories have been written about the many 14
brave individuals who went westward to our country's wild and unknown 28
western lands. The first pioneers have deserved and received sincere 42
praise and admiration for the efforts and sacrifices which were made. 56
There is a small group about which very little has been written. The 70
small group consisted of the news reporters and fine artists who drew 84
or recorded an exciting account of our nation's western growth. They 98
realized the new need and hunger for accurate news about the vast and 112
largely unexplored lands. Many eager reporters turned west to launch 126
newspaper publishing careers in smaller towns. They returned new and 140
detailed news back across the country; the accounts were exciting and 154
provided graphic descriptions of the new country and all its wonders. 170
News articles were the direct cause of the vast migration of families 184
across the nation. The desire for added knowledge about those rugged 198
and savage lands was great, indeed. Most people wanted to know about 212
the riches and not about the hazards of journeying westward. 224

Much knowledge was received from those early reporters. Because 238
each writer was quite unique, he or she observed and viewed the great 252
land differently. Many of the news reports or articles contained the 266
cold hard facts; others were simply far-fetched tales of pure fantasy 280
contrived merely to delight and intrigue some readers. Many of those 294
readers, however, really believed the author's tale of fantasy. They 308
thought the new country was an easy path to riches and fortune. Many 322
folks were unaware of the numerous perils, hazards, and horrors which 336
could be encountered when migrating to the far-off west coast. After 350
beginning the arduous journey, many were quite sorry they had come. 364

Many fine artists and illustrators played a constructive role in 378
recording the history and growth of the expansion. Many of the early 392
illustrations and drawings were very accurate, while others were dis- 406
torted. Quite like the writers, some artists viewed the land through 420
different eyes and consequently the final products were varied. Many 434
of the efforts of those very fine and skilled journalists and artists 448
have become a quite important and treasured part of our past history. 462
Indeed, there is a huge debt of gratitude that should be paid to this 476
unheralded and forgotten group of early settlers--they were the basic 490
foundation for the publishing industry of today. 500

----1----2----3----4----5----6----7----8----9---10---11---12---13---14

Task 16

Type as bound manuscript.

WHERE TO BUY-----Most cities have many stores selling similar, or identical, types of merchandise. The people of a particular city, therefore, have the choice of where to buy certain products. Several factors which may influence thidr decision of where to purchase may include cost, quality, style, and location. Usually if two items are of the same quality and style people will buy the item which coss the less. That is, if the individual knows which store is selling the tiem for less. Most consumers depend upon advertsing to eeep informed wherethe "bargins" may be located. Although this elejement is an important one for consideration, in too many instances it becomes the only deciding factor. The cnsumer forgets that there are 2 additional factors which must also be considered in relatinship to price. These two factors are the amount of time required to travel to obtain the item and the cost involved in the travel. If a consumer must spend quite a bit of time traveling to the store which has the merchandise fo the lowest price it becomes a major consideration. How much is time worth? Each individual must answer that question. The cost of travel, whether by private or public vehicle, continues to rise. Again, if the distance involved is quite far, it may be that a person spends more on transportation costs than saved on the item.

Timing 5-13

S.I. 1.56

During an earlier time in history, many houses had a very unique 14
feature which was not actually a physical portion of the house. This 28
unique creation was known as the gazebo. The homeowners preferred to 42
place the structure in a restful place, sometimes in an apple orchard 56
or among the flowers in a garden. The site of the gazebo was usually 70
one which was isolated from a disturbing view and any annoying sounds 84
or noises. The purpose of erecting the gazebo was to provide a haven 98
of rest for persons who wished to relax and meditate. 109

The gazebo was a quiet and restful place. The building was very 123
often painted a darker color which blended into the surrounding land- 137
scape or environment. The openings were all screened to keep out any 151
annoying pests or insects. In addition to being screened, all window 165
openings had some kind of window coverings, commonly sturdy draperies 179
which could be raised or lowered to adjust lighting. Those draperies 193
could also be used to compensate for any change in weather conditions 207
which might arise. The beautiful summer place was normally furnished 221
in a simple and tasteful manner. Because it was a spacious place, an 235
ample amount of furnishings could be arranged within the walls. Some 249
comfortable chairs, a sofa, and usually a table or two would comprise 263
the simple furnishings. The gazebo was a nice room in which a person 277
could think quietly, have afternoon tea, read, or even take a lengthy 291
nap. As a haven of rest, a gazebo provided a quiet, relaxing retreat 305
from a daily routine of hectic and busy living. 315

As technology rapidly progressed and the pace of everyday living 329
increased at a faster rate, the gazebo soon slipped into the past and 343
was forgotten. For some unknown reason, many people just didn't have 357
or want to take the time to relax. 364

Recently, people have begun to realize that there is obviously a 378
lack of restful interludes in their lives. The concept of the gazebo 392
is coming back into existence. It is quite possible for an inventive 406
person to construct a gazebo, patterned after earlier models. Larger 420
firms have even assembled some kits which contain the necessary parts 434
and materials for constructing a gazebo. A main problem is to select 448
a quiet and restful site on which to erect the gazebo. Another major 462
problem is making oneself take the time to relax and enjoy a few very 476
quiet moments each day. If one does not wish to construct a separate 490
building such as the gazebo for relaxation, perhaps one should select 504
a quiet room in the house to read, sew, think, or nap. 515

----1----2----3----4----5----6----7----8----9---10---11---12---13---14

Task 15

Type as left-bound manuscript.

Self-Confidence

Some people would define self-confidence as feeling comfortable in whatever you are trying to do. Others might say that it is simply a matter of believing in yourself and your ideals.

The problem is not in defining the term, but rather in how to attain the feeling of self-confidence. There are several methods commonly used; each works differently for each person.

One way to develop a new confidence in your ability is to be pleased with your personal appearance and the image you project to others. Feeling good about your clothing, hair style, and general appearance enhances self-confidence.

Another method of developing confidence is to be adept at your job. You must practice to attain efficient job skills so that you will be able to do your job well. After you have attained those skills, it is very important that you strive to maintain those skills. In addition, you may want to learn new skills that will enable you to get promotions in the future.

An integrated segment of continued confidence in yourself includes planning. You must make plans for the future, in regard to your job, what you want out of life, and how to reach your various goals. To be a slave to those plans, however, is not wise -- there must be some flexibility.

The last method is to get out and try something new. Breaking the routine not only gives you a new confidence in your abilities, but it gets you out of the proverbial "rut" of daily chores. You will have an opportunity to practice that new-found confidence in yourself.

Timing 5-14
S.I. 1.57

Most people are accustomed to shopping in the grocery market for 14
vegetables and fresh produce. We choose the health-giving vegetables 28
from rows of sterile storage bins. Many people cannot even recall or 42
remember the great flavor of vegetables that have been freshly picked 56
from a garden. Because of skyrocketing prices, too many persons can- 70
not afford to purchase the correct amounts of vegetables needed for a 84
person's good health and well-being. 91

A logical answer to the problem of obtaining an inexpensive, yet 105
flavorful, supply of vegetables is to grow our own. With some seeds, 119
a small parcel of land, a very few tools, and lots of energy, you can 133
experience the joy of gardening. You will receive many benefits with 147
a tasty supply of fresh vegetables which have a flavor that cannot be 161
obtained in any grocery store or market. 169

You should select a sunny location for the garden. It should be 183
one that has an adequate exposure to the sunlight, a supply of water, 197
and fertile soil. You might wish to locate your garden close to your 211
residence, for convenience. You should devise a planting arrangement 225
that blends and harmonizes with your surrounding landscape. Any plan 239
should include your favorite kinds of vegetables, in quantities which 253
are adequate enough to feed all the members of your family. The best 267
planting time will definitely depend upon the area in which you live. 281
In warmer climates, the produce is planted and harvested much earlier 295
in the year. In a colder climate, the growing season is much shorter 309
and the harvest is much later in the season. 318

Because there are periods during the year when you won't be able 332
to harvest vegetables directly from the garden, you should also think 346
of ways to preserve the produce for later use. Two very popular ways 360
of preserving produce are canning and freezing. Even if you have not 374
had experience in preserving produce, there are many good books, easy 388
tips, and other information available for you to follow. 399

Not only will you receive many benefits and extra enjoyment from 413
working outdoors in the garden, the joy and pleasure of eating really 427
fresh and tasty vegetables will truly be a wonderful experience. You 441
will quickly learn that gardening is one of the finest and by far the 455
most rewarding experience you have ever had. 464

----1----2----3----4----5----6----7----8----9---10---11---12---13---14

Task 13

Type as left-bound manuscript.

EVALUATING WHAT YOU READ / Many persons have the one basic fault of believing anything that is printed. How many times have you heard someone say, "I know it is true because I read it in black and white." These individuals are telling you that they lack the skill to evaluate and compare what they are reading. / (Para.) / It is important that you make it a practice to read one or several daily newspapers each day. In addition, to be an effective person, you will want to read current periodicals, books, and so on. This is a "must" if you want to become an intelligent citizen. Read a variety of material and views. Too many people make the mistake of reading articles that conform only to their own view and simply ignore any other view. As you read the current information, you must try to understand what the writer is attempting to tell you. This is called comprehension. / (Para.) / After you have comprehended or understood what the writer is trying to say, the next step is to evaluate the information. Is it backed up by facts or is it merely the writer's opinion? Is the writer a respected expert on the subject? / (Para.) / The last step after comprehension and evaluation is to compare the information you have just read to other types of information. This is basic to becoming an efficient citizen in matters of politics, consumer problems, and just simply becoming a knowledgeable person.

Task 14

Type as left-bound manuscript.

SELECTING A POST-SECONDARY INSTITUTION / People considering attending a post-secondary institution to further their education must take many things into consideration when making their final selection. The available institutions may be quite similar in nature, or so it woul seem upon the surface. What are some of the factors that people consider in making their final selection? / (Para.) / Some individuals have as a career objective and/or goal the attainment of a specialized field of knowledge or experience. The particular field may be so highly specialized that there will be only a few schools offering this particular curriculum. If this is true, this particular factor becomes the major deciding element./(Para.)/ Many people have to be concerned about the economic or financial factor. There are usually two deciding elements involved with the financial consideration—location of institution to the home, and type and amount of financial aid available. Post-secondary education can be quite expensive. Every individual has the desire and necessity to obtain the best education and experience at the lowest possible cost. / (Para.) / The third factor usually considered is the reputation of a particular institution. It may be highly recommended by parents, friends, or former educational instructors. / (Para.) / The last factor which some individuals may use in determining the place where they will seek their further education is a purely personal aspect. They may decide to attend an institution because their friend(s) have already selected that particular school.

Timing 5-15
S.I. 1.58

In the autumn, when the grass begins to turn brown and the trees 14
begin to lose their leaves, many persons turn their attentions to the 28
upcoming sports season. Appearing high on the list of sports fans is 42
professional football. Every weekend there are a variety of exciting 56
games to attend, watch, or listen to. As the season progresses, much 70
excitement is evident; the excitement culminates in the last big game 84
of the year--the Super Bowl. The top two teams with the best records 98
participate in the Super Bowl Game. The winning team is declared the 112
National Football League champion. 119

Other winter sports games draw the attention of many folks. Ice 133
hockey has grown considerably as a professional sport during the past 147
few years. The whizzing skaters, the delicate skills of the players, 161
and the element of competition will add to a winter spectator's joy. 175

Basketball draws its share of attention during the long winters. 189
The game of basketball is played at a faster pace and usually is very 203
exciting. As in other professional sports, the teams travel all over 217
the nation, giving the spectators one thrilling game after another. 231

Downhill or slalom skiing is always an enjoyable sport to watch. 245
The refined skills of the experienced skiers, combined with the great 259
action, make skiing one of the most beautiful displays for spectators 273
to watch. Some skiers also participate in another related event--ski 287
jumping. As a jumper soars through the cold air with grace and ease, 301
observers gasp at the magnificent sight. 309

Ice skating is also a wonderful winter sport. The keen competi- 323
tions include both figure and speed skating. Most of the skaters are 337
quite exciting to observe. During the short time of the competition, 351
spectators do not fully realize the years of tedious training and the 365
tremendous amount of effort the skater was required to devote for one 379
moment of glory. 382

From the professional to the rankest amateur, the whole realm of 396
fall and winter sports is becoming more popular each year. The spec- 410
tators and participants both benefit in enjoyment and excitement. To 424
receive maximum enjoyment from any sport, spectators should learn the 438
basic rules before the actual game begins. 445

---1----2----3----4----5----6----7----8----9---10---11---12---13---14

Task 12

Type as left-bound manuscript.

READING ABILITY

Many people in the United States today do not like to read because they are not good readers. In addition, these people who do not like to read have no wish to learn to read better. Some claim that the change started with the first general use of television approximately two and a half decades ago. Experts feel that before television, family members spent their time socializing and reading. When the majority of homes had a television installed, the amount of reading done was lowered.

Schools have tried to counter the trend toward nonreading. From all recorded statistical data, it would appear that trend has not been reversed. Even though a child spends more and more time in school reading, national averages of reading ability continue to fall. We have turned from the written to the spoken word of television.

Interviews with people who do not read seem to indicate that they feel reading is too hard and takes too much time. Obtaining information from a television set or radio is much faster than reading a daily newspaper, magazine, or a book. In addition, many poor readers feel that they can get much more out of seeing an event on television rather than having to fantasize or imagine it in their mind from written words.

Perhaps the saddest aspect of being a poor reader is that the person has no opportunity to exercise and stretch imagination. No opportunity is available to explore the wonderful world of reading. The nonreader will never experience the joy of "curling up with a good book."

Timing 5-16

S.I. 1.59

Our own century has been recognized as one of rapid change. One 14
area in which change is very obvious is in the amount of time workers 28
have for new leisure pursuits. Employees are now working fewer hours 42
every week. Advanced technology has had an impact on many employees. 56
In the home, many time-saving electric appliances have taken over the 70
back-breaking labor associated with homemaking. People no longer are 84
required to launder clothes by hand, carry water, beat carpets, scrub 98
floors, or expend much energy in house cleaning. A push of a button, 112
and the work is done magically. Automation has shortened the working 126
time of factory and office workers. Manual work is now done by huge, 140
complex machinery. As a result, many workers are now only working at 154
their jobs four days a week instead of the traditional five days each 168
week. The resulting three-day weekend is becoming a major part of an 182
existence for many individuals. 188

Increased amounts of leisure time has caused problems. Deciding 202
how to spend the wonderful extra hours can be a great problem to many 216
persons. For other people, there is not enough extra money to afford 230
a vacation or some other activity. Many people, for unknown reasons, 244
are unable to relax and are happy only while working. 255

People have responded to leisure time in a number of ways. Many 269
people have decided that the answer is a part-time job. They have an 283
opportunity to earn more money and purchase the goods and services in 297
greater quantities. For other persons, leisure time is used to relax 311
by going skiing, swimming, golfing, or fishing. Other people utilize 325
their extra time to catch up on reading and other quiet activities in 339
their homes. One quite exciting method of using leisure time is in a 353
health-related field. Strenuous activities such as jogging, running, 367
playing handball, and hiking all seem to lend themselves well to good 381
programs of physical fitness. 387

A new major problem facing most workers today is a direct result 401
of jobs that require a minimum of movement. This problem affects the 415
health of people. More people are suffering from overweight, related 429
health problems, and boredom than ever before known. Experts know an 443
effective and sure answer to many of these health problems lies in an 457
increased physical exercise program for all people. Each person must 471
try harder to improve general health and fitness in leisure moments. 485

----1----2----3----4----5----6----7----8----9---10---11---12---13---14

Task 11

Type as left-bound manuscript.

Start heading on line 13

Set left margin of 18 for elite type and 15 for pica (1½ inches).

Leave at least 12 spaces in the right-hand margin for elite type and 10 spaces for pica (1 inch).

A NEW WAY TO TRAVEL

T.S.

Reference: p. 236

There is a way to travel that doesn't cost much money, and uses very little energy. The only thing needed is time, a place to relax, and an imagination. This method of travel is commonly called "arm-chair" travel. People have been sitting at home and transporting their minds and imaginations all over the world and sometimes even into outer space simply by reading.

The simplest method of "arm-chair" travel is to sit back and relax and do a bit of daydreaming. From the age of a few years to a very old age, all of us indulge in daydreams at one time or another. Picture yourself in the one place in the world you would like to visit. What does it look like? The pictures in your mind are providing you with some arm-chair traveling. You can come home at any time and "take off" for another place quickly.

Another method of arm-chair traveling is provided through reading. You can travel along many roads by reading what others have written. It can be pure fiction, or a factual atlas describing the scenery. Soaring away into far-off lands using your imagination can be one of the greatest thrills ever experienced. The vivid words used to describe a unique spot on the earth can transport you beyond your wildest dreams.

An added benefit of arm-chair travel is that you increase your knowledge of your country, and the world, in general. And who knows? Someday you may just decide to travel physically to one of your favorite arm-chair travel spots!

Timing 5-17

S.I. 1.60

The unique lure of heights and a quest for an exciting adventure 14
has been the spark of joy and enthusiasm for several persons for many 28
centuries. During the very year in which our country was discovered, 42
the first attempt at climbing an inaccessible mountain range was also 56
recorded. Thus began the first experiences for mountain climbers who 70
assaulted rugged peaks purely for the joy of reaching the top. These 84
first attempts at climbing usually ended in unusual numbers of tragic 98
deaths due to faulty equipment and ineptitude. 107

As the years passed, the new mountaineers looked for peaks which 121
were higher and much more difficult to climb. The quest took them to 135
new points all over the world. The most difficult test came when the 149
high peaks of the Himalayas were climbed and explored. The winds and 163
the snowstorms were ferocious, threatening to sweep the cold climbers 177
right off the treacherous and dangerous icy ridges. In addition, the 191
quite inadequate oxygen supply was a constant problem with which many 205
climbers were not familiar. Because of vital research which has been 219
done in the area of safety and efficiency at high altitudes, climbers 233
of today ascend mountain peaks with a greater degree of safety. 245

In recent decades, one favorite pursuit of mountaineers has been 259
Mt. Everest, the world's highest mountain peak. An incredible number 273
of massive assaults were attempted on the brutal peaks of Mt. Everest 287
during the time between the two world wars. In terms of human lives, 301
the price paid for the renewed attempts was unusually high. Climbers 315
were certain that the mountain had a mysterious, invisible element at 329
the top which prevented the climbers from conquering the rugged peak. 343
After thirty years of futile attempts, that mysterious and forbidding 357
peak was finally conquered. 362

Once the peak of Mt. Everest had been conquered, any interest in 375
climbing the highest mountain in the world no longer existed. Rugged 389
climbers focused their endeavors and interests on methods of mountain 403
climbing. Where safety had once been a prime factor, very dangerous, 417
hazardous, and foolhardy attempts at climbing increased. Many rugged 431
climbers fell to their deaths trying to climb sheer rock faces, which 445
were clearly beyond anyone's ability and skill. It seemed as if some 459
mania or craze existed that drove climbers to the hazardous assaults. 471

Such foolhardy excesses, fortunately, are no longer common. The 485
mountain climbers of today pursue the majestic mountain peaks for the 499
pure joy of climbing and for the marvelous scenic beauty of nature. 513

----1----2----3----4----5----6----7----8----9---10---11---12---13---14

I'm not hungry!" It seems it is almost impossible to rpovide the quality, quantity and serving conditons to satisfy every individual. Most instutitions allow professional food service companies to offer bids for providning food service to students. Usually, and perhaps this may be part of the problem, the contract is given to the lowest bidder. The service is contracted to the food service company for a certain number of years, usually two to five years. Provding food to students also provides a large quantity of jobs. Usually the contrascting company hires many students as part-time workers. Although the pay is not the highest, it allows the students to earn enough money to help pay for their education.

Task 10

Type as unbound manuscript.

Note to student: Because a document has been edited, it doesn't mean that all errors have been detected. Be sure to read the item carefully to see if errors have been overlooked; make corrections.

Why Read? all caps

It would appear that the world is divided into the "non-readers" and the "readers." What exactly are the advantages enjoyed by those who would be classified as the "readers?" There are many, but tow must important advantages to reading well and often is that the reader is well informed and that he has a means of entertainment. Reading for informatin is probably one of the most important assets for any person. In this world of rapidly chainging eideas and technologies, every perons needs to be well informed and up-to-date at all times. The best way to keep in with the world is to read newspapers, current periodicals, and other literature. In addition, reading for information all invovles delving into past works of authors. One can learn much from past history, ideas, and ahppenings. Or, perhaps a person wishes to pursue a newhobby or career. Reading about it provides a new insight and knowledge. Another important reason for reading is becuae it has a unique entertainment value that can not be found anywhere else. One can lost himself in a book; he or she can travel anywhere in the world, any time in istory--future or past, and with almost anyone, simply by opening a book and reading. Reading relaxes away the everyday tensions experienced at times and gives one a whole new outlook on life. Typist - please type inserting correct paragraphs.

Timing 5-18
S.I. 1.61

In the past few years, the science of ecology has assumed a role 14
of importance in the lives of many human beings. A study of the sub- 28
ject involves learning about living organisms and their relationships 42
to the environment which surrounds and is a major part of their daily 56
living. A small action or inaction of one human could well determine 70
the fate of many other living organisms throughout our planet. Man's 84
good will, or the lack of it, coupled with stupidity, greed, and much 98
shortsightedness determines the fate of all living things on our tiny 112
earth. Man has the ability to preserve or to destroy nature. 124

Many individuals are not aware of the delicate balance of nature 138
that exists among all plants and animals. Many food chains which are 152
found in nature all are quite complex. A typical community of living 166
things consists of many species of plants and animals living together 180
in harmony. Their living habits, which seem to be quite orderly, are 194
bound by an interesting and complex byplay of forces. For centuries, 208
various species of plants and animals have existed on the earth, each 222
in its own unique habitat. The principle of the survival of only the 236
fittest has been operable from the time of life's first beginnings on 250
the earth. Nature has managed to survive undisturbed by human inter- 264
ference for centuries. The delicately balanced food chain of life in 278
which all animals and plants prey and are preyed upon has existed and 292
survived since the first beginning of life. Undisturbed, innumerable 306
living things have managed to survive and multiply on this earth. 319

Humans have needlessly destroyed natural habitats of animals and 333
plants. The constant intrusion into the world of nature by concrete, 347
asphalt, and steel constructions seems to be of more importance to an 361
uncaring human race than the preservation of nature. The destruction 375
of some living things is hastened by mindless and selfish hunting and 389
killing by human beings. It is true that if man did not kill certain 403
numbers of selected species, many animals would soon die from disease 417
due to overcrowded conditions. On the other hand, many of the deaths 431
can be traced directly to diseases caused by the great destruction of 445
habitats and natural environments of plants and animals. 456

Nature's creatures and plants will survive if humans are able to 470
make wise decisions and practice conservation. If only a few persons 484
are interested in protecting nature, the destruction of much wildlife 498
is a certainty. The combined efforts of all people residing on earth 512
is the key to protecting and preserving the world of nature. 526

----1----2----3----4----5----6----7----8----9---10---11---12---13---14

Task 7

Type as unbound manuscript.

COMPETITIVE PRICING IN THE BOOKSTORE / The purpose of any school bookstore is to serve students as effectively as possible. Do most school bookstores attain that function or do some of them take advantage of residents on campus who find it difficult to shop off the campus grounds? / (Para.) / Recent research studies have indicated, for the most part, that many school bookstore prices for most items are definitely higher than those prices charged by stores located off campus. These same studies have also revealed that, although students feel it is unfair for the bookstore to have higher charges, they also feel it is convenient for them to purchase certain items there. / (Para.) / Interviews with managers of selected bookstores indicate that most items are sold at the retail prices suggested by the manufacturers. Large stores located off campus, buying in bulk, can sell the same item for less because of the discount they receive from the manufacturer. Most bookstores do not sell enough to get a large volume discount. The same interviews reveal that most school bookstores do not make a large profit. / (Para.) / The major purpose of any school bookstore is convenience. It allows students to purchase necessities quickly. When there is not time to walk, bike, or ride the bus downtown or to the shopping mall, it is most convenient to walk over to the campus bookstore.

Task 8

Type as unbound manuscript.

ON THE JOB / This is a red-letter day for you! You have been hired for your first job. You have successfully passed the written and oral tests included in the application process. You have successfully interviewed for the position—and it is yours. / (Para.) / What now? Obviously you have the skills needed for that particular position—but do you have what it takes to stay on the job and become a successful worker? / (Para.) / The first thing that comes to mind is your personal appearance. In a sense, you are representing the company or firm for which you work. Is your manner of dress such that it is an asset to you rather than a liability? Personal grooming and an appropriate wardrobe often tell others about your self-confidence. Other items to be aware of are your voice, your health, and so on. / (Para.) / To be successful in any endeavor, however, you must be aware of others around you. This includes getting along with others with whom you work. The first step is to try to understand them and to understand their motives and actions. This will not always be easy, but it is necessary for good job-peer relations. / (Para.) / Another area of major importance is using common sense in all situations. Along with this, any firm for which you work expects ethical behavior toward the firm. This means that you avoid petty quarrels, gossip, and substitute loyalty to the company. It also means that you do your job efficiently and, in a sense, "earn your salary fairly."

Task 9

Type as unbound manuscript.

MEAL PLANS FOR STUDENTS Many schools require that students who elect to stay in residence halls ~~must~~ also pay for a meal contract of some type. The meal plan is a contract which provides a student a cetain ~~amount~~ number of mealsper week for a particular price. Many instutions ofer several different type meal plans. For example, it may be possible to contract for as many meals as twenty-one per seek. Or, the school also may offer an option whereby it is necessary to pay for as few as fifteen ~~mal s~~ meals per week. Regardless of the particular meal plan a student has available many students do not regard the food service at any particular institution too highly. It is quite common to hear a variety of compalints ranging from "the quality of the food is terrible," to "the times a day the meals are served are when

(cont'd. on next page)

Typewriting Techniques Module

There are four general classifications of typewritten communication. They are: (1) correspondence (letters, memorandums), (2) reports, (3) tabulated data, and (4) forms. It is not difficult to learn the guidelines for the preparation of various classifications of typewritten communication. It is, however, quite critical that you develop efficient techniques relating to the preparation of each kind of typewritten communication. Read the following information; then practice the exercises until you can do each efficiently.

Proofreading Techniques

One of the common needs of all who prepare typewritten communication is developing effective proofreading techniques. Proofreading, like typing, requires practice. The time required to proofread a document is less than the time required to retype it. The document should be read slowly, word for word. It is best to proofread the document three times: first, for spelling and typographical errors; second, for punctuation and grammar; third, for meaning.

The characteristics of an effective proofreader, which you want to develop, include:

1. Be a good speller.
2. Know the basics of punctuation.
3. Be willing to pay attention to detail.
4. Know and use the various methods of proofreading.
5. Know the types of errors most frequently overlooked.
6. Take the time to proofread.
7. Be conscious of error.
8. Use the dictionary when in doubt.

To master proofreading skills, follow the techniques illustrated below:

1. As much as possible, control the environment in which you proofread. Noise and movement are distracting. Be sure there is sufficient light.
2. It is best to proofread material before it is taken out of the typewriter. In this way, errors can be corrected without either retyping the document or reinserting and aligning the paper to make the correction.

DRILL 1

a. Set the Line Space Lever for double spacing.

b. Type the following paragraph just as it is shown. It contains a number of errors. Check the clock and jot down the time you begin.

> The implimentation of Word Proocessing Systems in busniess offices requires secretariel and clerical personnil to haev a greater knowledge of a veriaty of typing applications, since thier responsibility is too process the typing of material from many authors.

c. Remove the paper from the machine.

d. Proofread and write the correct word on the copy in longhand.

e. Insert another piece of paper and retype the entire paragraph, making the needed corrections.

f. Remove the paper from the machine. Check the clock; determine the time required to complete the initial typing, proofreading, and the retyping.

Task 6

Type as unbound manuscript.

THE TELEPHONE

The telephone has indeed become an indispensable item in modern living. Businesses depend upon the telephone as a major necessity in doing their daily routine of transactions. The telephone is quick, efficient, and quite inexpensive to use.

Customers often judge a business by the voice they hear on the other end of the telephone. The "telephone voice" instantly becomes the business or firm in the caller's mind. For example, an unfriendly, harsh voice may give the caller the impression that the business itself deals with customers in an unfriendly manner. On the other hand, a pleasant and friendly voice will enhance the image of the company. Sad as it may be, many business transactions have been lost because of the initial contact via the telephone.

Prompt answering of the phone will give the customer the idea that the business itself is very efficient. If the answerer identifies him or herself, it portrays a sense of security of knowing where one is going. Also, a quite considerate telephone personality will use common courtesies such as a warm "thank you for calling" at the conclusion of the conversation.

Practice developing your own telephone voice on calls made to you from your friends. With a little concentration and practice, you can have a very pleasing telephone personality. Remember, your voice is the only image the caller "sees" and hears.

DRILL 2

a. Insert a new sheet of paper.

b. Type the paragraph again, with errors. Check the clock and jot down the time you begin. Do not remove the paper when you finish.

c. Proofread the paragraph. When you find an error, roll the paper back and type the correct word above the incorrect one. When you finish, check the clock to determine the time required to complete the exercise.

d. Compare the time required for each exercise. Which one took less time?

3. Another technique to improve proofreading ability is to bring the paper beneath the Paper Bail of the typewriter. As you read a line, move the paper forward. Use the Paper Bail to guide your eyes along the line of typing. When using this method of proofreading, read for context. It will help you identify grammatical errors and words that do not make sense.

4. It is quite common for a typist to use a word similar in sound but different in meaning and spelling from one that should be used. Examples of incorrect usage include:

their	instead of	there
an	instead of	and
too	instead of	to

DRILL 3

a. Set the Line Space Lever for double spacing.

b. Type the sentences below just as they are shown. After you finish typing the sentences, proofread using the Paper Bail method. When you discover an error, type the correct word under the incorrect one.

He paid me a great complement.
Please except our apology for the delay in shipping your order.
Many of our correspondence request literature on the subject.
The state legislature holds sessions in a building called the capital.
Far to many errors are made as a result of our failure to listen to directions.
The personal in the Marketing Department planned an office party.
I strongly advice you to consult your attorney before signing the papers.
I do think that their are advantages to be gained from a variety of media.
Honesty is it's own reward.
The base of the bookend is weighted with led to prevent sliding.

5. Locating typographical errors is a difficult task for some people. Typographical errors include incorrect letters or letters transposed, repeated, or omitted. One method that will help you improve the detection of such errors is to read the copy backwards. Start at the right margin and read each word until you get to the left margin. Then move to the next line down and repeat the process. In reading the material in this manner, you cannot read context; you are forced to read for detail.

Following is a series of tasks to be typed. Notice that in this section there are reference pages indicated to the left of each task.

1. If this is the first time you have typed this particular kind of task, turn to the reference page(s) and:
   a. Read the information.
   b. Complete the drill material section (if any is provided). The drill will give you practice before typing the task.
2. If you have already typed this kind of task before (and consequently have already read the information and completed the drills), refer to the reference page only if you need help in completing the task.

Task 5

Type as unbound manuscript.

Begin heading on line 13. Set left and right margins of 12 spaces for elite type and 10 spaces for pica (1 inch).

Reference: p. 235

centered, all caps

GETTING ALONG WITH OTHERS

T.S.

Although an employee may be highly skilled and talented in a chosen job,

D.S.

he may fail dismally at the task simply because he could not get along with fellow workers. The ability to get along with others is probably one of the greatest single assets a worker can possess.

One of the first rules in getting along with others is to be courteous to everyone. Although the world is moving at a very rapid rate, the old-fashioned art, as some would call it, of good manners is not out-of-date. Remembering to use words such as "please," "thank you," and "excuse me," will take you a long way in your quest in getting along with others.

Another rule is to be interested in the other person. This will take an effort, at times, on your part. Perhaps the other person is interested in something that you utterly cannot stand or that you know nothing about. But, remembering a very common idea--that the other person is interested in himself and what he does--will help you gain a friendly "footing" with that person. And, who knows--you may learn something about a new subject!

Being a good listener and caring about others follows naturally in being interested. Perhaps it will take an effort on your part not to talk so much and listen more. Most of us have the bad habit of talking and carrying on a conversation with others and never listening to what the others say. Listening involves not only hearing words, but comprehending the meaning of those words and responding to them.

DRILL 4

a. Insert a clean sheet of paper.

b. Read the paragraph below using the method of reading from right to left. When you locate an error, type the word correctly.

Secretarial and clerical studenst should be provided with the opportunity for more variety and in-depth application traing. They should have knowledge of technology advances in offi e equipment used by business to rpocess typing. Todyas' keyboards are designed to reduce or eliminate many of the problems secretaries encounter. Problems such as reseatrs, deadlines, page-end presseres, revisions, and errors lower productivity. Magnetic media typewriters are designed to enable secretaries to type a document at routh-draft speed and correct erros by cbakspacing and striking over the erroor. They assist secredtaries to mroe efficienty process revisions by eliminating the need to retype eth entire document.

6. The typewriting errors you are most apt to miss are shown below. Study each one carefully.

COMMON PROOFREADING ERRORS

Conditions	*Examples*
• Confusion of similar words	now, not; on, of, or; than, that; yet, yes
• Confusion of suffixes and word endings	formed, former; pointing, point; type, types
• Omissions in sequence of enumerated items	a, b, d, e; 1, 2, 4, 5
• Transposition of digits in numbers	78, 87; 1967, 1976
• Transposition of letters within words	the, teh; tehir, their
• Misspelled words, names, and words sounding alike	Clark, Clarke; Reed, Reid; knew, new
• Omissions and additions of letters	though, thogh; write, wite
• Omissions in long words	reincorporate, recorporate; thoroughly, throughly
• Omissions, additions, and transpositions in headings and subheadings	Atheletic, Athletic; Development, Devlopment; Introductoin, Introduction
• Errors in words that fall near margins	(Because beginnings and endings of lines are often skimmed more rapidly)
• Omission of an entire line when a word appears in the same place in two consecutive lines	Turning it on is accomplished by moving the lever in. Turning it on is accomplished by (turning the dial to the left and) moving the lever in.
• Errors occurring at the bottom of the page	(Because the eye is tired or the reader skims too rapidly at the end of the page)

Task 1

Full sheet; Begin heading on line 13 (2-inch top margin), set left and right margins of 12 spaces for elite type and 10 spaces for pica (1 inch). When typing Roman numerals, be sure to right justify (align on period).

Reference: p. 233

THE OFFICE MANAGER

I. NEED

A. Business grown considerably
B. New employee--the office manager

II. CHANGES

A. Rising financial costs
1. Increased paperwork
2. Inflation
B. Employee change
1. Retiring workers
2. Lack of skills
3. Automated equipment
C. Career office managers
1. Definite need
2. Post-secondary school programs

Task 2

Full sheet; Begin heading on line 13.

HUNTING ANCESTORS CAN BE FUN / I. FAMILY SOURCES / A. Immediate relatives / 1. Direct interview / 2. Letter interviews / B. Family records / 1. Bible and other books / 2. Diaries and letters / II. OTHER SOURCES / A. Printed / 1. Public library / 2. Local records / 3. State and federal record sources / B. Miscellaneous / 1. Museums / 2. Gravestones

Task 3

Full sheet; Begin heading on line 13.

COLLECTING EARLY AMERICAN TOYS / I. COLLECTIBLE DOLLS / A. Patented / B. Head-only / C. Rubber / D. Wooden with ball joints / E. Rag / II. MECHANICAL TOYS AND BANKS / A. Toys / 1. Tin / 2. Iron / 3. Wooden / B. Banks / 1. Ceramic / 2. Tin / 3. Iron /

Task 4

OFFICE MANUALS

I. PURPOSE OF OFFICE MANUALS
A. Information sharing
1. Saved supervisory time
2. Available reference

II. ADVANTAGES + DISADVANTAGES OF OFFICE MANUALS
A. Advantages
1. Saves money
2. Eliminates errors
B. Disadvantages
1. Costly to produce
2. Reduces initiative

III. PREPARATION OF OFFICE MANUALS
A. Scientific method
1. Variety of writers
2. Duplicate + distribute
3. Revise
B. Annual evaluation + revision

- Omission of short words — (Short words such as *if*, *is*, *it*, and *in* when preceding word ends in similar letter or following word begins with same letter)

DRILL 5

a. Insert a clean sheet of paper.
b. Type the information below. When you discover an error, type it correctly.

You may not no this storey, but it is told by hunters talking about thier hunting experiences.

Every hear, during the deer hunting season, a certain farmer lost one or two cows to over zealous hunters. In their enthusism to bring back a prize buck or doe, some hunters would shoot at anything that moved or didn't mover.

It got so bad that the farmer and his family were afraid to come out of their house, for fair of being shoot. At first, the farmer put up signs warning the hunters not to hunt on his propety. This was not very successful be-use the hunters would shoot at the signs. All that mattered to the poor famer is that he new something had to be done or he would go broke, or get kilt.

One year, after a trip to the local hardware stor, the farmer beleived he had the solution to his problm.

With the usually excitement, the hunters invaided the area with the thoughts of bagging a prise dear. Of course, the first place they headed for was the the farmer's property. But this time, they were in for a surprise. The farmer had taken the precauiton of identifying everything he owed with large letters painted with bright yellow paint. Each cow had the word "cow" painte on it side, and the house and the bard and the tracter were also marked with yellow paint to identify them.

Needless to said, the hunters got the massage and the farmer stopped losing his cows.

Reprinted from ***IBM Transcription Skills for Word Processing; An Introduction to Machine Transcription,*** Student's Guide. Published by Science Research Associates, Inc., Chicago, Illinois.

Type as a table of contents.

DRILL

Space once after first line. Determine if "even" numbered space or "odd" numbered space. Always begin on same as first line! *Never* place a leader immediately before or after a word or number!

CONTENTS Type on line 13

TS

Leaders help the "eye" move to the right to the page number. Make sure they "line up."

7. Proofread technical or difficult material ***at least twice***. Read slowly; check for spelling and typographical errors. Read for errors in punctuation and grammar.
8. Proofread with another person; one person reads while the other makes proofreading changes. Read from the original and indicate difficult spelling, paragraphing, format, and decimal points. Read numbers digit by digit; for example, 4,230.62 should be read aloud as; "Four, comma, two, three, zero, point, six, two."
9. Proofread statistical tables by adding the numbers on the material from which you are copying. Then add the numbers on your typed copy. The totals should agree. If they do not, check the figures on your copy with the ones on the original to locate the error.

DRILL 6

Type the information shown below. After you finish, ask another student to read the copy to you while you proofread your typed copy. Then you read the information to the other student who proofreads the typed copy.

Mr. Smyth suggested that our selling price on Item #16-780-32 was entirely too high. He recommends that we reduce the price approximately five percent, from $14 to $13. I feel he has a good idea but I would like you to check it with Sandra Dennis in accounting. Perhaps she may have some additional recommendations that should be considered. Please get back to me as soon as possible. The new catalogs will have to go to the printers within the next two weeks. If something unexpected comes up, contact me at 734-1617. Thanks.
George Aspick

Using the following guides for line placement, type the cover sheet example given on this page. Be careful to center each horizontal line. Any attractive arrangement may be used.

DRILL

OFFICE MANUALS	Type on line 18
By	Type on line 32
John Smith	Type on line 34
O.A. 417, Section 01	Type on line 50
Office Management	Type on line 52
T/Th, 2 o'clock	Type on line 54
Dr. Johnson	Type on line 56
April 1, 1982	Type on line 58

Proofreader's Symbols

When correcting material that contains mistakes and/or errors (rough draft copy), practice showing the needed corrections with proofreading symbols.

Symbol	*Stands for*	*Example*
∽ S	transpose (change around)	See the play children. Second, is the . . . . . . First, is the . . . .
^ ∨	insert	Bring me the tub. big
⌢⌣	close up	book keeping
#	add a "space" or "line"	Let usnow begin. #
e /	delete (take out)	Bring me the big tub.
lc	lower case (small letter)	Look at Jack Run. lc
uc or ≡	upper case (capital letter)	Look at jack run. uc
[	move to the left	[Let me see the paper.
]	move to the right	Let]me see the paper.
ss	single space	ss See the man.
ds	double space	Why should I? Look at the cars. ds I see them.
ts	triple space	ts Look at the cars. I see them.
stet	let it stand (ignore marked change made previously)	See the man. old . . . See the man. old stet
¶ or ₱	begin new paragraph	¶ I see the man.

DRILL

Type each of the bibliographical entries below. Concentrate on the correct insertion of punctuation marks, quotation marks, and other display items.

Dart, Janell R. "The World is Not Going to the Dogs." Otis Flyer. May 9, 1982.

Davis, Dr. Claude. Interview. Nelson, Nebraska. February 28, 1982.

Hearthic, Olive T. "The Shame of Our Dog Population." Dogs Today. March 1982.

McKenzie, Dr. Phillip. Personal Correspondence. March 3, 1982.

Quick, Hiram P., Editor. Dogs and Cats. New York: Marshall and Hines Publishing Company, 1981.

-----. "Trends in Dog Management." Dog World. January 1982.

Star, Marvel E. and Ann Smith. Grooming Your Dog. Denver, Colorado: Allison Publishers, 1982.

Strage, Arthur J. Healthy Dogs. Dallas, Texas: Marston Printing Company, 1982.

Zich, Raymond R. The Problems of Our Canine Society Today. Madison, Wisconsin: Dane County Veterinarian Society, 1981.

DRILL

From the information below, type a correct bibliographical entry for each reference.

1. Twenty-Nine Ways to Please Customers—Barker Review (magazine) by Ms. Gladys Fox. Appeared in the March 1982 issue on page 29.
2. Book—Exciting Sales Techniques by J. R. Scott. Published by Winston Royal Pub. Co. in Havertown, New Jersey in 1980. Taken from page 14.
3. Interviewed Dr. Allie Joy in May 1982 at her home in Denver, Colorado.
4. Book by Joanne Dowl and Kenneth Eden. Title: Will Friday Never Come? Published in 1982 by the Fridley Pub. Co. in Dallas, Texas, Quoted information on pp. 196-200.
5. Quoted from the Sept. 19, 1981 issue of the San Jose Independent newspaper, page 17, column 3.
6. Office Equipment (book)—edited by Mark Nelson, published by Ralsten Publishers, Inc., in 1982—location, Des Moines, Iowa. Material quoted from p. 397.
7. Used quote from p. 86 in March last year's issue of Times & Trends magazine in article entitled Dynamic Decorating—no author given.
8. Report by Jane Green, Office Issues & Trends, put out by New York Office Managers Association, New York City in 1982, page 46.
9. Letter received from Mayme Goldstein dated August 16, last year.

General Guidelines

SUPPORTING PARTS OF A FORMAL MANUSCRIPT

Supporting parts, or pages, of a formal manuscript include the cover sheet and a table of contents. Illustrations of each, and instructions for preparation, are shown on pages 245 and 246.

Rough Drafts

It is not uncommon for the originator to request a rough draft of a letter, memo, or report. Such a request indicates that the originator anticipates revising the material before it is typed in final form.

Rough drafts are always typed on plain paper and double spaced, with three blank lines between paragraphs to allow space for writing in changes. Lines that will not be changed, such as the inside address and closing lines of a letter or the heading of a memo, can be single spaced.

Errors can be crossed out and a word can be added by typing a diagonal line, then typing the correct word on the line above. An illustration is shown below.

March 25, 19--

Mr. J. A. Thompson
WP Consultants, Inc.
4031 Wisconsin Avenue, N.W.
Washington, D.C. 20008

Dear Mr. Thompson:

The new WPTM Price List will be shipped directly to

you from hte printer.

to
The remaining 9000 will be ~~sent~~ shipped directly/ the

Central Distribution Center in Bethesda Maryland. Field
directly
Office ~~may~~ must order/ from the distribution center.

producing
The final cost for/ this price list is $18,000.

Sincerely,

S.A. Kemp
Advertising Consultant

SAK/jrf

General Guidelines

THE BIBLIOGRAPHY

1. A bibliography is a formalized listing of all the books, magazines, and other sources used in your report. The listing is placed at the end of the paper. The information given in a bibliographical entry contains the same facts as the footnote but is arranged somewhat differently.

   Joynter, Louise R. Living Values. Denver, Colorado: Marchant Press, 1982.

   Note: Author's last name is listed first.
   Second line is indented normal paragraph indention (author's name is thus readily apparent to the reader).
   No parentheses enclose publisher information.
   Page numbers are not included.

   The format for bibliographical entries used in this book is one of the more common styles. Other authors, institutions, and individuals may require a slightly different format. Consult your instructor or a style reference manual for further details.

2. Entries in the bibliography are listed alphabetically according to the author's last name. If there is no author information (magazine article or newspaper article), type five hyphens followed by a period as illustrated below:

   -----. "Time Marches On." The Los Angeles Flyer. March 10, 1982.

   Use the word ***Time*** to place this entry alphabetically.

Start on Line 13

BIBLIOGRAPHY

Armes, Jane, E. J. James, and Betty Jane Onis. Secretarial Systems. Cincinnati, Ohio: Poston, Inc., 1982.

Onie, George. Control in the Office. Chicago, Illinois: A-Z Publishing Company, 1982.

Prentis, Richard A., and James E. Johnson. Clerical Systems. Dallas, Texas: Weston Publishers, 1982.

-----. "Speed and Quality in Handling Workflow." Office Systems. January, 1982. Vol. 29, No. 3.

Wilson, James. Using Your Skills. New York: Creative Enterprises, 1981.

The originator indicates revisions by using proofreader's symbols. The typist proofreads for typographical errors, misspellings, punctuation, and grammar. An illustration is shown below.

March 25, 19--

Mr. J. A. Thompson
WP Consultants, Inc.
4031 Wisconsin Avenue, N.W.
Washington, D.C. 20008

Dear Mr. Thompson:

Two cartons containing 1000
~~The new~~ WPTM Price List s will be shipped directly to you from the printer — on April 1.

to
The remaining 9000 will be ~~sent~~ shipped directly/ the Central Distribution Center in Bethesda, Maryland. Field

directly
Offices ~~may~~ must order/ from the distribution center. The form number is 8327-9320.

producing
The final cost for/this price list is $18.000.

Sincerely,

S. A. Kemp
Advertising Consultant

SAK/jrf

Based on an estimated distribution of 1500 per month, this quantity provides only a six month supply. Please notify us no later than August 1 if the Price List needs to be reprinted.

General Guidelines

ANOTHER METHOD OF REFERENCING

When footnotes are located at the bottom of each page (as you have been practicing typing them), it is convenient for the reader to make quick and easy reference to them. A newer system of making reference is used in some instances. This system places all the footnote data at the back of the paper (bibliography), and each quotation refers to that page. This system is somewhat inconvenient for the reader but much faster for the typist to prepare. When typing a paper, always determine which style of referencing is required. Compare the examples of the two styles illustrated below.

OUR PAPER HIGHWAY

Records

The storing of valuable documents and records has had a place in history almost from the beginning of time. Even then, eary man sought to find a way to preserve and keep important records of his existence. As buying and selling evolved, the need to keep important records of business transactions also grew. Throughout history, records storage and retrieval has become an exciting and rather new career field.

Importance of Records Storage

Because of added productivity and correspondence of businesses of today, the sheer volume of paperwork has increased beyond one's wildest imagination. Business records take up more space than any other single item and more money is paid out for salaries and equipment than any other single item.[1] Not only has the need for additional space become critical, but the cost of maintaining the records' system has risen.

One expert indicated that if trends continue, the cost of filing just one document could rise to ten cents.[2] The problems increase, as one file drawer can hold only a certain amount of items. Not only do the

---

[1]Judy L. Holbreck and Vincent T. Marcus, Problems in Record Storage, (Dayton, Ohio: Western Publishing Company, 1982), p. 2.

[2]Deborah Dane, "The Rising Cost of Record Storage," Management and Money, (April, 1982), p. 52.

OUR PAPER HIGHWAY

Records

The storing of valuable documents and records has had a place in history almost from the beginning of time. Even then, early man sought to find a way to preserve and keep important records of his existence. As buying and selling evolved, the need to keep important records of business transactions also grew. Throughout history, records storage and retrieval has become an exciting and rather new career field.

Importance of Records Storage

Because of added productivity and correspondence of businesses of today, the sheer volume of paperwork has increased beyond one's wildest imagination. Business records take up more space than any other single item and more money is paid out for salaries and equipment than for any other single item (Holbreck and Marcus; 1982:2). Not only has the need for additional space become critical, but the cost of maintaining the records' system has risen.

One expert indicated that if trends continue, the cost of filing just one document could rise to ten cents (Dane; 1982:52). The problems increase, as one file drawer can hold only a certain amount of items. Not only do the records take up precious space, but the need for higher salaries and equipment soars. Quite obviously, any time or effort spent by office workers or any money spent by a business firm is totally

Typing Procedure:

1. Rather than use a raised (superior) number in the body of the paper to indicate it is a quotation, use author, date of publication, and page number.
   Example:
   ...and equipment.[1]
   ...and equipment (Holbreck and Marcus;1982:2).
2. Do not put anything at the bottom of the page; continue the typing of the text material down to the point where there are 6 to 9 blank lines at the bottom of the page (1 to 1½ inches).
3. If you should have more than one publication by the same authors with the same publication date, use *a, b, c,* etc., to let the reader know to which publication in the bibliography you are referring.
   Example:
   (Holbreck and Marcus;1982a:2) Listed first in bibliography
   (Holbreck and Marcus;1982b:16) Listed second in bibliography
   (Holbreck and Marcus;1982c:118) Listed third in bibliography
4. Use the title of the reference if there is no author.
5. The bibliography is typed in alphabetical order (see next page).

The document is typed in final form on the appropriate stationery, incorporating the changes. An illustration is shown below.

Parker Advertising Inc.

1750 NINTH STREET • BALTIMORE, MD 21201 • 301/493-4700

March 26, 19--

Mr. J. A. Thompson
WP Consultants, Inc.
4031 Wisconsin Avenue N.W.
Washington, D.C. 20008

Dear Mr. Thompson:

Two cartons containing 1000 WPTM Price Lists will be shipped directly to you from the printer on April 1.

The remaining 9000 will be shipped directly to the Central Distribution Center in Bethesda, Maryland. Field Offices must order directly from the Distribution Center. The form number is 5327-9320.

Based on an estimated distribution of 1500 per month, this quantity provides only a six month supply. Please notify us no later than August 1 if the Price List needs to be reprinted. The final cost for producing the Price List is $18,000.

Sincerely,

S. A. Kemp

S. A. Kemp
Advertising Consultant

SAK/jrf

Prepared Guide Sheet:

1. Insert paper into machine; count down to line 55. Type the number 12 three spaces from the left edge of the paper.
2. Single space and type the number 11; continue this procedure, typing down to the number 1. When completed, your guide sheet should look like the one illustrated below:

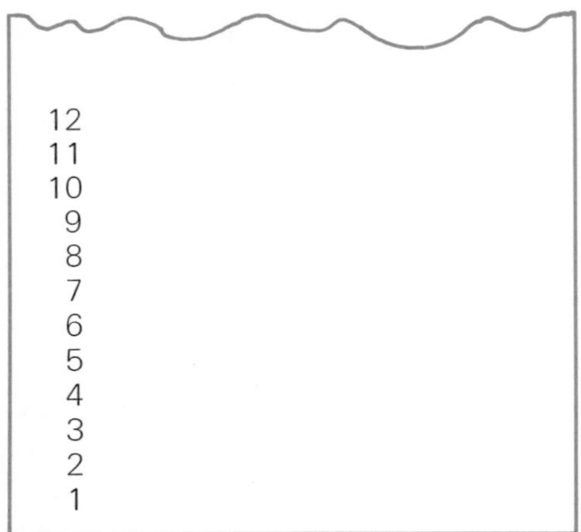

3. When ready to begin typing your manuscript, place guide sheet under a clean sheet of paper and insert into machine. After completing approximately two-thirds of the page, begin to watch for the numbers appearing through the paper in the left margin. Remember—you want to plan on three blank lines for ***each*** footnote, plus an additional blank line for the divider line.

Methods of Correcting Typographical Errors

Another common skill needed by anyone who prepares typewritten communication is the ability to select the best correction method for each situation and to correct typographical errors so that they are undetectable.

There are two major reasons for learning how to correct errors neatly:

1. The rising cost of preparing typewritten communication and the growing paper shortage are of major concern to employers. Every time you begin again on a new sheet of paper, the cost of preparing a typewritten document increases.
2. A typewritten document represents the individual(s) and/or the firm associated with the communication. The image projected to the reader of the document will be something less than positive if there are conspicuous corrections on the paper. It is critical that you develop the skill to correct errors so that they are undetectable.

It requires practice to develop the necessary skills and techniques for each correction procedure or method. No single method is satisfactory for all situations: one method may work better in one situation than another. When selecting a correction method, there are three things to consider.

1. ***How obvious is the correction?*** On original copy to be mailed, strive for undetectable corrections. A poor correction can compound your original mistake. On rough drafts or documents that are to be photocopied, an obvious correction or alteration may be acceptable.
2. ***How permanent is the correction?*** How the typewritten document is used determines whether a permanent correction is needed. For documents that are folded, mailed, stored, handled frequently, and checked in and out of files, a permanent correction method such as lift-off tape or an eraser should be used. Correction fluid, in time, can crack, and correction tape (which covers the error with a powder substance) can flake or rub off. Therefore, less permanent correction methods should be used only for short-term documents.
3. ***How costly is the correction?*** The major cost of any correction is the time that it takes you to make it. Therefore, you should practice until you can make undetectable corrections in a few seconds.

The basic error-correction methods are described below.

Correction Fluid

Correction fluid may be used to remove a single character, a word, or an entire paragraph. This method can be used on originals, carbon copies, or photocopies. Also, correction fluid can be used with fabric or carbon ribbons to correct typed mistakes, or it may be used to correct handwritten errors. Correction fluid may be used in or out of the typewriter, does not damage the paper, and is permanent. The fluid is available in white or can be color-matched to most colors of paper. To use correction fluid:

(cont'd. on next page)

General Guidelines

FOOTNOTE PLACEMENT

There are two common methods used for judging footnote placement on a page: (1) use of pencil marks in the margin, and (2) use of a prepared guide sheet.

Pencil-Mark Method:

1. Before inserting paper, place a small, light pencil mark in the left margin approximately 6 lines (1 inch) from the bottom of the page.

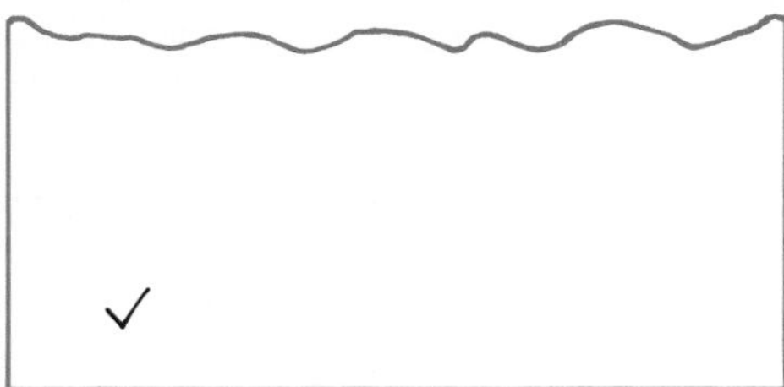

2. As you are typing the body of the text and come to material that is quoted that will require a footnote, roll the paper up until you come to the warning pencil mark. Roll the paper back three single spaces and make another mark. Then roll the paper back to your line and resume typing. Follow this procedure for each reference you type that must be footnoted in the text.

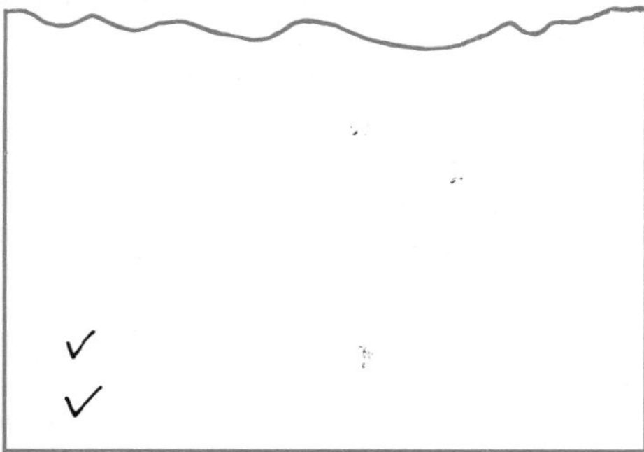

3. When you come to the pencil mark that you made last (the first one you will come to), stop typing, single space, draw a divider line, double space and indent, begin typing the first line of the first footnote.

OUR PAPER HIGHWAY

Records

The storing of valuable documents and records has had a place in history almost from the beginning of time. Even then, early man sought to find a way to preserve and keep important records of his existence. As buying and selling evolved, the need to keep important records of business trasactions also grew. Throughout history, records storage and retrieval has become an exciting and rather new career field.

Importance of Records Storage

Because of added productivity and correspondence of businesses of today, the sheer volume of paperwork has increased beyond one's wildest imagination. Business records take up more space than any other single item and more money is paid out for salaries and equipment than any other single item.[1] Not only has the need for additional space become critical, but the cost of maintaining the records' system has risen.

One expert indicated that if trends continue, the cost of filing just one document could rise to ten cents.[2] The problems increase, as one file drawer can hold only a certain amount of items. Not only do the

---

✓ [1]Judy L. Holbreck and Vincent T. Marcus, Problems in Record Storage, (Dayton, Ohio: Western Publishing Company, 1982), p. 2.

✓ [2]Deborah Dane, "The Rising Cost of Record Storage," Management and Money, (April, 1982), p. 52.

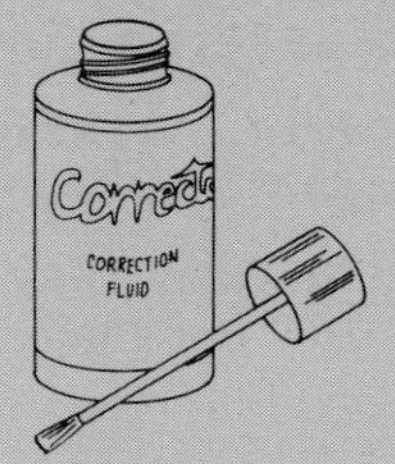

1. Roll the paper up or down so that the error can be easily reached.
2. Shake the contents of the bottle before opening. Open the bottle and wipe the brush on the inside of the bottle opening to remove any excess fluid.
3. Apply the fluid sparingly by dotting the errors with the tip of the brush, following the outline of the incorrect letter. Be sure to correct one character at a time. Do not paint the entire word (excess fluid attracts attention to the error).
4. Put the cap back on the bottle after each use.
5. Allow the fluid to dry thoroughly on the paper.
6. Return the paper to the proper position and type the correct letter or letters.

Correction Paper

Correction paper is quick and easy to use. By placing a strip of correction paper between the typing paper and the typewriter ribbon, the force of a key striking the correction paper transfers a chalklike substance from the correction paper to the typing paper. You are actually retyping your original mistake in order to cover it with the chalklike substance.

There are different correction papers produced for use on originals, on carbon copies, on colored papers, and for use with fabric or film ribbons. To use correction paper:

1. Backspace to the error.
2. Hold the correction paper over the error. Be sure the chalky side faces the typing paper.
3. Retype the error.
4. Remove the correction paper.
5. Backspace and type the correct letter. You may need to retype the correct letter more than once so that the correction has the same darkness as the rest of the typing.

Remember that excessive folding or handling of the paper may cause the chalklike substance to flake or rub off.

Correction Tape

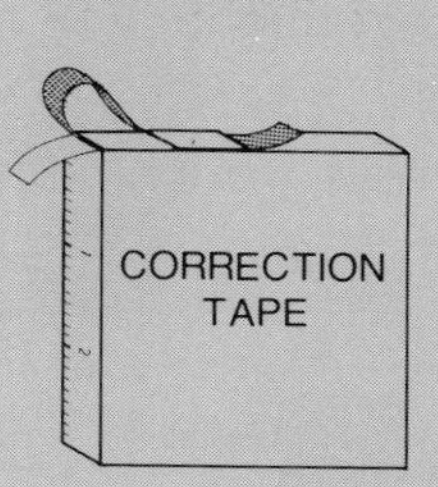

Correction tape is a continuous strip of white pressure-sensitive adhesive paper which can be attached to a document and typed over. The resulting document can then be photocopied. The tape is available in one-, two-, three-, four-, five, or six-line widths and may be used to cover a word or an entire paragraph.

While this is an excellent method for correcting documents to be photocopied or for correcting spirit masters, correction tape is not appropriate for correcting originals or carbon copies.

Eraser

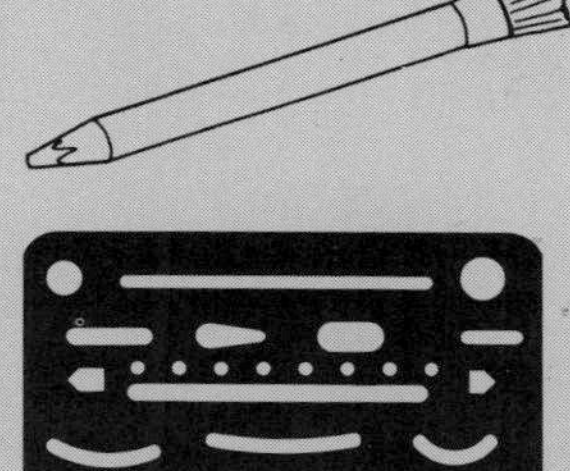

Although erasing is time-consuming, it is an alternative correction skill. To erase properly, you need an eraser and an erasing shield. The two basic types of erasers used are abrasive erasers (used for ink and originals) and soft erasers (used for carbon copies and pencil). To correct an original, use an abrasive eraser as follows:

1. Move the Carrier away from the error, so eraser dust will not fall on the Element.
2. Roll the paper forward or backward, so that the error is easy to reach.

REPORT	[5]Raymond R. Zich, The Problems of Our Canine Society Today (Madison, Wisconsin: Dane County Veterinarian Society, 1981), p. 39.
INTERVIEW	[6]Interview with Dr. Claude Davis, Veterinarian, Nelson, Nebraska, February 28, 1980.
EDITOR OF COLLECTION	[7]Hiram P. Quick, ed., Dogs and Cats (New York: Marshall and Hines Publishing Company, 1981), p. 123.
NEWSPAPER ARTICLE	[8]Janell R. Dart, "The World Is Not Going to the Dogs," Otis Flyer, May 9, 1982, p. 4, col. 2.
PERSONAL CORRESPONDENCE	[9]Dr. Phillip McKenzie, March 3, 1982, personal correspondence.

DRILL

From the information shown below, type a correct footnote for each illustration.

1. Twenty-Nine Ways to Please Customers—Barker Review (magazine) by Ms. Gladys Fox. Appeared in the March 1982 issue on page 29.
2. Book—Exciting Sales Techniques by J. R. Scott. Published by Winston Royal Pub. Co. in Havertown, New Jersey in 1981. Taken from page 14.
3. Interviewed Dr. Allie Joy in May 1982 at her home in Denver, Colorado.
4. Book by Joanne Dowl and Kenneth Eden. Title: Will Friday Never Come? Published in 1981 by the Fridley Pub. Co. in Dallas, Texas, Quoted information on pp. 196-200.
5. Quoted from the Sept. 19, 1982 issue of the San Jose Independent newspaper, page 17, column 3.
6. Office Equipment (book)—edited by Mark Nelson, published by Ralsten Publishers, Inc., in 1982—location, Des Moines, Iowa. Material quoted from p. 397.
7. Used quote from p. 86 in March issue of Times & Trends magazine in article entitled Dynamic Decorating—no author given (1982).
8. Report by Jane Green, Office Issues & Trends, put out by New York Office Managers Association, New York City in 1982, page 46.

General Guidelines

PLANNING FOR FOOTNOTES

When typing the final copy of your manuscript, you must determine when to stop typing the body to allow enough room to include the divider line and the footnotes. Follow the general rule: Leave three blank lines for each footnote and one additional blank line for the divider line.

To type a divider line, single space after last line.	xxxxxxxxxxxxxxxxxxxxxxxx __________________
"Divider" line is 18 spaces long for elite, 15 for pica (1½"). Use Underscore Key.	[1]xxxxxxxxxxxxxxxxxxxx xxxxxxxxxxxxxxxxxxx. [2]xxxxxxxxxxxxxxxxxxxx xxxxxxxxxxxxx.

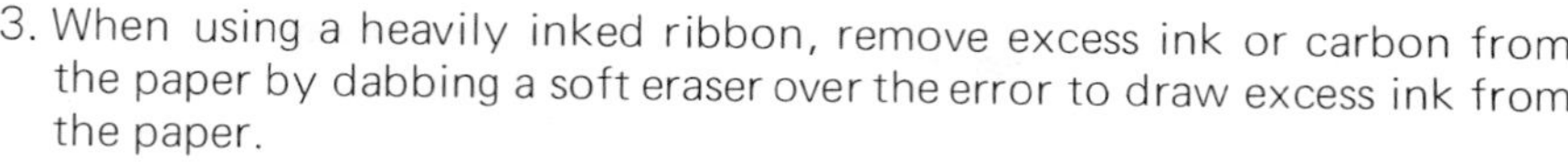

3. When using a heavily inked ribbon, remove excess ink or carbon from the paper by dabbing a soft eraser over the error to draw excess ink from the paper.
4. Position the eraser shield to protect adjacent letters.
5. Erase lightly in one direction; be careful not to tear the paper.
6. Roll the paper to the original position and type the correct character. Be sure that both the eraser and the eraser brush (if you use a brush to remove eraser dust) are clean before you use them.

To correct a carbon copy, use a soft eraser as follows:

1. Follow steps 1 and 2 for correcting an original.
2. Place an eraser guard (usually a card or a piece of metal) between the original and the first carbon copy. Avoid using small pieces of paper as they tend to leave black smudges.
3. After you have corrected the error on the original, place the eraser guard between the first and second carbon copies. Erase the error from the first carbon copy using a soft eraser and the same technique as on the original.
4. Continue the process for each additional carbon copy.
5. Return the paper to the original position and type the correct character.

Note: If you are using a copy set (which has a copy and carbon paper fastened together at one end), be sure to insert the open end of the copy set into the typewriter.

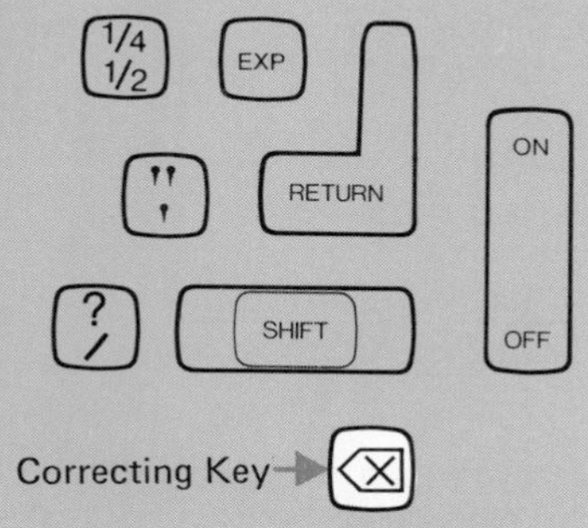

LIFT-OFF TABS AND SELF-CORRECTING TYPEWRITERS

Another correction method is the lift-off technique introduced with self-correcting typewriters. Rather than covering a mistake, the lift-off ribbon or tab pulls the ink off the page. This is a permanent correction method and requires a special carbon-film ribbon. It cannot be used to correct carbon copies. It is the fastest method of correcting typewritten errors on original copy.

ELECTRONIC ERROR CORRECTION

For electronic keyboards, with and without display screens, the typist backspaces and strikes over the incorrect character. The correct character replaces the incorrect character in the electronic memory of the system. Depending on the electronic memory capacity and the type of text-editing features available, extensive corrections that include inserting words, phrases, sentences, and paragraphs, deleting any of the preceding, moving sections of text, and reformatting documents are samples of the flexibility of electronic editing and revision.

DRILL

Type each of the statements below. Concentrate on inserting the quotation marks, superscripts, and other punctuation marks in the proper position.

In his latest book, Strage states, "Dogs should never be given more food than they can eat at one time."[1]

Star and Smith have said, "The coat of a healthy dog should be shining and glowing at all times."[2]

Hearthic has stated clearly, "There is no excuse for having an unhealthy dog in this day and age."[3]

According to the latest information, the one leading cause for animal neglect is human indifference.[4]

Zich has declared, "Nine million dogs are suffering each day in our country."[5]

Dr. Davis has emphasized the importance of early training of the young puppy. . . .[6]

There is an overwhelming need for continued control of our animal population, according to recent reports.[7]

General Guidelines

FOOTNOTES

1. Footnotes are used to tell your reader the exact source of your quoted material, and where additional information can be found.
2. The format for typing a footnote will vary slightly, according to various reference books. Choose one method and be consistent throughout the entire manuscript. Generally, a footnote must include:
   Author, title, facts of publication (place: publisher, date), page on which you found the information.

   Example: James L. Johnson, All You Wanted to Know About the Moon (Tucson, Arizona: Minute Publishing Company, 1980), page 117.
3. Remember—poems, short stories, chapters, essays, and articles in magazines are enclosed in quotation marks. Titles of books, newspapers, and magazines are underscored.

DRILL

Type each footnote example shown below. Concentrate on inserting the quotation marks, superior numbers, and other punctuation marks in proper position.

BOOK (one author) — [1]Arthur J. Strage, Healthy Dogs (Dallas, Texas: Marston Printing Company, 1981), p. 110.

BOOK (two authors) — [2]Marvel E. Star and Ann Smith, Grooming Your Dog (Denver, Colorado: Allison Publishers, 1982), p. 86

MAGAZINE ARTICLE (author named) — [3]Olive T. Hearthic, "The Shame of Our Dog Population," Dogs Today (March 1982), p. 267.

MAGAZINE ARTICLE (no author named) — [4]"Trends in Dog Management," Dog World (January, 1981), pp. 267-272.

(cont'd. on next page)

Reinserting Paper and Realigning for Corrections

If you find an error after you have removed the paper from the typewriter, it is more difficult to make the correction. To realign characters for a correction, use the markings on the Cardholder, the Paper Release Lever, and the Platen Variable.

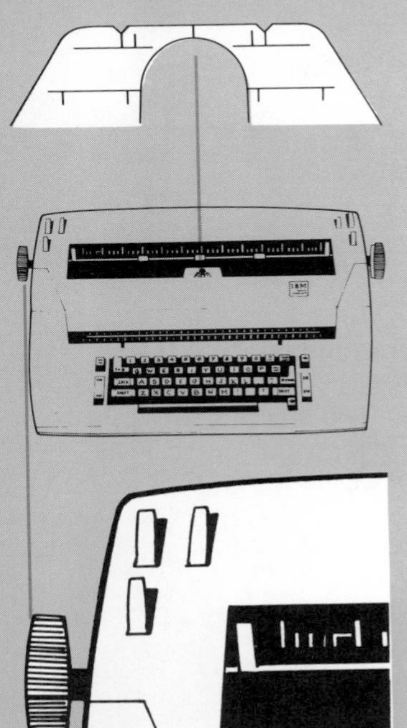

DRILL

1. Insert a sheet of paper and type: *Now si the time*.
2. Backspace to the *t* in *time* and note the position of the vertical line at the top center of the Cardholder.
3. Note where the typed line rests on the horizontal line toward the bottom of the Cardholder.
4. Remove the paper and erase the error.
5. Reinsert the paper and space to the *t* in *the*.
6. With the aid of the Paper Release Lever, align the vertical line at the top of the Cardholder over the *t*.
7. Use the Platen Variable to position the characters just above the line toward the bottom of the Cardholder.
8. Put the ribbon in stencil position and type the *t*. If the stencil *t* does not fall exactly over the *t*, adjust the paper further.
9. Move the ribbon out of stencil position, backspace, and type *is*.

Crowding and Spreading Type to Make Corrections

There are times when it will be necessary that you crowd (squeeze) or spread the type to make an acceptable correction.

Two methods of half spacing may be used on electric typewriters:

1. Reach over the cover with the right hand; press against the Carrier with the first finger until the Position Indicator (red arrow) is between two of the lines of the Margin/Pitch Scale. (Practice a few times so that you know about how much pressure is needed to make the Carrier half space).

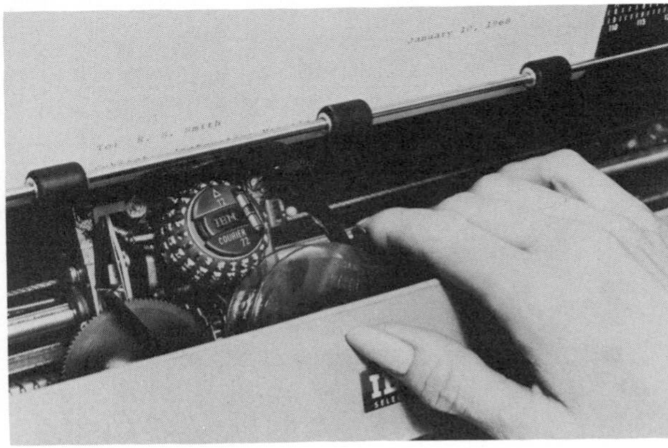

2. Position the Carrier as though you were going to type over the last correct letter. Place the right hand on top of the cover; drop the fingers to the right side of the Carrier and hold firmly. Tap the Space Bar; the Carrier cannot move. Release enough pressure so that the Carrier moves slightly forward a half space. Watch either the Position Indicator as it moves along the Margin/Pitch Scale *or* the line on the top of the Cardholder to judge when the Carrier has moved the right distance. Hold the Carrier in this half-space position and type the needed letter.

Example: PROPER TELEPHONE TECHNIQUES

The Business Image

Caller's Response

A prompt answer. Answering the telephone promptly will give the caller

Note: In a formal report that requires chapter headings, the format would differ slightly. Consult a reliable reference book for further details.

DIRECT QUOTATIONS, FOOTNOTES, AND BIBLIOGRAPHICAL ENTRIES

To use someone else's exact words or ideas in your written material and not give the other person credit for his or her ideas is known as *plagiarism*. In some cases it is against the law; and in all cases, it is considered unethical. You *must* give credit to another person if you are using his or her words. In a report or manuscript, credit to the original person is given through the use of quotation marks and a system of footnotes.

General Guidelines

QUOTATIONS

1. Direct Quotation. Use quotation marks to enclose the words and ideas of another person whom you are quoting directly.

   Example: Johnson stated, "If the moon be made of green cheese, I would be the first to say so."[1]

   or: "If the moon be made of green cheese," stated Johnson, "I would be the first to say so."[1]

   Note: A number called a *superscript* (or a superior number) is placed after the quote in the text of your written report; this same number is also placed at the beginning of the corresponding footnote.

2. Paraphrased Quotation. In formal writing, the material that has been directly quoted is enclosed in quotation marks as shown above. If you were to paraphrase (not quote the words exactly) you would not need the quotation marks, but you must still show the number and the corresponding footnote information.

   Johnson has indicated that he would have been the first to say that the moon was made of green cheese.[1]

3. In some situations you may have a quote within a quote. It should be typed as:

   Tom replied, "The airport is only fifty miles 'as the crow flies' from the beach."

4. In some printed material, you will notice a series of three evenly-spaced periods called an *ellipsis* indicating that some words have been omitted. An ellipsis is made by typing a period after the last word, then a space, period, space, period, and the next word. Four periods are used to indicate the end of a sentence.

   Example: The airport is only fifty miles. . .from the beach.
   The airport is only fifty miles "as the crow flies" from the beach. . . .

Send the ordr today.

Send the order today.

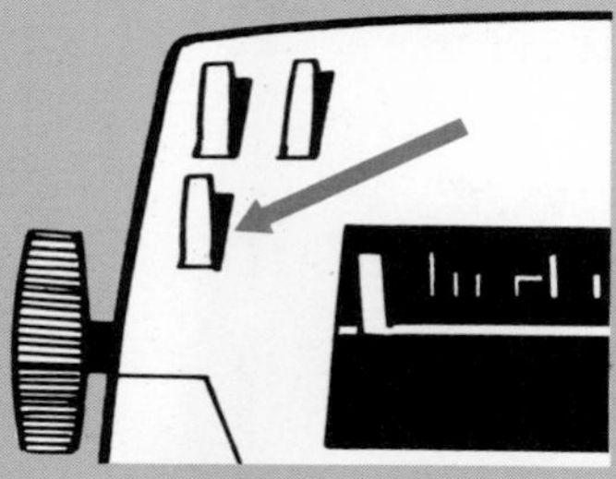

CROWDING LETTERS

1. Tab to the center and type the line:

   Send the ordr today.
2. Return the Carrier, tab, and type: *Send the*
3. Space, then reach over the cover and move the Carrier until the Position Indicator is between the black lines on the Margin/Pitch Scale (or move the Half Backspace Lever toward you).
4. Type: *o*.
5. Repeat step 3.
6. Type: *r*.
7. Repeat step 3.
8. Continue until the word is typed.

DRILL

Type each of the sentences below. Using the procedures illustrated on the previous pages, practice crowding letters until you are able to do it correctly.

1. (Insert an *e*.)	Th electrical wiring is worn out.
2. (Insert a *w*.)	The electrical iring is worn out.
3. (Insert a comma.)	If you can be sure to arrange the appointment.

He will send it.

He c a n send it.

SPREADING LETTERS

1. Tab to the center and type the sentence:

   He will send it.
2. Return the Carrier, tab, and type: *He*
3. Type the letter *c* (it will appear directly below the *w*).
4. Space twice and type the letter *n* (it will appear directly below the *l*).
5. Backspace once.
6. Reach over the cover and move the Carrier until the top line on the Cardholder is directly between the *c* and *n*. Type the letter ***a***.

DRILL

Type each of the sentences below. Using the procedures illustrated above, practice spreading letters until you are able to do it correctly.

1. The Carrrier Return operates quickly.
2. Oil paintings, in maany cases, have proven goood investments.
3. Space/~~twice~~ once and type the letter.

General Guidelines

LEFT-BOUND MANUSCRIPT

1. A left-bound manuscript is usually longer than three pages. It is usually placed in some type of cover or folder or stapled along the left side.
2. Because additional space is needed to allow for the left edge "binding," leave 18 spaces at the left margin for elite type and 15 for pica type (1½-inch left margin). Leave a right margin of 12 for elite type and 10 for pica type (1-inch right margin).
3. Because the left margin is wider than the right, it is necessary to move the "center" point of the paper three spaces to the right.

THE OFFICE MANAGER

Need

The office scene has changed considerably over the past few years. Business has grown, more transactions are taking place, and certain incidents have occurred that require most offices of today to hire a new type of employee--the office manager. His or her duties mainly are to see that the office is run as efficiently as possible.

Changes

There are many exciting and new changes that have taken place in the world of offices today. Some of them are inevitable and others have been developed to replace older methods.

Financial Costs

Many businesses have tended to view the cost of operating an office as a necessary, but unproductive, evil. Executives have seen the cost of operating an office rise rapidly.

Increased paperwork. One reason costs have increased is the fact the paperwork in an office has increased dramatically. Unless the flow of paperwork is carefully controlled, costs will skyrocket.

Inflationary times. During the past ten years, the pattern of constantly rising costs has been consistent. Many businesses are forced to cut costs in every conceivable manner. The

2

office manager is directly responsible for cost analysis and efficient production.

Change in Employees

There also has been a dramatic change in the characteristics of office personnel throughout the years.

Retiring workers. Many employers feel that there just aren't enough employees to replace older, experienced workers who have retired. New workers are costly to train and sometimes just can't do the job.

Lack of skills. Until a few years ago, office workers could usually obtain employment directly from high school. Many office positions, however, require more specialized training.

Automated equipment. Because of the development of highly automated equipment, many offices are using less employees. The new employee must be highly skilled in the use of automatic equipment and thoroughly understand the techniques and uses of data processing.

Career as Office Manager

Because of the changes that have taken place, there is a definite need for offices to use modern techniques and scientific methods. This in turn, increases the need for efficient office managers. The area of office management as a career can be profitable and productive. Training is available at most post-secondary schools which offer specialized courses in the "new method management."

General Guidelines

MANUSCRIPT HEADINGS

There are many suitable systems for handling *headings* within a manuscript. The main purpose of headings is to call the reader's attention to important ideas and portions of the manuscript. Companies, institutions, and individuals normally use a particular format that is unique to their purpose (or simply because they "like" a particular format). Regardless of which method you choose, you must be consistent throughout the entire manuscript. The heading format used in this text includes the following:

1. MAJOR TITLE: Start typing on line 13 of the first page; centered; all capital letters; triple space after.
2. First-Level Heading: center; capitalize first letter of each major word; triple space before and after.
3. Second-Level Heading: flush with left margin on separate line; capitalize first letter of each major word; underscore; triple space before and double space after.
4. Third-level heading: indent with paragraph; capitalize only first letter of first word; period following; underscore; triple space before.

Preparation of Copies

The technological advancements in copying machines and the increased use of these machines over the past decade have been phenomenal. Many of the typewritten documents that were once made with the carbon copy process are now made with copying machines.

Carbon Processes

Many offices today use both copying machines and carbons. Sometimes a carbon copy is made for the file and copies for distribution are made on a copier. Forms may come preassembled with carbon paper or printed on a specially sensitized paper which automatically reproduces information on a second or third sheet.

Copying Machines

The primary reasons for the increasing use of copying machines are quality, ease, and convenience.

1. The quality of the last copy is the same as the original.
2. Copiers are easy to use, and errors need only be corrected on the original, reducing correction time.
3. Copiers are convenient because the number of copies can be adjusted as needed. Copies can easily be made at any time.

Carbon Pack

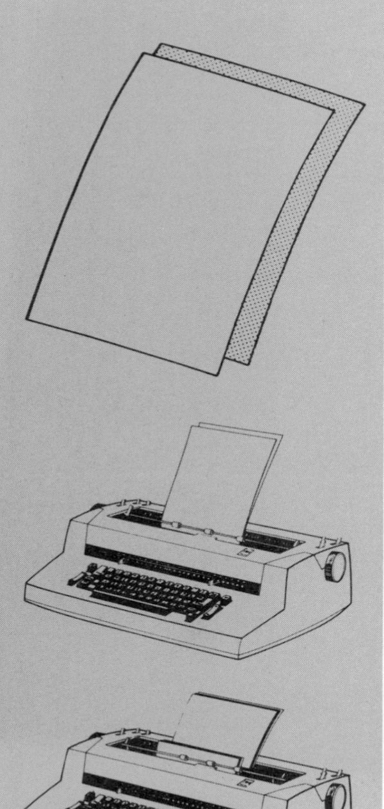

To make carbon copies, follow these steps:

1. First, you must decide on the number of copies to be made. Take out the number of second sheets or onionskin paper needed for copies and lay a blank sheet of regular typing paper on top. "Joggle" the pack so that the papers are all even.
2. Place the pack behind the Platen; be sure the yellow sheet or onionskin is facing you.
3. Turn the Platen Knob at least two clicks, until the pack is caught in the machine.
4. Insert a sheet of carbon paper between each piece of paper. As you insert the carbon paper, you should be looking at the shiny or inked side.

WHERE TO BUY

Most cities have several stores which carry similar, or identical types of merchandise. The neople of a oarticular city, therefore, have a choice of stores in which to buy certain products. Several factors which may influence their decision about where to purchase are quality, style, cost, and location. If two items are of the same quality and the same style, people will usually buy the item which costs less; that is, if they know which store is selling the item for less.

Most consumers depend upon advertising for information about sales and bargains. Although oricing is an important consideration, in far too many instances it becomes the only factor in a decision. The consumer forgets that there are two additional factors which must be considered along with price. These two factors are the amount of traveling time required to get to the store and the cost involved in the travel. Most oeople fail to recognize these added factors.

If a consumer must spend quite a bit of time traveling to the store which has the merchandise for the lowest price, travel time becomes a major consideration. How much is time worth? Each individual must answer that particular question.

The cost of travel, whether by private or oublic transnortation, has continued to rise. Again, if the distance involved is quite far, the consumer may spend more on transoortation than he or she saved on a "barrain" purchase; thus, will not save anv money.

2

The intelligent consumer must be aware of all factors involved with purchasing. Too many times the consumer considers difference in prices as only "cents" and not dollars. Yet, "cents" add up to dollars over the duration of a small period of time.

General Guidelines

UNBOUND MANUSCRIPTS

1. An unbound manuscript is usually a very short manuscript (three or fewer pages). If it is more than one page, the pages may be stapled in the upper left corner.
2. Set side margins of 12 spaces for elite type and 10 spaces for pica type (1-inch side margins for unbound manuscripts). An example of this is shown below.

WHERE TO BUY

Most cities have several stores which carry similar, or identical typed of merchandise. The people of a particular city, therefore, have a choice of stores in which to buy certain products. Several factors which may influence their decision about where to purchase are quality, style, cost, and location. If two items are of the same quality and the same style, neople will usually buy the item which costs less; that is, if thev know which store is selling the item for less.

Most consumers depend upon advertising for information about sales and bargins. Although pricing is an important consideration, in far too many instances it becomes the only factor in a decision. The consumer forgets that there are two additional factors which must be considered along with price. These two factors are the amount of traveling time required to get to the store and the cost involved in the travel. Most peonle fail to recognize these added factors.

If a consumer must spend quite a bit of time traveling to the store which has the merchandise for the lowest price, travel time becomes a major consideration. How much is time worth? Each individual must answer that particular question.

The cost of travel, whether by private or public transnortation, has continued to rise. Again, if the distance involved is quite far, the consumer may spend more on transportation than he or she saved on a "bargin" purchase; thus, will not save any money.

The intelligent consumer must be aware of all factors involved with purchasing. Too manv times the consumer considers difference in prices as onlv

The intelligent consumer must be aware of all factors involved with purchasing. Too many times the consumer considers difference in prices as only "cents" and not dollars. Yet, "cents" add up to dollars over the duration of a small period of time.

5. Turn the carbon pack to the first line of typing and proceed.
6. Should you make an error, roll the carbon pack forward or backward, whichever allows you to correct the error without removing the pack from the machine. If you are using correction paper, insert it between the shiny or inked side of the carbon and the copy. Place a piece of correction paper over the error on the original and proceed with the correction process.

   If you are using an eraser, place a card or a piece of metal that can be used as a guard between the shiny or inked side of the carbon paper and the copy. Start by erasing the error on the original and then correct the errors on the carbon copies, beginning with the first copy and proceeding to the last. Be sure to remove the piece of paper or card being used as a shield.
7. After the page has been completed, remove the carbon pack from the machine. With one hand, hold the pack in the upper left or right corner tightly; with the other hand, grasp the carbon paper that extends beyond the pack and pull. Put the carbon paper away and distribute the copies.

Copy Sets

Copy sets are preassembled copy paper and carbons which offer these advantages:

1. The copies are consistent and clear, since the carbon paper is used only once.
2. The collating and aligning of copy paper and carbon paper is already done. Filing of carbon after use is eliminated.
3. You do not have to touch the carbon in assembling or detaching the copy paper.

TYPES OF COPY SETS

1. Pad. One end is perforated so that the copy paper and carbon can be separated. A clean-end tissue leader is provided for removing carbon.
2. Single Sets. One end of the carbon is spot-glued to the copy paper; a clean-end tissue leader on the carbon permits easy separation.

ERASING ON COPY SETS

For ease in separating copy paper and carbon to erase, insert the open end of the copy set into the typewriter, particularly if using the pad form. To prevent papers from "bubbling," use your Paper Release Lever as you insert the copy set.

In summary, whether to use copying machines or the carbon copy process depends on individual circumstances. At this point, you should be aware of the advantages and disadvantages of each procedure and know how to prepare a carbon pack should the situation warrant this process.

Study the following example of an outline:

PLANTS

```
 I.   FLOWERING PLANTS

      A.   Tender perennial flowers
           1.   Gloxinia
           2.   Temple Bells
      B.   Hardy perennial flowers
           1.   Yarrow
           2.   Phlox

II.   FOLIAGE PLANTS

      A.   Low light-level plants
           1.   Schefflera
           2.   Nephthytis
                a.   High humidity
                     (1)   Calathea
                     (2)   Fittonia
                b.   Low humidity
                     (1)   Jade plant
                     (2)   Sansevieria
      B.   Bright light-level plants
           1.   Geranium
           2.   Azalea
           3.   Aralia
```

General Guidelines

MANUSCRIPT TYPING

1. Manuscripts are usually double spaced.
2. Paragraphs are indented from 5 to 8 spaces. Use a 5-space paragraph indention on the following typing tasks.
3. Center heading; type in all capital letters.
4. Triple space after titles.
5. Begin title on line 13 of the first page; place page number on second and succeeding pages on line 7 (1-inch from top) at the right-hand margin; triple space before beginning the first line.
6. Leave bottom margin of 6-9 lines (1-1½ inches).

(cont'd. on next page)

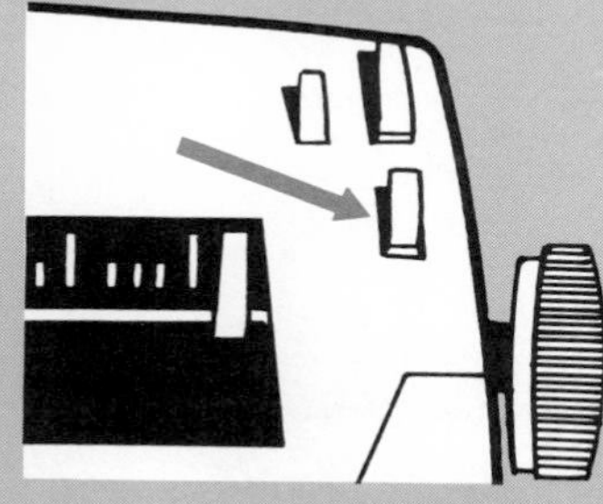

Superscripts and Subscripts

The Line Finder allows you to temporarily leave the original typing line to type a superscript, subscript, double underscore, or to draw lines.

Steps in making superscripts and subscripts:

1. Move the Line Finder toward you.
2. Turn the Platen Knob to move to the temporary typing line.
3. Type the information.
4. Push the Line Finder back and turn the Platen Knob to return to the original typing line.

DRILL

Using the Line Finder, type the following sentences.

1. H_2O is the chemical formula for water.
2. If x^2 equals 16, x must equal 4.
3. $M^2 + Y^2 = C^2$
4. [2]Hall, Kenneth R., The Joys of Traveling, Hyland Publishing Company, New York, New York, 1978.
5. The temperature was 90° last Monday.

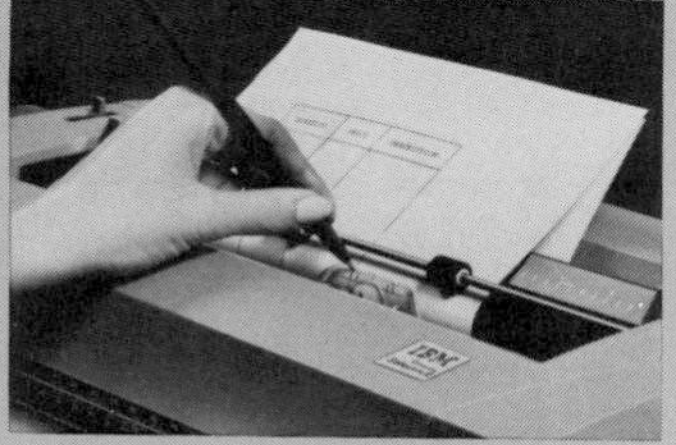

Drawing Vertical Lines

1. Place a pencil or pen in the notch of the Cardholder.
2. Move the Line Finder toward you to achieve a free, rolling motion.
3. Turn the Platen Knob manually.
4. Push the Line Finder back and turn the Platen Knob to return to the original typing line.

Task 17

Working Papers, pp. 165-66

TO — all employees FROM — Pat Ganser SUB. — Company Christmas Party The Truax-Vehlow Christmas Party will be held on Saturday, Dec. 20, at the downtown Lexington Hotel. Cocktails + hors d'oeuvres will be served commencing at 6:30 p.m. in the Embassy Room, located downstairs from the main lobby. Dinner will be served at 7:30 p.m. in the adjacent Concorde Room. An orchestra will begin playing at 9:00 p.m. for your dancing pleasure.

Parking is available in the hotel parking ramp. Entrance to the ramp can only be made from 51st St. between Hudson + Marquette Avenues. Attached is a list of those attending. Please let me know as soon as possible of any additions +/or corrections.

ATTACHMENT:

Mr. + Mrs. Anatole Jazbutis
Mr. + Mrs. Clarence Rothenburger
Ms. Edna Jayko + friend
Mr. Rudy Ewert + friend
Mrs. Sherrey Green
Mr. + Mrs. W. Houston
Mr. Aki Hoshida
Ms. Karen Jones
Mr. + Mrs. Dick Orrell
Mr. Al Riden + friend

Applications Production Module

You have learned basic typewriting skills and developed your speed and accuracy so that you are now ready to learn how to type letters, memos, manuscripts, reports, and forms. The material you will be typing is presented in different stages:

Introductory Level:

1. Copy, with instructions. A model will be shown that will include all instructions so that you can copy it successfully.

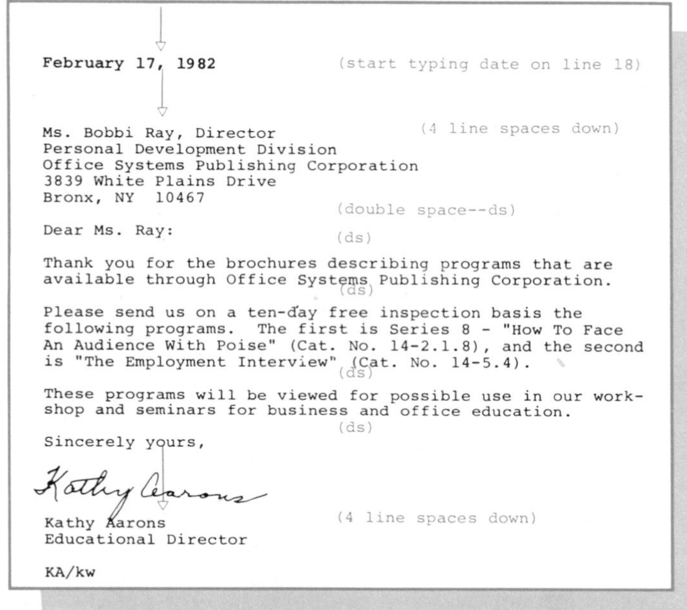

February 17, 1982 (start typing date on line 18)

(4 line spaces down)

Ms. Bobbi Ray, Director
Personal Development Division
Office Systems Publishing Corporation
3839 White Plains Drive
Bronx, NY 10467

(double space--ds)

Dear Ms. Ray:

(ds)

Thank you for the brochures describing programs that are available through Office Systems Publishing Corporation.

(ds)

Please send us on a ten-day free inspection basis the following programs. The first is Series 8 - "How To Face An Audience With Poise" (Cat. No. 14-2.1.8), and the second is "The Employment Interview" (Cat. No. 14-5.4).

(ds)

These programs will be viewed for possible use in our workshop and seminars for business and office education.

(ds)

Sincerely yours,

Kathy Aarons

(4 line spaces down)

Kathy Aarons
Educational Director

KA/kw

2. Copy, without instructions. This model can be copied also; however, it will not have the instructions printed on it. Try to complete the tasks without referring to the model with instructions.

1964 Showgate Way
Denver, CO 80219
Current Date

Mr. Tom Torrence
General Wolfe Secondary School
55 McCraney Street East
Oakville, Ontario, CANADA
L6H 1H9

Dear Mr. Torrence:

For the presentation in Toronto on March 8 I would like to have the following equipment: an overhead projector, a 35mm carrousel slide projector, and a large screen.

You need not worry about sending an advance for the cost of airfare as I will put the ticket on my credit card. It takes approximately 30 days for the bill to catch up.

By the way, would you give me an idea of the approximate number attending the workshop. I want to have sufficient materials to hand each participant.

Sincerely yours,

Paula Goldberg

Paul Goldberg

Task 20

Working Papers, pp. 171-72 and plain paper

Current Date

Selected

TO: ~~A Few~~ V.I.P. Clients

Patricia Ganser
Executive Director
ITG Program Bureau

AN EXCLUSIVE NEW ATTRACTION--DR. DAVID C. SHEPARD

our organization

Dr. David C. Shepard, acknowledged as one of America's most colorful and recognized writers, who is at the same time both enlightening and entertaining, has just signed an exclusive contract with ~~us~~. Dr. Shepard will be available for a very limited number of engagements throughout the country during the months of ~~September and~~ October & November this year.

His frequent appearances on talk shows and other popular television programs have ~~been~~ enchant~~ing~~ed millions of viewers, long familiar with his powerful and creative prose in numerous volumes of contemporary fiction. He is currently in Hollywood filming a ~~dramatic~~ motion picture in which he will have a major role.

We are suggesting the following two lecture subjects:

1. An Evening With Dr. David C. Shepard
2. Dr. David C. Shepard--The Writer's Life

In either program, Dr. Shepard will be talking about his life as a best-selling author and a unique national celebrity. His program will include a discussion of selected stories he has written, fascinating readings from his works, and some surprise anecdotes about his writings. The highlight, of course, ~~will be~~ the half-hour of questions and answers that ~~top off the~~ program. end each
We can ~~virtually~~ guarantee that your audience will be held spellbound throughout Dr. Shepard's talk.

Since this is a very limited tour, we strongly urge you to contact us immediately to discuss fees and availability. Call now at 612/488-6009.

~~A Few~~ V.I.P. Clients
Page 2 Selected
Current Date

As is our usual policy, we are continually adding new stimulating programs of wide reputation that will draw capacity crowds on campuses. Be sure to telephone us for your program needs. We ~~are grateful to you for your business~~ in the past, and we ~~are~~ look~~ing~~ forward to continuing this friendly relationship.
have enjoyed working with you.

your initials

Competency Level:

1. Unarranged: These tasks will be shown in typewritten copy. All the information will be included, but you will have to visualize the final document, since it will not be set up so that you can copy it.

> 23 Rock Place / Reno, NV 89504 / Current Date / Mr. Philip W. Ruehl / Center for Vocational, Technical, & Adult Education / Department of Public Instruction / Springfield, IL 62302 / Dear Mr. Ruehl: / I did not return my evaluation materials to you until Saturday. Consequently, my observations are not included in the enclosed materials. / I will not be able to attend the workshop in Rockford in June as I have another commitment. / If there is anything else I should do with these materials, please return them to me with the appropriate instructions. / Sincerely, / Cecile Conway / Evaluation Committee Member / Enclosure

2. Handwritten: These tasks will be unarranged and presented in handwriting. You will be required to type a final document or a rough draft.

> (Current date) / Dr. Carolyn Bonner / Department of Business Education / University of Southern Mississippi / Southern Station, Box 83 / Hattiesburg, MS 39401 / Dear Dr. Bonner / Dr. Livingston indicated that you would be serving as coordinator for the workshop that Dr. Ed Wanzer and I will be presenting in Hattiesburg in July. ¶ Could you please make arrangements to have the following equipment available for our presentations: (1) an overhead projector, (2) a 16 mm projector, and (3) a 35 mm carrousel slide projector. ¶ I will send you an outline of the program that we will be presenting. Also, we will be sending you materials to duplicate for distribution to the participants of the workshop. ¶ If there is anything else that you need from us, please drop me a line or give me a call at 312-864-5622. / Sincerely yours, / Dennis Czeslaw / President / c: Janet Livingston / c: Dr. Wanzer

3. Rough Draft: These tasks will be shown in typewritten copy with author changes marked on it. At times, you will be required to proofread and edit for additional corrections before you type the final document.

> Dr. James Moline Metropolitan Professional Building 5991
> Madison Drive, New York, NY 10055. Dear Dr. Moline: ~~It~~
> ~~was a pleasure to visit with you on the phone this morning.~~
> Truax-Vehlow Invenstment Services has been in the brokerage and
> investment banking busines s for over ~~25~~ 35 years and specializes
> in ~~new~~ growth companies. We firmly believe that such companies
> represent the greatest profit potential for individual investors. In
> recent years, we have devoted considerable attention to the medical
> industry through our research and investment banking activities.
> We have played an important role in the early stages of several
> ~~recently~~ emerging medical firms in the city of New York. ¶ Please
> give me a call whenever it is convenient, and I will be pleased
> to set up an appointment to discuss a mutually-satisfying business
> relationship. Sincerely, Roberta E. Thomas, Invenstment Consultant

Task 19

Working Papers, pp. 169-70

TO: Biological Research Association
c/o Mr. John Gardner
Kresge Laboratories
3661 51st Avenue
San Diego, CA 92101

FROM: Patricia Ganser
Executive Director
ITG Program Bureau

RE: Special Props/Equipment

We would like to request that the following audio-visual equipment and special props be available for our speaker's presentation at the Biological Research Association Convention on June 22.

/X / Podium
/X / Overhead projector
/X / Lavaliere microphone
/X / 35mm Carrousel slide projector
/ / 16mm Movie projector
/X / Screen
/ / Tables (No.:____)
/ / Chairs (No.:____)
/ / Electric typewriter
/ / Other (please indicate: ________________________________)

To be used
DATE/HOUR/PLACE June 22 1:00 p.m. Room 1404/05

April 10, 19--
Date

Signature

Correspondence

Goals of Correspondence Production

In this section of the book you will learn to type letters, memos, and envelopes. Your first goal is to be able to prepare a typewritten document that conveys a favorable image. To do this, you will need to learn guidelines for style and format in preparing correspondence and you will have to be able to correct typographical errors properly.

In addition to preparing correspondence that makes a positive first impression, you must be able to prepare typewritten correspondence that is without error in content. To accomplish this second goal, you will be given an opportunity to refine your proofreading, editing, and language arts skills, including spelling, punctuation, and grammar.

Finally, you must be able to prepare typewritten correspondence in mailable form at marketable production speed levels. Most people can write in longhand at the rate of 20-25 words a minute. Your goal will be to reach rates of over 25 words a minute on typewritten correspondence.

Letters

PARTS OF A TRADITIONAL STYLE LETTER

The traditional business letter has ten major parts. As each part is presented, refer to the letter to Ms. Madeline Serro, page 184, and also to the illustration appearing in the left-hand margin.

1. *Letterheads.* Letterheads come in all types of printing and colors, many of which include pictures, symbols, or other designs of varying sizes. Some of the items included in a typical letterhead are:
   a. the name and location of the firm or individual
   b. departments, divisions, or sections within the firm
   c. telephone number(s)
   d. the firm logo-a trademerk representing the firm
   Plain Paper. A personal letter is typed on plain paper.

2. *Date Line.* The first section of a letter is.the date line. Typically, the date is written as follows: the month, the day of the month followed by a comma, and then the year: January 12, 1982. Some individuals rearrange the order in which these items are presented. They may put the day of the month first, then the month and year. No commas are required when the date is presented in this manner: 12 January 1982. Canada and some other countries employ the metric system of dating, in which only numerals are used. In this system, the date is presented in this manner: 82/01/12 (year-month-day). If uncertain, check with your instructor for the appropriate method in your area. The date is usually typed 9-18 lines from the top of the page. The actual placement will vary, depending on the style of the letterhead and the length of the letter.

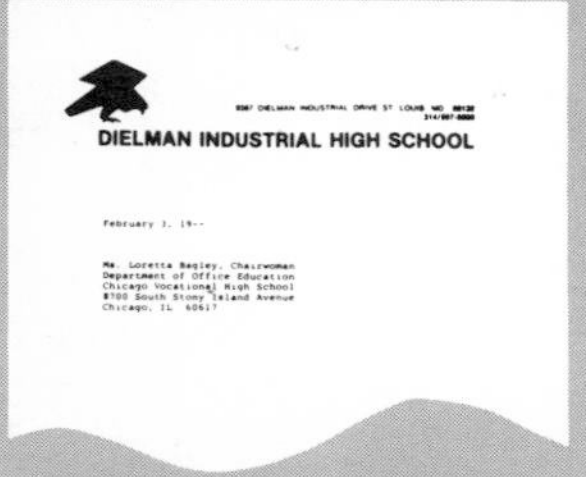

3. *Inside Address.* The inside address represents the person and/or organization receiving the letter. Included are: the name of the individual, the person's title, the department or office, and the name of the firm. This information generally takes two lines. The street address or post-office box number follows, with the city, state, and postal code making up the last line. (Many organizations use the inside address as the envelope address by using window envelopes when mailing correspondence outside the firm.)

Task 18

Working Papers, pp. 167-68

TO: All Employees

FROM: Pat G.

SUBJECT: Company Christmas Party

The Truax-Vehlow Christmas Party will be held on ~~Saturday, Dec. 20,~~ Friday, Dec. 19 at the downtown Lexington Hotel. Cocktails and hors d'oeuvres will be served commencing at 6:30 p.m. in the Embassy Room, located downstairs from the main lobby. Dinner will be served at 7:30 p.m. in the adjacent Concorde Room. An orchestra will begin playing at 9:00 p.m. for your dancing pleasure.

Parking is available in the hotel parking ramp. Entrance to the ramp can only be made from 51st St. between Hudson & Marquette Avenues. Attached is a list of those attending. Please let me know as soon as possible of any additions and/or corrections.

--------------attachment----------------

Mr. and Mrs. Anatole Jazbutis
Mr. and Mrs. Clarence Rothenburger
Ms. Edna Jayko and friend
Mr. Rudy Ewert and friend
Mrs. Sherrey Green
Mr. and Mrs. W. Houston
Mr. Aki Hoshida
Ms. Karen Jones
Mr. and Mrs. Dick Orrell
Mr. Al Riden and friend

Please redo this memo as date has been changed due to conflict. Send out over my name.

Pat Ganser

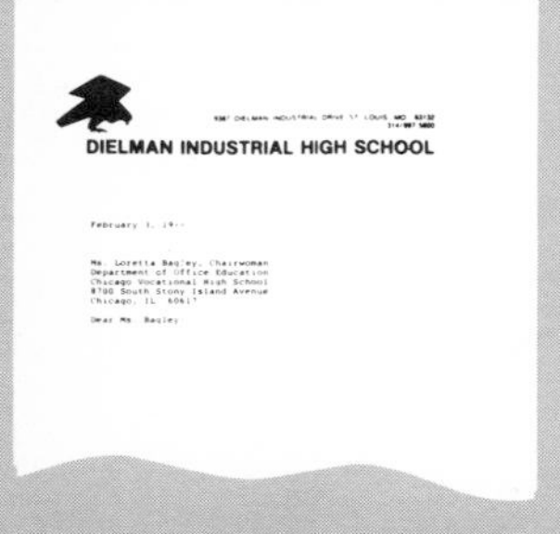

9387 DIELMAN INDUSTRIAL DRIVE ST LOUIS MO 63132

DIELMAN INDUSTRIAL HIGH SCHOOL

February 3, 19--

Ms. Loretta Bagley, Chairwoman
Department of Office Education
Chicago Vocational High School
8700 South Stony Island Avenue
Chicago, IL 60617

Dear Ms. Bagley:

4. ***Salutation/Greeting.*** Traditionally the salutation, or greeting, is placed on a line by itself following the inside address. Two punctuation styles are used—mixed, a colon is typed; open, no colon is typed after the salutation. Some samples of salutations include:

Open-Punctuation Style	Mixed-Punctuation Style
Dear Ms. Cebron	Dear Ms. Cebron:
Dear Ruth	Dear Ruth:
Dear Mr. Wiedmeyer	Dear Mr. Wiedmeyer:
Dear Robert	Dear Robert:
Gentlemen	Gentlemen:
Ladies	Ladies:

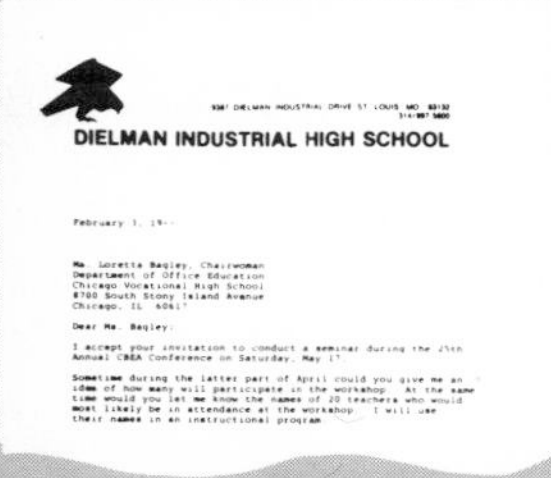

DIELMAN INDUSTRIAL HIGH SCHOOL

February 3, 19--

Ms. Loretta Bagley, Chairwoman
Department of Office Education
Chicago Vocational High School
8700 South Stony Island Avenue
Chicago, IL 60617

Dear Ms. Bagley:

I accept your invitation to conduct a seminar during the 25th Annual CBEA Conference on Saturday, May 17.

Sometime during the latter part of April could you give me an idea of how many will participate in the workshop. At the same time would you let me know the names of 20 teachers who would most likely be in attendance at the workshop. I will use their names in an instructional program.

5. ***Body.*** The fifth major part of the letter includes the body, or message, of the letter. This section represents the reason for writing the letter. The sender is sharing with the receiver of the letter a message on paper in lieu of a face-to-face or other form of oral communication. Notice that the body of a business letter is usually single spaced, with a double space between paragraphs.

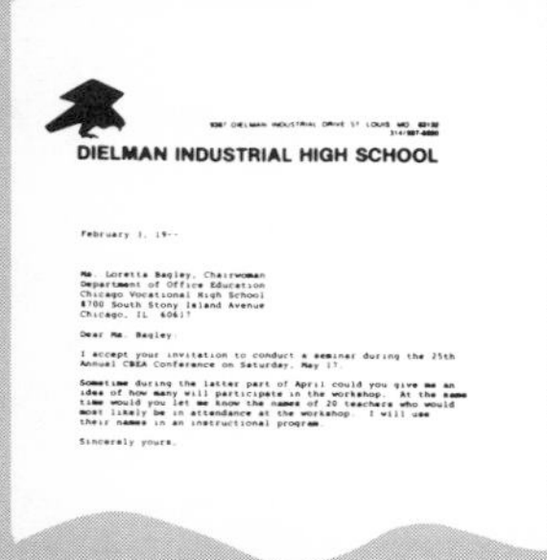

DIELMAN INDUSTRIAL HIGH SCHOOL

February 3, 19--

Ms. Loretta Bagley, Chairwoman
Department of Office Education
Chicago Vocational High School
8700 South Stony Island Avenue
Chicago, IL 60617

Dear Ms. Bagley:

I accept your invitation to conduct a seminar during the 25th Annual CBEA Conference on Saturday, May 17.

Sometime during the latter part of April could you give me an idea of how many will participate in the workshop. At the same time would you let me know the names of 20 teachers who would most likely be in attendance at the workshop. I will use their names in an instructional program.

Sincerely yours,

6. ***Closing.*** The next part of the letter is the complimentary close. Two punctuation styles are used—mixed, a comma is typed after the closing; open, no comma is typed. Some samples of a complimentary close include:

Open Style	Mixed Style
Sincerely	Sincerely,
Yours truly	Yours truly,
Very truly yours	Very truly yours,

DIELMAN INDUSTRIAL HIGH SCHOOL

February 3, 19--

Ms. Loretta Bagley, Chairwoman
Department of Office Education
Chicago Vocational High School
8700 South Stony Island Avenue
Chicago, IL 60617

Dear Ms. Bagley:

I accept your invitation to conduct a seminar during the 25th Annual CBEA Conference on Saturday, May 17.

Sometime during the latter part of April could you give me an idea of how many will participate in the workshop. At the same time would you let me know the names of 20 teachers who would most likely be in attendance at the workshop. I will use their names in an instructional program.

Sincerely yours,

William Walczak
Educational Consultant

7. ***Signature Line.*** Following the complimentary close is the signature line. This line includes the typewritten first name and the last name of the individual responsible for creating the correspondence. The typewritten signature line is important, since many signatures are difficult to read. And in responding to the writer of a letter, one wants to be sure that the proper spelling of the individual's name is used. Since letters may be originated by females or males, individuals are encouraged to use their first names rather than their initials, so that appropriate titles may be used in responding to the person.

8. ***Title Line.*** The next major part of the letter is the title line. Here you will find a business or professional title that is associated with the person who has prepared the message of the letter. In some cases, you may find that if a person has a short name and title, the signature and title lines are combined:

Guy Able, President

9387 DIELMAN INDUSTRIAL DRIVE ST LOUIS MO 63132

DIELMAN INDUSTRIAL HIGH SCHOOL

February 17, 1976 (start typing date on line 18)

Ms. Bobbi Ray, Director (4 line spaces down)
Personal Development Division
Office Systems Publishing Corporation
3839 White Plains Drive
Bronx, NY 10467

Dear Ms. Ray:

Thank you for the brochures describing programs that are available through Office Systems Publishing Corporation.

Please send us on a ten-day free inspection basis the following programs. The first is Series 8 - "How To Face An Audience With Poise" (Cat. No. 14-2.1.8), and the second is "The Employment Interview" (Cat. No. 14-5.4).

These programs will be viewed for possible use in our workshop and seminars for business and office education.

Sincerely yours,

(4 line spaces down)

Kathy Aarons
Educational Director

KA/kw

9. ***Reference Initials.*** Reference initials are the initials of the people who have prepared the communication. There are many differing styles and manners of typing these. One popular style has the initials of the person who dictated the correspondence in upper case letters followed by a slash or colon with the initials in lower case letters of the person who prepared the typewritten copy: KAS/pta or KAS:pta. (Another popular style does not repeat the initials of the preparer and simply shows the initials of the typist: pta.)

Manuscripts and Business Reports

Manuscripts

In an educational environment, a manuscript (term paper) is a frequent application; in business it is a report. The preparation of a term paper is somewhat different from that of a business report.

NOTE CARDS

Preparation of a report or manuscript involves several steps from beginning to completion. After you have selected a topic, you will want to spend an adequate amount of time researching the subject thoroughly. As you research your subject, make notes on pertinent information. Be certain you have recorded the following on each note card:

Author's complete name
Title of work (book, magazine, or so on)
Publishing facts (city, state, publisher, date, edition)
Page or pages on which the information was found

OUTLINES

From your note cards, prepare an outline. A good outline will give you direction from beginning to middle to end. You can spot inconsistencies in an outline easier than on a manuscript. An outline will help you establish clear, logical thinking and enable you to emphasize main points and minor points.

General Guidelines

PREPARING OUTLINES

An outline is a listing of major topics and subtopics. The method used for outlining may vary, but the following method is commonly used.

MAIN HEADING

I. (ROMAN NUMERALS) MAJOR DIVISION OR POINT
    A. Second-level division
        1. Third-level division
            a. Fourth-level division
                (1) Fifth-level division

Typing Format:

1. Set side margins of 12 spaces for elite type and 10 spaces for pica type (1-inch margins).
2. Start heading on line 13 (2-inch top margin).
3. Center the main heading, in all capital letters.
4. Capitalize all words in major divisions.
5. Capitalize the first letter of the first word in second-, third-, fourth-, and fifth-level divisions.
6. Set tabs every four spaces from the left margin; align the material in each division.
7. Space twice after the period following numerals and letters.
8. Triple space after the main heading. Double space before and after a major division. Single space before and after all other divisions.

SPECIAL LETTER NOTATIONS

There are a number of other notations that might appear at the bottom of the letter if they are appropriate to a particular letter. They would be typed after the reference initials. As each part is presented, refer to the letters on this page.

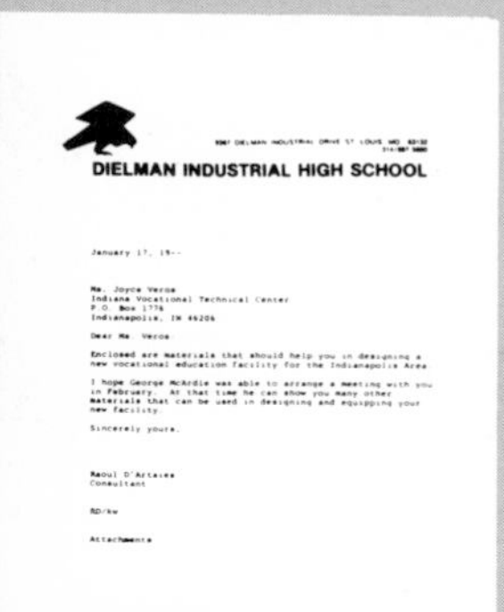
DIELMAN INDUSTRIAL HIGH SCHOOL

1. *Enclosures/Attachments.* The word ***enclosure*** or ***attachment*** typed at the bottom of the letter tells the reader that something has been included with the letter itself. (In some cases, there may be more than one enclosure. In this instance, it is appropriate for the typist to include the word ***enclosures*** or ***attachments***; you may list the title of each item underneath.)

DIELMAN INDUSTRIAL HIGH SCHOOL

2. *Copy Notations.* In some cases, individuals besides the person whose name appears on the inside address will receive copies of the letter. Traditionally, you will find the initials *cc*, representing "carbon copy," at the bottom of the letter. This, then, is followed by the name or names of the individuals to receive copies. Copies of letters today are made so frequently on copying machines that the words ***carbon copy*** may not be an appropriate reference. In this text you will find the letter ***c*** used to represent ***copy*** as an indication that more than one person received a copy of the letter.

   When two or more people receive copies of the correspondence, there may be a problem in determining whose name should be written first. It may not always be clear by job title which person is the highest ranking official. To eliminate this problem, list all persons receiving copies of the correspondence in alphabetical order.

3. *Enumerated Items.* In some letters, a list or section of enumerated items is included. The items may be typed at the left margin or indented five spaces. The second and additional lines are begun under the first word of the numbered line. The items are typed single spaced for each number and double spaced between the items.

4. *Miscellaneous.* There are other types of lines that may be included in particular letters.

   a. Attention Line. There are instances when correspondence is addressed to an organization rather than to a specific individual or division of the organization. If the individual or division name that will receive the correspondence is known, an attention line may be used. The attention line is typed at the left margin, a double space below the last line of the inside address. Double space after the attention line. There are various styles for typing the attention line.

      Attention Accounting Department
      Attention: Accounting Department
      Attention: Accounting Department
      ATTENTION: ACCOUNTING DEPARTMENT

   b. Subject Line. A subject line is used to draw the reader's attention to something of importance. The subject line is typed a double space below the greeting; it may begin at the left margin or be centered. Double space after the subject line. The subject line can be typed using the same styles used for an attention line.

in adding a touch of brilliance and zeal to your ~~previous clients in adding a touch of brilliance and zeal to your~~ convention program. Write or call today about the availability of a personal appearance by Dr. Carl Bishop.

Task 14

Working Papers, pp. 159-60

Type a memo to: Mark Powers, Financial Dept. FEES FOR SERVICES RENDERED. Make the memo from Pat Ganser, Ex. Director. The fee for the appearance of Connie Lochnew on Thursday, April 24 in the amount of ~~$400~~ $500 is now due from Metro Industries. Tell them to make their check payable to ITG Program Bureau after the engagement has been fulfilled. They should mail their check to: ITG Program Bureau, 730 Foshay Tower, 200 Eighth Avenue South, Minneapolis, MN 55402, and invoice for expenses incurred will be forwarded separately. Pat Ganser, Ex. Director

Task 15

Working Papers, pp. 161-62

TO: Jack MacPearson, Secretary/Treasurer Subject: Operations Report From: Jack Nelson Please prepare a "spread sheet" for the fiscal year ending November 31, 19--, which will include the following information:

1. Agency trades
2. Listed trades
3. Underwriting trades
4. Option "
5. Margin "
6. Bond "

From now on, this report is to be updated on a quarterly basis so that we can be fully aware of the income generated in the various categories.

Task 16

Working Papers, pp. 163-64

In some cases, rough copies are made of memos and then edited. For this task, assume Task 15 was typed in rough draft and then edited. Type in final form.

TO: Jack MacPearson, Secretary/Treasurer SUBJECT: Operations Report FROM: J. N. ¶ Please prepare a "spread sheet" for the fiscial year ending November 31, 19--, which includes the following information: ¶ 1. Agency trades ¶ 2. Listed trades ¶ 3. Underwriting trades ¶ 4. Option trades ¶ 5. Margin trades ¶ 6. Bond trades. From now on, this report is to be updated on a ~~quarterly~~ monthly basis so ~~that~~ we can be fully aware of the income generated in ~~the various categories.~~ each category.

LETTER STYLES

A variety of letter styles are being used today for both personal and business letter. The style you see on page 181 is referred to as the block, full block, or extreme block, depending on the reference source. The term ***block style*** will be used in describing the letter format in this section. In the block-style letter, all parts of the letter begin at the left margin. The block-style letter is popular because it is comparatively easy to learn, and it is the fastest letter style for the typist to set up.

Once you have mastered the block-style letter, you will have little difficulty adjusting to other letter styles. (Other letter styles are illustrated on page 176.) The examples you will see in this text will all be set up in the block style; your instructor may have you prepare some of them using other styles.

On page 184 you will find a letter to Ms. Madeline Serro. Take a moment to look it over and make a mental note of your reactions.

The letter should have registered a good first impression. The letter is well balanced, sections of it are clearly defined, and it has a "style" that is pleasing to the eye.

VERTICAL LETTER PLACEMENT

The vertical spacing on letters, regardless of style, is the same. Your goal is to place the letter on the page so that it is visually attractive. If the body of a letter is short, leave more space between the letterhead and the date line and between the date line and inside address. Less space is left in these two areas for medium and long letters.

Following the inside address, double space to the salutation and then double space to the body of the letter. The body of all letters is single spaced with a double space between paragraphs. Following the last line of a letter there is a double space to the complimentary close.

Following the complimentary close there are four single spaces to the signature line. Next there is a single space to the title line, then a double space to the reference initials. For additional notations at the bottom of a letter to include attachments and copy notations, double space from one section to the next.

There is another technique that can be used if you should happen to make a poor estimate in placing a letter on a page. After finishing the body of a letter, if you should find that it is going to end too high or low on the page, adjust the closing lines. For example, if the letter is going to end too high, drop down five or six lines to the signature line and three or four lines to the reference initials. If the letter is going to end too far down on the page, leave fewer line spaces between the closing lines of the letter.

MARGINS

To center a letter on a sheet of paper, you must provide for horizontal as well as vertical placement. Left and right margins of a letter should be approximately equal. A common practice is to allow for a line of 60 or 70 spaces. Another alternative is to set margins of 12 to 18 spaces (1-1½") for machines with elite type and 10 to 15 spaces for machines with pica type. To leave a left margin of 1 inch on elite type, set the margin at 13.

Task 10

Working Papers, pp. 151-52

(Current date)/ TO: Mr. John Kearney, Editorial Department/ From: Frances Dalton, Adm. Sect./ Subject: Information on Office Systems Seminar/ Jack, here is a revised copy of our Office Systems Seminar outline to highlight the conversation that we had regarding the programs available through our department. ¶ Also attached is a revised copy of the letter that we will mail to potential participants. ¶ Thank you for the opportunity to share these thoughts with you and your staff./ Your initials / Attachments

Task 11

Working Papers, pp. 153-54

(Current date)/ TO: Mark Mitchell, President/ From: Raymond Eaton, Vice-President/ Subject: President's Advisory Board/ Mark, on Friday a special meeting of our Department was held to elect a representative to your advisory board. ¶ Mr. Jim Quattrone was elected for a one-year term. I gave Jim the background you sent me regarding the duties and responsibilities of this board./ Your initials / c: J. Quattrone

Task 12

Working Papers, pp. 155-56

(Current date) / TO: Mark C. Olsen, Editorial Department / From: C. Jones / Subject: Seminar Handbook / Mark, here are 15 copies of the seminar handbook. Please give a copy to each of your staff members. It will give them a better idea of the steps we go through in setting up a seminar. Also, it may give them some ideas for developing materials for distribution to seminar participants / Your initials

Task 13

Working Papers, pp. 157-58

Type a memo to: Our Customers. From Patricia Ganser, Executive Director regarding THE SEARCH IS OVER FOR YOUR NEW PROGRAM SPEAKER We would like to introduce you to one of Americas' most outstanding motivational speakers, Dr. Carl Bishop. His acceptance by industry across the United States and Canada has been exceptional. We invite you to read the attached lettar of recommendation from Mr. John B. Suter of Pilgrim Industries describing Dr. Bishop's impace on his audiences. ¶ Dr. Bishop can make a valid contribution to your next conference or convention program. He spaks to the critical issue of skill application, which is a primary concern to every industrial leader. You will appreciate the humor incorporated within his presentation and will be pleased with his ability to speak the technical language of your people. ¶ We are most interested in working with you as we have with over a thousand previous clients

(cont'd. on next page)

To avoid the time necessary to adjust margins for long, medium, and short letters, decide on one line length or margin width for all correspondence. As noted in the preceding section on vertical letter placement, documents of varying lengths can be accommodated without detracting from letter placement.

FORM LETTERS AND PREPRINTED LETTERS

In some situations the typist is responsible for completing form letters and preprinted correspondence.

Form letter. A form (repetitive) letter is one which is sent to more than one individual. The typist must personalize the letter by including the inside address and the salutation.

(Date)

(Name)
(Street)
(City, State, ZIP)

(Salutation)

It is with special pride that I announce representation of the young British pianist, Sarah Phillips. I urge you to pay particular attention to this superbly gifted pianist. One of the great performers to emerge on the international circuit this season, she is that rarest of all human beings, a great artist. This is a critical consensus from the music capitals of Europe.

Although we are booking for next season, a number of requests for the current season are under consideration. I would urge your early inquiry in any event, and I look forward to hearing from you.

Sincerely,

Patricia Ganser
Executive Director

pan

Task 5

Working Papers, pp. 141-42

(Current date/TO: Ms. Pat Ganser, Editorial Department/ From: Amos Grant, Research Director/ Subject: Abstracts of Office Research Studies/ The National Business Educators' Association (NBEA) is calling for abstracts of research studies that were completed in office systems during the past calendar year. If you are interested in submitting your abstract, note the attached directions from Oscar Byrnside, Executive Director of NBEA. ¶ All abstracts must reach NBEA headquarters within the next 30 days./ your initials/ Attachments

Task 6

Working Papers, pp. 143-44

(Current date)/TO: John Haldrimson, Director of Publicity/ From: Marilyn Douglas, Assistant/ Subject: New Seminar Brochures/ John, here are rough drafts of the new seminar brochure for office systems. The ideas were developed by David Armbruster and Ellen Walch. ¶ Would you have your staff go over the material carefully. The brochure needs professional artwork and printing. What is your opinion of color pictures? Will it date the brochure if we use them?/ your initials/ c: David Armbruster/Ellen Walch

Task 7

Working Papers, pp. 145-46

(Current date)/TO: Otis Franke, Space Coordinator/ From: Preston Smeltzer, Dean/ Subject: Change in Office Assignments/ Otis, we have a change in office assignments starting the first of next month. ¶ Bob MacDonald has been transferred to the Computer Science Center. He will move to an office on the south side of the fourth floor. Larry Ozzello will indicate which office it will be. ¶ Please put Dave Armbruster in the office that Bob had been assigned—413./ your initials/c: Dave Armbruster/ Bob MacDonald/ Larry Ozzello

Task 8

Working Papers, pp. 147-48

(Current date)/TO: Mark Mitchell, President/ From: Estel Lawler, Personnel Director/ Subject: Seminar Evaluations/ Mark, at a special staff meeting our department voted to use a common evaluation instrument for rating seminars. ¶ In developing this instrument, our departmental committee contacted all speakers used in the past six months. I also obtained data from a variety of evaluation instruments being used by other consulting firms. ¶ For the record, our department voted to use this instrument on a trial basis for the next two weeks. At the end of the two-week period, we will meet to discuss changes that may be made based on our experience. A copy of the evaluation instrument is attached./ your initials/ Attachment

Task 9

Working Papers, pp. 149-50

(Current date)/ TO: David Mattes, Director/ Computer Center/ From: Maureen Burns, Research/ Subject: Computer Reports on Seminar Registration/ Dave, since we don't have a reader, please send us hard copies of the following reports on a regular basis: ¶ 1. Quarterly Seminar size report/ 2. Preliminary seminar registration report (listing)/ 3. Final seminar registration report (listing)/ Your initials

(Date)__________________

(Name)__________________
(Street)_________________
(City, State, ZIP)_______

Dear (Name)_____:

The enclosed new note represents the original dollar amount you have invested plus interest payments through __(1)____. The quarterly interest payment due for _(2)_____ will be added to the principal amount on ___(3)________.

Please send us the old note dated __(4)________, in the amount of ___(5)______, so that it can be cancelled.

Sincerely,

Robert E. Truax
Senior Vice President

pan

Enclosure

A form letter may have variable information inserted into the body in addition to the personalizing of the inside address and salutation.

Task 3

Working Papers, pp. 137-38

Current Date

TO: Harry Harder, Coordinator
Non-Occupational Programs

Franklin Washington, Dean

CONSIDERATIONS REGARDING GENERAL STUDIES SEMINARS

Our Department supports the General Studies Seminar program as it now exists. Our staff certainly appreciates the opportunity to assist you in developing these programs. Should the current General Studies format be changed, you can be sure that we will continue to support you.

your initials

c: General Studies Seminar Staff
Mark Mitchell

Task 4

Working Papers, pp. 139-40

Current Date

TO: Donald Ellickson
John Hunnicutt
Lawrence Ozzello
D. Wallace Weil

Julie Berrtleson, Space Coordinator

SPACE UTILIZATION - FOURTH FLOOR

To make more efficient use of office space on the fourth floor of our Headquarters Building, the following rooms will be assigned for department use:

400C Accounting

443 Computer Center

481 Edit and Work Flow

401 Editorial

Conference Room 440 is to be used by all departments located on the fourth floor. Contact Marcia Peterson, Ext. 2720, to reserve the conference room.

your initials

c: Otis Franke
Mark Mitchelll

We are pleased to announce that the new line of Mark Ten automobile will be presented on April 19, 19--. Our records indicate that you presently own a Mark Ten. We would like to invite you to our showroom on April 19 to inspect the new model. Refreshments will be served.

If you are unable to attend the April 19 showing, please contact me and I will attempt to make arrangements for a private showing sometime before April 19th.

Sincerely,

Edith Lane
Sales Division

pan

Preprinted letter. Preprinted letters are letters that have been duplicated and lack only the date, inside address, and the salutation. In order that the letter look original, it is necessary that your typewriter have the same style Element that was used in preparing the duplicated copy.

Task 1

Working Papers, pp. 133-34

(Start typing on line 7)

Reference: p. 220

Current Date

(ds)

Reference: p. 220

TO: Ron Decker, Editorial Department

(ds)

Reference: p. 221

Bill Walczak, Educational Consultant

Reference: p. 221

SEMINAR OUTLINE

(ds)

Reference: p. 221

Ron, attached is the revised seminar outline for the program on Organizational Communication.

(ds)

Ned Ostenso, Bill Sleep, Randy Smith and I collaborated on this revision. Please note that we changed the name of the program. We feel that this is really a better description of the content of the seminar.

(ds)

Please let us know when you are ready to review the program.

(ds)

Reference: p. 222

your initials

(ds)

Reference: p. 222

Attachment

(ds)

Reference: p. 222

c: Mark Mitchell
Ned Ostenso
Bill Sleep
Randy Smith

Task 2

Working Papers, pp. 135-36

Current Date

TO: Max Poole, Media Development Center

April Williamson, Building Representative

USE OF ROOM 204B

This will confirm our conversation of Tuesday, August 27, regarding the use of room 204B.

I previously had told Don Burke that I thought we could share this facility with the Department Media Development Center. This has created a number of problems.

We have enough equipment and supplies to completely fill this facility. It is important for us to have access to this equipment from the corridor as our seminar rooms are on the second floor of the building.

your initials

c: Don Burke
Otis Franke

Dear

According to our discussion, enclosed is an
which sets forth our relationship in assisting you in

Please sign one copy and return it to us for our files. We appreciate this opportunity to be of assistance to you and hope that our efforts will be successful in achieving your objectives.

Any communication in regard to this matter will be treated as strictly confidential.

Sincerely,

Robert E. Truax
Senior Vice President

Enclosure

Another variation of the preprinted letter is one in which space has been left in the body for variable information to be inserted.

On page 224 is a memo from Bill Walczak to Ron Decker. Review it carefully. Be sure to note the various sections of the memo.

Memos that are routed to other departments in the same building, as well as those to other locations, should be placed in envelopes. These can be either internal envelopes or external envelopes requiring a full mailing address.

Internal envelopes are marked ***internal mail*** or ***company mail***. There are two styles: those that can be used only once (example 1), and those that can be used several times (example 2).

Example 1

FROM Ray Lyons
Room 141
Nelson Hall

Internal Mail

TO
Elaine Williams
Room 10-A
Schneider Hall

Example 2

Internal Mail

Name	Elaine Williams	Name	
Location	Schneider Hall	Location	
Department	Room 10-A	Department	
Name	Bob James	Name	
Location	Room 16	Location	
Department	Accounting	Department	
Name		Name	
Location		Location	
Department		Department	
Name		Name	
Location		Location	
Department		Department	
Name		Name	
Location		Location	
Department		Department	
Name		Name	
Location		Location	
Department		Department	

POPULAR LETTER STYLES

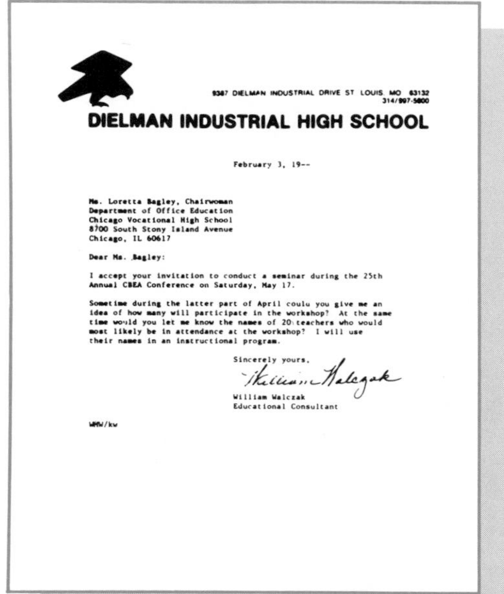

9387 DIELMAN INDUSTRIAL DRIVE ST LOUIS MO 63132
314/997-5800

DIELMAN INDUSTRIAL HIGH SCHOOL

February 3, 19--

Ms. Loretta Bagley, Chairwoman
Department of Office Education
Chicago Vocational High School
8700 South Stony Island Avenue
Chicago, IL 60617

Dear Ms. Bagley:

I accept your invitation to conduct a seminar during the 25th Annual CBEA Conference on Saturday, May 17.

Sometime during the latter part of April coulu you give me an idea of how many will participate in the workshop? At the same time would you let me know the names of 20 teachers who would most likely be in attendance at the workshop? I will use their names in an instructional program.

Sincerely yours,

William Walczak
Educational Consultant

WMW/kw

Modified block style: date, closing, signature line and title line begin at the center of the paper.

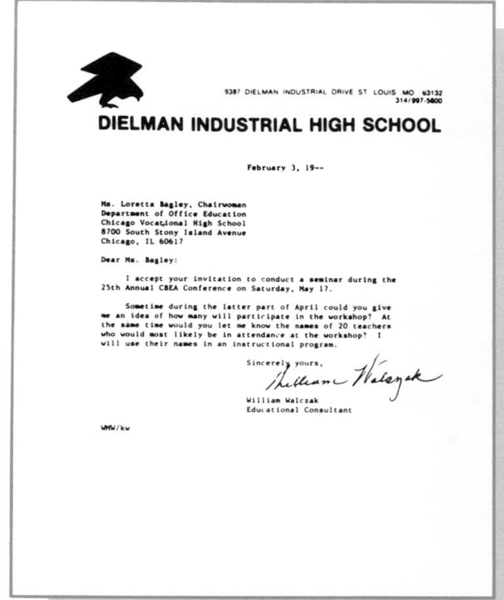

9387 DIELMAN INDUSTRIAL DRIVE ST LOUIS MO 63132
314/997-5800

DIELMAN INDUSTRIAL HIGH SCHOOL

February 3, 19--

Ms. Loretta Bagley, Chairwoman
Department of Office Education
Chicago Vocational High School
8700 South Stony Island Avenue
Chicago, IL 60617

Dear Ms. Bagley:

I accept your invitation to conduct a seminar during the 25th Annual CBEA Conference on Saturday, May 17.

Sometime during the latter part of April could you give me an idea of how many will participate in the workshop? At the same time would you let me know the names of 20 teachers who would most likely be in attendance at the workshop? I will use their names in an instructional program.

Sincerely yours,

William Walczak
Educational Consultant

WMW/kw

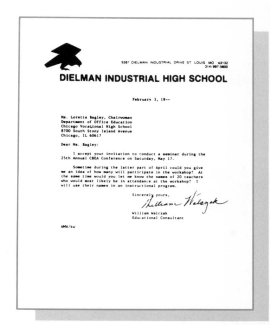

Modified block style with paragraph indentions: date, closing, signature line and title line begin at the center of the paper; the first line of each paragraph is indented 5 spaces.

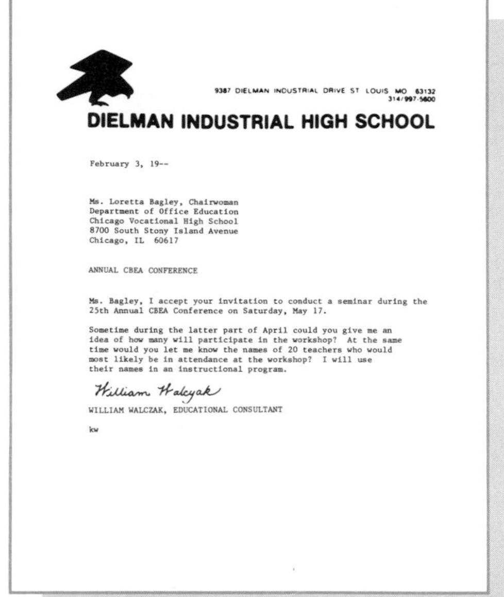

9387 DIELMAN INDUSTRIAL DRIVE ST LOUIS MO 63132
314/997-5800

DIELMAN INDUSTRIAL HIGH SCHOOL

February 3, 19--

Ms. Loretta Bagley, Chairwoman
Department of Office Education
Chicago Vocational High School
8700 South Stony Island Avenue
Chicago, IL 60617

ANNUAL CBEA CONFERENCE

Ms. Bagley, I accept your invitation to conduct a seminar during the 25th Annual CBEA Conference on Saturday, May 17.

Sometime during the latter part of April could you give me an idea of how many will participate in the workshop? At the same time would you let me know the names of 20 teachers who would most likely be in attendance at the workshop? I will use their names in an instructional program.

WILLIAM WALCZAK, EDUCATIONAL CONSULTANT

kw

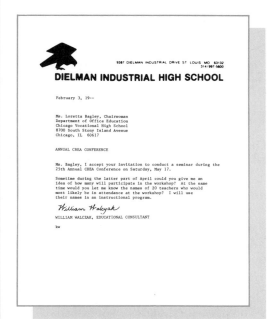

AMS (Administrative Management Society) simplified: No salutation; subject line in all capitals, a triple space before and after it; no closing; signature line and title all in capitals, 3 blank lines before; reference initials in lower case, a double space below signature line.

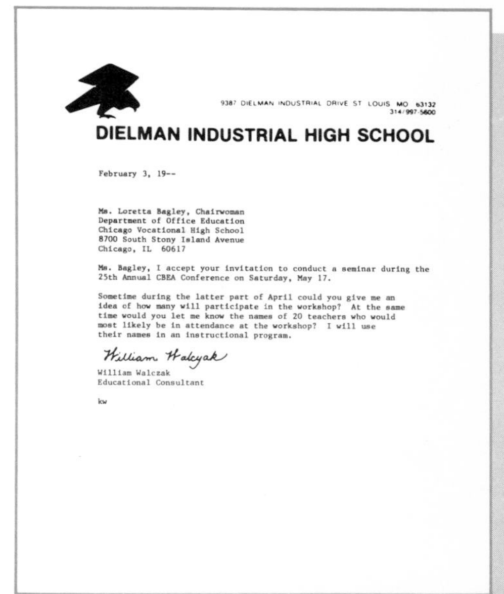

9387 DIELMAN INDUSTRIAL DRIVE ST LOUIS MO 63132
314/997-5600

DIELMAN INDUSTRIAL HIGH SCHOOL

February 3, 19--

Ms. Loretta Bagley, Chairwoman
Department of Office Education
Chicago Vocational High School
8700 South Stony Island Avenue
Chicago, IL 60617

Ms. Bagley, I accept your invitation to conduct a seminar during the 25th Annual CBEA Conference on Saturday, May 17.

Sometime during the latter part of April could you give me an idea of how many will participate in the workshop? At the same time would you let me know the names of 20 teachers who would most likely be in attendance at the workshop? I will use their names in an instructional program.

William Walczak
Educational Consultant

kw

Simplified: date on line 20; no salutation; first line of body begins a double space after last line of inside address; no closing; signature line begins 4 line spaces down from last line of last paragraph; reference initials in lower case, a double space below title line.

WALCZAK CONSULTING CO.

date: February 9, 19--

to: Ron Decker, Editorial Department

from: Bill Walczak, Educational Consultant

subject: SEMINAR OUTLINE

Ron, attached is the revised seminar outline for the program on Organizational Communication.

Ned Ostenso, Bill Sleep, Randy Smith and I collaborated on this revision. Please note that we changed the name of the program. We feel that this is really a better description of the content of the seminar.

Please let us know when you are ready to review the program.

kw

Attachment

c: Mark Mitchell
Ned Ostenso
Bill Sleep
Randy Smith

DATE: February 9, 19--

TO: Ron Decker, Editorial Department

FROM: Bill Walczak, Educational Consultant

SUBJECT: SEMINAR OUTLINE

Ron, attached is the revised seminar outline for the program on Organizational Communication.

Ned Ostenso, Bill Sleep, Randy Smith and I collaborated on this revision. Please note that we changed the name of the program. We feel that this is really a better description of the content of the seminar.

Please let us know when you are ready to review the program.

kw

Attachment

c: Mark Mitchell
Ned Ostenso
Bill Sleep
Randy Smith

---

5. ***Body***. The body or message of the memo is single spaced with double spacing between paragraphs. Double space before typing reference initials.
6. ***Reference Initials***. Reference initials identify the person who typed the memorandum.
7. ***Enclosure or Attachment***. The word ***enclosure*** or ***attachment*** is added to the memorandum if something is to accompany the message.
8. ***Copy Notation***. The letter ***c*** followed by one or more names listed alphabetically in columnar form tells the recipient of the memo who else has received a copy of it.

Note that there is no place for a signature on a memo. The person who prepared the message simply writes his or her initials following the name typed in the ***FROM***: section of the memo.

Envelopes

There are two popular envelope sizes for letters:

1. The smaller size is approximately 3½ inches wide, 6½ inches long, and is known as a "small" or "personal-use" envelope.

2. The larger size is approximately 4¼ inches wide, 9½ inches long, and is known as a "business" or "large" envelope.

The upper left-hand corner of an envelope is reserved for the return address (address of the sender). The address of the person or firm to receive the contents of the envelope is typed in the lower right section.

The Postal Service uses a machine called an optical character reader (OCR) to scan mail electronically. Mail that is not properly addressed is rejected by the machine and set aside until it can be read.

To avoid delays in the delivery of the mail:

1. Type the address single spaced and in block form in the ***read zone.*** It should be in three or four lines and be the same as the inside address.
2. Type the two-letter state/province abbreviation in capital letters with no periods. Space either once or twice and then type the zip code/postal code.
3. Notations such as ***confidential*** are typed in all capital letters three or four lines below the return address.
4. Special mailing instructions such as ***registered*** and ***special delivery*** are typed in all capitals in the upper right-hand corner, below the postage area.
5. Business envelopes usually have the return address printed on the envelope. If not, type it in the upper left-hand corner, block style, single spaced, approximately two lines down from the top and three spaces in from the left edge.

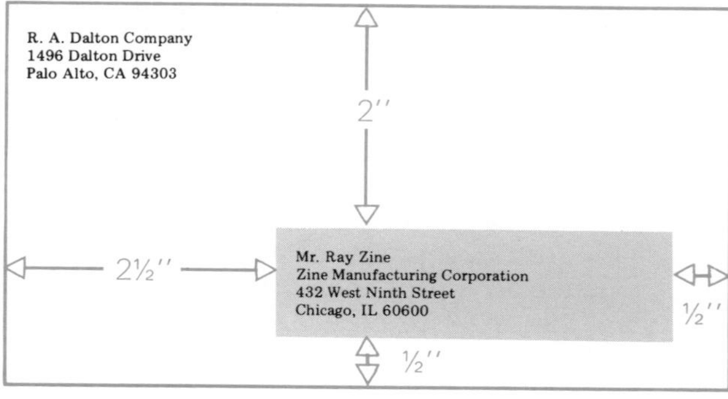

Small Envelope

WALCZAK CONSULTING CO.

4816 STONE AVENUE ● DENVER, COLORADO 80201 ● 303/737-8330

date: February 9, 19--

to: Ron Decker, Editorial Department

from: Bill Walczak, Educational Consultant

subject: SEMINAR OUTLINE

DATE: February 9, 19--

TO: Ron Decker, Editorial Department

FROM: Bill Walczak, Educational Consultant

SUBJECT: SEMINAR OUTLINE

2. ***Recipient***. The recipient is the person or persons to receive the memo. On preprinted forms the word ***TO***: is included. If you use blank or letterhead paper, type the word ***TO***: and then add the name of the individual(s) receiving the memo. Double space after the recipient line(s).

3. ***Sender***. The sender is the person who prepared the message. On preprinted forms this area is labeled with the word ***FROM***: with space to fill in the data. On blank or letterhead paper, the word ***FROM***: can be typed followed by the name of the sender. In order to conserve time in preparing the document, the word ***FROM***: is not included in the memos shown in the text—see page 224. The name of the sender starts at the left margin. Double space after the sender line.

4. ***Subject Line***. The subject line identifies the purpose of the memo. On preprinted forms you will find a variety of designations for this section of the memo. ***SUBJECT***, ***SUBJ.***, ***REGARDING***, and ***RE*** are some examples. If you are using blank or letterhead paper, you may use one of the above designations and then type the appropriate information. In the samples shown in your text, the designation SUBJECT is eliminated to save time, and the information representing the subject is typed in all caps—see page 224. Triple space after the subject line.

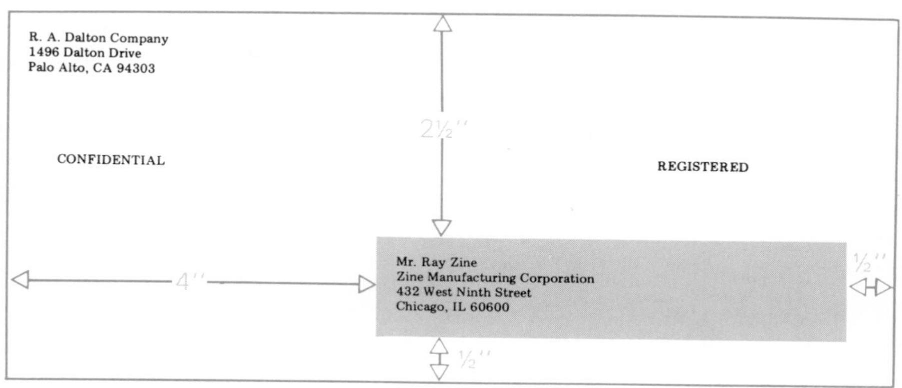

Large Envelope

If you are preparing envelopes to accompany letters that must be signed by someone else, place each letter under the flap of the envelope, then give both the letter and the envelope to the person who is to sign the letter.

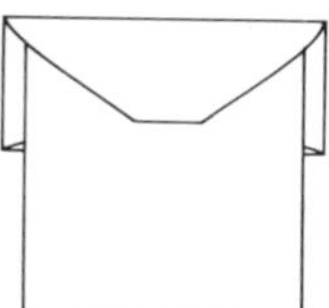

A letter should be inserted into an envelope so that when it is removed and unfolded it will be in a normal reading position.

For the large (business) envelope:

1. Place the letter flat on the desk in the normal reading position.
2. Fold a little less than a third of the letter up from the bottom and crease.
3. Fold upward again to within ½ inch of the top and crease.
4. Insert the last fold into the envelope first. The top of the sheet of paper will be at the top of the envelope.

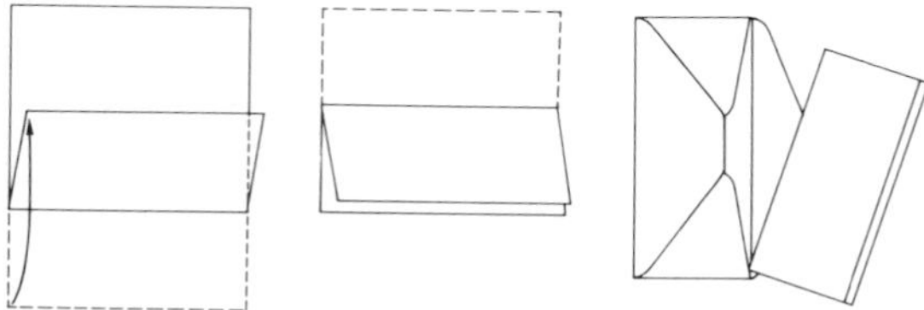

For the small (personal) envelope:

1. Place the letter flat on the desk in the normal reading position.
2. Fold from the bottom up to ½ inch from the top.
3. Fold the right third over to the left.
4. Fold the left third over to about ½ inch of the last crease.
5. Insert last-creased edge into the envelope first.

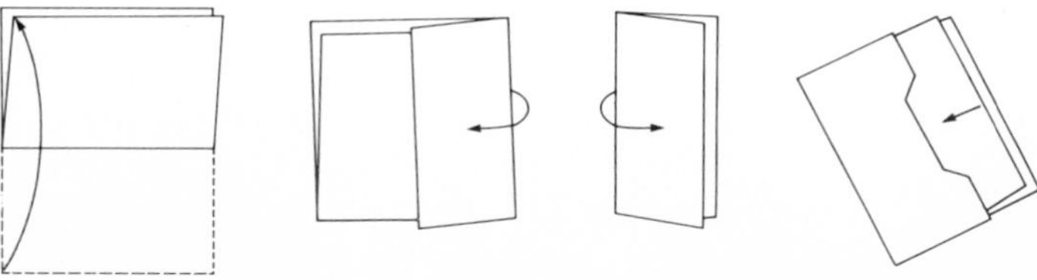

On letterhead

WALCZAK CONSULTING CO.

4816 STONE AVENUE ● DENVER, COLORADO 80201 ● [illegible]

date:	February 9, 19--
to:	Ron Decker, Editorial Department
from:	Bill Walczak, Educational Consultant
subject:	SEMINAR OUTLINE

Ron, attached is the revised seminar outline for the program on Organizational Communication.

Ned Ostenso, Bill Sleep, Randy Smith and I collaborated on this revision. Please note that we changed the name of the program. We feel that this is really a better description of the content of the seminar.

Please let us know when you are ready to review the program.

kw

Attachment

c: Mark Mitchell
Ned Ostenso
Bill Sleep
Randy Smith

On blank paper

DATE:	February 9, 19--
TO:	Ron Decker, Editorial Department
FROM:	Bill Walczak, Educational Consultant
SUBJECT:	SEMINAR OUTLINE

Ron, attached is the revised seminar outline for the program on Organizational Communication.

Ned Ostenso, Bill Sleep, Randy Smith and I collaborated on this revision. Please note that we changed the name of the program. We feel that this is really a better description of the content of the seminar.

Please let us know when you are ready to review the program.

kw

Attachment

c: Mark Mitchell
Ned Ostenso
Bill Sleep
Randy Smith

HORIZONTAL PLACEMENT

The information on a memorandum is to be centered horizontally. Some pre-printed forms are set up so that the length of the writing line is predetermined. If you are using blank or letterhead paper, the margins are the same width as those of a letter—12-18 spaces for left and right margins for elite type; 10-15 spaces for pica type (1-1½ inches).

PARTS OF A MEMORANDUM

1. *Date Line*. The date line includes the current date. If you are using a printed memo form, the word *DATE* is printed with sufficient space provided to fill in the information. If you are using blank or letterhead paper, you can type the word *DATE*: in all capitals and then follow with the month, day of the month, and year. Set a tab stop 10 spaces from the left margin and then type each leading line at that setting. To reduce the time to prepare the memo, you can eliminate typing the word *DATE*: This procedure has been used in the samples shown in your text—see page 224. Double space after the date line.

For window envelopes:

1. Place the letter flat on the desk in the normal reading position.
2. Fold one third of the letter up and crease.
3. Turn the letter over and fold the top up, so that the address shows, and crease.
4. Insert the letter in a window envelope with the address facing the front. Check to make sure the complete address shows in the window.

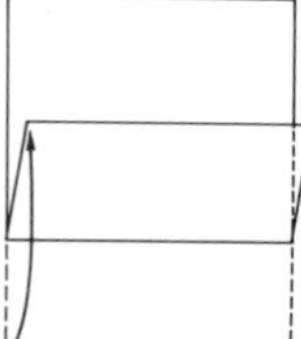 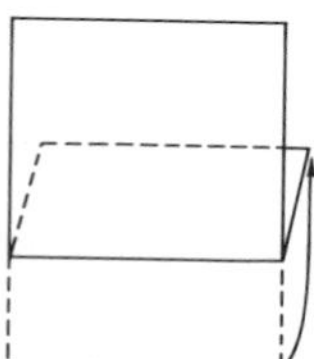 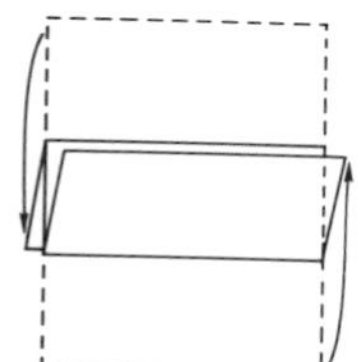 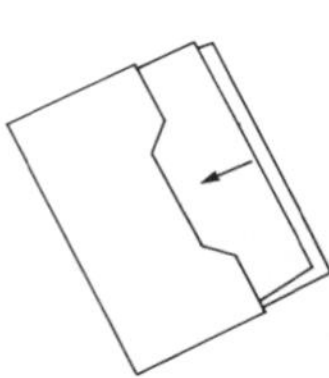

Memorandums

The memorandum (or memo for short) is a means of communication used within an organization. It has many of the same characteristics of a letter, but it also has some unique features.

STYLE/FORMAT

Some organizations have preprinted memo forms, so that the person preparing the document has no decisions to make regarding vertical and horizontal placement, what information to include in the heading, and where to place the body or message of the memo.

Memorandums are usually typed in blocked style with all parts starting at the left margin.

When guide words in the heading are aligned on the left, set a tab stop two spaces after the colon in the longest line as a margin for the heading information. Align the left margin for the body with the guide words (see example 1 below).

When guide words are aligned on the right, set the left margin two spaces after the colon to type the material in the heading and body (see example 2 below).

Example 1

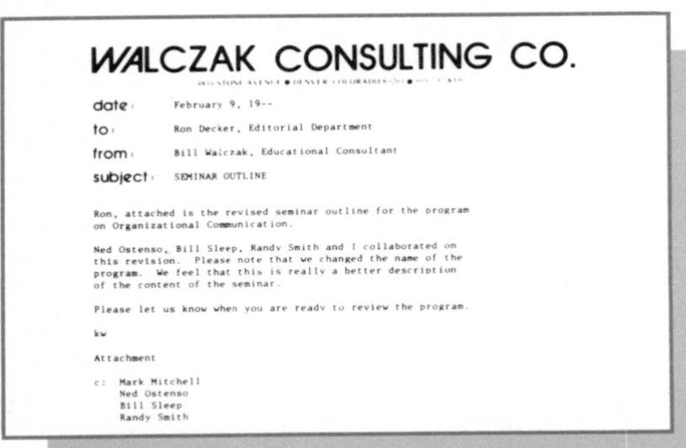

WALCZAK CONSULTING CO.

date: February 9, 19--
to: Ron Decker, Editorial Department
from: Bill Walczak, Educational Consultant
subject: SEMINAR OUTLINE

Ron, attached is the revised seminar outline for the program on Organizational Communication.

Ned Ostenso, Bill Sleep, Randy Smith and I collaborated on this revision. Please note that we changed the name of the program. We feel that this is really a better description of the content of the seminar.

Please let us know when you are ready to review the program.

kw

Attachment

c: Mark Mitchell
Ned Ostenso
Bill Sleep
Randy Smith

Example 2

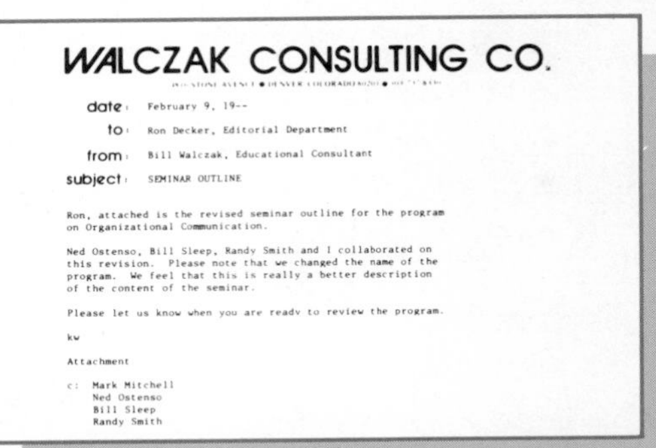

WALCZAK CONSULTING CO.

date: February 9, 19--
to: Ron Decker, Editorial Department
from: Bill Walczak, Educational Consultant
subject: SEMINAR OUTLINE

Ron, attached is the revised seminar outline for the program on Organizational Communication.

Ned Ostenso, Bill Sleep, Randy Smith and I collaborated on this revision. Please note that we changed the name of the program. We feel that this is really a better description of the content of the seminar.

Please let us know when you are ready to review the program.

kw

Attachment

c: Mark Mitchell
Ned Ostenso
Bill Sleep
Randy Smith

VERTICAL PLACEMENT

Unlike the letter, the memorandum is not centered vertically on the page. Whether you are using a printed memo form, blank, or letterhead paper, the parts of a memo begin at the top of the page, and no attempt is made to center the message vertically on it. If you are using a blank sheet of paper to prepare a memo, the top margin should be between 6-9 lines (1 and 1½"). If you are using letterhead paper, start the memo 3 lines below the last line of the letterhead. Double space between each part of the memorandum.

On letterhead

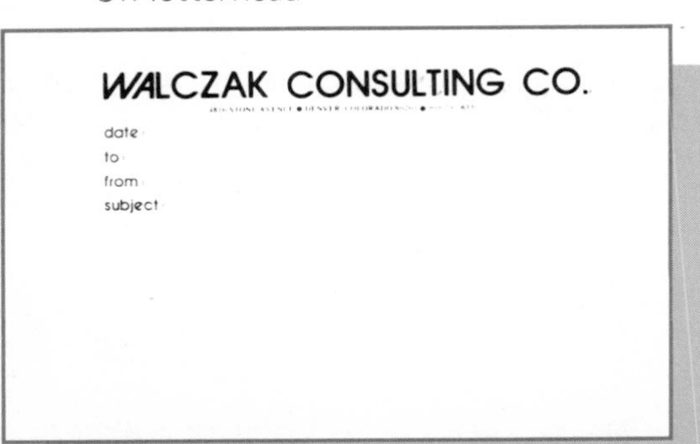

WALCZAK CONSULTING CO.

date
to
from
subject

On blank paper

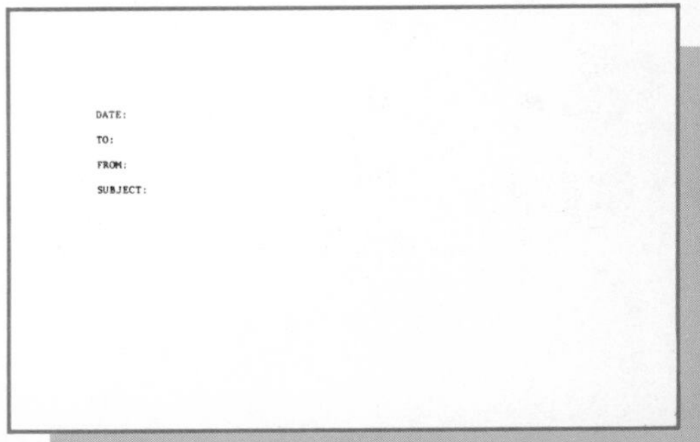

DATE:
TO:
FROM:
SUBJECT:

The Personal Business Letter

The personal business letter follows the same format of a business letter, but it is not usually typed on letterhead stationery. It is necessary that you add your return address as follows:

2350 Catalina Drive Line 13
Denver, CO 80219
February 12, 19--

Mr. Barth Trimble, Manager
Creative Printing Service
4950 Heights Drive Circle
Denver, CO 80219

Dear Mr. Trimble:

Our communications class is planning a series of intense studies on various aspects of word processing. As part of this series, we would like to visit a printing firm that is known for modern and innovative practices.

Our class meets every day from 8:00 a.m. to 11:30 a.m. Would it be possible for our class to visit your firm sometime during the month of April? If so, please contact me at 303/777-9462 any day after 3:30 p.m.

Sincerely yours,

Margo Hillman

Margo Hillman, Chairman
Communications Series 1190

NOTE: No reference initials are necessary, since you prepared (composed) and typed the letter yourself.

Task 9

Working Papers, pp 131-32

Ms. Theresa Bently, 680 Yorkshire Terrace, Bay View, CA 94124 / Ms. Bently, John Forrester has asked if it would be possible to bring in his assistant to help demonstrate during his lecture at the convention for the American Society of Engineers. This would be particularly valuable for the audience participation portion of the workshop. However, if this arrangement is not acceptable, Mr. Forrester will be able to work just fine on his own. / Also, Mr. Forrester has asked if he could receive his check immediately following the program. The other checks can be sent directly to the bureau. If this is a problem, let us know, and we will work out some other arrangement for his payment. / The speakers will be staying overnight in San Francisco on the 17th. Could you please make hotel reservations for the five individuals at a nearby hotel? / All of the participants are thrilled to be a part of this convention and are planning spectacular programs for the day. It just might be possible for me to make the trip as well, in order to meet you and the other regional directors. It's been such a pleasure working with you, and we want to assure you of a smooth and successful presentation. / Patricia Ganser, Executive Director

Following is a series of letters to be typed. Notice that in this section there are reference pages indicated to the left of each task.

1. If this is the first time you have typed this particular kind of task, turn to the reference page(s) and:
   a. Read the information.
   b. Complete the drill material section (if any is provided). The drill will give you practice before typing the task.
2. If you have already typed this kind of task before (and consequently have already read the information and completed the drills), refer to the reference page only if you need help in completing the task.

Task 1

Personal business letter
Plain paper
Personal size envelope
Working Papers, p. 3
Reference: p. 180

3103 Eddy Lane
Eau Claire, WI 54701
Current Date

(Begin first line of return address on line 13. This will vary from letter to letter, depending on length.)

(4 line spaces down--this will also vary, depending on length)

Reference: p. 168

Ms. Bobbi Ray, Director
Personal Development Division
Office Systems Publishing Corporation
3839 White Plains Drive
Bronx, NY 10467

(double spaces--ds)

Reference: p. 168

Dear Ms. Ray:

(ds)

Thank you for the brochures describing programs that are available through Office Systems Publishing Corporation.

(ds)

Reference: p. 169

Please send me, on a ten-day free inspection basis, the following programs. The first is Series 8--"How to Face an Audience with Poise" (Cat. No. 14-2.1.8) , and the second is "The Employment Interview" (Cat. No. 14-5.4).

(ds)

These programs will be viewed for possible use in our workshop and seminars for business and office education.

(ds)

Reference: p. 169

Sincerely yours,

Kathy Aarons

Reference: p. 169

Kathy Aarons

(4 line spaces down)

Envelope
Reference: p. 177

Task 7

Working Papers, pp. 127-28

Ms. Beverly Kellogg, Treasurer, North America Publishers Association, 1660 Whitney Way, Suite M10 Hayworth Center, Portland, ME 04104/ Ms. Kellogg, on April 2 at the NAPA Convention in Quebec, a check for $1,100 was given to Katherine Edmund as payment for her engagement at the Princeton Hotel. Ms. Edmund presented a very successful lecture/workshop for the members of the association. / We have been advised by Ms. Edmund that after she deposited the check, she received notice that $44 was deducted from the deposit to cover the Canadian exchange. A copy of the notice is enclosed. / Since our negotiations have consistently been with NAPA in the United States, we had no way of knowing that the check would be drawn on a Canadian bank. The bureau's invoice was accepted by NAPA for $1,100 payable to Ms. Kellogg at the time of the engagement. We feel that an adjustment should have been made to assure her of her entire contract fee. / This misunderstanding is no doubt unintentional. We would appreciate hearing from you on this matter. / Patricia Ganser, Executive Director

Task 8

Working Papers, pp. 129-30

Mr. Duane Anderson, Illinois Transport Services Association, 620 Commerce Building, Rockford, IL 61106 / Mr. Anderson, we are pleased to enclose contracts for the appearances of Deborah Berg, Sid Whitney, and Kim Thomas for November 13. Each speaker is looking forward to being with you on that date. / Enclosed are contracts for these programs. After filling in the information requested, please sign all four copies of each contract and return them as soon as possible. We will send you a copy of the fully-executed contract for your files. / Two weeks prior to the engagement, we will send you and each speaker a reminder notice which will summarize all the last-minute details. At that time we will also send you an invoice, but this will not be payable until the engagement has been fulfilled. / Patricia Ganser, Executive Director

Task 2

Personal business letter
Plain paper
Personal size envelope
Working Papers, p. 3

1964 Showgate Way
Denver, CO 80219
Current Date

Mr. Tom Torrence
General Wolfe Secondary School
55 McCraney Street East
Oakville, Ontario, CANADA
L6H 1H9

Dear Mr. Torrence:

For the presentation in Toronto on March 8 I would like to have the following equipment: an overhead projector, a 35mm carrousel slide projector, and a large screen.

You need not worry about sending an advance for the cost of airfare as I will put the ticket on my credit card. It takes approximately 30 days for the bill to catch up.

By the way, would you give me an idea of the approximate number attending the workshop. I want to have sufficient materials to hand each participant.

Sincerely yours,

Paula Goldberg

Paula Goldberg

Task 4

Working Papers, pp. 121-22

Mr. Marvin T. Wright, 363 Jefferson Boulevard, Patterson, NJ 07509 / Dear Marv: Enclosed is a data sheet on your investment status to date. / According to recent public information on Dorchester Corporation, their sales and earnings are simply phenomenal! Indications are that Flavor Foods ended their fiscal year with a strong performance, too, with actual results to be reported in January. / Also enclosed are a quarterly report and news release on A.B. Butler Company. I rate this company as an outstanding investment opportunity at present levels (12 1/4 - 12 3/4). If you have some cash available for investment purposes, please let me know; we can discuss this matter when we meet in Chicago next month. / Sincerely, Robert E. Truax, Senior Vice President

Task 5

Working Papers, pp. 123-24

Mr. Patrick C. Shields, 3228 Glenview Circle, Staten Island, NY 10302 / Dear Mr. Shields: In accordance with your request, enclosed is an agreement which sets forth our relationship in assisting you in finding an appropriate business investment. Please sign one copy and return it to us for our files. / We appreciate this opportunity to be of assistance to you and hope that our efforts will be successful in achieving your objectives. / Any communications in this regard will be treated as strictly confidential. / Sincerely, Robert E. Truax, Senior Vice President

Task 6

Working Papers, pp. 125-26

Mr. & Mrs. Edward Hopkins, Jt. Ten., Route 7, Box 144, Rockville Centre, NY 11571 / Dear Mr. and Mrs. Hopkins: Attached is a statistical summary of your 19__ taxable stock transactions. Be sure to examine these figures for accuracy prior to submission to the Internal Revenue Service. Also, you should consult with your attorney or accountant regarding tax laws pertaining to stock transactions. / I have also included a summary of the performance of your securities portfolio since coming under my supervision. / Best wishes to you and your family for the upcoming holiday season. / Sincerely, Robert E. Truax, Senior Vice President

Task 3

Personal business letter
Plain paper
Personal size envelope
Working Papers, p. 3

23 Rock Place / Reno, NV 89504 / Current Date / Mr. Philip W. Ruehl / Center for Vocational, Technical, & Adult Education / Department of Public Instruction / Springfield, IL 62302 / Dear Mr. Ruehl: / I did not return my evaluation materials to you until Saturday. Consequently, my observations are not included in the enclosed materials. / I will not be able to attend the workshop in Rockford in June as I have another commitment. / If there is anything else I should do with these materials, please return them to me with the appropriate instructions. / Sincerely, / Cecile Conway / Evaluation Committee Member / Enclosure

Task 4

Personal business letter
Plain paper
Personal size envelope
Working Papers, p. 5

1152 West Third Street / Portland, OR 97223 / Current Date / Mr. Jerry King / 1421 Columbia Street / Broadmor, LA 70125 / Dear Mr. King: / Several of the participants of the March 30 program in New Orleans have asked about the evaluations which were conducted at the conclusion of the seminars. So much excitement was generated that they would very much like to hear what reactions were received./ Also, Sam Marsh would like to know whether it is possible to obtain a transcript of the tape that was recorded by the monitor during his presentation. If so, please let us know what arrangements have to be made. / Sam also mentioned that he had neglected to thank the staff (coordinator, hostess, and monitor) as he had to leave so quickly following his program. Would you please pass on the message for him that he really appreciated all the cooperation, preparation, and assistance they provided./ Sincerely, / Patricia Grant

Task 5

Personal business letter
Plain paper
Personal size envelope
Working Papers, p. 5

726 Langdon Street
San Francisco, CA 94119
Current Date
Mr. A. R. Bradford, Credit Manager, Office Administration
Book Company, 24 Conrad Road, Waterford, CT 06385. Dear Mr.
Bradford: The Office Systems text is being returned to you
under separate cover. The material is outdated and does not
contian the types of exercises that would be helpful in our
training ~~paorgams.~~ program. ¶ If you publish a new text in office
systems that has inbasket exercises, I would be happy to
consider it as a handout for the office systems workshops I
conduct throughout Canada and the United States. Sincerely yours,
Peter Quattrone, Business ~~Teacher~~ Instructor

Task 1

Working Papers, pp. 115-16

Sinclair Electric Company, P.O. Box 43092, Atlanta, GA 30319 / Dear Sirs: Truax-Vehlow Investment Services has been claimed for the January 2 dividend of Sinclair Electric on certificate numbers 2623-4860 for 8 shares and 8132-8075 for 61 shares in the name of our customer, Henry Vosen. However, Mr. Vosen has stated that he never received the dividend on the 69 shares. / Could you please verify whether a check in the amount of $65.55 was issued to Henry Vosen on these certificates for the February 1 payable, and whether or not the check is outstanding. Please note the enclosed letter from Mr. Vosen giving us authorization to proceed in this matter for him. / Sincerely, Robert E. Truax, Senior Vice President

Task 2

Working Papers, pp. 117-18

Mr. Henry Vosen, Roseville Estates, Apartment #803, Charleston, SC 29402 / Dear Hank: Enclosed is a copy of the canceled check for the Sinclair Electric dividend of $65.55. Since the stock was sold prior to the dividend date, we must remit the payment to the proper owner of the stock. You already have a credit in your account of $57.37; therefore, you need only send us a check for $8.18. / Hank, since this payment must also be reported on your income tax statement, it is important that you maintain a record of all dividends that you receive. / We are always pleased to be of service to you. / Sincerely, Robert E. Truax, Senior Vice President

Task 3

Working Papers, pp. 119-20

Mr. Mark Mitchell III, 5126 Golden Valley Road, Great Neck, NY 11022 / Dear Mr. Mitchell: We have delivered 160 of the 1975 shares of Niagara Mining and Manufacturing stock to the various charitable organizations as requested in your letter of December 1. The 15-share certificate for the New York Multiple Sclerosis Foundation was incorrectly registered by the transfer agent and is being returned for correction. This final transfer should be completed within a week. / I have enclosed copies of our correspondence to these organizations for your file, as well as the remaining 25-share certificate registered in your name. / Sincerely, Robert E. Truax, Senior Vice President

Task 1

Business letter
Letterhead
pp. 7-8

THE ASLOW COMPANY

1448 QUIMBY LANE • KELLY, LOUISIANA 71441 • (318) 716-9200

Reference: p. 168

Current Date

(Since this is a short letter, begin on line 15.)

(6 line spaces)

Reference: p. 168

Ms. Madeline Serro
Office Systems Publishing Company
280 Fulton Avenue
Hempstead, NY 11550

(double space--ds)

Reference: p. 169

Dear Ms. Serro:

(ds)

Our department administrative assistant, Cynthia Brummond, has talked with you on two occasions about your instructional cassettes and slides for office inservice programs that were sent to us.

(ds)

Reference: p. 169

I previewed these materials myself and felt that they were not the calibre we had in mind. In fact, some of the slides are quite out of date.

(ds)

These materials were returned to you more than 45 days ago.

(ds)

Reference: p. 169

Sincerely yours,

Barbara Caserza

(4 line spaces)

Reference: p. 169

Barbara Caserza
Research Assistant

(ds)

Reference: p. 169

BC:your initials

Envelope reference: p. 177

Task 4

Working Papers, pp. 111-14

Typist — please send this form letter to:
Ms. Judy Fuller, Rinehart–Newman Associates,
2184 Barclay Drive, Newburg, Ohio, 48762

Insert #1—Ms. Fuller
#2—Dayton, Ohio

Mr. Juston Wilson, Wilson Associates
94 Hanover Drive, Emerald, Penn. 18048

Insert #1 — Mr. Wilson
#2 — Dallas, Texas

(INSERT #1), thank you for your inquiry regarding those speakers and programs we have to offer for your conference in (INSERT #2). We are pleased to forward some supplemental material about each of the programs discussed. / Also enclosed is information on speakers who have joined us since the distribution of our current brochure. Our new business convention folder is now at the printers, and we will be sending you a copy as soon as they are ready for mailing. / We are anxious to work closely with you in order to bring in one or more of our exciting speakers. Keep in mind that we also have some of the top musical groups of today and just about any type of entertainer you might have an interest in. / We're looking forward to hearing from you soon. / Patricia Ganser / Executive Director / pjg / Enclosures

Reference: p. 173

Task 2

Business letter
Letterhead

Working Papers, pp. 9-10

THE ASLOW COMPANY

1448 QUIMBY LANE • KELLY, LOUISIANA 71441 • (318) 716-9200

Current Date

Mrs. Dorothy M. Sobota
Collection-Book Department
Office Systems Publishing Company
280 Fulton Avenue
Hempstead, NY 11550

Dear Mrs. Sobota:

We have checked again with our mail center and our local Post Office. The materials are not in either place. We did not insure the programs returned to you, so we have no record of the mailing.

As I mentioned to Ms. Serro, the programs were returned to you over a month ago. We cannot use these programs. If they are returned, I will send them to you immediately.

Sincerely yours,

Barbara Caserza

Barbara Caserza
Research Assistant

BC:your initials

Envelope Reference: p. 177

Task 3

Working Papers, pp. 107-110

TYPIST— please send letter below to these 2 people. Put in inserts

Alvin Shepek Suite 101A Cameron Building Ashland, Louisiana 71002	Insert # 1 – January 1, 19-- 2 – Jan., Feb., + March 3 – April 1 4 – December 10, (last year's date) 5 – $25,000
Ms. Alice Barker Barker and Smith 909 North Wilson Natchez, Mississippi 39120	Insert # 1 – February 1, 19-- 2 – Dec., Jan., Feb. 3 – March 1 4 – Jan. 1, (this year's date) 5 – $100,000

Dear ______: / The enclosed new note represents the original dollar amount you have invested plus interest payment through ___(1)___. The quarterly interest payment due for ___(2)___ will be added to the principal amount on ___(3)___. / Please send us the old note dated ___(4)___ in the amount of $___(5)___ so that it can be cancelled. / Sincerely, / Robert E. Truax / Senior Vice President

Reference: p. 173

Task 3

Business letters
Letterhead
Working Papers, p. 12

Business envelope
Working Papers, p. 11

(Current date)/ Mr. John C. Rohrscheib/ General Manager/ Western Company/ 8 Walts Rd./ North Ryde, 2113 N.S.W. AUSTRALIA/ Dear Mr. Rohrscheib/ We really appreciate the letter that you sent to the 3M Corporation regarding our offices systems seminar. If we can be of help to you on next year's program, please let us know. ¶ I believe Bill mentioned that you may want to have someone review your records system. We would be happy to do this for you./ Sincerely yours/ Bernard Berbalian/ Editor/ BB/ your initials

Task 4

Business letters
Letterhead
Working Papers, p. 14

Business envelope
Working Papers, p. 13

(Current date)/ Dr. Melton Jones/ Roundtree Medical Clinic/ Ware Road/ Henley-on-Thames/ Oxfordshire RG9 1 EW ENGLAND/ Dear Dr. Jones:/ Thank you for the opportunity to meet with you during your trip to discuss the growing demand for cardiovascular devices and to observe a pacemaker implant./ I sincerely appreciate the time you took to stop by. It is through such direct communication that non-medical people such as myself can help develop seminars for the advancement of medical science./ I hope we will have an opportunity to meet again./ Sincerely,/ Ralph C. Jacob, President/ RJ/ your initials

Task 5

Business letters
Letterhead
Working Papers, p. 16

Business envelope
Working Papers, p. 15

(Current date)/ Mr. Robert Carlson/ American River College/ 4700 College Oak Drive/ Sacramento, CA 95841/ Dear Bob/ Thanks for your hospitality and all the arrangements that you made for my presentation at the CBEA meeting in Lake Tahoe. ¶ Here are the titles of two presentations that might be considered for the National Business Education Association meeting to be held in San Francisco: (1) "Innovative Software and Hardware in Business Education" and (2) "Office Systems and Ergonomics." ¶ The first presentation provides an emphasis in methods and procedures. The second presentation is content-oriented and includes items that teachers should know to make their classes in business education more meaningful. ¶ If you have any questions about either of these presentations, please drop me a line or give me a call at 312-864-5622./ Sincerely/ Laura Chong/ Educational Representative/ LC: your initials

Task 6

Business letters
Letterhead
Working Papers, p. 18

Business envelope
Working Papers, p. 17

(Current date)/ Mr. Peter Jennings/ Stock Transfer Department/ Florida National Bank/Second & Gulf Streets/ Miami, FL 33161/ Dear Mr. Jennings:/ A client of mine, Dr. Simon Knott, has 110 shares of Miami Steel, Inc., common stock on record with your bank. Dr. Knott received the shares as a gift from Mr. Paul Gray, who is now deceased. Dr. Knott, however, never received a certificate for the shares./ I would like to request that the stock be placed against the certificate and the necessary papers forwarded for the shares to be replaced. The papers should be sent to Dr. Knott at the following address: Albany Medical Center, 290 Broadway, New York, NY 10046/ Your promptness in handling this matter will be appreciated./ Sincerely/ Robert E. Truax, Senior Vice President/ RT/ your initials

Task 1

Working Papers, pp. 93-102

Reference: p. 175

Typist: Please send copy of preprinted letter to people below. The first variable for each letter is "investment portfolio"; the second variable is "investing in money market securities."

1. Mrs. Hazel Flick / 415 Mingus Street / Huntsville, Texas 77340
2. Dr. Lyle Waterman / P.O. Box 97 / Forbus, Tennessee 38561
3. Mr. Ray Linwood / 18 Little Creek Road / Narka, Kansas 66960
4. Ms. Lucille Forsyth / 1469 Brown Blvd. / Swan Lake, Idaho 83449
5. Mr. Douglas Dunberry / 50 Post Lane / Cedartown, Georgia 30125

Task 2

Working Papers, pp. 103-6

Reference: p. 172

TYPIST—please send letter below to: (1) Ms. Ann Leonard / Program Chairman / SRAT International / 415 South Peters Drive / Hilo, Hawaii 96720 / (2) Mr. Arnold Rhodes / Services Office / Miller College / Golden, Colorado 80401

It is with special pride that I announce the representation of the young British pianist, Sarah Phillips. I urge you to pay particular attention to this superbly gifted pianist. One of the great performers to emerge on the international circuit this season, she is that rarest of all human beings, a great artist. This is a critical consensus from the music capitals of Europe. / Moreover, we are pleased to offer you an opportunity to judge her talent for yourself. A taped excerpt of her most recent recital will be made available to you upon request. You will be able to mark the rich and imaginative creativity which distinguishes all the interpretations of Sarah Phillips. Such musical talent is rare indeed. / Although we are booking for next season, a number of requests for the current season are under consideration. I would urge your inquiry in any event, and I look forward to hearing from you. / Sincerely, / Patricia Ganser / Executive Director / Enc.

Task 7

Business letter
Letterhead
Working
Papers, p. 20

Business envelope
Working
Papers, p. 19

Dr. James Moline Metropolitan Professional Building 5991 Madison Drive, New York, NY 10055. Dear Dr. Moline: It was a pleasure to visit with you on the phone this morning. Truax-Vehlow Invenstment Services has been in the brokerage and investment banking busines-s for over 25 years and specializes in new growth companies. We firmly believe that such companies represent the greatest profit potential for individual investors. In recent years, we have devoted considerable attention to the medical industry through our research and investment banking activities. We have played an important role in the early stages of several recently emerging medical firms in the city of New York. Please give me a call whenever it is convenient, and I will be pleased to set up an appointment to discuss a mutually-satisfying business relationship. Sincerely, Roberta E. Thomas, Invenstment Consultant

Task 8

Business letter
Letterhead
Working
Papers, p. 22

Business envelope
Working
Papers, p. 21

Mr. Howard Young, Esquire

West, Young & Stern

4200 Exchange Building, new yourk, NY 10014

On November 29, a non-qualified stock option was issued to Mr. Del Stewart for 2,500 shares of Life Devices, Inc. common stock. You have informed us that these shares, when issued, bear a two-year restrictive legend. Life Devices, Inc., engaged in the manufacture and sale of implantable neurological pain-relieving devices, has been in business less than five years ahd has a limited sales and earnings history. The company's common stock is currently traded on the national over-the-counter market. On November 20, the stock closed at 14 5/8 bid and 15 1/8 asked.

Based on the two-year restriction as well as the speculative nature of the company, it is our opinion that the fair market value, for the purpose of the stock option described above, would be a 50 percent discount from the market praice. The mean between the bid and asked prices on Nobember 20 was $14.875, resulting in our valuation of $7.44 per share. Robert E. Truax, Senior Vice President

Line 7 (1") Top Margin

Mr. Alex Chester
Page Two
Current Date

Triple Space

to their chairs and to pass out materials provided by the speakers. If you have materials that you would like duplicated for your seminar, please send them directly to Miss Mami Lou Tyler, 5500 The Main Building, Houston, TX 77002. She will have sufficient copies available for distribution.

If you have other questions about the program, please drop me a line or give me a call at 715-836-4320.

Kayleen Neitzel

Kayleen Neitzel
Program Coordinator

your initials

Attachment

c: Francis Jakes
Mami Lou Tyler
Leonard Wilkom

Task 5

Working Papers, pp. 91-92

Mr. Daniel Robinson, Assistant Director, Midway Civic Association, 449 High Street, Elizabethtown, PA 17022/ Thank you, Mr. Robinson, for asking us to make a suggestion for your association's dinner dance on September 5./ First of all, I would recommend the Big Band of Russ Williams. Mr. Williams' group broadcasts the Big Band sounds every Sunday night on one of our local FM stations from the Parkway Hotel and is exceedingly popular./ I'd also like to suggest a slightly different format for your evening affair. Enclosed is material on Mr. Wayne Todd, who does an after-dinner speaker impersonation. You would promote him and make a convincingly serious introduction. Within the first four or five minutes of his after-dinner presentation, the audience becomes aware that it is a "put on," and the rest of his presentation then becomes a hilarious evening of comedy./ I'm also making one additional suggestion which I think would make your dinner dance unique: a photographer, Mr. Roger Silverman. He would be set up during the entire evening to take pictures of your guests at no charge to them. He brings in all the costumes, props, etc.; dresses the people on a stage; takes their pictures; and gives them a print. While this is a relatively new program offering, we have received many favorable comments on this addition to a dinner dance./ I am not certain at the moment how adequate the sound system at the Devonshire Downtown Hotel in Elizabethtown would be. Therefore, my quotation is based simply on the entertainment; we could always discuss additional sound equipment needs later./ We would propose to furnish the 12-piece Big Band of Russ Willimas, Miss Sharon North, Mr. Wayne Todd, and Mr. Roger Silverman for a total fee of $2,325. What I would like to do is allow you a few days to go over this and then give you a call the first part of next week to discuss the arrangements in more detail./ Patricia Ganser, Executive Director/ Enclosure

Task 1

Business letter with enclosure or attachment
Letterhead
Working Papers, p. 24

Business envelope
Working Papers, p. 23

CONSULTANTS UNLIMITED
806 BOYCE STREET • SALT LAKE CITY, UTAH 84106 • 801/223-4151

Current Date (Begin typing on line 13 or 14.)

(5 line spaces)

Mr. Ronald A. Christner
Chief Administrator
Lincolnwood Manor
4762 W. Tauky Avenue
Lincolnwood, IL 60646

(double space--ds)

Dear Mr. Christner

(ds)

Attached are the resumes, pictures and outline for the Time Management seminar to be held in January at the Hilton Hotel.

(ds)

The program will be geared to the needs of nursing home administrators. If you have questions about the program, please give me a call at 846-5622.

(ds)

Dr. John Schillak of the University of Illinois and I will present the program.

(ds)

Sincerely yours,

S. Ferrari (4 line spaces)

Sandra Ferrari
Division Chairman

(ds)

SF:your initials

(ds)

Attachments

Reference: p. 170

Task 4

Working Papers, pp. 89-90
and plain paper

Current Date

Mr. Alex Chester
Senior Vice President
Houston Natural Gas Corporation
P.O. Box 1188
Houston, TX 77001

Mr. Chester, thank you for the conditional acceptance to speak at our International Convention in Houston, Texas. Assuming that your calendar will be clear, here are the details regarding the convention. The convention hotel is the Hyatt-Regency Houston. Our Association will pay you an honorarium of $150 plus expenses.

Attached is a list of the ten seminars and the areas that will be included in each of the programs. The program is scheduled for Monday afternoon, July 19. The 10 seminars will be given between 1:30 and 3:00 p.m.(the last 15 minutes might be used as a question-and-answer period), followed by a 30-minute break; and each program will be repeated between 3:30 and 5:00 p.m. There might be a slight adjustment in this time format.

I have asked our Headquarters staff to limit the number of participants in each program to approximately 200. Every attempt will be made to limit each program to 200 participants.

Would you please send me the following items by February 20, 19--:

1. A glossy print.

2. A paragraph describing your background (150 words or less).

3. A paragraph describing your program (150 words or less).

4. A one-page outline with the highlights of your program.

5. If you have a title for your seminar other than the one I have listed for you on the attached sheet, please let me know what it is.

For those speakers coming from outside Houston, the Headquarters staff will be sending you hotel reservation forms. Also, they will send you a form to fill out for audio-visual equipment needs as well as desired seating arrangements.

For each of the ten seminars, we will have a coordinator to introduce the program, a recorder, and several host/hostesses to direct people

Be careful where you stop typing on first page.

General Rule — leave at *least* 2 lines of paragraph at bottom of page and always carry at *least* 2 lines to the second page.

Task 2

Business letter with enclosure or attachment
Letterhead
Working Papers, p. 26

Business envelope
Working Papers, p. 25

CONSULTANTS UNLIMITED
806 BOYCE STREET • SALT LAKE CITY, UTAH 84106 • 801/223-4151

Current Date

Ms. Joyce Veros
Indiana Vocational Technical Center
P.O. Box 1776
Indianapolis, IN 46206

Dear Ms. Veros:

Enclosed are materials that should help you in designing a new vocational education facility for the Indianapolis Area.

I hope George McArdle was able to arrange a meeting with you in February. At that time he can show you many other materials that can be used in designing and equipping your new facility.

Sincerely yours,

Raoul D'Artaies
Consultant

RD/your initials

Enclosures

Task 3

Working Papers, pp. 87-88

(Current date)/ Mr. Gary Wenner/ Business Publications/ 510 Third Avenue/Toronto, Ont. CANADA/M2H 2S6/ Mr. Wenner, your letter regarding the proposal by Mrs. Darlene Jones arrived while I was on vacation. I've reviewed the proposal carefully, and here are my observations./ 1. The sequence for the proposed textbook is oriented to one job occupation, namely, the secretarial profession. However, this may be what you are shooting for./ 2. Textbooks in the following areas are not included: a. Data Processing/ b. Office Systems, Layout, and Design/ c. Office Management/ 3. The business communications text that was recommended does not include anything about oral communications./ 4. In the secretarial procedures textbook, the emphasis is devoted to legal secretary and medical secretary work. However, a large number of secretaries today are working in manufacturing and government firms. It would seem that simulation programs in these areas would be more appropriate./ 5. I would include the following items in one textbook: word processing, transcribing machines, and administrative support./ 6. In the filing and records management text, nothing was mentioned about electronic filing systems or the cost of maintaining and disposing of recorded information. I believe this should be added./ 7. The textbook that Mrs. Jones recommends on adding and calculating machines is purely traditional. I would refer only to ten-key electronic calculators./ 8. As far as the principles of accounting text, it doesn't seem to go far enough. No mention is made of managerial accounting./ 9. The duplicating processes text doesn't cover intelligent copier/printers. Also, it seems that there should be more emphasis on how to prepare material for these machines rather than on how to operate them./10. As far as the typewriting text is concerned, I believe it should include materials for in-basket exercises./ I hope that these comments will help in your decision to publish in the office education area. I certainly would promote this venture and would be happy to help you in any way possible./ If you have any questions, please write or call me. My telephone number is 312-864-5622./ Lorraine Misslingham/ Editor/ your initials

Task 3

Business letter with enclosure or attachment
Letterhead
Working Papers, p. 28

Business envelope
Working Papers, p. 27

Current Date/ Mr. Robert Wilson/ University of Toronto/ Toronto/ Toronto, Ontario, CANADA/ L3J 6N4/ Dear Bob:/ The OBEA workshop was a fantastic experience for me. It's a tremendous pleasure to work with teachers who are so appreciative of ideas and materials presented to them./ Enclosed is a copy of our seminar schedule for office systems, layout, and design. In your travels you might find an opportunity to spend several days in our area and attend one of the workshops./ My travel expenses for the workshop are attached. Thanks for taking care of the meals and hotel bill./ Sincerely/ Victor Neal/ Division Head/ VN/ your initials/ Enclosure

Task 4

Business letter with enclosure or attachment
Letterhead
Working Papers, p. 30

Business envelope
Working Papers, p. 29

Current Date/ Mr. Anthony P. Evans/ 8123 Red Fox Road/ Hempstead, NY 11551/ Dear Tony:/ Enclosed are the necessary forms to enable you to sell additional shares of Diamond Supply Company restricted stock under Securities and Exchange Commission Rule 144-B./ Please review and sign Form 144-B, the stock-selling questionnaire, and the five stock powers and return them in the envelope provided. Also, we will need a stock certificate sufficiently large to cover the number of shares you desire to sell./ As soon as you return these forms, I will submit them to Diamond Supply's attorney for his review. Upon receipt of the legal opinion, we will then be in a position to sell the shares in accordance with Rule 144-B and will have 90 days to do so under the current application./ Should you have any questions regarding these forms or procedures, please give me a call. My telephone number is 212/269-5432./ Sincerely,/ Janet E. Jones/ Stockbroker/ your initials/ Enclosure

Task 5

Business letter with enclosure or attachment
Letterhead
Working Papers, p. 32

Business envelope
Working Papers, p. 31

Mr. John Gardner, Kresge Laboratories, 3611 51st Avenue, San Diego, CA 92101 Dear Mr. Gardner: Attached is your form ~~memorandum~~ which has been completed to show the audio-visual equipment needs for our program at the Biological Research Association Conventin to be held in San Diego ~~on~~ June 22. -25 The equipment may be picked up for return immediately following the program. ¶ Our first preference for seating arrangements would be theater style, with calssroom seating as our second choice. ¶ You are to be ~~highly commended~~ congratulated for your thorough convention preparations. This certainly will ehlp assure a smooth-rinning porogram. Paul Ganser, Executive Director Attachment

Mrs. Shirley England
Page 2
Current Date

By the way, you might tell Tom that I called Bill Metzger in Milwaukee and gave him the titles to use in addition to Word Processors and Word Originators. Also, I have talked with Jim Smola. He will send you a letter of application and a resume within the next few days. After you have had a chance to look over Jim's application, give me a call if there are any questions I can help you with.

Sincerely,

Denzel E. Williams

Denzel E. Williams
Project Director

your initials

c: Bob Hendrickson

Task 6

Business letter with enclosure or attachment
Letterhead
Working Papers, p. 34

Business envelope
Working Papers, p. 33

Ms. Donna Cujmings
1201 Wilshire Boulevard
Schenectady, NY 12301

Dear Ms. Cummings:

Enclosed is a copy of Dorchester Corporation's latest press releats announcing results for their fiscal year. Please note that despite this year's difficult economy, Dorchester has been able to continue to make progress in both sales and profitability. Their annual report, which fully covers fiscal 19-- results, is now coming off the press and will be sent to you by the end of this month. Earlier documents mailed to you explained how important it was to Dorchester to build strong and effective management and that therewere several new progrmas under way in the area of management development. Enclos3d is a reprint of an article published recently in U. S. Business News which covers one of these programs. I'm sure you will find it interesting. I continue to recommend this company's stock as a sound investment. Sincerely, Robert E. Truax Senior Vice President, your initials, Enclosures

Task 2

TWO-PAGE LETTER

Business letter
Letterhead
Working Papers, p. 86 and plain paper

Business envelope
Working Papers, p. 85

460 HOPEWELL CIRCLE
HACKENSACK, NEW JERSEY 07601
201/443-1026

Current Date

Mrs. Shirley England
Educational Director
Kansas City Occupational Center
2450 Pershing Road
Kansas City, MO 64108

Dear Shirley:

This letter will confirm our telephone call earlier this week. Bob Hendrickson and I will spend a day at the Kansas City Occupational Center on Tuesday, August 20. It is suggested that the day go as follows:

1. During the morning hours, we would present to you and your school administrators an overview of business and office education and realistic expectations for the students that you are working with. Perhaps we could have lunch together and discuss the items that were presented in the morning session on an informal basis.

2. After lunch we would like to meet for one to two hours with your counselors. The emphasis will be on which students to channel into the office occupations program and what area of the office occupations program would be best for each student.

3. The remainder of the afternoon, or for however long they can stay, we would like to talk with the business and office education teachers. In this portion of the program we would emphasize methodology. We plan to leave on the 9:45 p.m. flight to Chicago so we would be available to talk with the business education teachers until approximately 8:00 p.m. if they would be available.

If you want to change the day's activities around, by all means do so. I know that you may have difficulty getting the administrators together first thing in the morning.

Task 1

Business letter with copy notation
Letterhead
Working Papers, p. 36

Business envelope
Working Papers, p. 35

3609 EAST MARSHALL STREET • CHICAGO, ILLINOIS 60602 • (312) 495-6134

Current Date (Begin on line 12.)

(6 line spaces)

Mr. Timothy Palmer
Wagoner Consultants Corporation
2091 Front Avenue
Rochester, MN 55904

(double space--ds)

Dear Mr. Palmer:

(ds)

RE: Ms. Margaret Lloyd

(ds)

Enclosed is a contract for the above attraction. Please sign all four copies of the contract and return them addressed to my attention. We will mail you one copy of the fully executed contract for your records.

(ds)

Also enclosed is the Requisition for Advertising Materials. Please fill in the information requested and return the completed form as soon as possible.

(ds)

We appreciate your prompt attention to these matters and urge you to write or telephone if we may be of any further assistance.

(ds)

Sincerely yours,

Pedro Garcia (4 line spaces)

Pedro Garcia
Advertising Director

(ds)

your initials

(ds)

Enclosures

(ds)

c: Margaret Lloyd

Reference: p. 170

Line 7 (1") Top Margin

Mr. Thomas Quaker, Jr.
Page 2
December 3, 19__

T.S.

The exact terms of the underwriting will be set forth in an underwriting agreement to be entered into by Quaker Business Machines and Truax-Vehlow Investment Services. The underwriting discounts and commissions will not exceed 10 percent of the public offering price.

Except for any reimbursement provided for in this letter, Truax-Vehlow Investment Services will pay its own expenses and the expenses of its attorney. The underwriters will also pay the expenses of running the customary advertisements in various publications following the offering.

Quaker Business Machines will pay the fees and expenses of its legal counsel; all printing charges relating to the registration statement, prospectus, and underwriting agreements; postage; SEC, state, and federal filing fees; and the reasonable costs of a due diligence meeting.

Following conclusion of the public offering, Quaker Business Machines agrees to furnish quarterly unaudited financial statements to its shareholders and the underwriters, with audited reports to be issued annually.

We look forward to working with you and your associates on the proposed public offering. This letter is accepted by Quaker Business Machines and Truax-Vehlow Investment Services as a statement of mutual intent to carry out the proposed transactions, but does not constitute a firm commitment on the part of either the Company or the underwriters.

If this letter correctly sets forth your understanding of our arrangement, please contact us.

Sincerely,

Robert E. Truax

Robert E. Truax
Senior Vice President

Task 2

Business letter with copy notation
Letterhead
Working Papers, p. 38

Business envelope
Working Papers, p. 37

49 ROYAL WAY
ST. LOUIS, MISSOURI 63101
314/456/7219

Current Date

Ms. Sheila Graham
Midwest Learning Center
1308 South Wabash Avenue
Chicago, IL 60605

Dear Sheila

Here is a booklet from TSM on aptitude tests. Note that there are several items that may be of help to you.

These items include the Stenographic Skill Dictation Test shown on page 4, the Typing Skill Test shown on page 5, and the Iowa Personnel Test shown on page 9. Notice that the Iowa Test complies with EEOC and OFCC guidelines.

Sincerely

Renee Jewett

Renee Jewett
Testing Evaluator

RJ/your initials

Enclosure

c: Jim Levi
Tom O'Malley

Task 1

TWO-PAGE LETTER

Business letter
Letterhead
Working Papers, p. 84 and plain paper

Business envelope
Working Papers, p. 83

Reference: p. 170

TRUAX–VEHLOW INVESTMENT SERVICES

10 KEARNEY DRIVE
KEARNEY, NE 68847
(402) 554-6314

December 3, 19__ (Begin typing 2-3 lines below letterhead)

(4 line spaces)

Mr. Thomas Quaker, Jr.
President
Quaker Business Machines
2401 Lincoln Boulevard
New York, NY 10037

(double-space—ds)

Dear Mr. Quaker:

(ds)

This is to record the mutual intention of Quaker Business Machines and Truax-Vehlow Investment Services to undertake a public offering of common stock of Quaker Business Machines (the "Company").

(ds)

It is our intention to form an underwriting syndicate to purchase up to 250,000 shares of new common stock from Quaker Business Machines and to reoffer the shares to the public at a price mutually agreed upon. This agreement is subject to the following:

(ds)

1. the assurance that no materially adverse change in the affairs of the Company and its prospects occurs which appears sufficient, in our opinion, to threaten the success of our effort

2. the market conditions at the time of the offering

3. the filing of a prospectus with the Securities and Exchange Commission and its subsequent notification of effectiveness

We will not be bound to receive and pay for your shares until:

1. Blue Sky qualifications have been met in a reasonable number of states of our mutual selection

2. a final underwriting agreement satisfactory to each of us is executed

3. the registration statement is declared effective by the Securities and Exchange Commission

It is our intent to work with management to obtain a distribution of the common stock which will be beneficial to the Company and be consistent with securities industry practices.

6-9 lines (1″ to 1½″) bottom margin

Task 3

Business letter with copy notation
Letterhead
Working Papers, p. 40

Business envelope
Working Papers, p. 39

(Current date) / Mr. Jack P. Ancona / PMI Corporation / Office Services Division / Ryders Drive / New York, NY 06006 / Dear Mr. Ancona: / I would be most happy to participate in the ANSI X4 Standards Committee Subcommittee to investigate and develop user-oriented standards and guides for Word Processing. In order for me to receive reimbursement from the university, it will be necessary for you to send a letter informing my division chairman of the purpose of the meeting. / Of the possible meeting dates listed in your letter, I find that January 15 would fit my schedule best. / I am most excited about participating in this endeavor. / Sincerely, / Rick Uno / Professor / RU / your initials / c: Dr. William F. Hanrahan

Task 4

Business letter with copy notation
Letterhead
Working Papers, p. 42

Business envelope
Working Papers, p. 41

(Current date) / Mr. David E. Rowen / 5068 University Avenue / Kalamazoo, MI 49001 / Dear Mr. Rowen: / Burton Pyle has asked us to send you a copy of his brochure. We're happy that you enjoyed his presentation and that you are looking forward to booking him for another appearance in the near future. / If you have a specific date in mind for a special function, I would suggest that you contact us as soon as possible, since Mr. Pyle's calendar does fill up very rapidly. / If we can be of any help to you in arranging dates, please do not hesitate to call. We are always anxious to be of service to you. / Sincerely, / Palo Rodriquiz, Executive Director / PR: your initials / Enclosure / c: Burton Pyle

Task 5

Business letter with copy notation
Letterhead
Working Papers, p. 44

Business envelope
Working Papers, p. 43

(Current date) / Dr. Carolyn Bonner / Department of Business Education / University of Southern Mississippi / Southern Station, Box 83 / Hattiesburg, MS 39401 / Dear Dr. Bonner: / Dr. Livingston indicated that you would be serving as coordinator for the workshop that Dr. Ed Wanzer and I will be presenting in Hattiesburg in July. ¶ Could you please make arrangements to have the following equipment available for our presentations: (1) an overhead projector, (2) a 16 mm projector, and (3) a 35 mm carrousel slide projector. ¶ I will send you an outline of the program that we will be presenting. Also, we will be sending you materials to duplicate for distribution to the participants of the workshop. ¶ If there is anything else that you need from us, please drop me a line or give me a call at 505-864-5622. / Sincerely yours, / Dennis Czeslaw / President / c: Janet Livingston / c: Dr. Wanzer

Task 6

Business letter with copy notation
Letterhead
Working Papers, p. 46

Business envelope
Working Papers, p. 45

(Current date) / Mr. Michael D. Watts / 62 Wood Drive / Greenwich, CT 06830 / Dear Mr. W.: / Thank you for your interest in giving a presentation at our international convention in Houston. Unfortunately for us, it looks as though we will not be able to utilize your services for this year's convention, as our program has already been finalized. A list of programs + speakers is attached. / Should any of the seminar speakers withdraw from the program, I will contact you immediately. / Sincerely yours, / Malcome LaForrest / Sales Manager / Attachment / c: Francis Jakes / Mami Lou Tyler / Leonard Wilkom

Task 6

Letter with enumeration
Letterhead
Working Papers, p. 80

Business envelope
Working Papers, p. 79

First Fidelity Bank + Trust Co. / 2400 Central Avenue N.E. / New York, NY 10026 / Gentlemen— Re: Account #102-31106 / ¶ Our auditors, Smithburg + Johnson, Inc., are presently going over our year-end financial statements. In connection with this examination, they request that you furnish them with the following:

1. The information requested on the enclosed Standard Bank Confirmation Sheet.
2. A statement of any securities held by you for collections, in safekeeping, or as agent or trustee for our account, as of November, 19--.
3. Monthly bank statements of our account + the related paid checks as of the close of business on Dec. 15, 19--.
4. The names of persons authorized to sign checks on each of our accounts according to your records.

¶ Your reply should be sent directly to our auditors at the following address: Smithburg + Johnson, Inc., 871 Baker Building, 100 North Sixth St., NY, NY 10003. An addressed envelope is enclosed for your convenience. Sincerely, Robert E. Truax, Senior Vice President

Task 7

Letter with enumeration
Letterhead
Working Papers, p. 82

Business envelope
Working Papers, p. 81

(Current Date) / Mr. Gerald Smith / 402 Century Parkway / White Plains, NY 10603 / Dear Mr. Smith: / Many highly successful people devote nearly all of their time and effort to their careers and tend to neglect their private financial affairs. If you are one of these success-oriented people, you probably have consulted with your attorney, accountant, insurance agent, stock broker, and/or real estate agent for advice. Each of these advisers, however, sees only a segment of your situation. / We at Truax-Vehlow Investment Services can evaluate and coordinate all the complex areas of financial and estate planning for your benefit. We can provide expert advice and assistance in the following areas: / 1. Tax Planning / 2. Investment Counseling / 3. Insurance Planning / 4. Estate Conservation Planning / 5. Estate Tax Valuations / 6. Employee Benefit Planning / 7. Disability Planning / 8. Pension, Profit Sharing, and Deferred Compensation Planning / If you are interested in realizing savings on your taxes and insurance premiums, a greater return on your investments, and true peace of mind, contact us for further details. / Sincerely, / Robert E. Truax / Senior Vice President

Tasks 1 and 2

SPECIAL INSTRUCTIONS:

1. Type a rough draft, double space.
2. Edit, using proofreader's symbols.
3. Retype, using proper line spacing and making all corrections.

Use plain paper for rough draft.
For final copy:
Letterhead
Working Papers, p. 48

Business envelope
Working Papers, p. 47

Reference: p. 155

Ms. Michele Zukaitis, 7887 Cherry Grove Road, Fargo, ND 58102/ Dear Ms. Zukaitis— Thank you very much for returning the contract covering the appearance of Barry Livingston in Fargo on Dec. 3. Enclosed is a fully-executed contract for your files/ I appreciate your cooperation; if there is any way this office can be of assistance, please do not hesitate to write or call. / Sincerely / Patricia Ganser, Executive Director

Tasks 3 and 4

SPECIAL INSTRUCTIONS:

1. Type a rough draft; double space.
2. Edit, using proofreader's symbols.
3. Retype, using proper line spacing and making all corrections.

Use plain paper for rough draft.
For final copy:
Letterhead
Working Papers, p. 50

Business envelope
Working Papers, p. 49

Mr. William Carlson / Executive Director / Executive Program Center / 705 Minnesota Avenue / St. Paul, MN 55107 / Dear Mr. Carlson: / Enclosed is an outline for the self-contained seminar entitled "Time Management for Managers." The purpose of this program is to help managers concentrate on making optimum use of one of their most valuable resources -- time. I have used this format in at least a dozen presentations during the months of Jan., Feb., + March; it has been thoroughly field tested. / As soon as the seminar outline has been edited, revised, + the final format approved, I will provide the text + supporting materials. These materials will include transpar-encies, slides, cassettes, a set of guidelines for conducting the seminar, + handouts correlated with the seminar program. / We at the ITG Program Bureau are excited about the introduction of self-contained seminars to our special program offerings. / Sincerely / Patricia Ganser, Executive Director / c: Frank Nelson

Task 3

Letter with enumeration
Letterhead
Working Papers, p. 74

Business envelope
Working Papers, p. 73

(Current date)/ Mr. Dennis Long/ Department of Music/ Loyola University/ 820 North Michigan Avenue/ Chicago, IL 60655/ Mr. Long, enclosed is a brochure showing Miriam Rydell's current season in Chicago. Ms. Rydell is available in 19-- through the ITG Program Bureau for:/ 1. college residencies of one or one-half week/ 2. one-night engagements/ 3. one or one-half week performances as a soloist with local symphony orchestras/ 4. summer festivals/ Please contact us if you wish a complete press book on this popular singer or information on availability and fees./ James Cody/ Booking Agent/ JC/ your initials/ Enclosures

Task 4

Letter with enumeration
Letterhead
Working Papers, p. 76

Business envelope
Working Papers, p. 75

(Current date)/ Dr. Marcella Reicherter/ Division of Business and Business Education/ Emporia State University/ 1200 Commercial/ Emporia, KS 66801/ Dear Marcella:/ Here are the four topics for the workshop scheduled for June:/ 1. "An Alternative Approach to Introducing the Keyboard"/ 2. "The Topical Approach to Building Production Typewriting"/ 3. "The Effect of Word Processing on Typewriting" / 4. "Technological Changes in Office Systems and Procedures"/ There will be time provided within each of the four programs for group discussion activity./ Please count me in on the opening night banquet scheduled as part of the program. A copy of my resume and picture are enclosed for publicity purposes./ Sincerely,/ Harry A. Scheffel/ Lecturer/ HAS: your initials/ Enclosures

Task 5

Letter with enumeration
Letterhead
Working Papers, p. 78

Business envelope
Working Papers, p. 77

Mr. Russell Hes s, University Activities Chairman, NYC Community College, 300 Willougby, Brooklyn NY 11201 Mr. Hess, as you check your lecture / and concert plans for the coming year, I ~~do~~ hope ~~that~~ you will find an open date or two on ~~the~~ your schedule so that it will be possible for you to include one of these: ~~fine enroute suggestions~~

1. Margaret Lloyd, September 20. 2. Rodney Oleson, September 23. 3. Miriam Rydell, November 17. 4. Dr. Martin Lee, December 4-5.

¶ Individual folders are enclosed on these suggestions. The fees listed include all expenses. If you have a particular date to fill or need a special program, let me know; ~~and~~ I will be glad to check ~~my~~ our tours for additional, special suggestions. I look forward to hearing from you. Leslie Brown, Director JB/your initials

Task 1

Simplified business letter
Letterhead
Working Papers, p. 52

Business envelope
Working Papers, p. 51

World-Wide Consultant Service

40 PLAZA CENTER
SAN FRANCISCO, CALIFORNIA 94104
415/712-6400

Current Date (Begin 3 line spaces below letterhead.)

(4 line spaces)

Mrs. Carol Eastman, Chairperson
Talks 'N Topics Committee
The State College of Kentucky
SCK Union
Louisville, KY 40201

(double-space—ds)

Reference: p. 176

Thank you very much, Mrs. Eastman, for including us on your mailing list of speakers bureaus and allowing us to submit our ideas for your next year's Talks 'N Topics Series. Enclosed is literature on our wide selection of lecturers, performing artists, and special programs.

(ds)

I would single out Ms. Phyllis Bates as a high recommendation for your particular needs. I'm sure she would "fill the bill" for the vacancy you described in your letter of April 7. Therefore, I am also including detailed information about Ms. Bates's excellent program.

(ds)

By the way, Ms. Bates was recently honored on network television as the Woman of the Year in Communications by a national magazine. Her fee is $1,250 plus travel expenses from Minneapolis. Ms. Bates would certainly be a fantastic addition to your series.

(ds)

Should you be interested in any of our other offerings, please drop me a line or give me a call at 612/488-6009.

Reference: p. 176

David Shoemaker

David Shoemaker (4 line spaces)
Division Head

(ds)

your initials

(ds)

Envelope reference: p. 177

Enclosures

Task 2

Letter with enumeration
Letterhead
Working Papers, p. 72

Business envelope
Working Papers, p. 71

3609 EAST MARSHALL STREET • CHICAGO, ILLINOIS 60602 • (312) 495-6134

Current Date

Mr. Sheldon Josephs
Editor
Minneapolis Chronicle
P.O. Box 8045
Minneapolis, MN 55438

Mr. Josephs, enclosed are publicity materials for the four seminars to be presented on Thursday, May 8, as part of the Regional Realtors Forum. The materials include:

1. a glossy photograph of each speaker

2. a paragraph describing the presentation for each speaker

3. a paragraph describing the speaker's background

Should you need any additional materials, please feel free to contact me.

J. Sampson

Julie Sampson
Public Relations

your initials

Enclosures

Task 2

Simplified business letter
Letterhead
Working Papers, p. 54

Business envelope
Working Papers, p. 53

World-Wide
Consultant
Service

40 PLAZA CENTER
SAN FRANCISCO, CALIFORNIA 94104
415/712-6400

Current Date

Ms. Roberta Melrose
Los Angeles City College
855 North Vermont Avenue
Los Angeles, CA 90029

Ms. Melrose, here are the Word Processing slides. A check for $25 to cover processing and duplication may be sent directly to me.

Note that I have added a few slides to the series since the presentation at the California Business Education meeting.

I do not have a script for the slides. If you have questions about any of them, please drop me a line or give me a call at (715) 865-4320. Note that I have numbered the slides. If you should have a question, you can refer to them by number.

Dale Roble

Dale Roble
Sales Director

your initials

Enclosure

Envelope reference: p. 177

Task 1

Letter with enumeration
Letterhead
Working Papers, p. 70

Business envelope
Working Papers, p. 69

TRUAX–VEHLOW INVESTMENT SERVICES

10 KEARNEY DRIVE
KEARNEY, NE 68847
(402) 554-6314

Current Date

Dr. Richard Yates, Dean
Birnamwood Law School
733 Main
New York, NY 10032

Dear Dr. Yates:

We have received from the transfer agent the 100-share certificate of Essex Industries common stock which was donated to your institution by Mr. and Mrs. William M. Larson.

You have indicated that you would like to sell the shares. We will be in a position to proceed with the sale as soon as we receive the following:

(double space—ds)

1. A resolution stipulating who is authorized to act in such matters for your institution.

(ds)

2. A stock power signed by the authorized person.

Sincerely,

Robert T. Shaw

Robert T. Shaw
Senior Consultant

RS/your initials

Reference: p. 170

Task 3

Simplified business letter
Letterhead
Working Papers, p. 56

Business envelope
Working Papers, p. 55

(Current date)/ Mrs. Violet Tolstoy/ Syracuse University/ 103 Waverly Avenue/ Syracuse, NY 13210/ Mrs. Tolstoy, attached are my resume and photo for the Educational Office Personnel Conferences on September 25 and 26. Next week I'll send you the handouts to be duplicated./ By the way, I'll need an overhead projector, a 35mm carrousel slide projector, and a large screen for the presentation in Syracuse and Watertown./ Evelyn Kaluza/ Speaker Representative/ your initials/ attachments

Task 4

Simplified business letter
Letterhead
Working Papers, p. 58

Business envelope
Working Papers, p. 57

(Current date)/ Mrs. Violet Tolstoy/ Syracuse University/ 103 Waverly Avenue/ Syracuse, NY 13210/ Mrs. Tolstoy, the check covering my expenses and honorarium arrived this morning. Thank you for being so prompt./ Attached is a copy of my work analysis for the week of October 6. We use these materials in conjunction with time management. I'm sure that it has made me at least 50 percent more efficient than I was./ Thank you for sending me the practical business communications problem./ Evelyn Kaluza/ Speaker Representative/ your initials/ attachment

Task 5

Simplified business letter
Letterhead
Working Papers, p. 60

Business envelope
Working Papers, p. 59

Ms. Isabelle Martinez, Consumer Representative Supervisor,
Office Products Corporation, P.O. Box 3168, Dallas, TX 76231
Ms. Martinez, our Seminar program speakers have already been
contracted for this year's Convention. A list of the speakers
and their programs is attached. Should any of them withdraw
from the program, I will contact you as a possible alternativ-. e
¶ By the way, have you considered renting an exhibit booth at
the Convention in Houston? This would give you an opportunity
to display your products. Our executive Board is currently
making a decision regarding the revision of the Office Techniques
Manual. Should this manual be revised, you can be sure that
your material will be listed. ¶ You refereed to the possibility
of having your products listed in the "Weekly Division
Newsletter." To my knowledge, there is no such publication.
However, there is a monthly organizational report that is sent
to all divisions. If you are interested, I can submit your
material to the editor for possible inclusion in the report.
Diane Plendleton, Editor Attachment c: Francis Jakes,
Robert McCauley, John A. Walsh

Tasks 9 and 10

SPECIAL INSTRUCTIONS:

1. Type a rough draft; double space.
2. Edit, using proofreader's symbols.
3. Retype, using proper line spacing and making all corrections.

Use plain paper for rough draft.
For final copy:
Letterhead
Working Papers, p. 68

Business envelope
Working Papers, p. 67

Ms. Hilda Tripley / Assistant Professor / College of the Virgin Islands / St. Thomas, VI 00801 / Ms. Tripley, attached are a description + the first five pages of the Coordinators' Outline for the seminar package entitled "Decreasing Paperwork Costs of the Secretary/Management Team by 20 Percent." These materials should give you an idea of the scope of the seminar program. / In addition to the Coordinators' Outline, you can receive a set of 20 transparencies, 25 slides, 4 cassettes, a set of guidelines for conducting the seminar, + a packet of handouts correlated with the seminar. These materials can be ordered directly from our headquarters at a cost of $125. / We certainly appreciate your interest in the program. / Jose Tamiyasu, Editor

Task 6

Simplified business letter
Letterhead
Working Papers, p.62

Business envelope
Working Papers, p.61

Dr. ~~Donald~~ John Lundeen, Business Education Department, DePaul University, Chicago, IL 60607, ~~Don,~~ John, do you have individuals graduating from your program in Business Education who do not have jobs? Mr. Thomas O'Malley, one of the directors of the Midwest Learning Center, is interested in employing qualified ~~B~~business teachers. ¶ Midwest has programs in office occupations to include word processors, stenographers, and key tape operators. They are making application to the International Business School Association for accreditation. This means, of course, that their program is being expanded. ¶ ~~Why don't you~~ Give Tom O'Malley a call at the Midwest Learning Center. The number is 922-2094. They are also interested in any courses that you offer in the evening or on weekends that would be of particular interest to their ~~B~~business faculty. Lupe Van Straaten, Personnel Services, c. Tom O'Malley

Task 7

Simplified business letter
Letterhead
Working Papers, p.64

Business envelope
Working Papers, p.63

(Current date) / Mr. Hal Wimberley / Educational Director / Pacific West Occupational Educational Center / 1540 Page Mill Road / Palo Alto, CA 94304 / Hal, since I will be out of the office the next few days, I wanted to reconfirm our meeting on Tuesday, August 20. ¶ Earl Ames and I will be on United Airlines Flight 245 arriving at 9:10 p.m. on Monday, August 19. Would you please pick us up at the Western Star Motel at 8:30 a.m. on Tuesday, August 20. ¶ We have many materials and ideas to share with the administration, counselors, as well as the business and office education faculty. / Bruce Quatt / Vice-President / jiv / c: Earl Ames

Task 8

Simplified business letter
Letterhead
Working Papers, p.66

Business envelope
Working Papers, p.65

(Current date) / Mrs. Ruth Carter / Inservice Training Director / Reynolds Metals Company / Reduction Research Division / Box 191 / Sheffield, AL 35660 / Ruth, Northerners do not really appreciate Southern hospitality until they have been exposed to it firsthand. Nothing was spared in making my brief stay at the Joe Wheeler State Park Resort during the Reynolds Seminar a fascinating experience. Your division is certainly setting an example for industry to follow. / I hope that you will submit your name as a candidate for the Training in Business & Industry National Board. When your name is submitted, please let me know and I will do what I can to support your candidacy. / Jeanette Ahran / Personnel / pec

Index

G

H

I

J

L

M

N

O

P

Q

R

S

T

U

V

W